Technology Management

C.S.V. Murthy
B.Sc., B.E., MIE, Charteted Engineer
Industrial Consultant,
Visiting Faculty at Various Management Colleges
Executive Director,
INTAL Quality Certification Pvt. Ltd.,
(A Certification Body for ISO 9001:2000)

Himalaya Publishing House
ISO 9001:2015 CERTIFIED

First Edition : 2006
Reprint : 2012
Edition : 2017
Edition : 2018
Reprint : 2020

Published by : Mrs. Meena Pandey for **Himalaya Publishing House Pvt. Ltd.,**
"Ramdoot", Dr. Bhalerao Marg, Girgaon, Mumbai - 400 004.
Phone: 022-23860170, 23863863; **Fax:** 022-23877178
E-mail: himpub@bharatmail.co.in; **Website:** www.himpub.com

Branch Offices :

New Delhi : "Pooja Apartments", 4-B, Murari Lal Street, Ansari Road, Darya Ganj, New Delhi - 110 002. Phone: 011-23270392, 23278631; Fax: 011-23256286

Nagpur : Kundanlal Chandak Industrial Estate, Ghat Road, Nagpur - 440 018. Phone: 0712-2721215, 3296733; Telefax: 0712-2721216

Bengaluru : Plot No. 91-33, 2nd Main Road, Seshadripuram, Behind Nataraja Theatre, Bengaluru - 560 020. Phone: 080-41138821; Mobile: 09379847017, 09379847005

Hyderabad : No. 3-4-184, Lingampally, Besides Raghavendra Swamy Matham, Kachiguda, Hyderabad - 500 027. Phone: 040-27560041, 27550139

Chennai : New No. 48/2, Old No. 28/2, Ground Floor, Sarangapani Street, T. Nagar, Chennai - 600 017. Mobile: 09380460419

Pune : "Laksha" Apartment, First Floor, No. 527, Mehunpura, Shaniwarpeth (Near Prabhat Theatre), Pune - 411 030. Phone: 020-24496323, 24496333; Mobile: 09370579333

Lucknow : House No. 731, Shekhupura Colony, Near B.D. Convent School, Aliganj, Lucknow - 226 022. Phone: 0522-4012353; Mobile: 09307501549

Ahmedabad : 114, "SHAIL", 1st Floor, Opp. Madhu Sudan House, C.G. Road, Navrang Pura, Ahmedabad - 380 009. Phone: 079-26560126; Mobile: 09377088847

Ernakulam : 39/176 (New No. 60/251), 1st Floor, Karikkamuri Road, Ernakulam, Kochi - 682 011. Phone: 0484-2378012, 2378016; Mobile: 09387122121

Cuttack : New LIC Colony, Behind Kamala Mandap, Badambadi, Cuttack - 753 012, Odisha. Mobile: 09338746007

Kolkata : 108/4, Beliaghata Main Road, Near ID Hospital, Opp. SBI Bank, Kolkata - 700 010. Phone: 033-32449649; Mobile: 07439040301

DTP : Simple Logic Pvt. Ltd. Bangalore.

Printed by : Shri Krishna Offset Press, Delhi. On behalf of HPH.

PREFACE

The Value of a company in the past was assessed mostly on the basis of its capital and physical assets such as land, buildings, inventory, equipment etc. Technology adds value to the assets of a company in the present era. It resides in the company's people and its technology systems. An organisation can be thought of as a vehicle for introducing one or multiple technologies to society. The goal is to achieve a set of objectives. The technologies also varies in level, from being very basic on one end of the scale, its being super highly technologies at the other end. Though there are several factors that have been associated with improvement in technological competitiveness, one factor of undeniable value is the education and training of human resources needed for the ever-changing technical organisation.

The text has been written to aid the technology management users with numerous methods and techniques. It is important for the manager to understand how economic conditions affect the chances for success of the technology he/she manages and it is crucial that decisions take into account the present and expected future states of the economy. Technology and economy are closely interrelated. The rate of technological change is considered by many to be the primary variable in economic growth.

The success of the organisations is increasingly dependent on the top leader's ability to properly manage resources in a world of rapidly changing technology. Business enterprises must compete in a dynamic global market for their survival as well as for their success.

I hope this book will be useful to the university students to understand the basic principles of technology management. Many of the important and fundamental topics have been covered in this book. I presume that this book would be useful not only to the engineering and management students, but also for the industries as the book provides fundamental concepts to enable them to understand the subject.

Continued.....

The book has been organised in 14 chapters and with a vast number of illustrations.

CHAPTER

I ask for reader's feed back on possible improvements and suggestions for additional materials that could be included in future revised editions.

I am highly indepted to the excellent DTP work undertaken by Mr. Raghavendra, in bringing out the book in a limited time.

I also thank Shri Neeraj Pandey and Vijay Pandey of Himalaya Publishing House who took keen interest at every step in publishing this book. On the Home front, I want to thank all my family members and close relatives for the help rendered to me at times in numerous ways.

- C.S.V. Murthy

CONTENTS

Technology

Chapter - 1

1.1 Definition:

(i) The definition of **technology** as per dictionary is the systematic knowledge of **industrial arts;** a discourse or treatise on the arts; an explanation of terms employed in the arts; The branch of knowledge that deals with industrial arts, applied science, or engineering; the terminology of an art or science or a technological process, invention, method and the like and some of the ways in which a social group provides themselves with the material objects of their civilisation.

(ii) **Technology** is defined to be know how physical things and procedures used to produce products and services. (Fig 1.1)

(iii) **Technology** is defined as all the knowledge, products, processes, tools, methods and systems employed in the creation of goods or in providing services. It is the way we do things.

(iv) **Technology** is the systematised knowledge applied to alter, control or order elements of our physical and social environment.

1.2 Meaning of technology:

The meaning of **technology** is as shown in Fig 1.1

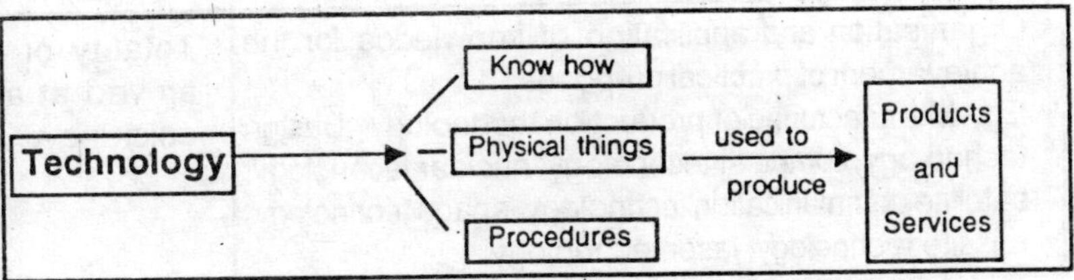

Fig. 1.1 The Meaning of Technology

Technology has a number of meanings, varying from **'product'** to the various disciplines of **Science and Engineering.**

- **Knowhow** means **knowledge** and **judgement** of how, when and why to employ equipment, processes and procedures

Knowledge includes:

- Craftsmanship
- Experience

Knowledge lies at the heart of economic progress.

- **Physical things include:**
  - Equipment
  - Tools
- **Procedures** are the rules and techniques for operating the equipment and performing the work.

Technology is the practical implementation of knowledge, a means of aiding human endeavour.

1.3 Requirement of Technologies

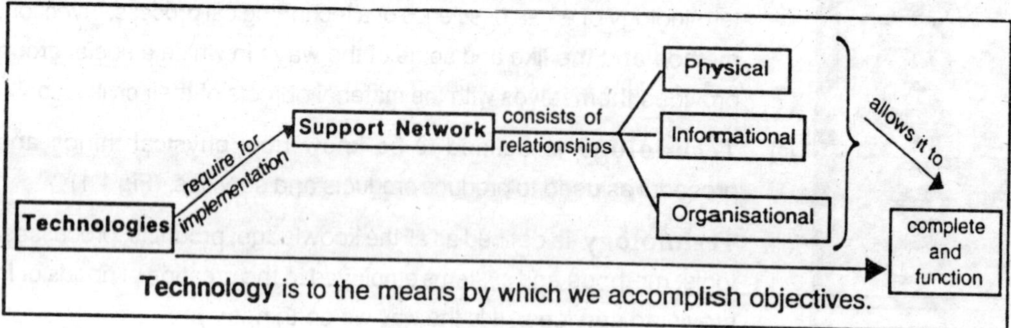

Fig. 1.2 Technologies and Relationship

1.4 Technology vs Technique

They are not the same

Technology	Technique
• Organisation and application of knowledge for the achievement of practical purposes. Eg:- Manufacturing or production technology, Design technology, computer technology, nuclear technology, satellite communication technology, space technology, missile technology, laser technology.	• Totality of methods rationally arrived at and having absolute efficiency.

Fig. 1.3 Technology vs Technique

1.5 Characteristics of Technology

Technology is socially constructed and **Technology development (TD) at all levels** is a process of social construction. Four characteristics of technology are:

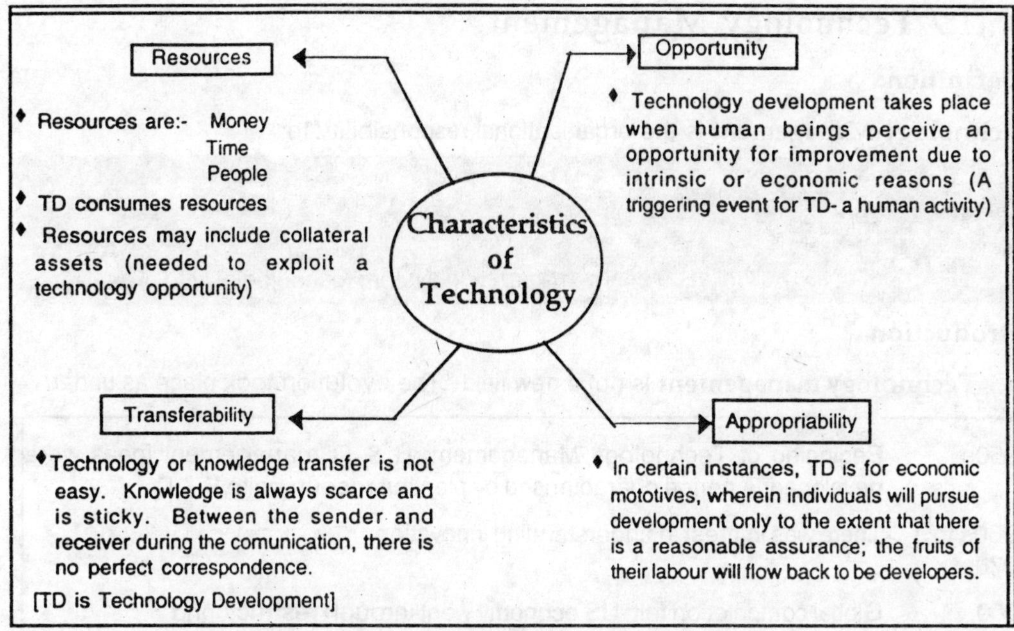

Fig. 1.4 Characteristics of Technology

1.6 Technology Development(TD)

Several levels of activity are included in TD. Three levels could be considered in general.

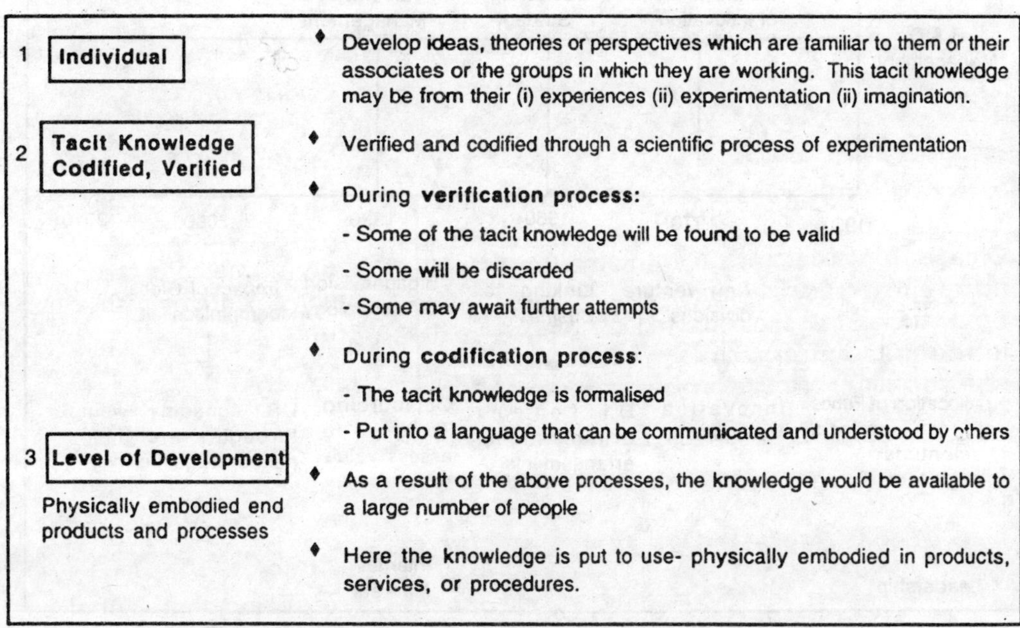

Fig. 1.5 Technology Development in Three Levels

1.7 Technology Management

Definition:

Technology Management is the organisational responsibility to:

- identify
- introduce
- monitor the assimilation of new information system technologies into organisation

Introduction

Technology management is not a new field. The evolution took place as under:

1950s	Beginning of Technology Management; R & D management ideas were developed; A period characterised by plentiful resources to R & D
1960s to 1970s	There was interest in understanding innovation
2000	Global compeletion felt; US economy went through restructuring

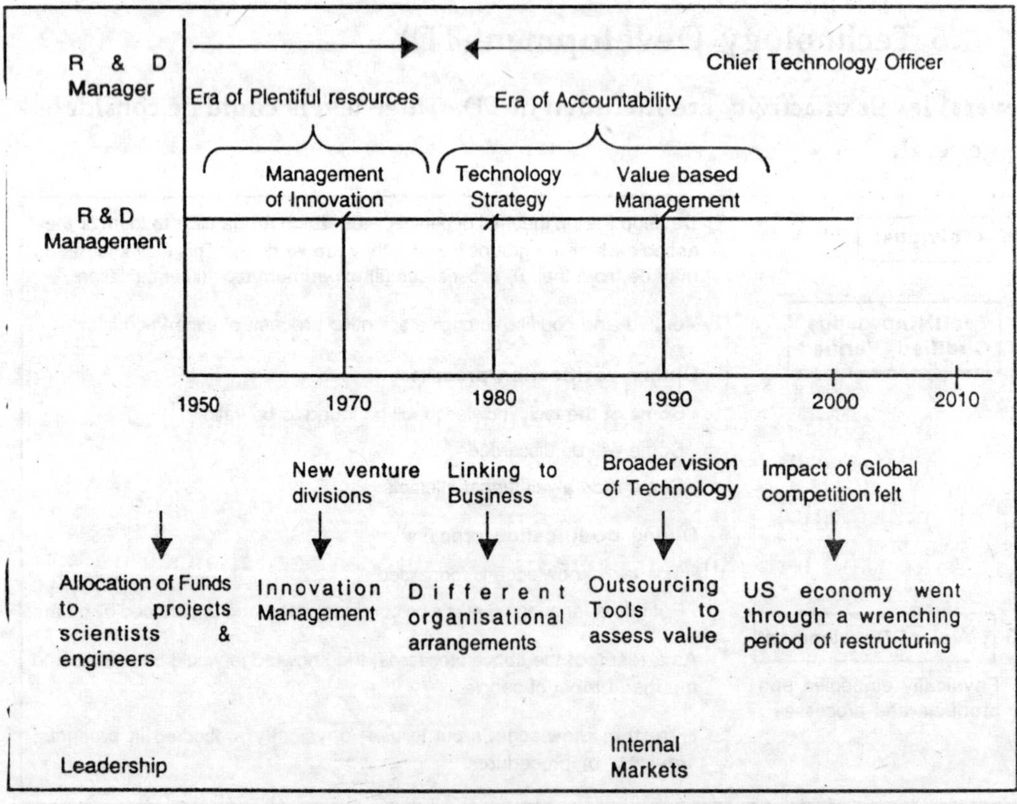

Fig. 1.6 Evolution of Technology Management

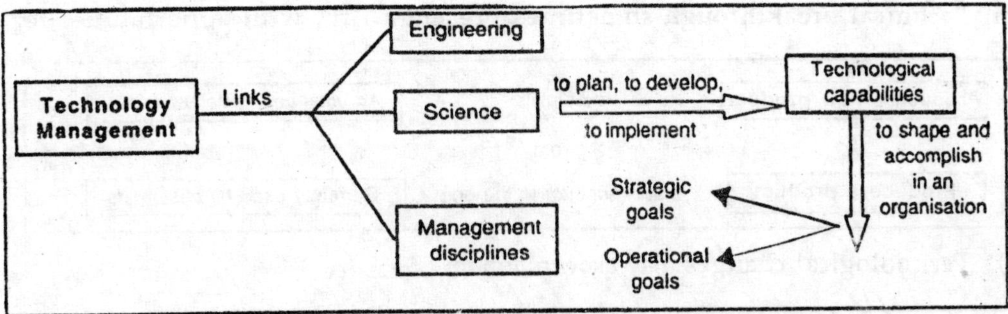

Fig. 1.7 Technology Management Vis-a-vis Goals

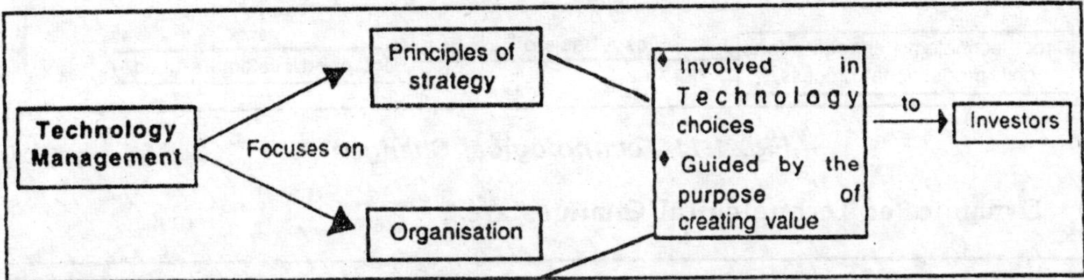

Fig. 1.8 Relationship Between Technology Management and Investors.

1.8 Process of Technology Change

(i) **Technology management** focuses upon creating competitive advantage for firms by finding effective means to fulfil the wants and needs of customers in the market place.

Fig. 1.9 Technology Management Focuses on Competitive Advantage

For achieving these, the firm has to create or acquire technical capabilities to deploy in new products or processes and hence our focus is to be on application of knowledge as the central technological change activity.

(ii) Technological Changes

(a) Successful technological changes takes place in the following ways:

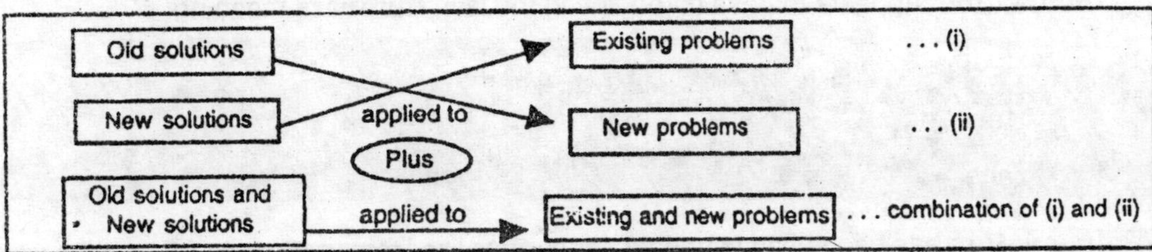

Fig. 1.10 Successful Technological Changes

(b) Technical breakthrough sometimes present a firm with opportunities to:

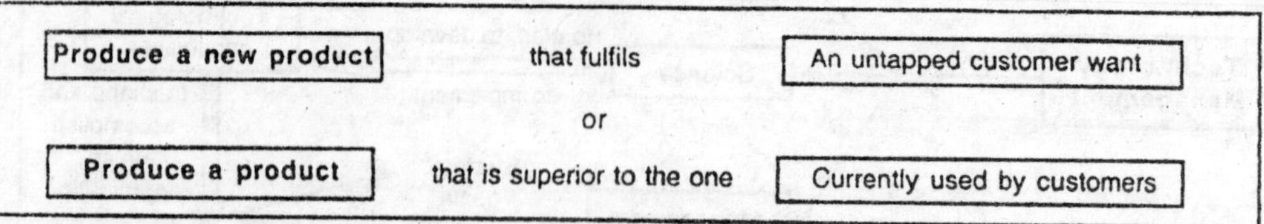

(c) Technological changes may allow a firm to:

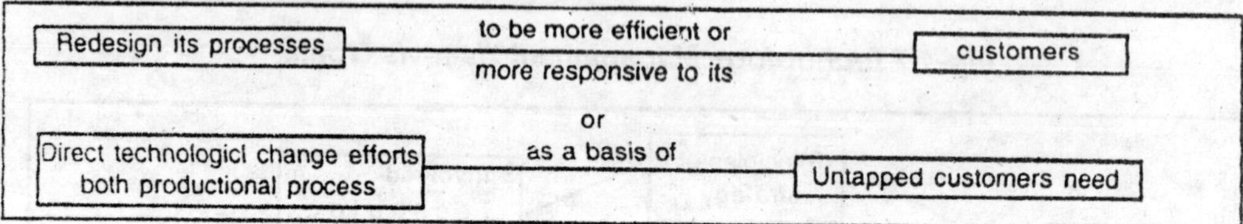

Fig. 1.11 Technological Changes

d) Dynamics of Technological Changes are:

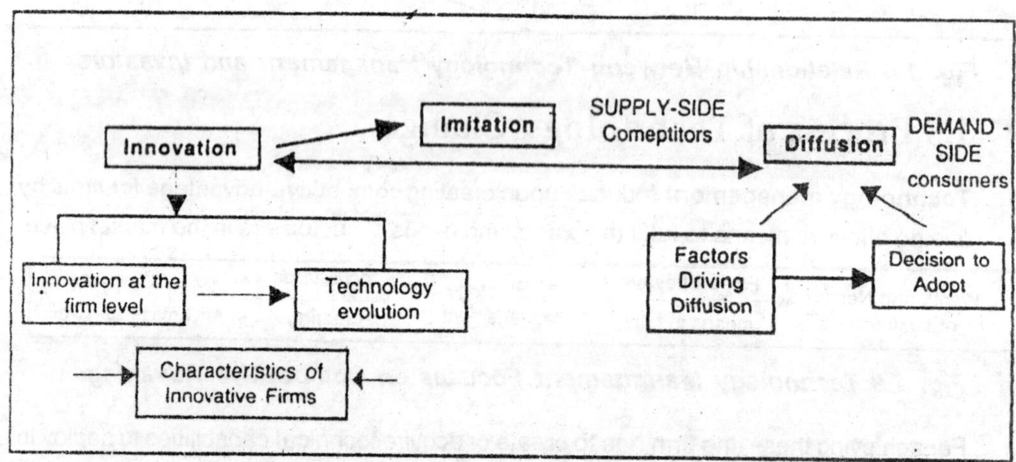

Fig. 1.12 Dynamics of Technological Changes

(iii) Innovation

Definition of Innovation

- 'Innovation' appears to have its origins in the latin **innovare** meaning
  - to renew
  - to make new
  - to alter

Innovation has been used in various languages like Roman (data as far back as the Roman empire), French, the old English and the colonial USA.

♦ **The dictionary meaning** of **innovation** is to bring in new methods, ideas etc; to make changes

Invention and Innovation are different

Invention is a more subtle concept.

If an enterprise produces a good or service or uses a system or procedure that is new to it; it makes an **'Innovation'**

In this view, Invention - if present - is part of the process of innovation.

❖ **Innovation** includes both:

- A change that has diffused into the economy and is adopted by the firm (eg; the adoption of computers by printing firms for type setting services)

What is the focus of the term Innovation?

Is it a process or does it refer to an artifact?

❖ **Innovation** refers both the output and the process of arriving at a technologically feasible solution to a problem triggered by a technological opportunity or customer need.

Innovation term is used in two ways:

(i) **Process** - Here individuals or organisations arrive at a technical solution; To describe different processes of innovation . **Problem solving model** is used as a frame work to have an overview of the dynamics of technological change.

(ii) **Output** - To refer to a product or service.

(iv) Technological changes occurrence at levels;

These occur at two levels:

- At the level of the individual firm
- At the level of the technology.

At the level of the individual form, **technological change** may be described as a process of **problem solving**. The four stages identified in the process of problem solving are:

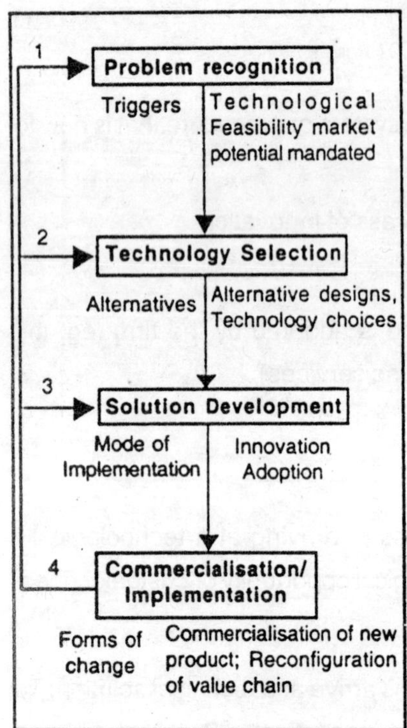

Fig. 1.13 Problem Solving

- Successful technological change begins when a firm recognises the potential of a technology for new products or process or when it recognises a market need that needs to be fulfilled.
- If technical feasibility dominates design, we call the process **technology push;** If market demand drives the process, we call it **market pull:**
- The firm formulates several design concepts that will serve the market needs. The design concepts are based on different technologies tends to be a creative act that also includes s strong judgemental input so that firm can decide to commit resources to the next stage. Technology the choice culminates in the selection of a particular design concept for development.
- It consists of actually fleshing out the chosen design concept. In the case of products, it may be the development of a prototype. In process innovation it may involve finalising a general approach or a blue print for organisational change. A new solution is formulated within the innovating firm or a ready made solution is adopted by the firm from outside.
- The economic benefits of an innovation are never fully realised until an item is actually introduced into the market or cost reductions from the process change are achieved. A firm fleshes out the operations and market strategy in the case of products, or implements the process change within the organisation.

1.9 Technology Transfer

(i) Definition

Technology Transfer is the process by which **commercial technology is disseminated.** This will take the form of a technology transfer transaction, which may or may not be a legally binding contract but which involve the communication by the transferor, of the relevant knowledge to the recipient.

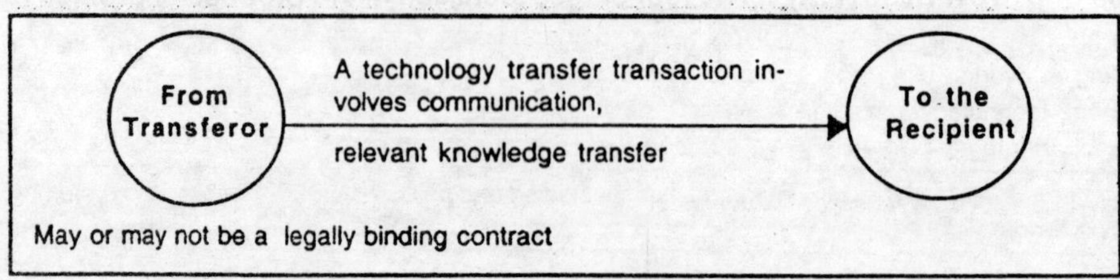

ii) Draft transfer of Technology (TOT) by UNCTAD

The **draft transfer technology** (TOT) code by UNCTAD has listed the following:-

- The assignment, sale and licencing of all form of industrial property; except for trade marks, service marks and trade names when they are not part of TOT transactions.
- The provision of know how and technical expertise in the form of feasibility studies, plans, diagrams, models, instructions, guides, formulae, basic or detailed engineering designs, specifications and equipment for training, services involving technical advisory and managerial personnel, and personnel training.
- The provision of technological knowledge necessary for the installation, generation and functioning of plant and equipment, and turn key projects.
- The provision of technological knowledge necessary to acquire install and use of machinery, equipment and/or raw materials which have been acquired by purchase, lease or other means.
- The provision of technological contents of industrial and technical cooperation arrangements.

The above list excludes **non-commercial technology** transfers as focused in international cooperation agreements between developed and developing states. Such agreements may be related to:

- Infrastructure
- Agricultural development
- International cooperation in the fields of:
  - Research
  - Education
  - Employment
  - Transport

Internalised form of TT	Externalised form of TT
♦ Refer to investment associated TT where control resides with the technology transfer. The latter, normally holds majority of full equity ownership] ♦ The transferer has a significant and continuing financial stake in the success of the affiliate, allows it to use its brand names and to have access to its global technology and marketing networks, exercises control over the affiliates investment, technology and sales decisions, and sizes the affiliate as an integral part of its global strategy.	♦ Refers to all other forms such as: - Joint ventures with local control - Licensing strategic alliances - International sub contracting ♦ Lack one or all of these features, with repercussions on the TT process.
Over time, the array of TT arrangements has diversified and particular modes have also become more flexible. The dividing line between these two forms or modes are becoming less easy to draw.	

Fig: 1.15 Internalised Form of TT Vs Externalised Form of TT

(iii) Forms of Technology Transfer (TT)

There are two forms of TT: **Internalised** and **Externalised.**

The TTs by MNCs, however is mostly internalised and therefore it does not help the domestic forms much.

(iv) Technology Transfer Levels

Four levels of Technology Transfer are:

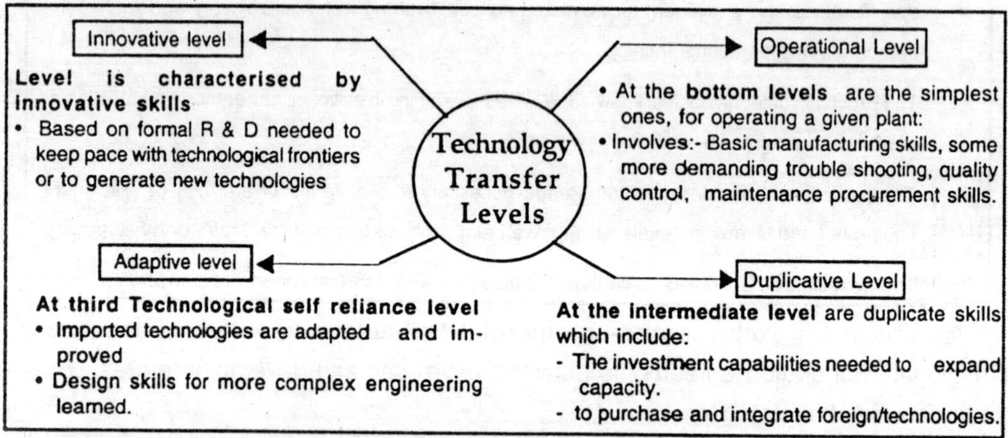

Fig. 1.16 Technology Transfer Levels

(v) Technology Flow Channels

Important channels for the flow of technology are Foreign Investment, Technology licence agreements and Joint Ventures.

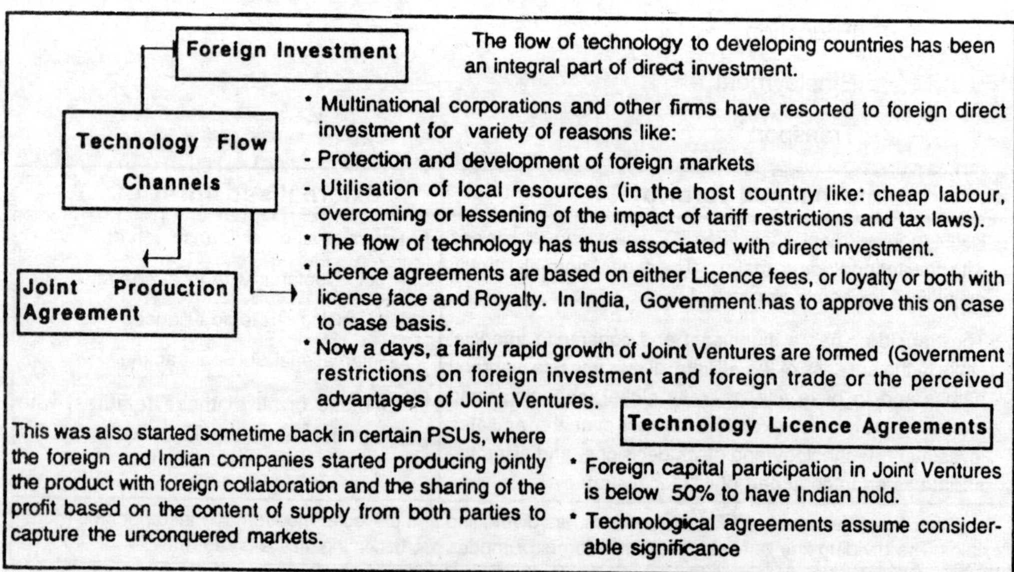

Fig. 1.17 Science/Technology Push

(vi) Technology Transfer methods

The methods are many. It takes a variety of firms depending on:

- Type of TT
- Nature of technological assistance
- Extent of technological assistance

Following methods of TT are adopted:

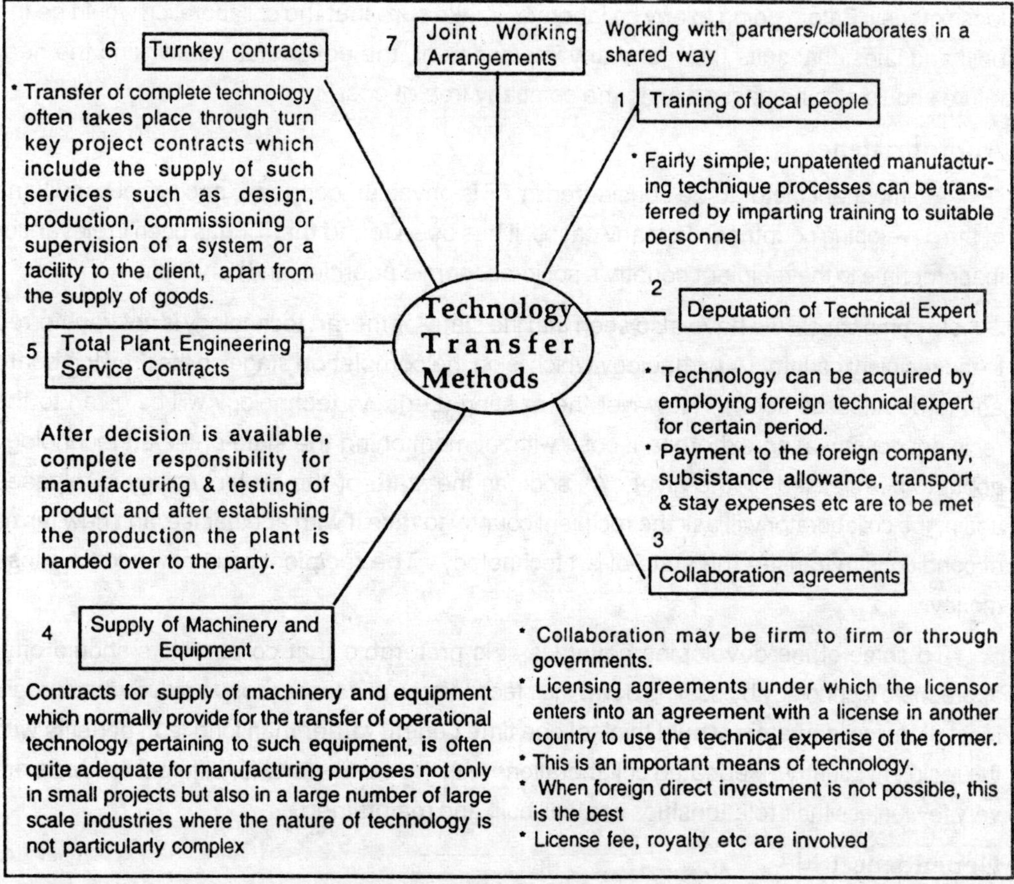

Fig. 1.18 Technology Transfer Methods

Many a times, a combination of two or more of the above methods undertaken: **Turnkey contracts** are the most comprehensive of such combinations.

(vii) Technology Transfer issues:

Transfer of technology has four important issues:-

(i) Cost (iii) Dependence

(ii) Appropriateness (iv) Obsolescence

Cost:

To obtain a foreign technology generally from a developed country to a developing country involves high prices. In a number of cases of foreign direct investment associated with technology transfer, the net outflow to capital by way of dividend, interest, technical fees, royalty etc has been found much higher than the corresponding flow. As Technology is fast changing and if the collaborator does not give the latest current technology to the company who goes in for collaboration, the cost benefit analysis would not work in a proper way. Again, if the company has to take another collaboration with the same or different collaborator, they loose money. Before going to any collaborator, make sure that the collaboration would be the best and latest that suits them and any improvement, the collaborator is thinking the near future should also be passed on to the company free of cost.

Appropriateness:

An important factor to be considered in TT is physical, economic and social conditions of the developing countries. In many cases, it has been found that TT has been irrelevant or inappropriate to the recipient country's socio-economic priorities and conditions.

In some cases, we have also seen that the state-of-the-art technology is not transferred to the recipient country (A technology which is on the completion stage on the drawing board and to be released soon). However the existing (Legacy) technology will be given to the recipient country at an exhorbitant cost, without mentioning the state-of-the-art technology about to be released by the giver. As soon as the state-of-the-art technology is released again, the collaborator will ask the recipient country to take it with another fee, and new terms of conditions to transfer the state-of-art technology. The recipient country would thus lose money.

To some of the developing countries, it is preferable that collaborators should offer appropriate technology by scaling down their technology, at a lesser cost to reduce the burden. Most of the collaborators would think of one time benefit rather than long term benefits with the recipient country. Repeated collaborations with the same party for different products are very few unless their relationships are well built and maintained.

Dependence:

Heavy reliance on foreign technology may lead to technological dependence.

Obsolescence:

It has also been observed that there is a tendency to transfer outdated technology to the developing countries which is a much worst case. Thus the recipient countries would not enjoy the advantages of the latest technology and would still technologically lag behind and are exploited. It is unfortunate that the owners of modern technology view the developing countries as a means to salvage technology that is obsolescent in the advance countries, even when they possess more advanced technology.

1.10 Import of Modern Sophisticated Technology

This has tended to displace the traditional indigenous technology which has been improved under a different set of policies. The steady stream of new products and processes introduced by multinationals into developing countries has been unfavourable to the promotion of domestic technological capacities and has discouraged local scientists and technicians from devoting themselves to practical development problems.

1.11 Twentieth Century Technologies with their scientific bases

Technology	Person Responsible	Year	Details
Nuclear Energy	**Einstein's** paper	1905	Established the equivalence of mass and energy
Transistors	**A H Wilson's** theory	1931	Based on his theory of Semiconductors
Electronics	**Maxwell's** theory of Electromagnetism	1980s	Theory of Electromagnetism developed
Genetic Engineering	Watson and Crick	1952	Discovered the structure of DNA

Fig. 1.19 Twentieth Century Technologies

1.12 Science/Technological Push opened new vistas for industrial development and economic growth

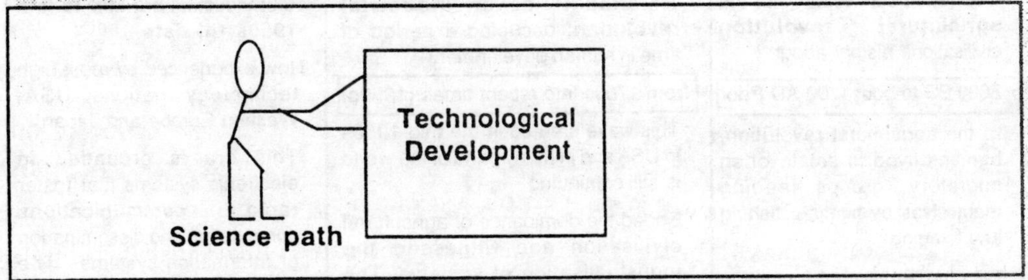

Fig: 1.20 Science/Technology Push

1.13 Technology Life Cycle

Similar to a product which has its life cycle, **technology** also has a **life cycle**. The various phases or stages in a **technological life cycle** are:-

(i) **Innovation** (in which stage, a new technology (product or process) is developed)

(ii) **Syndication** - during which stage, the technology is demonstrated and slowly commercialised.

(iii) **Diffusion** - Stage in which a new technology gradually replaces the current technology

(iv) **Substitution** - stage in which the current technology becomes obsolete and is completely replaced by the new technology.

The early stage of the technology life cycle is as per S-curve of innovation, the era of embryonic technologies, where the uncertainty surrounding the development of technology is quite high.

1.14 Technological Environment Changes

(i) **Definition:** The **Technological Environment** is defined as institutions linked to technology development activities.

The **Technological Environment** is dynamic and evolves over time. The technological environment can be thought of as a subset of the system of the following:

- Social Philosophies
- Norms
- Dogmas
- Ideologies

which comes under the broader heading of civilisation

Each phase of civilisation is grounded in its own system; These systems change slowly over long periods of time.

First wave of change ⟹	Second wave of change ⟹	Third wave of change
* Occured in connection with the **agricultural revolution** civilisations history about 8000 BC to bout 1700 AD Prior to the agricultural revolution, humans lived in small, often migratory, groups feeding themselves by hunting, fishing and foraging. • With the agricultural revolution the technologies that allowed people to take root at one place assured of a reasonably constant food supply (to create a civilisation) * Eg: Technologies included levers and hoists, wedges, winches, swords, knives- simple machines designed to amplify the renewable energy sources of human and animal muscle power, wind, sun and water.	* Referred to as an **industrial revolution;** occupied a period of time in human development from 1700s into recent times (1950s) This wave created in the mid 1950s in USA and in many parts of the world is still continuing * Ended the dominance of agricultural civilisation and witnessed the industrialisation of society. The technologies introduced with this wave, generally based upon electromechanical machines powered by non-renewable fossil fuels, produced wide spread changes in the makeup of society. eg:- These technologies include the steam engine, the automobile and electricity. Families became smaller; work shifted to the factory from field and education of the young shifted from home to organised class rooms.	* Post industrial era **Mid to late 1950s till date** * Now experienced by most high technology nations USA, Western Europe and Japan. This era is grounded in electronic systems that foster rapid communications computation and dissemination of Information systems. The wide availability of technologies such as computers, telecommu nications, robotics and bioengi neering has begun to leave its social mark on the social characteristics of society. Fundamental changes in social behavior is seen in such areas as the organisation of the work force, the education of the young, and the diversity in family form.

Fig. 1.21 Toeffler's Three Waves

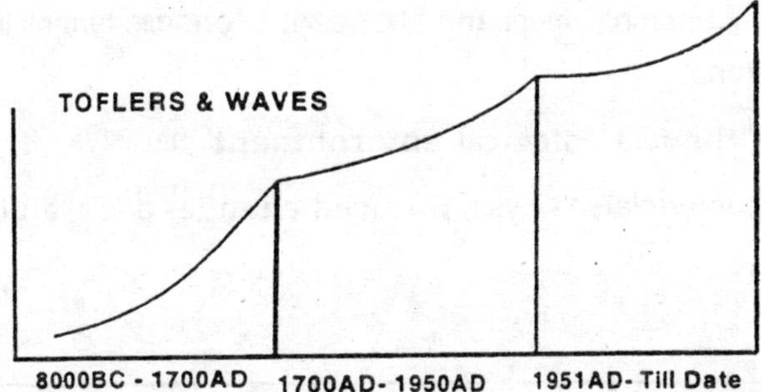

(ii) Waves of change in 1980, **Alvin Toeffler** summarised three 'Waves of Change' and the monumental impact that these waves had on civilisation in his book entitled **"The Third Wave".** He divided the history of civilisation into three distinct periods of time that he called **"Waves".** Each of these waves has its own distinct technosperes or its energy, production and distribution systems.

The question now is **'Is there a fourth wave?'**

Many believe so, but opinions regarding the nature of the **fourth wave** are different. Two different types proposed are:

- **Green wave**
- **Biological wave**

Authors like **Herman Maynard** and **Susan Mehrtens** envisioned a **yet to be achieved fourth wave** for the future after the three waves concept of **Toeffler.** The fourth wave where the other authors present a view of the corporation as this steward of global concerns. These organisations will appear more as communities than as business entities with decisions made in a consensual manner based upon the needs of all people and environment. Technologies pursued will be **'appropriate'** to the needs of a world community and in consort with the needs of the planet. Quality of life and alignment with the natural order will be the primary resources of corporate wealth.

Alternatively, few believe that beyond the information revolution or toeffler's third wave lies to **biological revolution.** In the core of this wave, lies the scientific advances in our understanding of human **genetic code. Human genome projects (HGP)** and other efforts at mapping the genetic code are expected not only to bring about medical advances but also to fundamentally change the way we go about living our daily lives. This has already created ethical dilemma, especially pertaining to cloning.

New industries formed around these markets, and contained innovations in these newly formed industries expand the market.

Third as technology matures, many competitors enter internationally, eventually creating excess capacity that in turn decreases profitability.

Finally, business failures, unemployment and attendant economic turmoil in financial markets may lead to depressions.

(iii) Types of changes in the technological environment

This comes about in two interrelated ways i) **induced changes** and ii) **autonomous changes**.

What is environment?

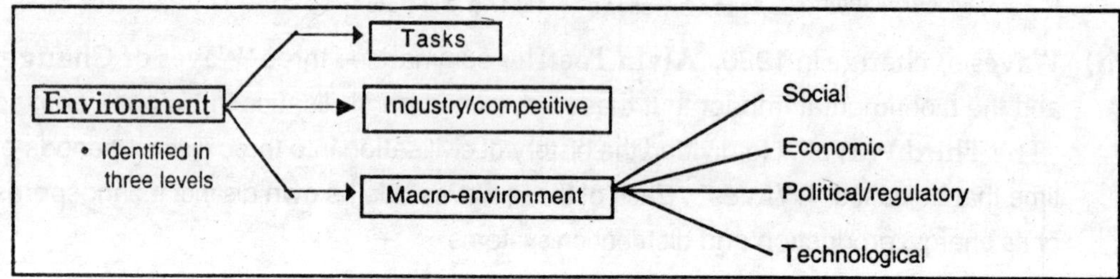

Fig. 1.22 Environment and its Levels

(iv) Institutions involved in the technological environment

These are classified along two dimensions:

- **Public Vs Private**
- **Developers Vs Facilitators**

Technology development in **public** organisations is in general more transparent than in **private** organisations. **Technology developers** are engaged in one or more stages of technology development from basic research to development, engineering and operations. **Facilitators** may be resource providers, policy analysts or linking organisations.

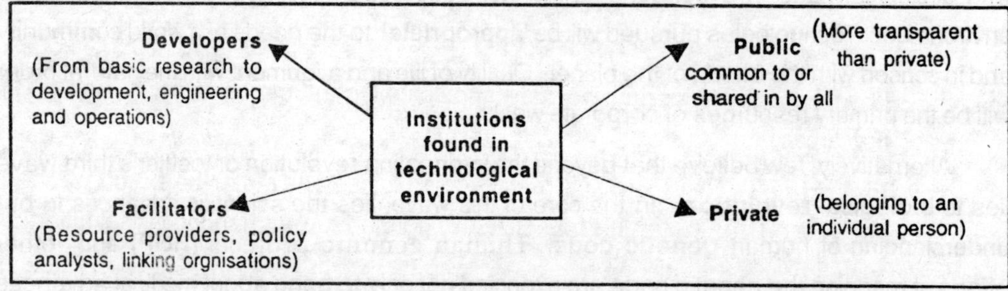

Fig. 1.23 Institutions Found in Technological Environment

Different nations have different interconnections among various organisations in the technological environment.

Classification of Technologies

Technologies can be classified in number of ways and the same is as per the following:

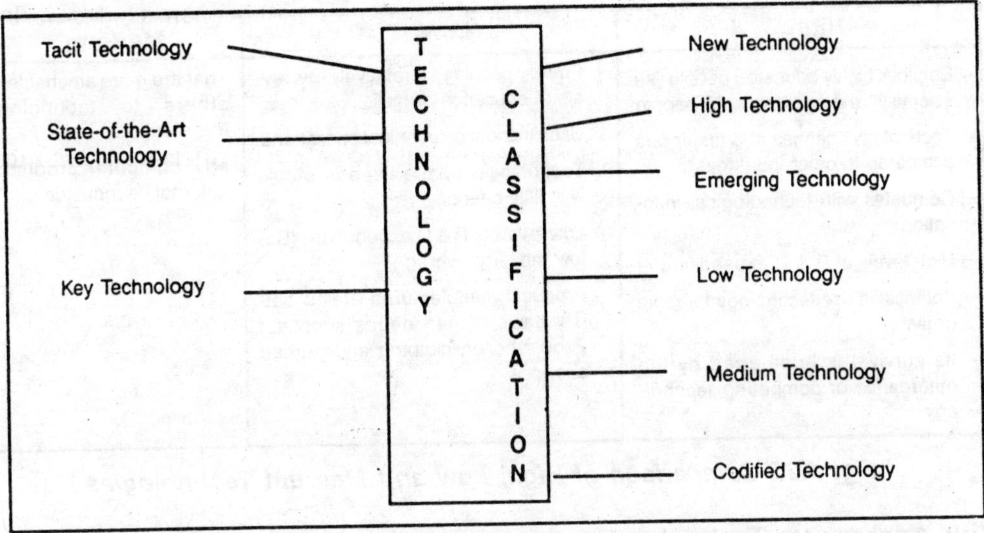

Fig. 1.24 Technology Classification

(i) **New Technology** It is the one which **newly introduced** or implemented technology that has an explicit impact on the way a company produces products or provides services.

eg:- A new company software to develop engineering drawings or Internet web site for marketing the company's products.

This technology need not be new to the world but new to the company. It might have been developed long back and used elsewhere. For the company it is new, whenever it is introduced for the first time in a new situation.

(ii) **Emerging Technology:-** It is any technology that is not yet fully commercialised but will become so within span of five years. It may be of limited use currently but is expected to evolve in a bigger size.

Eg:- Genetic engineering, cloning, nanotechnology, super conductivity, and the Internet new areas.

Emerging Technologies Create new industries and make the existing technologies obsolete. They have the potential of triggering large changes in institutions and in society.

(iii) High Technology, Low technology and Medium Technology

High	Low	Medium
• Refers to advanced or sophisticated technologies • Utilised by wide variety of industries having certain characteristics:	• Refers to technologies that have permeated large segments of human society • Used by a wide variety of industries having the following characteristics:	• Refers technologies that fall between the other two: high and low technologies. • Usually refers to mature technologies .

High	Low	Medium
- Employs highly educated people like scientists and engineers, IT people - Technology changes at a faster rate compared to other industries - Competes with technological innovation - High levels of R & D expenditure - Potential to use technology for rapid growth; - Its survival is threatened by the emergence of competing technology.	- Employ people with relatively low levels of education or skill. - Uses manual or technical operations. - Technological base used is stable with little change - Low levels of R & D expenditure (Below industry average) - Products manufactured are to satisfy basic human needs such as: Food, shelter, clothing and human services.	That are more amenable to others to technology transfer. eg:- computer products, automotive industries.

Fig: 1.25 Comparison of High, Low and Medium Technologies

(iv) Appropriate Technology:

It is the technology which is used to indicate a good match between the technology utilised and the resources required for its optimal use: The technology could be of any level; low, medium or high.

Eg:- To use high technology, when there is a lack of necessary infrastructure of skilled personnel.

Utilising this technology, results in better use of labour resources and better production efficiency. Developing countries have this dilemma to get to technology transfer from industrial developed countries. The latter may push for the acquisition of high technologies to a country where medium level of technology is sufficient.

(v) Codified Technology and Tacit Technology:

Technology can be preserved and effectively transferred among users if it is expressed in a coded form.

Eg: Engineering drawing is coded form which expresses shape, dimensions, and tolerances about product. A computer program is another example.

(vi) Tacit Technology is a non-articulated knowledge. There is no uniformity in the way it is presented or expressed to a large group of people. It is usually based on experiences and therefore remains within the minds of its developers. Tacit knowledge is transmitted by demonstration or observation, followed by assimilation by those who seek the knowledge. Tacit Technology transfer occurs by close contact and interaction between the source and the host-apprenticeship programs.

Questions

1. Define technology.
2. What do you mean by know how?
3. What does knowledge include?
4. What are the requirement of technologies?
5. What is the difference between Technology and Technique?
6. Explain the characteristics of technology.
7. Which are the three levels of technology development?
8. Define Technology Management.
9. How does the evolution of technology management took place?
10. Distinguish Technology management with goals.
11. Discuss on Relationship between Technology Management and Investors.
12. 'Technology Management focuses upon creating competitive advantage for firms' what are your views?
13. Discuss on the subject 'Dynamics of Technological changes'.
14. How does successful technological changes takesplace?
15. Define innovation.
16. Define invention.
17. In which two levels technological changes occur?
18. At the level of the individual firm, technological change is described as what?
19. Which are the four stages identified in the process of problem solving?
20. Define Technology Transfer.
21. Describe Technology Transfer levels.
22. Define Technology Flow channel.
23. Explain Technology flow channel.
24. Which are the Technology Transfer methods?
25. What do you mean by 'Total plant engineering service' and 'Turnkey Contracts'?
26. Mention Technology Transfer issues, Explain each one of them.
27. Which are the twentieth century technologies, Name a few of them.

28. Describe Science/Technological push which have opened new vistas for industrial development and economic growth.
29. Explain Technology Life Cycle and its stages.
30. Define Technology Environment.
31. Discuss Technology Environment changes.
32. What do you mean by waves of change? Explain the three waves of change happened during the three periods till date, stating from 8000BC.
33. When we talk about 3 waves regarding the history of a civilisation, is there any 4th wave yet to be achieved?
34. What is Environment? What are its levels?
35. Explain the types of changes in the technological environment.
36. Which are the institutions involved in the technological environment? Explain each one of them.
37. Which are the different types of technology? Explain them.

Chapter - 2

Planing and Forecasting

2.1 Preview

Chapter two deals with the following:

- *A model of the planning/decision making process*
- *Importance of defining an organisation's mission, strategy, goals, objectives as a prelude to planning.*
- *Management by objectives.*
- *Planning concepts*
  - Premises or assumptions
  - Planning horizon
  - Distinction between policies and procedures
- *Forecasting using :-*
  - Sales estimates
  - Moving average methods
  - Regression models comparison
  - Summarisation of Technological Forecasting
- *Introducing a few concepts essential to managing technology*
  - Invention
  - Innovation
  - Entrepreneurship

2.2 Importance of planning

(a) Management Functions

Many management gurus or experts have analysed the management funcitions. But they have not arrived at a common classification of managerial functions. Each expert has discussed the management function by studying different organisations from different levels. You may see the comparison of the views of the various experts as shown below.

<table>
<tr><th>Henri Fayol
(Father of principle of Management)</th><th>Gulick and Urwick</th><th>R. C. Davis</th><th>Koontz and O' Donnell</th></tr>
<tr><td rowspan="3">♦ Planning (including Forecasting)
♦ Organising
♦ Commanding
♦ Coordinating
♦ Controlling</td><td rowspan="3">♦ Planning
♦ Organising
♦ Staffing
♦ Directing
♦ Coordinating
♦ Reporting
♦ Budgeting
(POSDCORB)
For easy remembering, we can call it as POST CARD (Seven letters)
(Similar to POSDCORB)</td><td>♦ Planning
♦ Motivating
♦ Controlling</td><td>♦ Planning
♦ Organising
♦ Staffing
♦ Directing
♦ Contolling</td></tr>
<tr><td>G. R. Tery</td><td>Professor Haimann</td></tr>
<tr><td>♦ Planning
♦ Organising
♦ Activating
♦ Controlling</td><td>He finds the activities as a continuous circular movement. The functions are same as Koontz and O' Donnell</td></tr>
</table>

Fig. 2.1 Comparision of the Views of Various Experts regarding Management Functions.

From the above experts analysis, we can state the functions from **three to eight** and there is unanimity only in respect of the functions VIZ **Planning, Organising** and **Controlling.**

The functions of 'directing' which is concerned with the directing of the human behaviour for getting things done has been called by various authors as :

- **Commanding**
- **Motivating**
- **Communicating**

Some authors have introduced **staffing** functions by splitting the social aspect of **organising** because of the great importance the human resources acquired in organisation

The functions of management can be broadly classified as :-

- Planning
- Organising
- Staffing
- Directing
- Controlling

Planning provides a method of identifying objectives and designing a sequence of programs and activities to achieve these objectives. **Planning** implies **'decision making'** as to what is to be done? How it is to be done ? When it is to be done. and Whom it is to be done ? Planning involves setting of objectives, strategies, policies, programmes, and procedures for achieving them. Planning must obviously precede doing! Planning function is performed by managers at every level because planning may either be for the entire enterprise or for any action or department thereof. Planning pervades the entire gamut of managerial activity and also it is continuous and never ending. While the managers at the top level devote more time on planning (on thinking and deciding), the managers at the lower level follow the policies, programmes and procedures laid down by the top management.

For any business activity, planning is a pre-requisite for doing anything and also to ensure the proper utilisation of the resources of the business concern to achieve the desired goals. Plans can be classified into (I) Standing plans and (II) Single use plans :

(I) **Standing plans** include objectives, policies, procedures, methods and rules.

(II) **Single use plans** include budgets, programmes, strategies and projects.

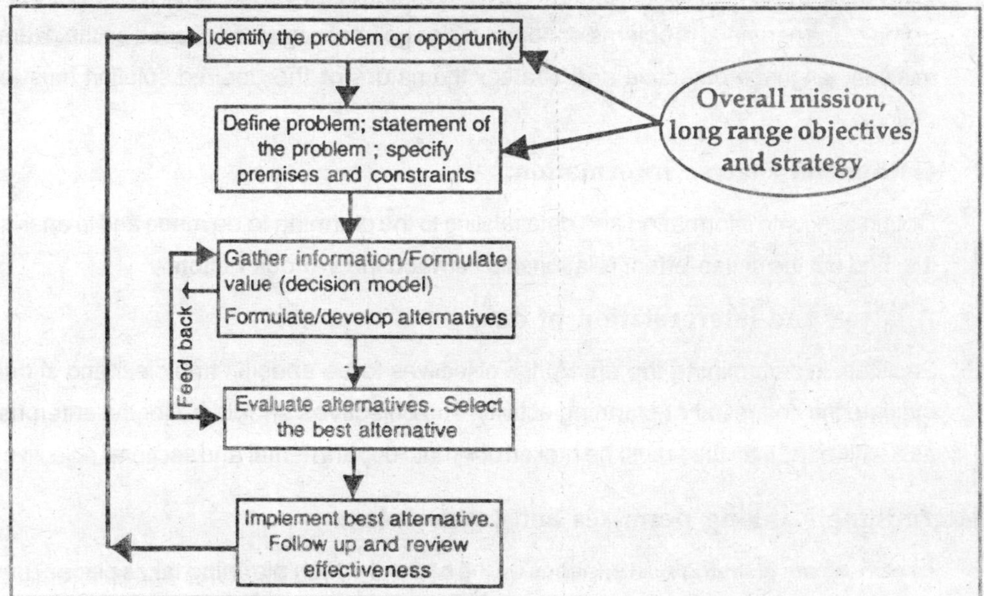

Fig. 2.2 Planning/Decision-making Process.

Planning/Decision-making Process

A logical method of solving the problems in to be adopted depending upon :

- The Application
- The Planning process
- The decision making process
- The scientific method

A model of this process is as shown Fig: 2.2

1) **Awareness of opportunities and problems:**

The first step in planning is the awareness of the unexploited business opportunities or the problems to be provided for in future. The following types of questions will help in ascertaining clearly the opportunities and problems.

(a) What business opportunities or problems are likely to arise in future?

(b) What is the plan to be performed to exploit such opportunities or such problems ?

(c) Whether it is necessary to advise a new plan or will it be sufficient to modify the existing plan ?

(d) By effectuating the plan, what benefit the organisation will get?

2) **Define problem:**

The problem is to be clearly defined. A problem cannot be solved untill it is recognised. Some of the perennial problems or opportunities go unrecognised. Based on the overall mission, language objective and strategy the nature of the desired solution must be defined.

3) **Gather and analyse information:**

Obtain adequate information and data relating to the planning to be made and to analyse it to find out the cause-effect relationship between the various factors.

4) **Analysis and interpretation of data:**

Facilitate in determining the enterprise objectives to be specific and clear and should indicate the end result of planning activity. The objectives should be for the enterprise as a whole and then they must be broken down into departmental and sectional objectives.

Determining planning permises and constraints

Premises are planning assumptions on the basis of which planning takes place. Thus, it is a **forecast** of conditions like :

- Trends in population
- Political and economic environment
- Production cost
- Advertising policy
- Availability of labour, material, power etc.

Some of the premises like population growth and political environment are uncontrollable while some degrees of control can be exercised on the technology to be used, availability of raw materials etc. Further, there will be constraints like government control which affect the plans. Plans should be formulated by the management in the backdrop of such premises and constraints.

Finding out the alternative courses of action

The next step is to find out the various **alternative courses of action.** For every plan, there are a number of alternatives and hence, all possible alternatives to work out a plan for achieving the desired objectives should be found out for their evaluation. Identification of the alternatives often leads to a search for more information.

Evaluation of alternatives and selection

The next step is to evaluate all possible alternatives with reference to cost, speed, quality etc and select the best course of action. Simply stating an alternative is not enough; each concept must be flushed out in enough detail so that its benefits and disadvantages can be effectively evaluated. At the same time, some 'Value model' or measure of merit (quantitative or qualitative) needs to be defined against which alternatives can be evaluated. The solution that best satisfies this value model is then recommended. Evaluation often needs to modification or combination of alternatives to find a new one that combines the advantages of several.

Implement best alternative

After the solution is implemented, it is important to check back later to determine if the problem as stated was really resolved by the solution. Often there will be unexpected secondary effects. This has to be defined as a new problem and the process once again begins.

It is therefore problem solving/decision making is an interactive process, involving feed back at several steps before the best resolution is found.

Methods of Planning

Planning consists of several individual plans. Depending on their nature and scope, plans can be broadly classified as follows :

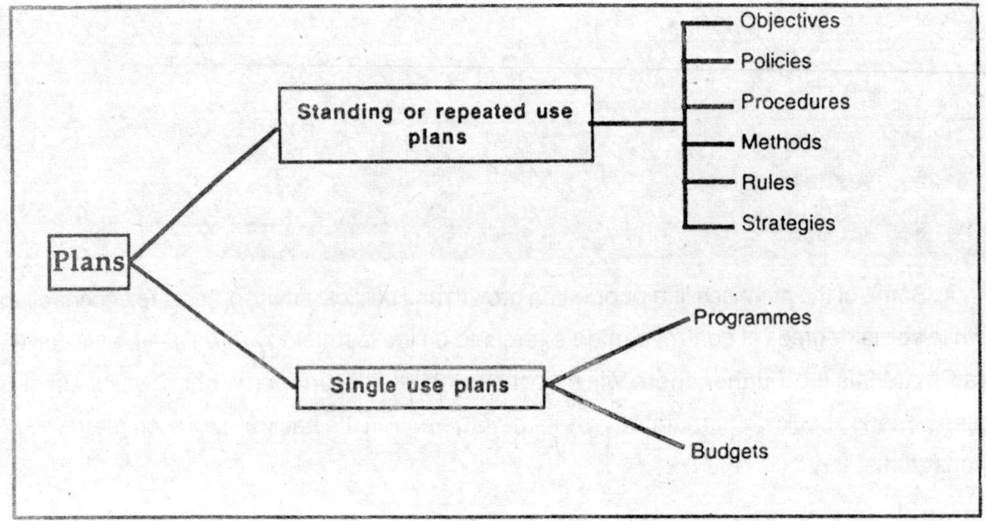

Fig. 2.3 Classification of Plans

On the basis of stated objectives, an organisation develops **standing plans and single use plans.**

- **Standing plans** which are to be used over and over again lead to the development of policies, procedures, methods, rules and strategies.
- **Single-use plans** which are to be used in specific situations only produce programmes and budgets.

Objectives :- The Foundation for planning

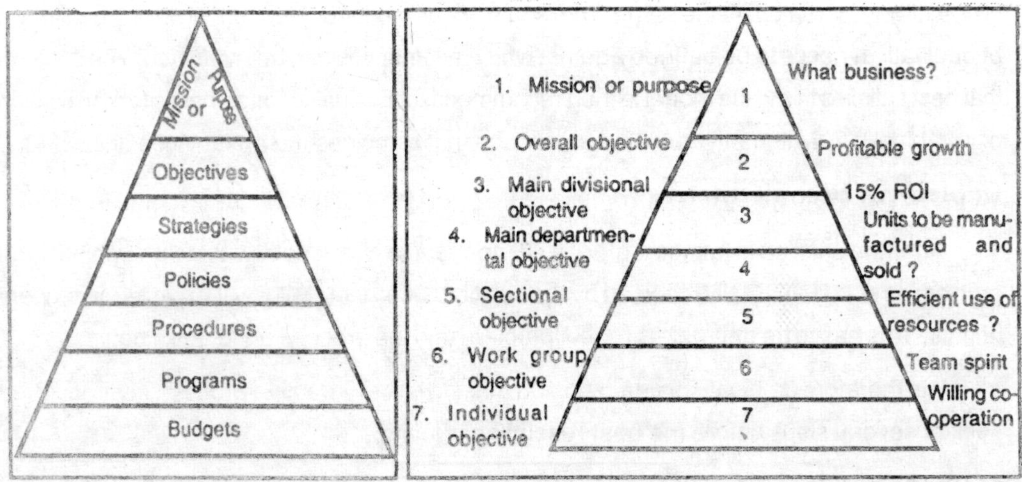

Fig. 2.4 Hierarchy of Plans *Fig. 2.5 Hierarchy of Objectives*

The hierarchy of plans and objectives are as shown above in figures 2.4 and 2.5

Important characteristics of business objectives	Requirement of sound objectives
♦ Multiple in nature ♦ Objectives have hierarchy ♦ Objectives may be long-range or short range ♦ Objectives are interdependent ♦ Objectives are either tangible or intangible ♦ Objectives have a priority ♦ Objectives sometimes may clash with each other	♦ Objectives must be clear ♦ Objectives must support one another ♦ Objectives must be precise and measurable ♦ Objectives should always remain valid ♦ Objectives should be result centered ♦ Objectives should encourage high performance, yet be realistic ♦ Objectives must be balanced

a) Mission or Purposes

Every Kind of an organised group should have meaningful purposes or missions. In every society, enterprises have a basic function which are assigned to them by society. We have generally come to realise the purpose of a business is the production and distribution of economic goods and services. The **purpose of a State Highway Department** is the Design, Building and Operation of a system of state highways. The **purpose of a university** is Teaching and Research and so on. It is true that in some Business, the specific purposes or mission often becomes fussy. In some of the larger conglomerates such as Tatas, missions related to the product line do not appear to exist. However, many of the conglomerates have regarded their mission as "SYNERGY" which is accomplished through the combination of a variety of companies. Some Business never makes clear to themselves or their organisation what their purposes are. Such Business often lack a guiding spirit for their actions.

People sometimes think that the mission of every business as well as its objectives is to make profit. It is true that every kind of enterprise must have profit in business to survive and grow. But this objective is accomplished by undertaking activities, by going in clearly defined directions and then accomplishing the mission or the duties owed to the society.

For eg: A Bulb manufacturing co. had a mission of lighting every village in its vicinity by providing quality goods and lighting systems.

b) Strategies

Market		Market share	
		Small	Large
	Fast growth	Question marks	Stars
	Slow growth	Dogs	Cash cows

Fig. 2.6 Business Portfolio Matrix

Three definitions are indicative of the most common usages of the term **'Strategies'**:

1. General programs of action and deployment of emphasis and resources to attain comprehensive objectives.
2. The program of objectives, resources used to attain these objectives and policies governing the acquisition use and disposition of these resources and
3. The determination of the basic long term objective of an enterprise of the adoption of courses of action and allocation of Resources necessary to achieve these goals.

For example, A company may have an objective to increase the market share of its product (say Toilet soap) by 10% in 2 years, the strategy it adopts may be to promote the product agressively by advertising campaigns and also give discounts on bulk purchase. Thus through this strategy the company has determined the broad course of action for achieving its objective.

The **purpose of strategies** then is to determine and communicate through a system of major objectives and policies a picture of what kind of action the enterprise will take in the future course to achieve its goal.

Stategies do not attempt to outline exactly how the enterprise is to accomplish the objectives, since the broad strategy will be supported by a number of major and minor programs. But the strategies furnish a framework for guiding thinking and action. A successful enterprise needs to develop effective strategies for achieving their ultimate goals. Strategic planning is the organised process for selecting these strategies.

For example, A few years ago, a forgeign Automobile Manufacturer selected the strategy of offering in the highly competitive American Automobile market a low priced, small car, easy to park, in order to meet a demand by consumer who were not then being served in these respects by domestic manufacturers. This kind of strategy helped the manufacturer to gain an increased profit each year which was his objective.

A **Business Portfolio matrix** is a tool for identifying the business the corporations are in and the ones they want to be in the future and to define a strategy for getting from the first set to the second. This is shown in Fig: 2.6.

c) Goals and Objectives

Objectives or Goals (terms can be used interchangebly or synonymous) are the ends toward which the activity is aimed. They represent not only the end point of planning but the end toward which organising, staffing, leading and controlling point. While enterprise objectives are the basic plan of the firm, a department may also have its own objectives. The objectives of each and every department naturally contribute to the attainment of enterprise objectives.

For example: The objective of a business might be to make a certain profit by producing colour Television sets (Their mission could be to provide entertainment to community through production and sale of TVs) whereas against this objectives of the business, the manufacturing department of the company may be to produce the required number of TV Sets of a given design and quality at a given cost. These objectives of Business at large and the manufacturing department are consistent, but they differ in that manufacturing department alone cannot ensure accomplishing the company's objectives.

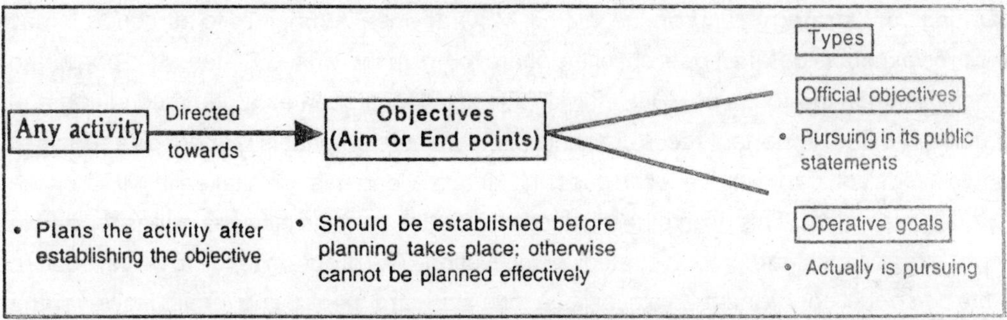

Fig . 2.7 Activity, Planning, Objectives and its Types

Peter Drucker talks about eight key result areas, objectives are to be established in all these areas:

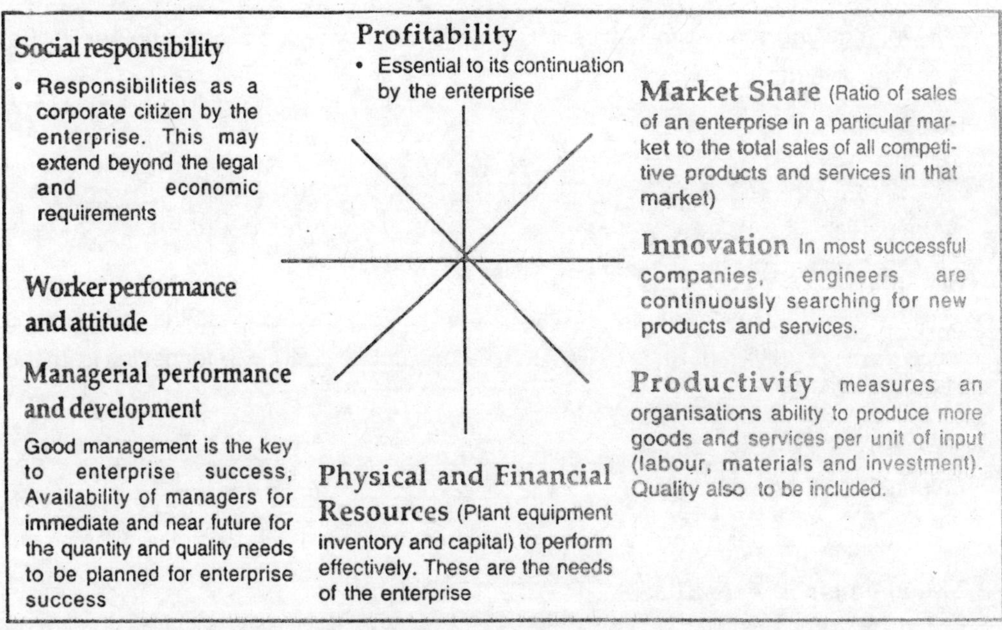

Fig. 2.8 Key Result Areas of the Organisation for Survival

2.3 Management by objectives of Management by Results

In 1954, Drucker formulated the concept of **'Management of objectives'** which has been widely adopted. **Management by objectives** is a powerful management tool and may even be considered a method of managing. Its abbreviation, "MBO" is known to most managers and will continue to be. The ideas behind MBO were popularized by Peter Drucker in the early 1940's. The name most associated with MBO currently in the United Sates in George Odiorne. Kingdom MBO has a very great emphasis on what is called **"corporate planning"** or **"strategy"** and on the internal MBO adviser. A program to introduce it may take twelve months before it gets out of the board room. In the United States while corporate planning is often the focus of MBO, individual motivation is seen as a prime condition and appraisal is still an important focus of attention. Much more emphasis is spent on aspects of human needs and participative techniques. In Canada a lead has been taken in MBO by the Federal government. This as in other such administrative settings elsewhere, has tended to emphasize appraisal rather than strategy or motivation. The program tends to be introduced by the personnel department as a substitute for a standard merit rating forms. However the underlying approach to all three methods is the same. It includes the clarification of managerial position outputs and then the derivation of specific measurable objectives. How the objectives are derived and what overall emphasis is put on individual commitment or appraisal are, however, major differences to be considered.

So, while having many similarities, MBO systems do vary from one another in the emphasis they give to:

Corporate planning

Manager planning

Appraisal link

Rewards link

Position analysis

Motivation element

Participation element

Emphasis on future

Versions of MBO go under a variety of names. The most widely used are:

Management by results

Goals management

Whatever it is called, MBO is now in use around the world and in many major corporation - to name only a few:

General Motors

Du Pont

General Electric

Air force Logistics Command

Radio Corporation of America

Socony Mobil Oil

Standard Oil

General foods

There must be something to it. What is MBO? What is common to all MBO systems? What are the major differences among them? This chapter will answer these questions.

Peter Drucker believes that objects are to be established in all areas on which the organisations survival depends. He distinguished eight key result areas. These are:-

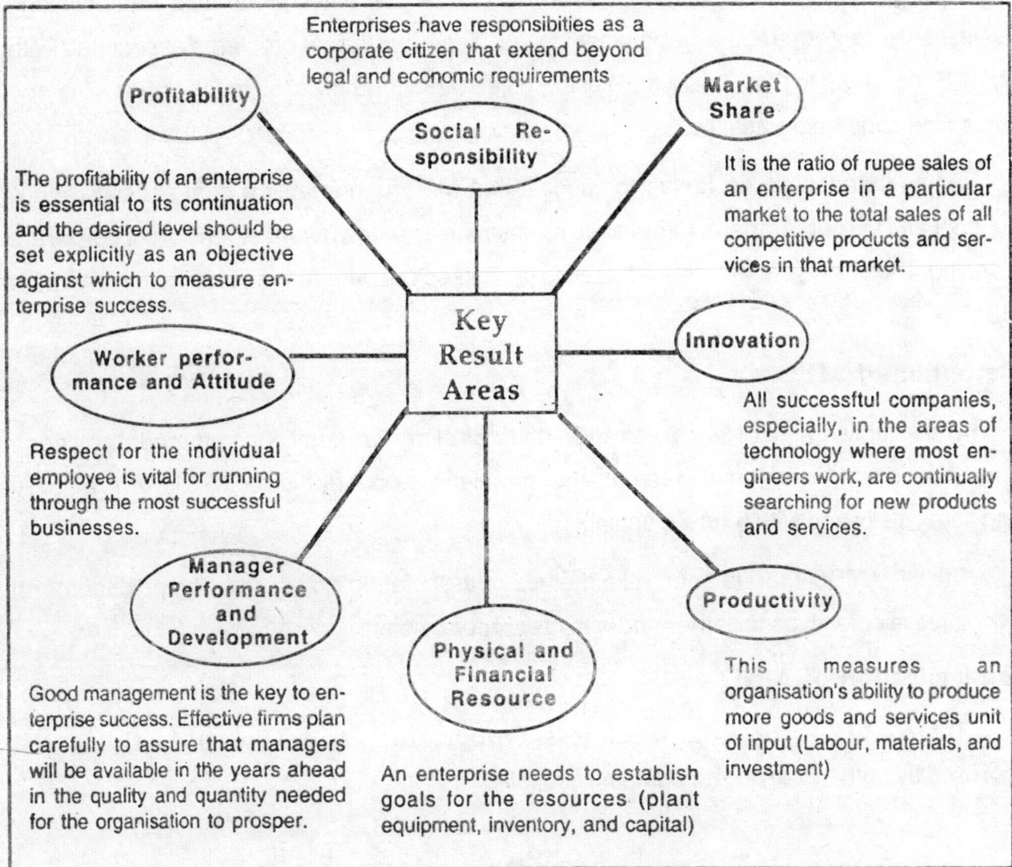

Fig. 2.9 Key Result Areas

The setting of objectives is no new idea, but until recently there has been little evidence of companies making systematic and sustained attempts to relative objectives to performance as measured by quantified profits. **Management by objectives** (MBO) goes a stage further in that it involves not only the establishment of realistic targets, but also the full support of management at all levels, in the achievement of those targets. The whole process is thus one of active involvement from the board of directors downwards.

MBO is a method of associating peoples positions with objectives and linking the objectives to the corporate plan. Peter Drucker proposed this management tool in the early 1950's as a method of managing the complexity of the growing organisations. The common elements in MBO are **objectives** that are established for positions. Managers and subordinates negotiate to set the objectives. Objectives are linked with corporate goals and emphasis is placed on measurement and control and on the establishment of a review and recycle system. Generally, the manager is more involved than the subordinate in setting the objectives, commonly establishing and setting them. MBO can be perceived either as a way of linking evaluation to performance or as a planning aid. There are a few problems associated with MBO. People tend to play it safe and set low objectives. It requires too much paper work and it is a time consuming activity.

Some theories go so far as to suggest that MBO is primarily a contract between a superior and his subordinate. Others see its essence as a downward extension of corporate planning. These kinds of differences need to be worked out prior to the decision to implement MBO.

Definition of MBO

The establishment of key areas and standards of performance for managerial positions and the periodic conversion of these into measurable time-bounded objectives linked vertically and horizontally and with future planning.

Effective MBO then is seen as a method of associating objectives with positions and linking these objectives together and with the corporate plan.

Implemetation of MBO

The **SWOT (Strength, Weakness, Opportunity and Threat) Analysis** is a tool used by both by corporate planning and MBO.

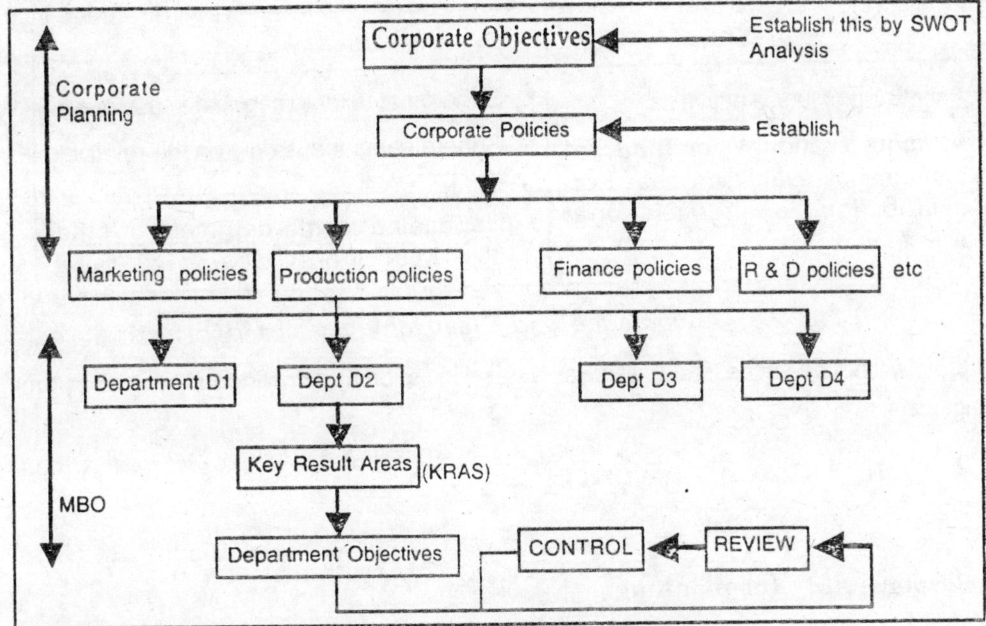

Fig. 2.10 Implementation of MBO

1. **Operational and Tactical Plans** first prepared
2. **Key result areas** at the operating level (Sectional or departmental level) are identified eg. Worker absentism, rejection rate, machine idle time etc.
3. **The objectives of section or department** are set jointly by the section head and his subordinates. Eg. To reduce of time per worker per month etc
4. **Action plan** for every manager describing his talks in quantitative terms, specifying resources, fixing standards for performance (contains KRA, Objective, Action needed by whom and when with review date)
5. **Implementation** of the Action plan.
6. **Performance review** with the expected and actual; short falls identified and corrective action suggested

Advantages and Disadvantages of MBO

Advantages	Disadvantages
♦ Greater commitment at the lower level	♦ Extensive paper work
♦ Satisfaction on the past of subordinates through involvement	♦ Time involvement
♦ Enforced Planning	♦ Misuse when superiors assign

Advantages	Disadvantages
♦ Prioritising of future activities ♦ A more rational method of performance evaluation based on contribution to organisational objectives	♦ Subordinates try to negotiate easy goals. ♦ Subordinates focus only on the relatively few (verifiable) ♦ Negotiated to the detriment of other objectives both quantitative and qualitative.

Fig. 2.11 Advantages and Disadvantages of MBO

MBO will not be successful until it has a good initiation and continuous support by top management.

2.4 Some planning concepts

These are:

(I) Responsibility for planning

Here the responsibility of every manager in planning function is needed. The higher the level, the more time they have to spend in planning with regard to long term planning. Strategic planning is at the higher level of the managers to meet competitive advantage, wider market, gather and analyse information on the economy etc.

(II) Planning premises :

This has been explained in the earlier paragraphs. Future of technology and competition are to be planned on the technology side. Contingency plans are to be developed whenever uncertainities found.

(III) Planning Horizon (Also known as Time Horizon)

This asks how far into the future one should plan. This varies widely depending on the nature of the business and the plan.

eg. High technology products, Information technology products may have short lives and therefore short planning horizons.

The following chart gives the time horizon that a large enterprises of heavy investments (aircraft company etc) normally covers the various planning stages.

Types of planning	Time span	Organisational unit	Objectives
Corporate Planning	15-20 Years	Corporate office	Mission, Corporate objectives
Long range planning	10 Years	Division	Organisational goals
Aggregate planning	5 Years	Factory	Program/Project goals

Types of planning	Time span	Organisational unit	Objectives
Budgetting	3 Years	Factory	Product Deliveries
Production plan	1 Year	Department	Departmental Targets
Central scheduling	1-2 Years	Shop	Shop Targets
Operational Scheduling	1-2 days	Work centre	Start and Finish dates for operations
Loading	1-2 shifts	Machine	Output in manhours

Fig. 2.12 Example of Time Horizon in the Case of A Large Enterprise.

2.5 Systems of plans

A **system of plans** may have to be involved in large firms in complex projects into yearly forecasts and ten yearly forecasts and revised once in 5 years. This was suggested in 1916 by **Henri Fayol**. Different types of plan are :-

- Production plan
- Tooling plan
- Make/Buy plan
- Distribution plan
- Servicing plan
- Quality assurance plan
- Facilities plan
- Reliability plan
- Training plan etc.
- Logistics support plan

2.6(1) Policies

Policies are also plans in that they are general statements or understanding which guide or channel thinking and action in decision making. All policies are not statements since they are often merely implied from the actions of a manager. For example, The president of a Company may strict follow, perhaps for convenience rather than as policy, the practice of promoting from within the Organisation, this practice may than be interpreted as policy by his subordinates and carefully followed by subordinates. In fact, one of the problems of managers is to make sure that subordinates do not interpret as policy, minor managerial decisions that are made without being intended to serve as patterns.

Policies limit an area within which a decision is to be made and ensure that the decision will be consistent with, and contribute to an objective. Policies help to decide issues before they become problem, make it unnecessary to analyse the same problem every time it comes up and unify other plans, thus permitting managers to delegate authority and still maintain control over what their subordinates do.

Policies exist on all levels of the organisation and range from major company policies through major department policies to minor policies applicable to the smallest segment of the organisation. They may also be related to functions such as Sales & Finance, or merely to a project such as that of designing a new product. There are many types of policies. Examples include policies to hire only University Trained Engineers or to encourage suggestions for improving cooperation, to promote employees from within to fill the higher posts or to conform strictly to a high standard of business ethics etc.

(II) Procedures

Procedures are plans that establish a required method of handling future activities. They are truely guides to action, rather than to thinking and they detail the exact manner in which a certain activity must be accomplished. They are chronological sequences of required actions.

Procedures are found in every part of an organisation. The board of directors follow many procedures different from those of the supervisor, the expense account of the vice president may go through quite different approval procedures than that of salesperson, the procedure for carrying forward the sick leave and earned leave may vary in different throughout an organisation, even though we might expect they become more numerous in the lower levels.

Like other types of plans, **procedures exist in a hierarchy of importance.** Thus, in a typical company we may find a manual called "Corporation Standard Practice" outlining the procedures for the corporation as a whole and an operating instructions manual for carrying out the work on the machines aimed at the Direct Workers.

Procedures often cut across department lines. For example, in a manufacturing company, the procedure for handling orders will certainly involve the sales department (for the original order), the finance department (for acknowledgement of receipt of funds), the Accounting Department (for recording the transaction) and the Production Department (to produce goods). Thus every time an order is received by the company the same procedure has to be followed by the company's officials and they need not wait for instructions to do their activity.

Let us look at few examples of the relationship between procedures and policies. Company policy may grant employees vacations. Procedures established to implement this policy will provide for scheduling vacations to avoid disruption of Work, maintaining records to assure each employee of a Vacation and spelling out the means for applying for a vacation. A Company may have a policy of shipping orders quickly, particularly in a large company, careful procedures will be necessary to ensure that orders are handled in a specific way.

2.7 Forecasting

Forecasting is a tool for technology management and presents managerial requirements imposed on Forecasting.

Given the uncertainly inherent in the future, expectations placed upon forecasts should be realistic.

Forecasts in our opinion are as under :

Expect results	Do not expect results
♦ To delimit the extent of uncertainty ♦ Establishing correct vectors of change ♦ Providing valuable information to the would-be-manager of technology ♦ Indicating ranges of future possibilities	♦ Perfectly accurate ♦ Highly precise ♦ Point values

Fig. 2.13 Results Under Forecasting

Forecasting involves the task of laying out possible evolutionary paths of anticipated change in the Technology environment

Technology Forecasting

Forecasting requires many **elements** as under :

As per **Roman and Marvin Cetron**, a **technology forecast** is a prediction based on confidence, that certain technical developments can occur within a specified time period with a given level of resource allocation.

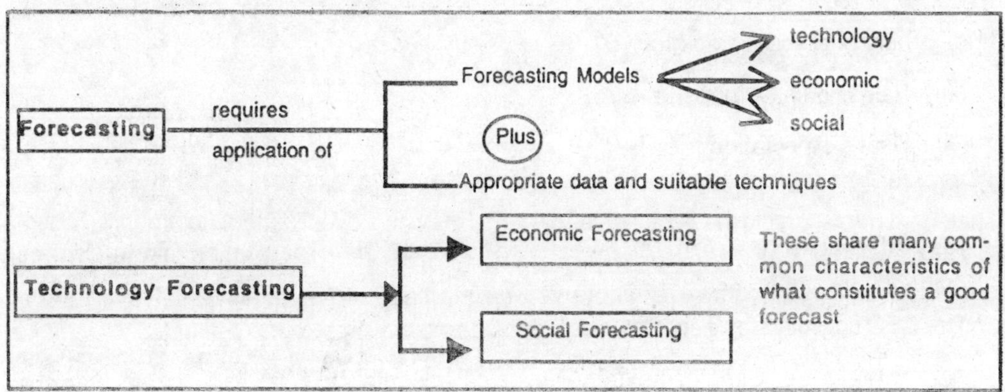

Fig 2.14 Elements of Forecasting

According to **Henry Fayol**, the first management function as **'Prevoyance'** meaning **'foresee'** and **'prepare for' action**, which is an essential preliminary to planning-it is therefore foreseeing or forecasting what the future will be like.

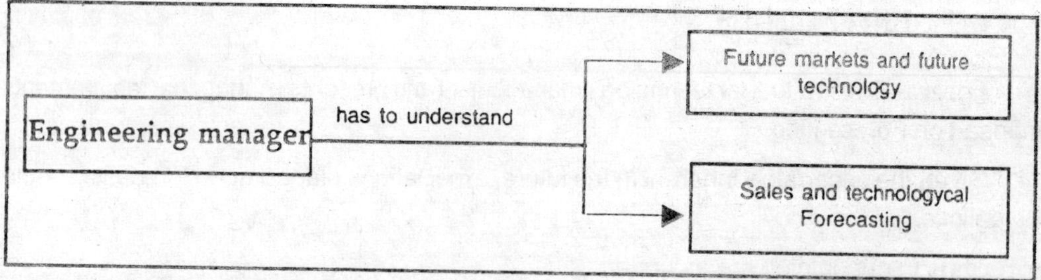

Fig. 2.15 Engineering Manager to Understand Forecasting

(I) Sales Forecasting

a) **Using Sales Estimates** : It is the most important premise in planning and decision making in the level of future sales (for non-profit activities of future operations). For everything, our plan is based on this assumption.

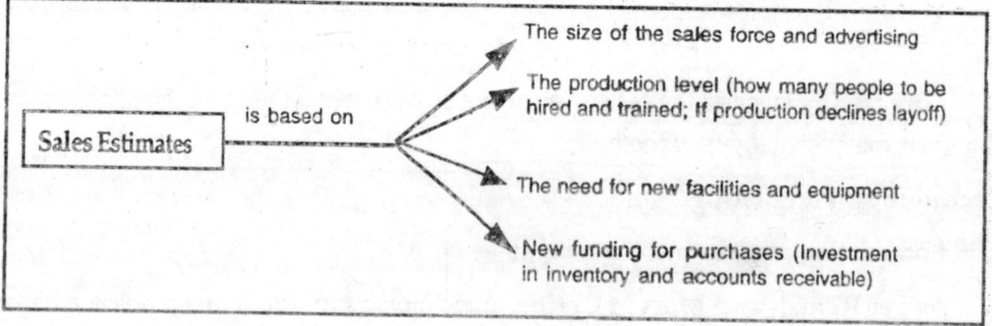

Fig. 2.16 Sales Estimate

Ways of doing sales estimates :-

(I) Jury of executive opinion

(II) Sales Force Composite

(III) User's expectations

(IV) Choice of method

- **Jury of executive opinion :-** Each executive of the organisation, say a general manager provide an estimate of future volume (A guess work done called gestimate). The CEO consolidates and provides a considered average of the estimates.

  Advantages are : Simple; inexpensive; quick; acceptable by all; if the future conforms to the assumptions made by the executives in gestimation.

- **Sales Force Composite :-** Members of the sales force estimate sales in their regions. Regional sales managers adjust these estimates for their opinion of the optimism or pessimism of individual sales people. The general sales manager again uses his experience and knowledge to trim the figures to account for new products or factors of which the 'regional' sales manager or individual sales men are aware. Advantages are :- commonly used method, better accuracy since the field sales force is close to the customer. The disadvantage is each sales person may be asked to achieve this goal. Hence the sales man in his own interest may come down with low/high figures to his advantage depending on the situation.

- **User's expectation:** If the company's products are sold to only a few customers, the simplest method is to ask them and take their opinion about their needs for the future period. Customers also need the product from reliable sources of supply. Hence communication will be the best for both the parties. For consumer goods, it is difficult to adopt this as they are scattered, more in numbers, and do not know what they will purchase in the future.
- **Choice of method**

  Companies have effective planning to combine a variety of methods to arrive at the best sales forecast.

  - Qualitative estimates (From the sales force and customer surveys)
  - Quantitative estimates (By adopting moving average or regression models)

  These two are compared. The chief executive with the help of other officers will establish a sales forecast to be used in future planning.

a) Moving Average Forecasts :

(I) Simple moving average (II) Weighted moving average

(II) Exponential Smoothing

b) Regression Models

(I) Simple regression model

(II) Multiple regression

Simple moving average :-

When the values of a parameter show no clear trend with time, a forecast for the next period can be taken as the simple average of some number (n) of the most recent actual values (AT). An example of the simple moving average method is shown as under :

Months	Actual	Forecast
January	4,800	-
February	4,900	-
March	4,950	-
April	-	4,883

In the above example, taking a 3 months moving average, the forecast for April is

The formula is : n

$$Fn + 1 = \frac{1}{n} \sum_{t=1} At$$

$$\frac{4800 + 4900 + 4950}{3} = 4883$$

Weighted moving average :

This method gives more weightage to recent past months and less to distant past. For example, the weights are shown as under :

Months	Weights	Sales	Weighted sales
January	2	4,800	9,600
February	3	4,900	14,700
March	5	4,950	24,750
Total	10		49,050

$$\text{Forecast for April} = \frac{49,050}{10} = 4905$$

The preceding method is simple moving average method has the disadvantages:

The earlier value (December previous month) has no influence at all; but value n years in the past January is weighted just as heavily as the most recent value (March). In this model, by assigning a set of weights with which total unity (1.0) to the previous n values.

$$Fn+1 = \sum_{t=1}^{n} W_t A_t \qquad \text{Where} \qquad W_t = \sum_{t=1}^{n} = 1.0$$

Exponential Smoothing

The weighted moving average techniques have some disadvantages. You or your computer must record and know 'n' previous values and 'n' weights for each parameter being forecast. If n is large it is burdensome. The simple exponential smoothing method continuously reduces the weight of a value as it becomes older, yet minimises the data that must be retained in memory.

FT = FT-1 + a (AT-1-FT-1)

Where FT = Forecast demand for the current period

FT-1 = Forecast demand for the previous period

AT-1 = Actual for the previous period

a = Smoothing Factor

(AT-1-FT-1) is the error in forecasting for the previous period and α moderates this error.

Example

FApril = FMarch+0.12 (AMarch-FMarch)

α value is assumed as 0.12, but based on the accuracy of forecasting. This can be raised or lowered.

$$F_{April} = 4950 + 0.12(5000 - 4950)$$
$$= 4950 + 0.12x50 = 4356$$

Summary

The results based on the previous methods are compared under :

	Sales of April
Simple Moving Average	4883
Weighted Moving Average	4905
Exponential Smoothing	4956

Expanding the right hand equation, using similar expressions for FT, FT-1 etc gives us

$$F_{T+1} = \alpha AT + (1-\alpha)(\alpha AT1 + (1-\alpha)F_{T-1})$$
$$= \alpha AT + \alpha(1-\alpha)AT - 1 + (1-\alpha)^2 F_{T-1}$$
$$= \alpha AT + \alpha(1-\alpha)AT - 1 + \alpha(1-\alpha)^2 AT - 1 + (1-\alpha)2A_{T-2}$$
$$+ \alpha(1-\alpha)^3 AT - 3 + - - -$$

We can see that the weight put on past values continues to decrease but never becomes zero. To start the forecast sequence we must set the first forecast equal to the actual value of the preceding year.

c) Regression Analysis

Regression is the formation of an equation for a line that best fits the **scatter diagram** of historic data. (The scatter diagram is as explained below). The equation can then be used for forecasting the values explained below). The equation can then be used for forecasting the values of the dependent variable. The relationship between x and y could be **linear** or **curvi linear** as seen from the following equations.

y = a + bx (Linear)

y = a + bx + cx² + dx³ + ... (Curvilinear)

So far, only the relationship between one independent and one dependent variable was considered. There are situations where more than one independent variable are responsible for the change in the values of the dependent variable.

The weight and the speed of an aircraft have an impact on the manhours required to produce the aircraft.

The crop output will depend on : Rainfall, Irrigation, Fertiliser. In such cases, **multiple regression** is used (Also called partial regression analysis-partial means that while maintaining the other variables constant, the influence of the required independent variable is examined. The multiple regression formula takes the following form :-

$y = a + bx_1 + cx_2 + dx_3$ etc. where x_1, x_2, x_3 are independent variables.

Simple Linear Regression (Simple regression model)

Method of Least squares

Consider a scatter diagram containing only 3 points a, b, & c

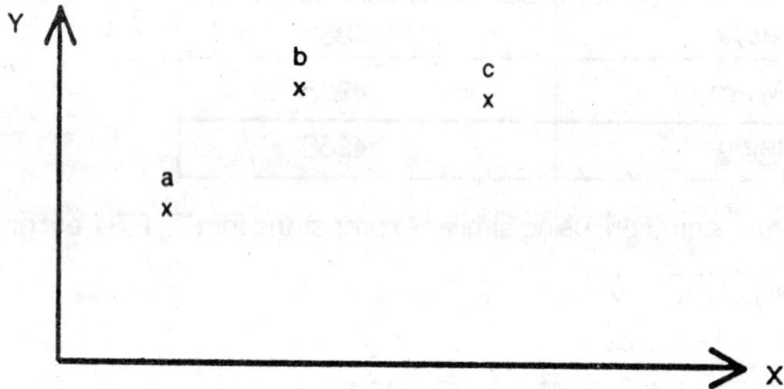

The object of linear regression analysis is to draw a straight line which either passes through all the points or lies closest to the maximum number of points

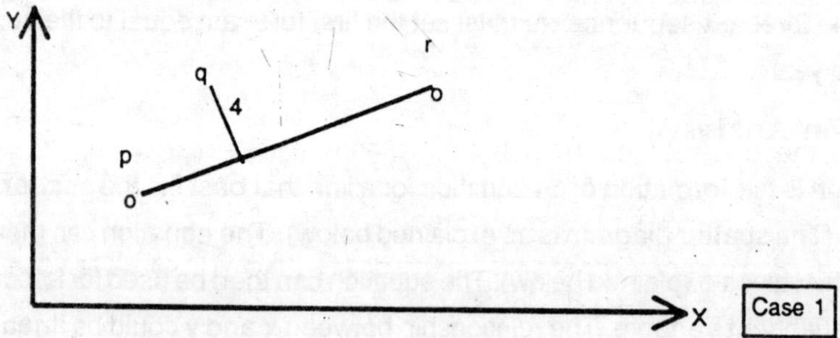

The direct approach suggests drawing a line connecting 'P' and neglecting the influence of 'q' altogether. A more sophisticted would be to shift to line upwards so that the vertical distance between q and the line is reduced in the first instance to 3 and next to 2. Correspondingly, the distance between points P & Q and the line would become -1 and -2 respectively. These two cses are shown below:

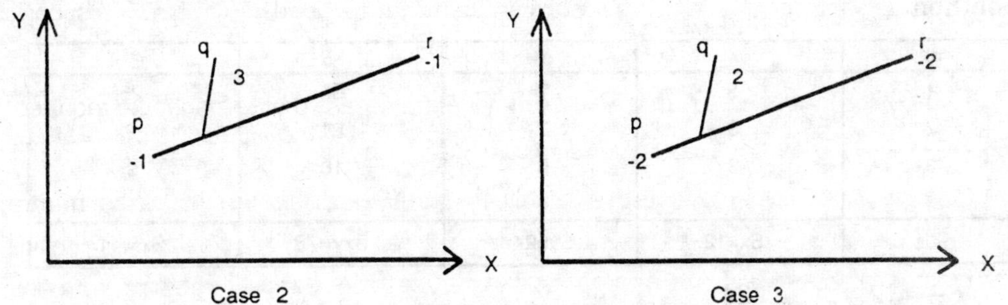

Now, the issue is which of the 3 cases gives the best fit. The **method of least squares** answers this question as shown below:

"Y" values are the vertical distances between the points and the regression line.

Points	'Y' Absolute values			'Y' Squared values		
	Case 1	Case 2	Case 3	Case 1	Case 2	Case 3
P	0	1	2	0	1	4
Q	4	3	2	16	9	4
R	0	1	2	0	1	4
Total	4-Best	5	6	16	11-Best	12

If one goes by absolute values, case 1 seems to be the best fit-Misleading

If one goes by squared values, case 2 seems to be the best fit-**As per statisticians, this is correct**

Regression formula for values of a & b

If Y = a+bx is the equation of a regression line, then the values of 'a' and 'b' are given by the following formulae

$$b = \frac{\sum xy - n\overline{x}\overline{y}}{\sum x^2 - n\overline{x}^2} \qquad a = \overline{y} - b\overline{x}$$

The utility of these formulae is brought out in the following example

Example

A Furniture moving company operating 4 lorries desires to have a relationship established between the years of service of their lorries and the annual repair expenses. It has collected the following statistics :

Truck no	Years of service	Repair charge (1000's Rs)
101	5	7
102	3	7
103	3	6
104	1	4

Solution

n	x	y	xy	x^2
1	5	7	35	25
2	3	7	21	9
3	3	6	18	9
4	1	4	4	1
n=4	Sx=12	Sy=24	Sxy=78	Sx^2=44

$$\overline{X} = \frac{12}{4} = 3^2; Y = \frac{24}{4} = 6$$

$$b = \frac{\Sigma xy - n(\overline{X})(\overline{Y})}{\Sigma x^2 - nx^2} = \frac{78 - 4x3x6}{44 - 4x3^2} = 0.75$$

$$a = \overline{y} - b\overline{x} = 6 - 0.75 = 3.75 \ \hat{y} = 3.75 + 0.75x$$

$\hat{Y}$ is pronounced as 'Yhat' and represents the estimated value of Y as distinct from the actual value of Y.

Multiple regression

As we have seen simple regression is a fore-casting tool. Such an overview is necessarily brief and omits many important assumptions and calculations,

Multiple regression often can provide a better explanation of the past behaviour of the forecast (dependent variable and a better basis for predicting its future levels)

A **multiple regression** with two explanatory variables has the form Y=a+bx+cz+e

The estimates of a, b and c once again are determined by the regressing procedure so as to minimise the sum of the squared errors.

Two independent variables will specify a two dimensional plane in a three dimensional space (Y, X and Z)

However, the procedures can be generalised to provide for any number of independent variables as long as there are adequate numbers of observations available.

There are many computer packages available that will generate results similar to those for simple regression.

Another way time can be included in regression is by using dummy variables (a variable with a value of either 0 or 1) to seasonally adjust data and forecasts.

Example: Summer (S), Fall (F), Winter (W) Variables could be included in the equation adopted for simplest naive extrapolation. (Indian cable TV subscribers in thousands and for different years)

$$Y = a + b_1X + b_2S + b_3F + b_4W + e$$

2nd example is a manufacturer of replacement automobile tyre must find that:

- The demand for tyres varied with the cost of gasoline
- The current unemployment rate
- Sales of automobiles 27 years previously
- Weight of those automobiles

d) Technological Forecasting

Technological Forecasting has already been explained earlier.

However, the eleven commandments for technology forecasting are explained below.

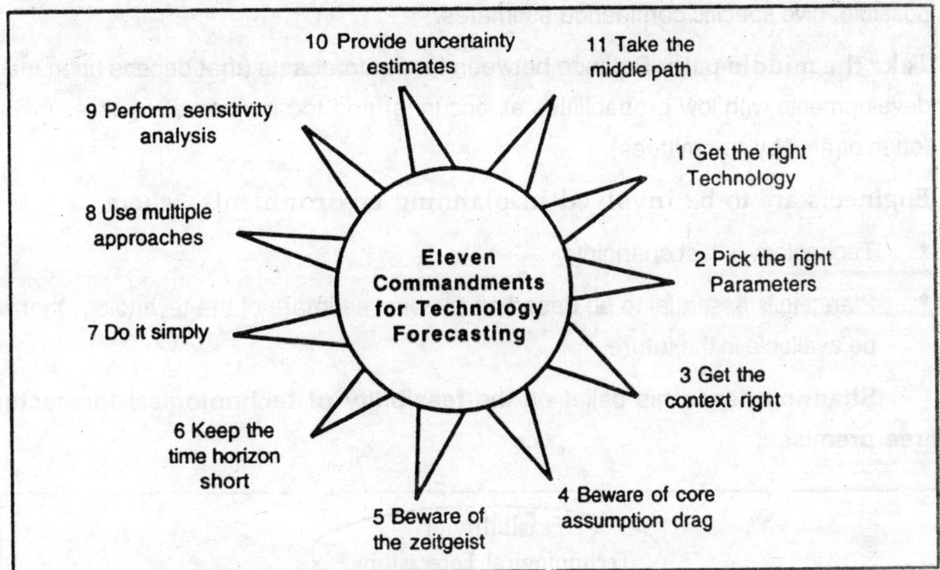

Fig: 2.17 Eleven Commandments for Technology Forecasting

1. **Get the right technology:** Understand the technical domain sufficiently to address the essential functions at the right level of aggregation.
2. **Pick the right parameters:** Technological parameters must pertain to the decision to be made; data must be attainable
3. **Get the context right:** Identify the institutions involved, socio-economic influences, and critical decision points now and in the future.
4. **Beware of core assumption drag:** Technical myopia or ideological fixation can miss qualitative changes from past patterns.
5. **Beware of the Zeitgeist:** Challenge the conventional wisdom; Try out alternative perspectives; do not allow the forecast to just mirror the prevailing mood of the moment
6. **Keep the time horizon short:** This suggests that frequent, lower cost forecasts be conducted rather than more substantial, but less freqent studies.

7. **Do it simply:** Invest study resources in reducing the most critical uncertainties, rarely will these respond to elaborate modeling.

8. **Use multiple approaches:** Seek convergence from diverse approaches with complementary strengths.

9. **Perform sensitivity analysis:** Deliberately estimate how the forecast would change if assumed initial conditions, influential variable levels, functional relationships or milestones change.

10. **Provide uncertainity estimates:** Give ranges of parameter projections over time; if possible, give specific confidence estimates.

11. **Take the middle path:** Balance between far-out forecasts (that depend upon many developments with low probabilities all occuring) and too conservative assessments (often offered by committees)

Engineers are to be involved in planning environments, where

- Technology is fast changing
- Planning is essential to be based on the best estimate of the technology that will be available in the future.

Shannon bases his belief on the **feasibility of technological forecasting on three premises:**

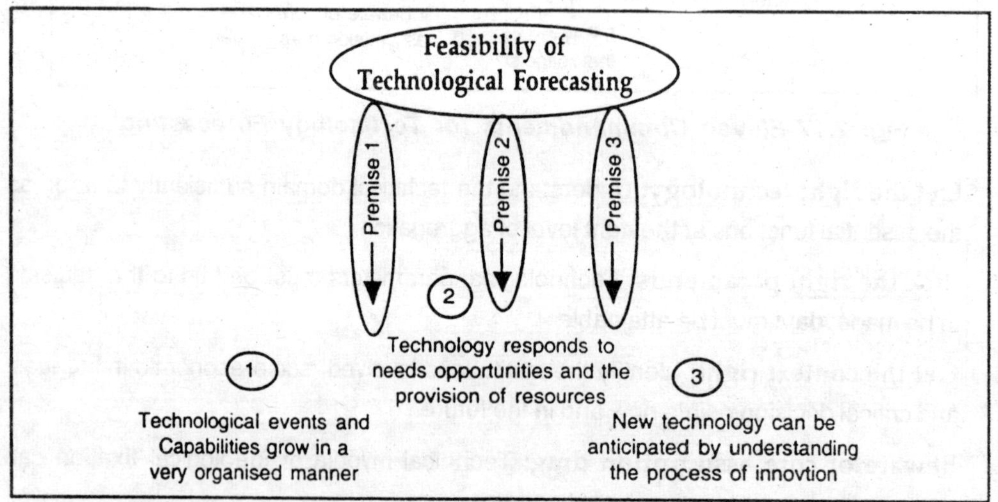

Fig. 2.18 Feasibility of Technological Forecasting

Technology forecasting categories apart from economic and social forecasting, can be classified as:

- **Normative**
- **Exploratory**

These two are polar types view points that may be blend in intermediate cases.

a) Normative technological forecasting:

This describes a desired future in line with the goals a nomative future. Following steps are adopted.

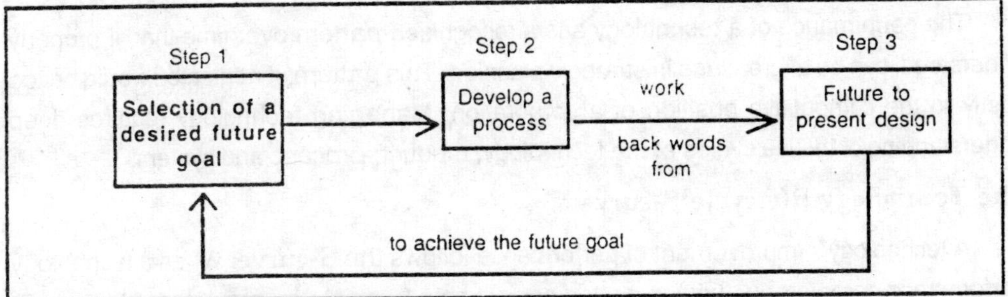

Fig. 2.19 Normative Technological Forecasting Steps.

Example: (i) Power availability from nuclear fusion in commercial quantities in the year 2020.

- Work backwards to establish a schedule for a full scale demonstration plant
- Then a smaller pilot plant.
- The research tasks that must precede them.
- Finally develop the overall budget and schedule required to reach the normative goal.

(ii) The decision taken in 1961 at USA by president kennedy to land a man on the surface of the moon needed normative technological forecasting.

b) Extrapolar Technological Forecasting

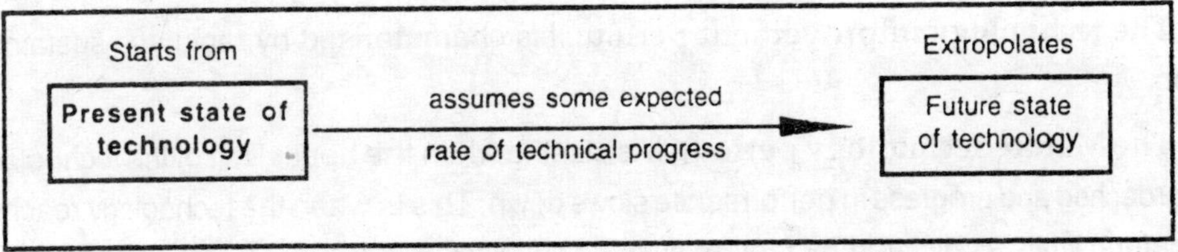

Fig. 2.20 Extrapolar Technological Forecasting

A common forecasting method is the use of a panel of experts in the technical field involved. Panels are sometimes consulted using the **'Delphi process'**

In the **extra polative future case**, the manager accesses studies of the future in the form of forecasts or impact assessments in areas over which his organisation exerts little or no direct control. Organisational goals may need to be adjusted in response to such a forecast.

Example :- If you want to dominate the US alluminium market, you have to look to the future. By beating the Canadian competition (Canada has cheaper energy and raw materials). You need to adjust that goal. (to dominate the US aluminium market).

Important Model for Technological Forecasting (Technology S-curve)

The performance of a technology has a recognised pattern over time that, if properly understood, can be of great use in strategic planning. This pattern, if neglected would be too costly to the competitive position of a corporation. Managing technology requires deep understanding of the life cycles of the technology, product, process and system.

The Technology life cycle S-curve

A technology's improvement of performance follows the **S-curve**. When a technology performance parameter (y axis) is plotted against time (x axis), the result resembles an S-shaped diagram called the **S-curve**. Technological performance can be expressed in terms of any attribute, such as density in the electronic industry (number of transistors per chip) or aircraft speed in miles per hour.

Technology progresses through a **three stage** technology life cycle (TLC)

- **The New invention period** (Embryonic stage)
- **The Technology improvement period** (Growth stage)
- **The Mature technology period** (Maturity stage)

The Technology becomes vulnerable to vulnerable to substitution or obsolescence when a new or better performing technology emerges.

The new invention period: It is characterised by a period of slow initial growth. This is the time when experimentation and initial bags are worked out of the system.

The technology improvement period: It is characterised by rapid and sustained growth.

The Mature-technology period:- It is starting when the upper limit of the technology is approached and progress in performance slows down. This is when the technology reaches into natural limits as dictated by factors such as physical limits.

Example:- The vaccum tube technology was limited by the:

- Tubes size
- Power consumption of the heated filament

Both of the above factors were natural barriers to electron conduction in a **Vaccum tube**. Electronic engineers could not overcome with these limitations. The arrival of the **solid**

state technology or **transistor** which permitted electron conduction in solid material, changed the physical barriers of size and power. The transistor technology started a new technology life cycle and rendered the Vaccum tube technology obsolete.

When the technology reaches its natural limits it becomes a **mature technology** vulnerable to substitution or obsolescence. This is a very important concept of **Management of technology (MOT).**

The **S-curve technology progress** is a very useful model in technological forecasting, as shown by **Fisher and Pry (1971).**

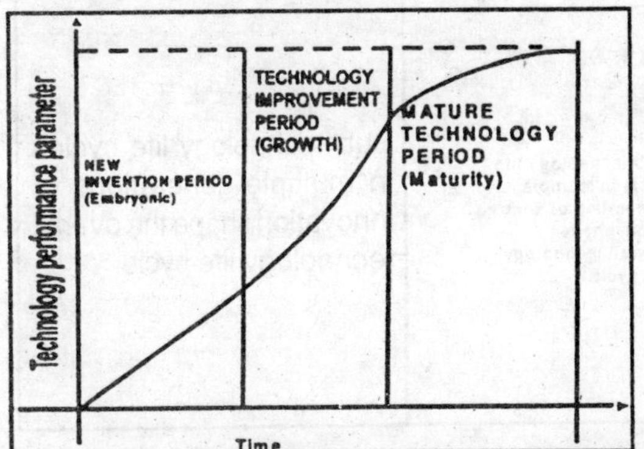

Fig. 2.21 The S-curve of Technolological Progress

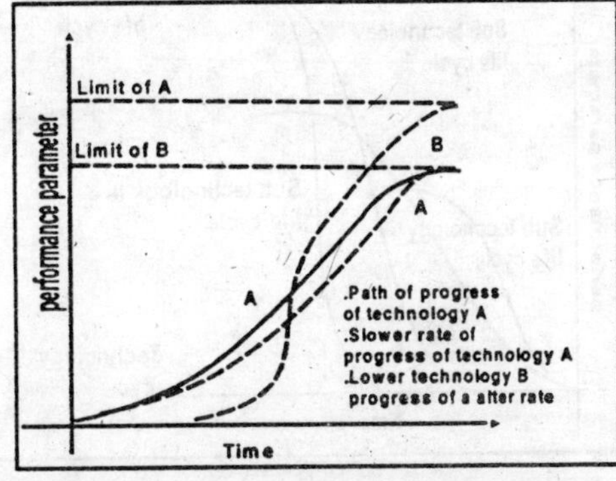

Fig. 2.22 Changes in Natural Limits of Technology (The rate of performance improvement is shown for two technologies)

A technology's rate of performance improvement is dependent on the effort devoted to its development. A technology may progress on curve A or A[1] depending on a number of factors, including:

- The type of the technology itself
- The cost and time devoted to its development

A **newer technology** (B) has a higher limit of performance for the same parameter. It may progress at a faster rate and will influence the progression of the older technology. At a certain point of time, it will replace the earlier technology (A)

Multiple Generation Technologies

Technology like other systems has also a hierarchy. A system can consist of a number of subsystems, and each subsystem may have a number of components or sub sub systems.

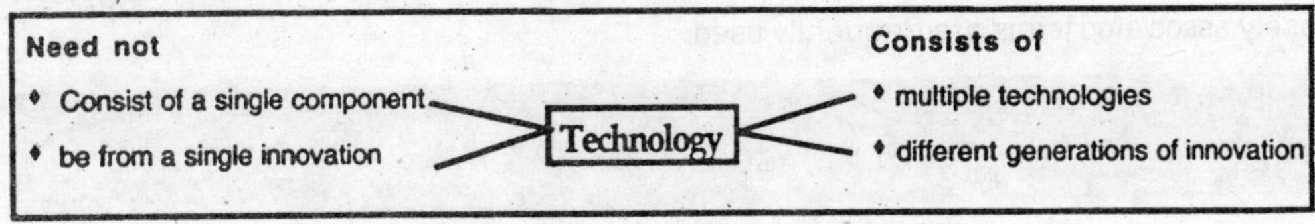

Fig. 2.23 Technology Features

Example

Personnel Computer (PC) is a technology and has a technology life cycle. It consists of several subtechnologies. One such subtechnology is the **micro processor** (defined as a technology with a technology life cycle all its own). In turn, the **micro processor** has its own **multigeneration technologies** or subtechnologies. Intel has under gone several generations of changes like 8088, 286, 386, 486, pentium. Each of these generations of innovation helped boost the technology life cycle of the micro processor and in turn that of the PC.

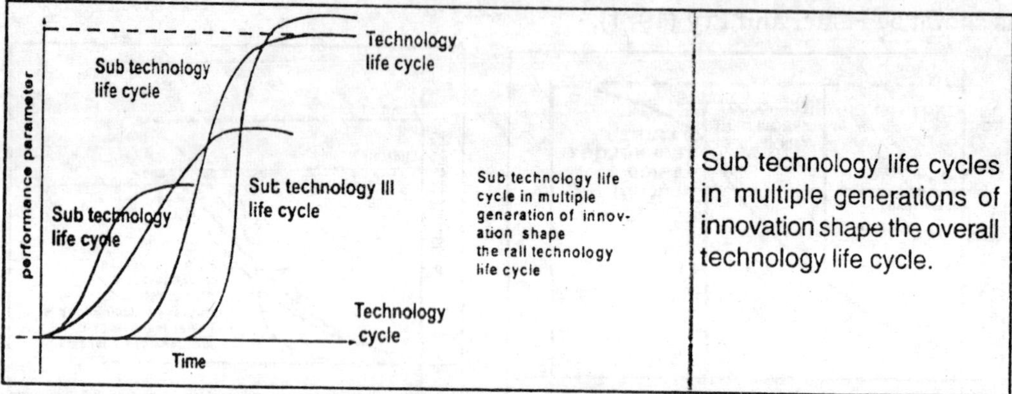

Fig. 2.24 Multiple Generation Technologies

2.8 Strategies for Managing Technology

Technology is an expression of **human creativity**. Managing technology involves:-

- Continuous effort in creating technology
- Developing novel products and services
- Successfully marketing them.

This requires great creativity with a system designed to exploit it. It also requires an investment in R & D (Research and Development), which is a costly endeavour - a risky investment which is to be managed well. However, it is an **investment in the future** that cannot be neglected nor can its value be underestimated. Technology creation and exploitation require a chain of events, starting with inventions and ending at the market place.

(1) Invention

When the subject of creativity is discussed in the context of technological change, two closely associated terms are frequently used:

- Invention
- Innovation

Invention is either a concept or the creation of novel technology

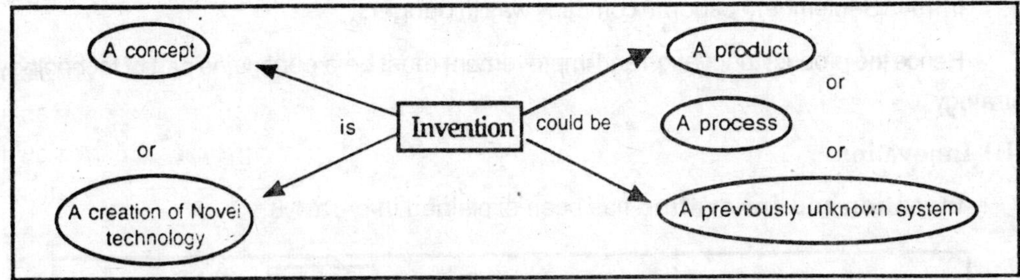

Fig. 2.25 Invention

Eg., Telephone, Steam Engine, Transistor or a xerox machine are important inventions. It can be either a new composite material, a new manufactured product, new process (New implies here new to the world)

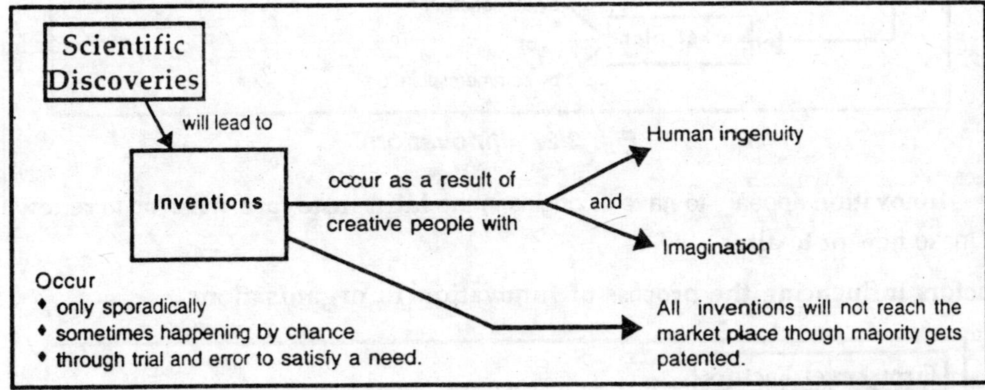

Fig.2.26 Inventions Occurence

In modern days, most **inventions** have followed **scientific discoveries** eg., See Einstein's discovery of the relationship between mass and energy in the early 1900's resulted in inventions in the **nuclear field.** There will be always a time lag between scientific discoveries and Inventions and may take more years to move the invention to the market in the form of a product or service. Producing the first successful product is not the desired one. It must keep the product line competitive.

Example:

In july 1981, **Adam osborne** - Entered the market of PC as the 1st person to market the PC as a complete package (computer, disk drive, monitor, printer and software); It was an instant success monitor was only 5" in size (diagnolly) and would hold only 52 characters across as against 80 on a typed page.

Competitors moved quickly to correct this deficiency

In 1983 September - osborne company was in danger.

Hence the product innovation and improvement must be a continuing part of technology strategy.

(II) Innovation

Invention and Innovation has been explained in para 1.8

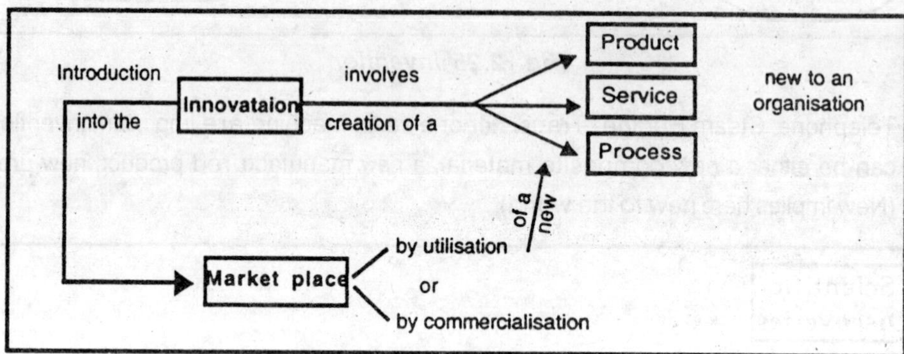

Fig. 2.27 Innovation

Innovation appears to have its origins in the **latin innovare**, meaning **to renew, to make new or to alter**

Factors Influencing the process of Innovation in organisations

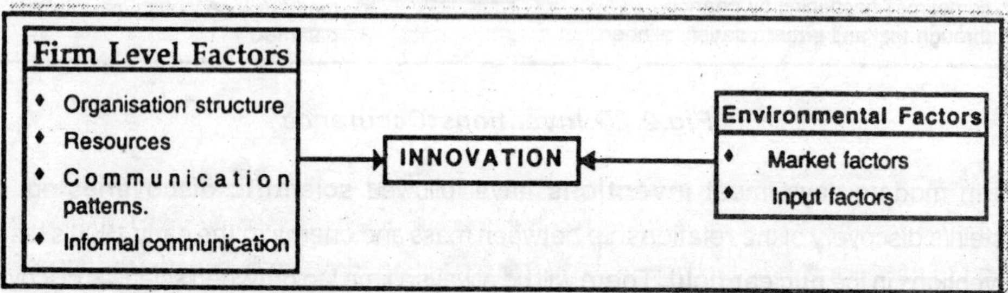

Fig. 2.28 Factors influencing the Process of Innovation

In 1939, **Joseph Schumpeter** proposed that innovative success might be related to the size of a firm. He outlined two types of innovation from a micro-economic perspective:

- **Entrepreneurial innovation**
- **Managed innovation**

Entrepreneurial innovation: occurs when new technologies and scientific development yield economic opportunities for proactive entrepreneuns. Small, dynamic, fast growing firms emerge and become the primary engine of innovation and often generate modular and architectural innovations.

Managed innovation: When the markets mature, the firms that survive tend to become larger, and competition shifts to price. This leads to an era of managed innovation, which firms attune their research and development efforts - innovation - to market forces; Several incremental innovations result from R & D activity, mainly of large firms. During this era, innovation efforts also become directed away from products and towards cost-reducing process technologies. Inventions and Innovations are intimately related; but they are not the same. An invention can be thought of as an event. Innovation can be thought of as a process. Inventions are not as common and one invention usually precedes a number of innovations. Innovation represents the important connection between an idea and its exploitation or commercialisation

Entrepreneurship

Webster defines the **entrepreneur** as:

- A person who organises and manages a business undertaking assuming the risk for the sake of profit.

Betz extends this as:

- The **entrepreneur** is a kind of business hero; and like all heroes they have qualities to be admired: initiative, daring, courage, commitment. These values are especially admired in turbulent business conditions, when initiative is required for survival. Technological progress is frequently sparked by entrepreneurs and entrepreneurial spirit.

Chester carlson and Joseph Wilson of xerox, **steve jobs** of Apple, **Laxmi Mittal** of UK, and **Bill Gates** of **Microsoft are but a few examples of successful entrepreneurs.** Entrepreneurs are a special breed of people who have the ability to sell or market ideas to others. They posess a particular set of qualities, including vision, courage, initiative, commitment, persistence, independent thinking, drive to succeed, and ambition. Most entrepreneurs have:

- an appreciation for a particular technology branch
- good motivational skills
- A commanding personality

They tend to deviate from mainstream thinking, enjoy being the center of attention, and savor recognisation. They could be compulsive in seeking their goals or perfection.

Enterpreneurs are not necessarly inventors. Their skill usually lies in bringing innovation to the market place.

Successful Entrepreneurs:	
Bill Gates	**Steve Jobs (Teamed with Stephen Woznaik)**
♦ He has been able to lead a company that started with 2 people (Gates and paul allen) and guide it through a technology revolution to become the largest software company in the world (Gold blatt, 1995). ♦ In 1996, Bill Gates networth was greater than the GNP of Nicargua (starling 1996) ♦ Between 1996 and 1997 his networth increased from $ 18 bl^n to more than $ 36 bl^n ♦ In 1999 it was more than $ 90 bl^n and with the continued growth of his technology sector company, his networth is greater than GNP of several countries combined. Bill Gates is one of the richest in the world.	♦ He created apple computers. ♦ Once an entrepreneur is always an entrepreneur. Jobs were forced out of the company in a power management struggie in the mid 1980 s. ♦ He moved on to a new venture buying and leading pixar, a successful computer based animation company that produced the very successful movie 'Toy story'. ♦ He paid $ 10 ml^n to buy pixar from George Lucas. He invested another $ 50 ml^n in the company. ♦ In 1995, pixar went for public offering Steve Job's stake in it was valued at $ 1.2 bl^n (warshah, 1996)

Fig. 2.29 Successful Entrepreneurs

Key role of Entrepreneurs:

Entrepreneurs play a key role:

- in creating and advancing technology
- sparking economic growth
- job creation.

Job creation

- The entrepreneurial spirit of silicon valley helped create thousands of new jobs in that region of USA and else where 1978-1992, 85% of the new jobs in Canada were created by small entrepreneurial firms (firms with 200 , or ferwer employees). Large corporations (500 employees or more) recorded no growth at all.

Entrepreneurship however is not limited to individuals or small companies. It exists in large corporations too if the corporation has to maintain its vitality and ensure its long term survival. Entrepreneurship within the confines of an organisation is called as **entrepreneurship (internal entrepreneurship)** in which the entrepreneurial process of combining resources remain rested in the larger resource combination constituted by the firm.

Management of Technology (MOT)

MOT is an interdisciplinary field that integrates:

- Science
- Engineering
- Management knowledge and practice.

MOT treats technology as the seed of the wealth creation system.

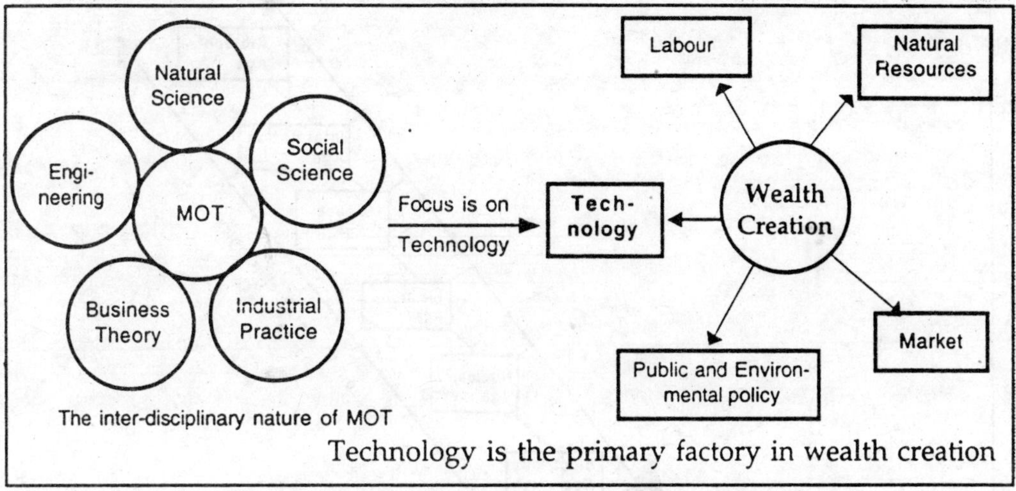

Fig. 2.30 MOT focuses on Technology

Wealth creation involves more than just money. It encompasses factors such as:

- enhancement of knowledge
- intellectual capital
- effective exploitation of resources
- preservation of the natural environment.
- other factors contributing to raising the standard of living and quality of life.

Managing technological change

The difference between the **world today** and the **world of yesteryear** is the **rapid pace of technological change**. This pace is combined with variation in the scope of technology deployment. Global competition is also new. Competitions have intensified between nations in 1980 s and 1990s compounded by the emergence of new countries on the 'playing field'. This contributes to a continuous shift in the balance of economic power. Most countries now pursue free global trade and trade blocs are becoming a defining feature of the time.

Technology is reshaping our world at a speed unimaginable just a few decades ago. Technological changes have been of such magnitude that it is difficult for individual and often for institutions, to follow them.

In several technological sectors, say information sector, more changes have occured in the last few decades than in th previous thousand years. The rate of change is increasing exponentially.

Evolution by age of Technology

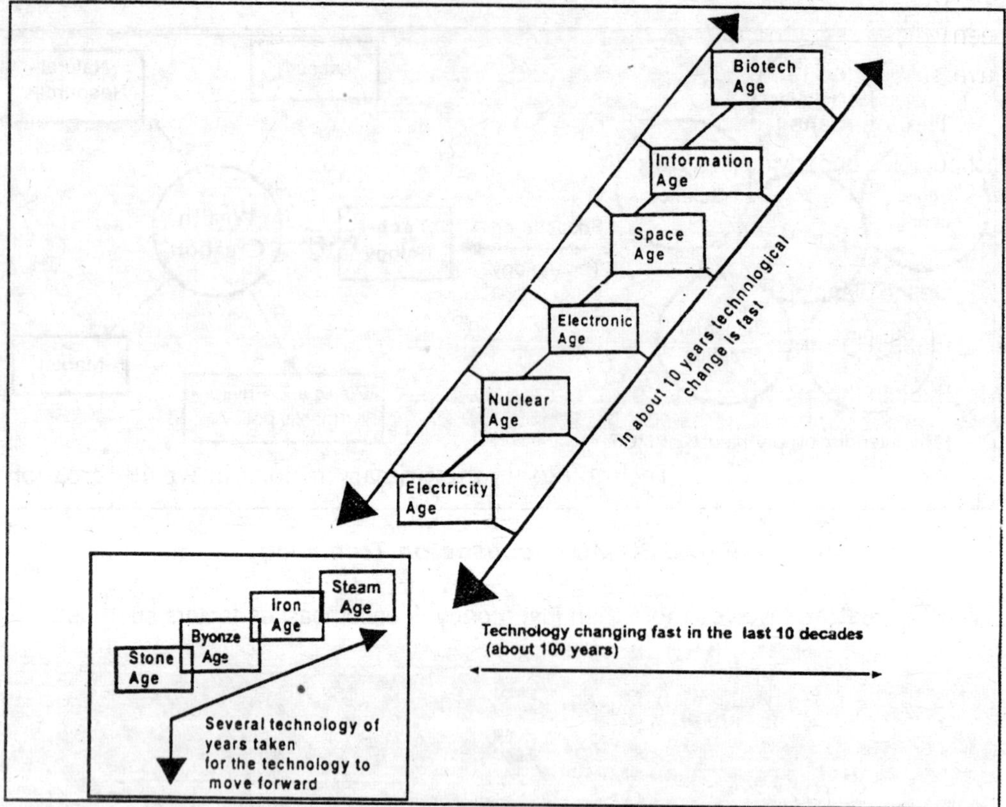

Fig. 2.31 Evolution by Age of Technology

In the late 19th and early 20th centuries, science and technology became increasingly interwined. Scientific discoveries and methodologies triggered technolgical break throughs, while technological devices and know how helped advance science.This closer linkage created an explosion in technology development.

The technology and sustainable growth.

These are as shown below:

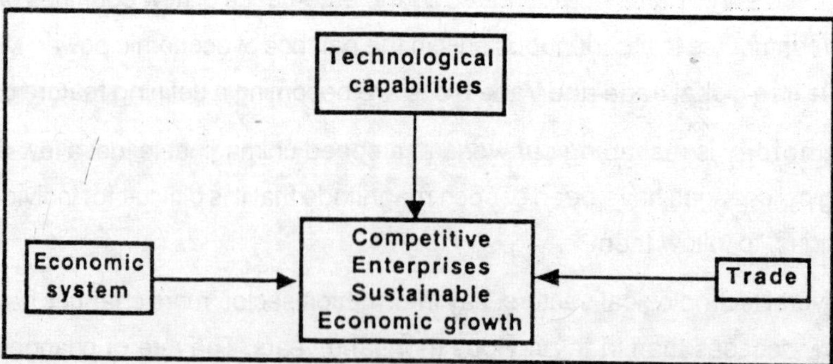

Fig. 2.32 Sustainable and Economic Growth of Competitive Enterprises

Companies like Infosys and Wipro have maintained leadership in India or have at least been vigorous early followers as technology changes, and they have prospered because they have succeeded in **integrating technology strategy** into **business strategy**.

The top management in technological enterprise should be constantly look into the technologies underlying their business and the potential for change.

Questions

1. Define planning.
2. Explain the importance of planning.
3. Explain the management functions as per various experts in this field.
4. How are the plans classified?
5. Explain Planning / Decision making process.
6. What do you mean by premises?
7. How do you determine planning premises and constraints?
8. Explain the hierarchy of plans.
9. Explain the hierarchy of objectives.
10. Compare important characteristics of business objectives with requirement of sound objectives.
11. Explain 'mission or purposes'.
12. Explain what do you mean by Objectives or Goals.
13. Explain what do you mean by Management by Objectives (MBO).
14. Which are the world wide companies used MBO and were successful?
15. What are the different view points about MBO?
16. What do you mean by Key Result Areas? Which are they? Explain them briefly.
17. Define MBO.
18. Explain how MBO is implemented.
19. What are the advantages and disadvantages of MBO?
20. Explain some of the Planning concepts.
21. What do you mean by Planning premises?
22. What do you mean by Planning Horizon? Give an example.
23. What do you mean by systems of plans?
24. Explain strategies and strategic advantage and competitive advantage.

25. What do you mean by a business portfolio matrix? Explain.
26. What do you mean by policies and procedures?
27. Distinguish policies with procedures.
28. Define forecasting.
29. Give the meaning of Forecasting.
30. Define Technology forecasting.
31. What are the elements of Forecasting?
32. What is that engineering manager has to understand about forecasting?
33. What do you mean by sales forecasting?
34. Explain sales estimates.
35. Explain the ways of doing sales estimate under forecasting.
36. What do you mean by Moving Average Forecasts? Which are the types?
37. Explain Regression Model. What are the types?
38. Explain simple moving average method in Forecasting.
39. Explain weighted moving average method in Forecasting.
40. Explain exponential smoothing.
41. What do you mean by Regression and Regression Analysis?
42. What do you mean by scatter diagram?
43. Explain a simple regression model (Method of least squares).
44. Explain multiple regression.
45. List down eleven commandments for Technology Forecasting. Explain each one of them.
46. What do you mean by feasibility of Technological Forecasting? Explain its three premises.
47. What do you mean by Normative technological forecasting? What are its steps? Give an example.
48. What do you mean by exploratory technological forecasting? What are its steps? Give an example.
49. Describe an important model for technological forecasting: Technology S-curve, with examples wherever needed.
50. How does the S-curve changes in natural limits of technology by changing the technology? Explain this change with a sketch.

51. What do you mean by multiple generation technology?
52. Explain technology features. Mention what does it involve and do not involve.
53. Explain the strategies of managing technology.
54. Explain the terms 'Invention' and 'Innovation'.
55. 'In modern days, most inventions have followed scientific discoveries'. Substantiate this statement.
56. Which are the factors influencing the process of innovation?
57. Which are the two types of innovation?
58. Joseph Schumpeter in 1935, said that innovative success might be related to the size of the firm. Give your views.
59. What do you mean by Entrepreneurial innovation?
60. What do you mean by managed innovation?
61. Who is an entrepreneur?
62. What do you mean by entrepreneurship?
63. Compare and contrast two successful entrepreneurs Bill Gates and Steve Jobs.
64. What is the Key role of Entrepreneurship?
65. Explain Management of technology (MOT).
66. 'MOT treats technology as the seed of the wealth creation system' Comment.
67. What does wealth creation involves?
68. What does MOT involve?
69. Discuss on Managing technological change.
70. Explain evolution by age of technology with a sketch.
71. Discuss on sustainable economics and technological growth of competitive enterprises.

Decision Making

Chapter - 3

3.1 Preview

This chapter deals with:

- *Nature of decision making*
  - Relation to planning
  - Types of Decisions
  - Concept of satisfying
  - Management of Science
    - Origins
    - Models and their analysis
  - Tools for Decision Making
    - Use of linear programming for decision making under certainty of expected value.
    - Decision trees, queuing theory, simulation for decision making under risk, games theory for decision making under uncertainty.
  - Discussions of integrated data bases
  - Management Information system
  - Decision support system
  - Expert system
  - Comment on the need for effective implementation decisions.

3.2 Decision making to planning

Every manager has to take decisions quite often. Everyday, we find hundreds of decisions are made in a company by managers.

Definition of Decisions:- As per simon, a **decision** is defined as being objectively rational if in fact it is the correct behaviour for maximising given values in a given situation.

Decision is a solution selected after examining several alternatives chosen because the decision maker foresees that the course of action he selects will do more than the other to further his goals and will be accompanied by the fewest possible objections and consequences.

Peter F. Drucker says "Whatever a manager does, he does through making decisions".

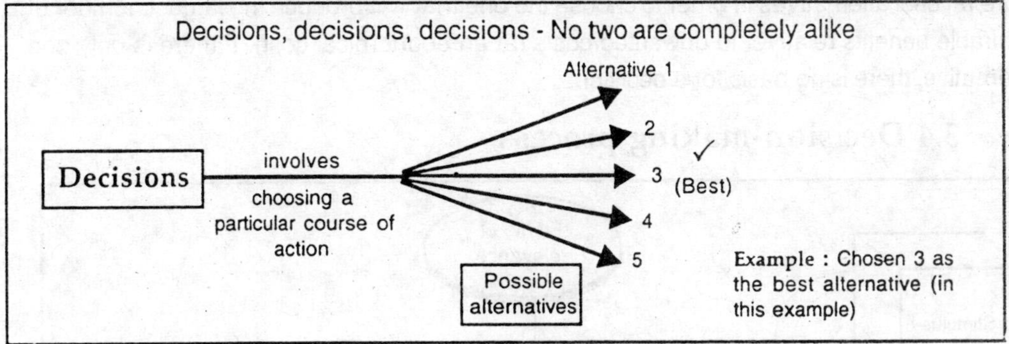

Fig. 3.1 Decision

A Decision involves choosing a particular course of action after considering the possible alternatives (may be expressed in words or it may be implied from behaviour).

Making the right decision is fundamental to good management practice. Some decisions can be made easily, by precedent, or from wide experience, but others demand a detailed investigation first. The ability to make right decisions depends to a great extant on adopting a logical method of approach.

3.3 Decision Making

Managers use the tool of decision making for discharging their duties. All management functions such as planning, organisation, direction and control are settled by managers with the tool of decision making. **Decision-making** is necessary in a business concern because there are many alternative courses of action to most business situations.

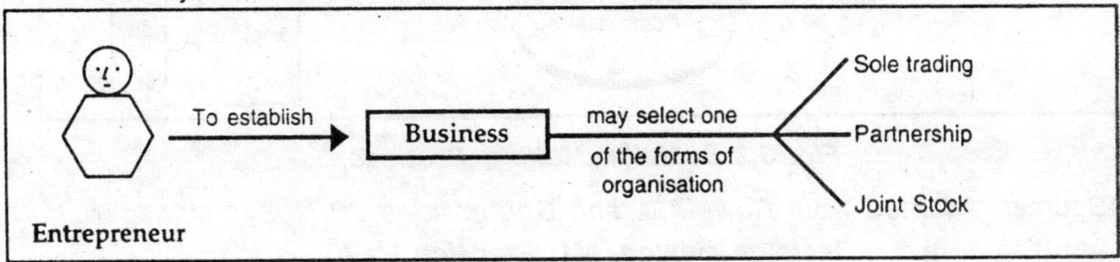

Fig. 3.2 Forms of Organisation

- For raising money, he may:
  - issue shares
  - debentures
  - borrow from financial institutions
- For selling the product, he may:
  - sell through a retailer
  - through middlemen
  - through his own retail shops.

This **decision making** is vital to all management activities

Decision making is the process of making a **conscious choice** between two or more rational alternatives in order to choose the one that will produce the largest number of desirable benefits relative to unwanted costs (at an economical cost). If there is only one alternative, there is no basis for a decision.

3.4 Decision-making process

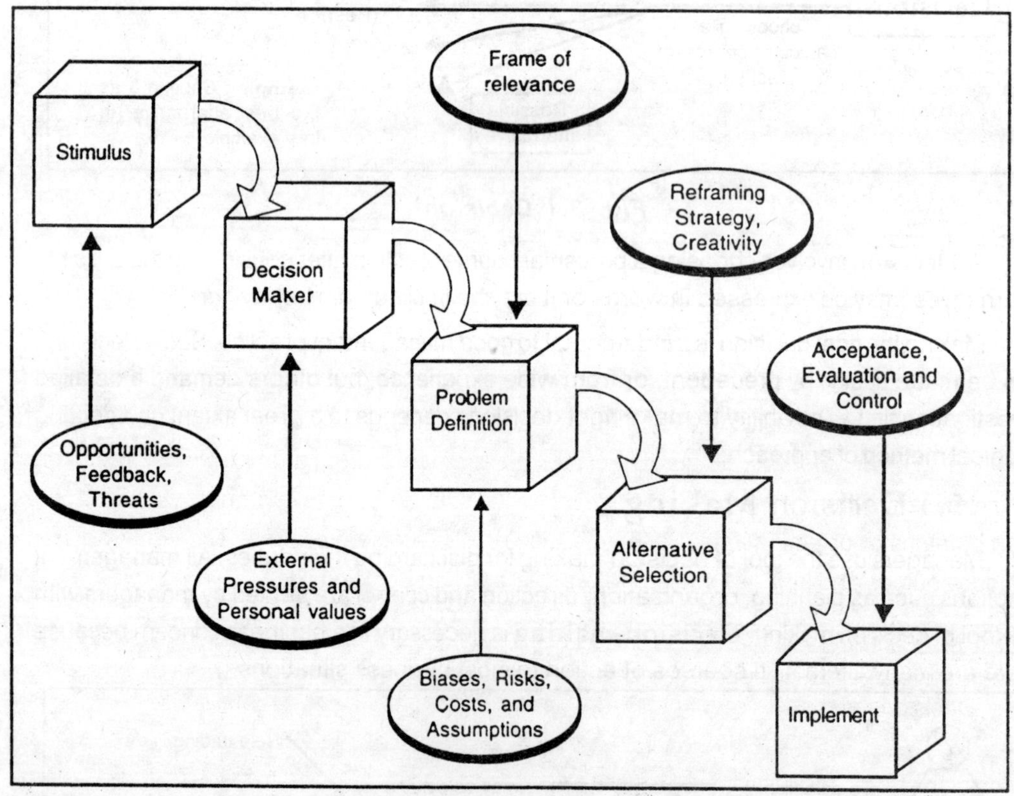

Fig. 3.3 Decision Making Process.

[Source:- Adapted from Rowe A.J. and Boulgarides JD (1994), Managerial Decision Making, NJ: Prentice Hall,]

Fig 3.3 shows a profile of the many ways that a decision is made. The reason this model must be described in this way is that in the real world of decision making, a decision is rarely, if ever, made in exactly to order suggested by the model or even by using all the steps contained in the model. The process depicted is a static representation on of a **distinctly dynamic operation**. The specific conditions and circumstances of the problem to be solved will ultimately dictate the way in which the decision is made. Fig 3.3 model serves as a basis for understanding what should be going on in a typical decision context ?

3.5 Decision makers classification

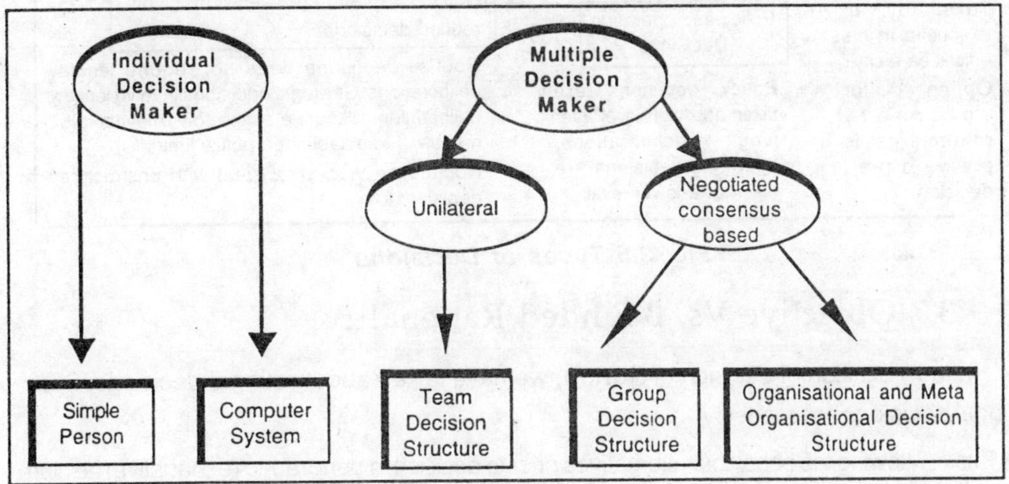

Fig. 3.4 Decision Makers Classification

Individual decision maker is understandable. Multiple class of decision makers is made up of multiple individuals interacting to reach a decision. We differentiate multiple decision makers and group or team decision makers.

While all people may be created equal, all decision makers are not. Decision makers come in many different forms. Some are individuals. Others come in groups, yet others are part of teams or organisations. Each type face unique problem contexts and each requires unique sources and kinds of support to read a particular decision.

3.6 Types of decisions

Decisions are of several types : Classification of these types is as follows:

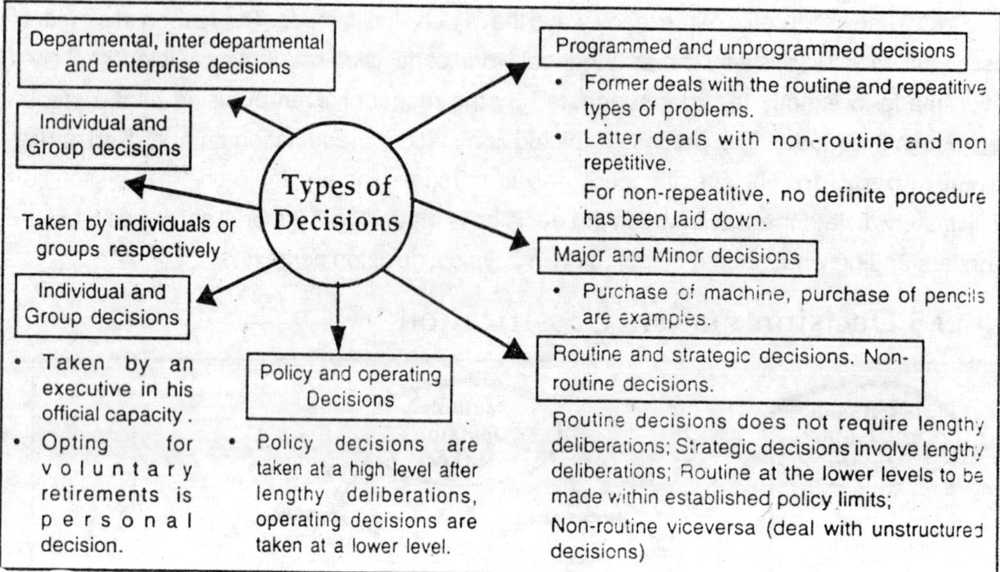

Fig. 3.5 Types of Decisions

3.7 Objective Vs. Bounded Rationality

In the definition of decision of **Simon**, we have talked about rational decisions. Such rational decisions are made by:

i) Viewing the behaviour alternatives prior to decision in panoramic (exhaustive) fashion

ii) Considering the whole complex of consequences that would follow on each choice.

iii) With the system of values as criterion singling out one from the whole set of alternatives.

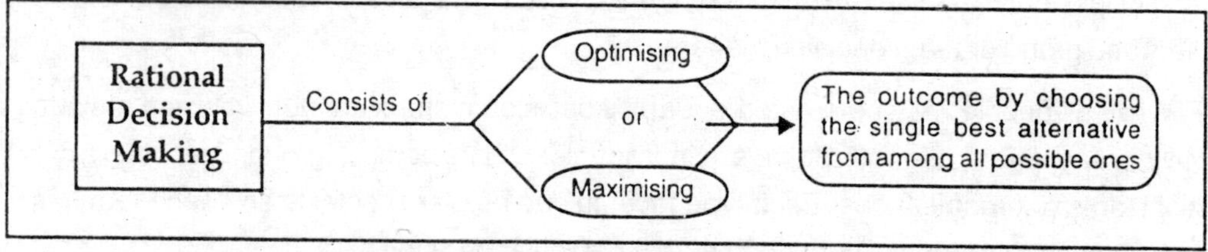

Fig. 3.6 Rational Decision Making

Herbert A. Simon believes that actual behaviour fall short, of objectives rationality - - - - :

(i) **Rationality** requires a complete knowledge and anticipation of the consequences that will follow on each choice. In fact, knowledge of consequences is always **fragmentary**.

(ii) Since these consequences lie in the future, imagination must supply the lack of experienced feeling in attaching value to them. But values can be only imperfectly anticipated.

(iii) Rationality requires a choice among all possible alternative behaviours. In actual behaviour, only a few of the possible alternatives ever come to mind.

Herbert A. Simon, Noble prize-winning scholar succeeded for a more practical theory of problem - solving behaviour than the rational model. In his early work, he questioned the concepts of:

- Optimisation
- Maximisation

as they were applied to normative economic models. If man truly wanted to maximise profit, then each transaction would be a negotiation for the highest possible price. While some buyers would obtain the product at a lower price than the last buyer, others must be willing to pay much higher prices. This would, over time, theoretically result in optimised profits. So why doesn't 'economic' man do this ?

The cognitive limitations of man as per simons argument has made it impractical to consider all possible alternatives to a particular problem. Even if we could review all relevant alternatives possible, we would not be able to assimilate all the information so that we could make an appropriate decision. Instead, simon suggested that we tend to "simplify reality" by focusing our energy on finding a solution that meets our pre-conceived notion of what an acceptable solution looks like. When we find such a solution, we immediately adopt it and stop looking for a better one. Simon used the term **satisfying** to refer to the search limiting strategy. Further, because decision makers are bounded by the cognitive limitations of human decision makers, they actually do make rational decisions that are bounded by often uncontrollable constraints. Simon referred to this as **bounded rationality**.

Problem Space and Search Space

Simon's concept of bounded rationality can best be understood by an example. Fig 3.7 contains a graphical representation of a typical **problem space**.

Assume that the graphic on the left represents the boundary of the identified problem at hand and all positive solutions so that problem;

- Good ones
- Bad Ones
- Ok Ones
- Great Ones etc.

In addition, the problem space contains the **'best'** or **optimum solution** to be identified problem. The rational model of decision making suggests that the problem solver would seek out and test each of solutions found in the problem space until all solutions were tested and compared. At that point, the best solution would be known and identifiable.

Simon argued that this is not what really happens in a typical decision making. The graphic on the right illustrates his approach. What the decision maker actually does is to develop a model of what an acceptable solutions to the problem looks like. Then he or she searches the problem space for a sufficient match to that preconceived solution model. When such a match found, the search ends and the solution is implemented. Thus the decision maker will not choose the optimal solution because the narrowed search of the problem space makes it improbable that the best solution will ever be encountered. Using this approach, the decision maker settles for a satisfactory solution to the given problem rather than searching for the best possible solution.

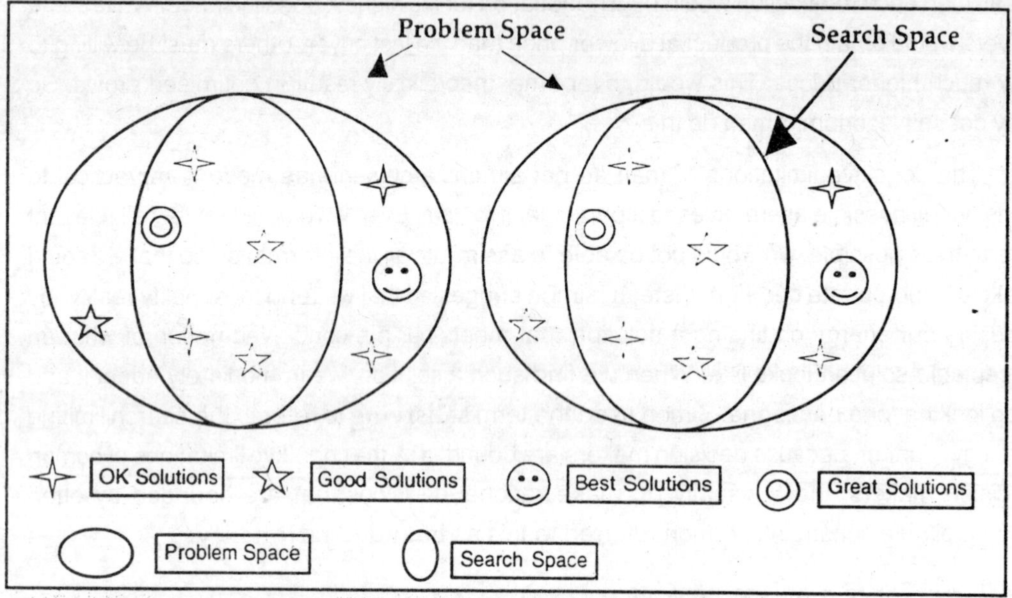

Fig. 3.7 Problem Space and Search Space

Categories of Decision Making

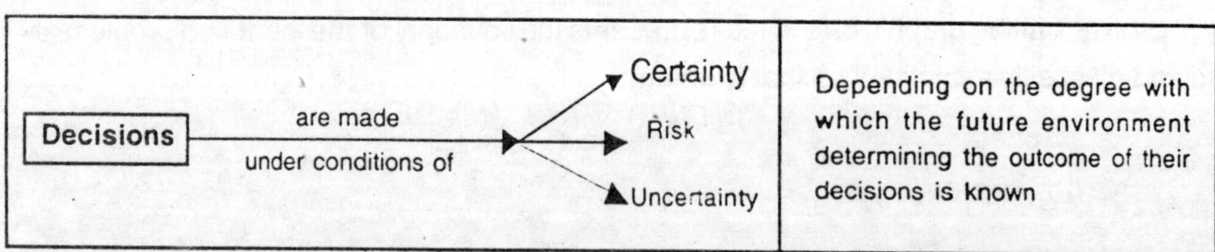

Fig. 3.8 Categories of Decision-Making

3.9 Tools for Decision Making

Decision making under certainty involves:-

- Linear programming
- Computer solution for the same

Decision making under risk involves:

- Decision Trees
- Queuing (waiting line) theory
- Simulation

Decision making under uncertainty involves:

- Game theory

	Certainty	Risk	Uncertainty
(i) Dictionary Meaning	Not to be doubted; Sure ; A certain person implying some degree of contempt	To venture, to take the chance of.	State of being doubtful or uncertain; want of certainty, that which is uncertain.
(ii) Meaning	Common decision structure involving those situations where the trade off among the various objectives and risk is not a significant consideration.	An action can result in more than one outcome, depending on external conditions with known probabilities of occurence. (eg. Forecasters of weather in a city agrees that there is a 50 : 50 chance for rain or sun next day)	An action can result in more than one outcome, depending on external conditions of unknown probability (eg. Weather forecasters disagree on the chance of rain/sun next day as under: Forecasters 1- 10% 2 - 50% 3 - 90% Average is 50% still there is considerable uncertainty in their estimates
(iii) Concerned with	—	Chances of injury (human injury) major	Due to many cases inherently randon processes, measurement error, model imperfections.

Fig. 3.9 Certainty, Risk, Uncertainty

Linear Programming

In 1947, **George Dantzig** and his associates of Stanford university while working in the US department of Air Force, observed that a large number of military programming and planning problems could be formulated as maximising / minimising a linear form of profit / cost functions whose variables were restricted to values satisfying a system of linear constraints.

A linear form is meant a mathematical expression of the type $a_1x_1+a_2x_2+$ .... + a_nx_n, where a_1, a_2, ... a_n are constants. x_1, x_2 ...... x_n are variables.

The term **'programming'** refers to the process of determining a particular programme or plan of action. So **linear programming** (LP) is one of the most important optimisation (maximisation / minimisation) techniques developed in the field of **Operation Research** (OR), also known as **Management Science**. It is a common technique for **decision making under certainty**.

Example

Old hens can be bought at Rs 2 each and young ones at Rs 5 each. The old hens lay 3 eggs per week and the young ones lay 5 eggs per week ; each egg being worth 30 paise. A hen costs Rs 1 per week to feed. I have only Rs 80 to spend for hens, how many of each kind should I buy to give a profit of more than Rs 6 per week, assuming that I cannot house more than 20 hens.

Solution :- **Formulation:** Let x_1 be the number of old hens and x_2 be the number of young hens to be bought.

Since old hens lay 3 eggs / week and the young ones lay 5 eggs / week, the total number of eggs obtained per week will be = $3x_1 + 5x_2$

The cost of each egg being 30 paise, the total gain will be

= Rs. $0.30 (3x_1 + 5x_2)$

Total expenditure for feeding the $(x_1 + x_2)$ hens at the rate of Rs 1 each will be = Rs $1 (x_1 + x_2)$

The total profit Z earned per week will become;

Z= Total gain - Total expenditure = $0.30 (3x_1 + 5x_2) - 1(x_1 + x_2)$ ---------------------------- (2)

$Z = 0.5x_2 - 0.1x_1$ (objective function) -- (1)

Since old hens can be bought at Rs 2 each and young ones at Rs 5 each and there are only Rs 80 available for purchasing the hens, the constraint is $2x_1 + 5x_2 \leq 80$ --------------------- (2)

Also since it is not possible to house more than 20 hens at a time

$x_1 + x_2 \leq 20$ -- (3)

Also since the profit is restricted to be more than Rs 6. This means that the profit function Z is to be maximised.

$0.5x_2 - 0.1x_1 \geq 6$

Again, it is not possible to purchase negative quantity of hens, therefore

$x_1 \geq 0 ; x_2 \geq 0$ -- (4)

So the problem becomes:

$Z = 0.50X_2 - 0.10X_1$-------------------(1)

subject to constraints:

$2x_1 + 5x_2 \leq 80$ -------------------------- (2)

$x_1 + x_2 \leq 20$ ------------------------------ (3)

$x_1, x_2 \geq 0$ ---------------------------------- (4)

Graphical solution

Plot the straight lines $2x_1 + 5x_2 = 80$ and $x_1 + x_2 = 20$ on the graph and shade the feasible region as shown in the figure.

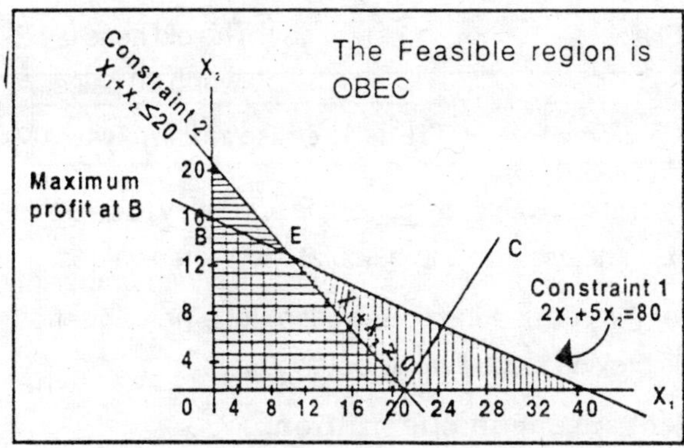

Fig. 3.10 Linear Program Example: Constraints and Solution

The Coordinates of the extreme points of the feasible region are :-

0 = (0, 0) C=(20,0) B=(0,16)

E= (20/3 , 40/3)

The value of Z at the vertices are

Zo = o. Zc= 0.50 x 0 -0.10 x 20 = -2

ZB = 0.50 x 16 - 0.10 x 0 = 8

ZE = 0.50 x 40/3 - 0.10 x 20/3 = 6

Since the maximum value of z = Rs 8 which occurs at the point B = (0, 16) the solution to the given problem is $x_1 = 0$, $x_2 = 16$ **max Z = Rs 8 Hence only 16 young hens, I should buy in order to get the maximum profit of Rs 8 which is > 6.**

Computer solution

The Simplex method was developed by **George Danzig.** A technique in mathematical algorithm that permits computer solution of linear programming problems having many variable (not just two)

AT & T telephone demand had 42000 variables - 4 to 7 hrs for a single run needed.

80000 variables - Weeks needed

Bell Laboratories has recently developed a short cut method based on "an arcane discipline known as projective geometry -50-100 times fast finding a solution to the larger problem in less than an hour. This is management science methodology. The new method showed AT & T how to squeeze an extra 9%, to 10% of capacity out of $15 bl^n system.

Another way to deal with risk is to use higher discount rates, for riskier projects. However, if the discount rate of one project is increased significantly to account for its risk, then other projects may be chosen due to their more attractive risk-adjusted present values.

Introducing risk into the analysis is a simple approach, but it has drawbacks. Adding a risk adjustment to the discount rate reduces present and thus the relative attractiveness of a project. However the effects of the adjustments are compounded with time.

eg:- 10,000 Rs in one year at 10% discount rate is Rs 9091.

Same 10,000 Rs in one year for a risk - adjusted discount rate say 14% is 8,772 Rs.

However, after 20 years, the present value for the higher discount rate will be less than one - half that for the lower rate. Such a compounding of risk adjustment is severe and unlikely to be appropriate for many projects.

Returns, or benefits, and sometimes costs as well, are not certain. One way to take this account is to make explicit risk estimates and use these to calculate expected values.

For instance, suppose your company is considering construction of a new liquefied natural gas processing facility. Experts provide the following estimates:-

- Annual chances of an accident are one in one million.
- Annual chances of sabotage are three in one million.
- The costs of either an accident or sabotage are valued at Rs 100 bl$^{n.}$

These estimates translate into an expected cost of

Expected value = Likelihood x Magnitude

$= [(1 \times 10^{-6}) + (3 \times 10^{-6})] \times [100 \times 10^{9}]$

= Rs 4,00,000

This annual cost combined with other costs in determining Net present value (NPV), for instance as under:-

$NPV = Bo - Co + (B - C) F$ [This entails considerable calculation unless one uses a computer program or spread sheet]

Where C = Actual Cost ; Bo = Benefit

B = Benefits ; Co = Initial cost

Short cut form of the equation can be used when the Actual costs (C) and Benefits (B) are the same each year.

$$F = \frac{(1+d)^n - 1}{(d)(1+d)^n}$$

d = discounted rate (or interest rate)

n = develpments life in years

This form assumes no salvage benefits or costs at the end of the development life.

Assume that there are no **initial benefits** and that co = 500 ml^n Rs

Assume also the annual benefits are 100 ml^n Rs ; Annual costs are Rs 40ml^n ; the facility life is 20 years and d = 10 %

$$F = \frac{(1+0.1)^{20} - 1}{(0.1)(1+0.1)^{20}} = \frac{6.73 - 1}{0.1 \times 6.73} = 8.51$$

NPV = - Rs 500 ml^n + (Rs 100ml^n - Rs 40 ml^n - Rs 0.4 ml^n) x 8.51

- Rs 500 ml^n + Rs 59.6 x 8.51 ml^n

- Rs 500 ml^n + Rs. 507.196 ml^n

= Rs 7.196 ml^n

Thus the developments NPV is positive, but only modestly so. Does such a small return warrant such a big risk (Rs 100 bl^n) ? Insurance might be considered to reduce the risk at somewhat higher cost (for instance) perhaps an insurer would charge Rs 1ml^n annually instead of the expected value of Rs 0.4 ml^n or other options of reducing risk might be explored (for instance, perhaps hiring a security force could reduce the chances of sabotage greatly)

Uncertainty

Another inherent factor to note is **uncertainty**. It is likely that the risk estimate for sabotage, for instance, is far from certain. Bounds on the risk estimate (analogous to the confidence intervals) could be determined. NPV calculations could then be carried out under extreme scenarios with various facility life, discount rate and risk estimates to provide management with a set of well-rounded benefit / cost / risk estimations.

Such a compounding of risk adjustment is severe and unlikely to be appropriate for many projects. Another problem with simple discount rate adjustment is that is implicitly assumes the independence of returns in each time period. In reality, however, early success might generally increase the certainty of net benefits in subsequent years, while **early losses**, could **completely destroy the projects future.**

Scenario strategy

One solution to the above problems is to adopt a **scenario strategy**. This approach will complicate in Fig 3.10, since instead of one column of net benefits for each project there will be several.

Project: A might have one column that portrays terrible losses, another that depicts terrifically high benefits and several others between these extremes. Perhaps to streams of benefits depicted in fig 3.10....... is the most likely (that is, has the highest probability) and lower probabilities can be assigned to the other outcomes. Projects Band C could have similar or quite different outcome distributions.

For example : Sometimes, there may be almost equal probabilities of great success of terrible failure and almost no chance of a middle ground. The array of possibilities depends upon :-

- the nature of the projects
- the judgement of the manager who makes the decisions.

Fig. 3.10 - Present the results of an analysis of alternate outcomes. The horizontal axis of each figure shows the present value of net benefits that might result ; the vertical axis show the probability of each value. Each scenario uses the same cost of money discount rate that is, the return possible on a riskfree investment.

Eg: when comparing projects over a time horizon of six years, it might be a appropriate to use the current annual interest rate paid by the government securities with a six - year maturity, or if the firm has debts, the interest rate paid on those could be used, since avoiding these costs is an alternative to investing in a new project. The discount rate chosen is intended to introduce the appropriate figure for the time value of money.

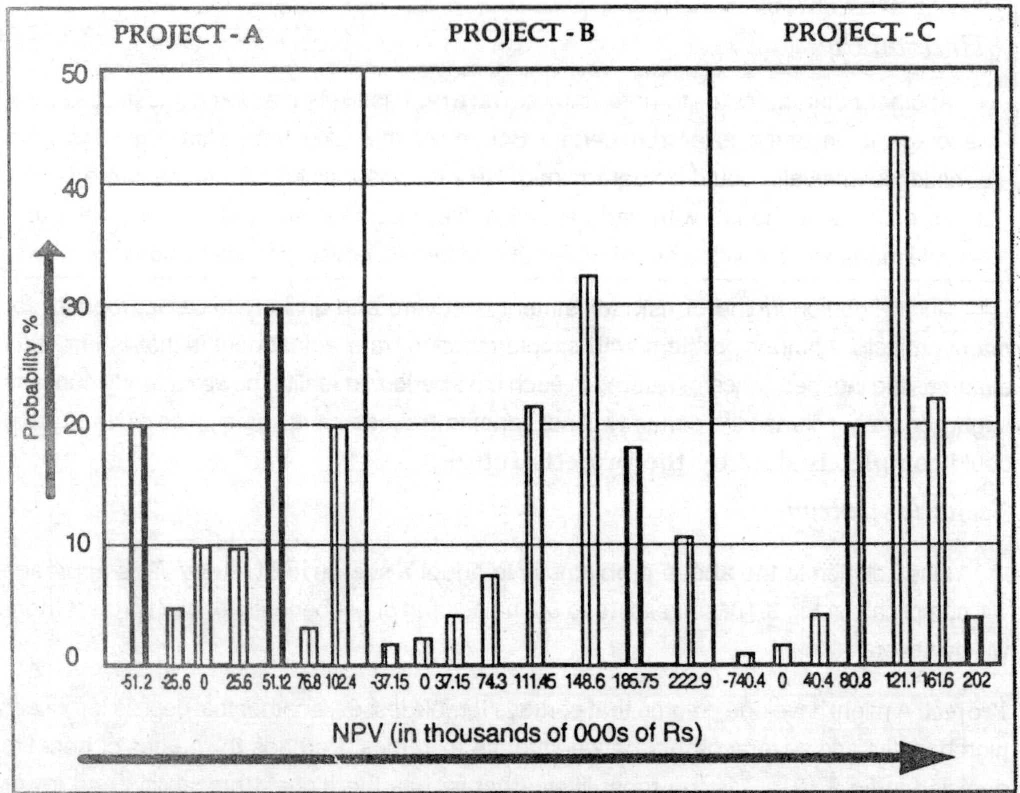

Fig. 3.11 Investment Analysis Under Uncertainty - Projects A, B, C (8% discount rate)

The benefits displayed by the scenarios in the above figure depict both pattern of the returns and the effects of the different probabilities of occurrence. This representation should be viewed as a **probability distribution.** The procedures for generating such distributions can range from simply using the judgement of one analyst to applying complex computer simulations and collections of expert opinions to determine the likelihood of the various outcomes.

The approach provides a much richer basis for decision making than merely using present values of the most likely outcome. It is also more realistic because no one is really certain about the future.

The choice of the best project, using the **scenario approach**, however is no longer so clear. Under conditions of certainty, selection of a discount rate identifies the highest present value and thus indicates a clear direction for the decision maker. With uncertainty, however, somewhat arbitary values must be applied, and even then, results can be ambiguous. Although there may be cases in which the array of outcomes for one project clearly dominate those of others, it is more likely that the best choice will depend on the degree to which the manager is committed to risk aversion. **Usually projects with the highest potential rewards also carries high risk.** Different individuals may make equally rational choices based on differencing preferences for risk and return.

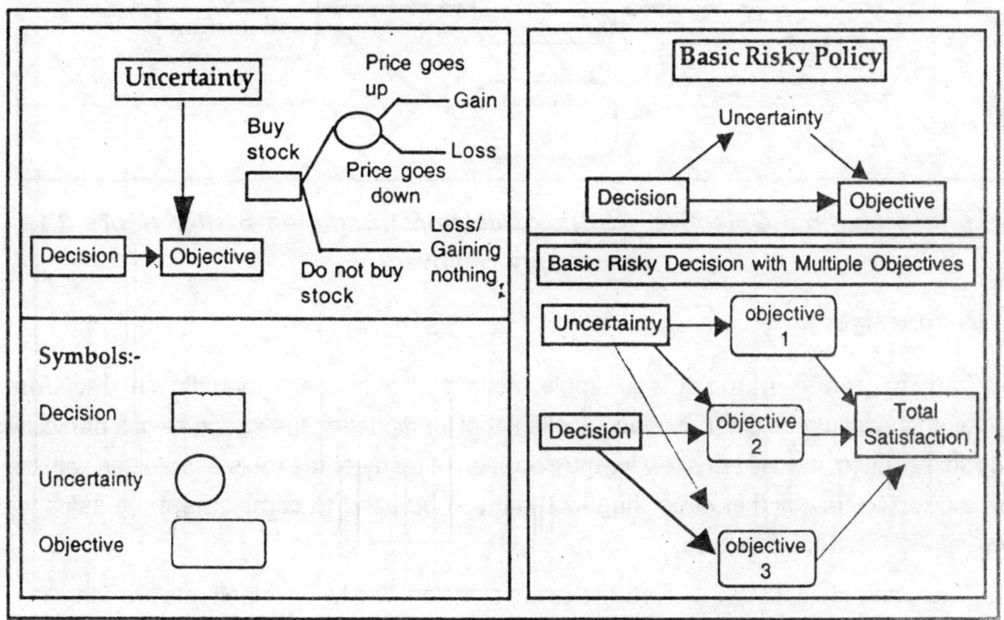

Fig. 3.12 Basic Risky Decisions and Model ***Fig. 3.13 Basic Risky Decisions with Multiple Objectives***

I) As shown in figure 3.11, the basic risky decision structure, a successful decision is a function of both the correct selection from the choice set and outcome of an uncertainty. Many problems faced by a decision maker necessitate a choice selection in the face of some uncertainty. Figure shows an example of how thus decision structure could be used to model a decision to buy stock

II) As shown in the figure 3.12 above, the basic risky policy variation describes a problem context where the choice made from the set of alternatives has a direct influence on the probabilities of an uncertainty as well as the objective. This problem is still modeled with three components but their relationship differ slightly from the basic risky decision structure. Here, the basic risky decision with multiple objectives, the decision maker is faced with making a trade off between objectives in order to manage the uncertainty present in the decision context. The best solution will be the one that results in the greatest measured success (known as total satisfaction)

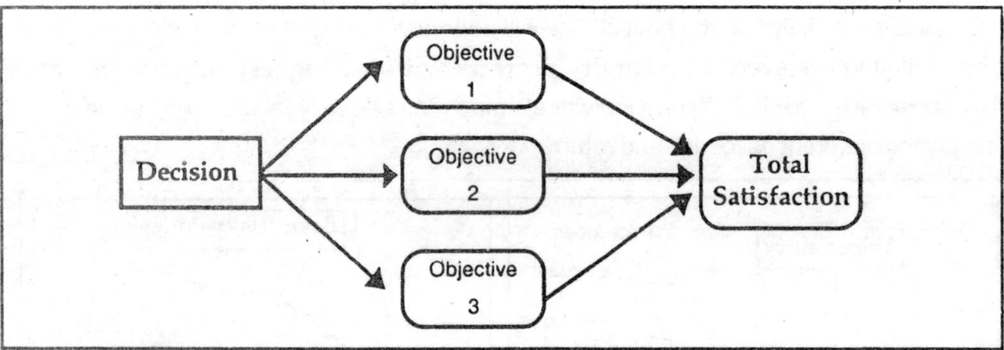

Fig. 3.14 Multiple Objective, No Risk Decision (Same as earlier figure 3.12, uncertainty removed)

Decision Trees

An **influence diagram** is a simple method of graphically modeling a **decision.** Although the influence diagram is an excellent tool for modeling the structure of a particular decision context, it does not allow for the depiction of many of the tools associated with the decision at hand. Another structuring tool that can be used to complement the influence diagram is the **decision tree.**

Here only **choices** and **uncertainties** are modeled. The two components are connected by lines referred to as branches. The branches radiating from an uncertainty node represents the possible out comes from a particular event. The value of each out come is attached to the end of each out come branch. Fig. 3.15 shows an example of a simple decision tree.

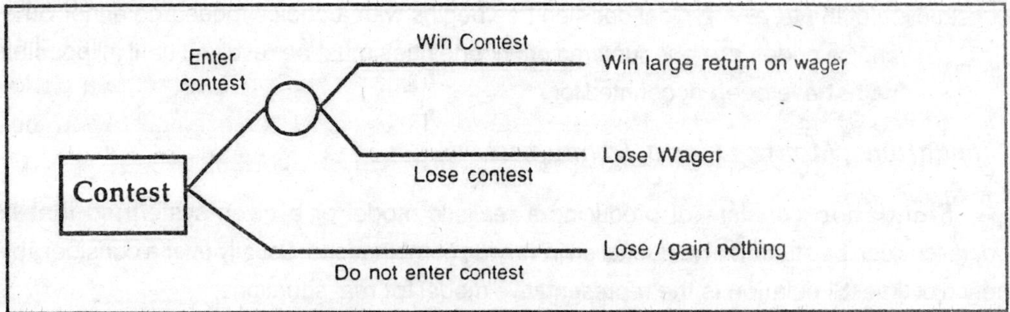

Fig. 3.15 A Simple Decision Tree

Similar to influence diagram, a decision tree can be thought of as similar to a rail road. It is specially constructed to be read beginning on the left and continuing to the right until an out come is reached. In addition, several 'rules' must be followed while constructing to ensure that the diagram clearly represents the details of the decision context.

(i) First the branches extending from a choice node must be constructed so that the decision maker can choose only one option. No branch can be modeled as a combination of choice options.

(ii) Next the branches radiating from an uncertainty node must represent a set of outcomes that are both **mutually exclusive and collectively exhaustive** (**Mutually exclusive** mean that only one of the possible outcomes can occur)

In this, an example would be an uncertainty node with two branches representing success or failure. In this case, the rule is followed because a project can either succeed or fail but not both.

'Collectively exhaustive' means that the branches represent all possible outcomes, no other possibilities exist. Together, these two conditions require that when the uncertainty is resolved one and only out come will prevail.

(iii) Third rule of decision tree construction is that all possible paths that can be followed over time by a decision maker are fully mapped in the tree, including all:

- Possible choices
- Uncertainty out comes

If we start with a choice node with three branches, each with two outcomes, we have a total of six possible out comes. If however, we add one additional choice node with three alternatives after each an certainty in the model, we increase the total number of possible out comes from **six to eighteen**. This exponential growth is often referred to as the 'Tree getting bushy'

(iv) The decision tree must be constructed to depict an accurate chronology of events over time. This is best accomplished by strictly adhering to the left to right construction of the tree. A typical decision tree begins with a choice mode and either other choice nodes are encountered or uncertainties must be resolved until all possible paths have been accounted for.

Simulation (Monte - Carlo Techniques)

Simulation consists of producing a realistic model of a given system so that its operations can be studied and quantified in varying combinations, usually over a considerable period of time. Simulation is the representative model for real situations.

Simulation analysis is a natural and logical extension to the analytical and mathematical techniques used for solving the problems in **Operation Research.** Simulation is one of the earliest tools of management science to use, but probably one of the hardest to apply properly and perhaps most difficult from which to draw accurate conclusions. Simulation is used when all else fail. This method is viewed as a **'method of last resort'.**

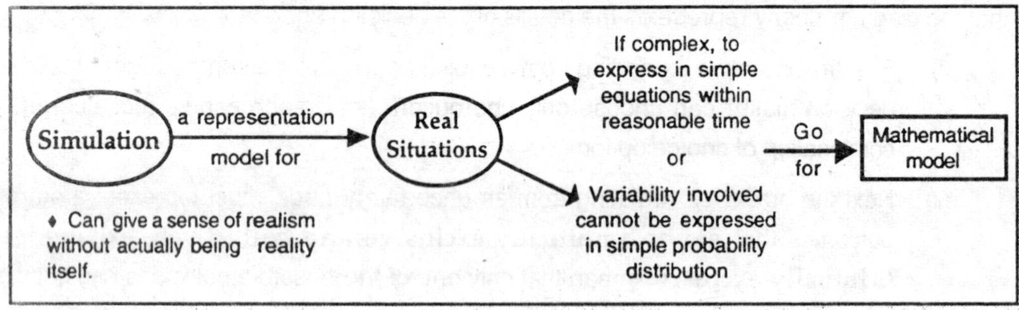

Fig. 3.16 Simulation

Eg:-

(i) A children's cycling park with various signals and crossing in the exhibition is a simulated model of city traffic in real system.

(ii) Testing of an aircraft model in a wind tunnel from which the performance of the real aircraft is determined for being fit under real operating conditions.

(iii) In the laboratories, we often perform a number of experiments on simulated models.

(iv) Flight simulator for training pilots.

Monte-Carlo Simulation

Monte-Carlo is a city in the south of France known for its gambling Casinos. As in this technique, random numbers are used, which is akin to gambling (a chance phenomenon), this technique has come to be called the **Monte Carlo Simulation technique.**

Applications of simulation:- Many applications are there.

- It can be used for reproducing workshop situations of all kinds.

- It can be a mock ship counter.
- It can be a model branch of a bank.

The war time R.A.F Link trainer was an early example whereby the cockpit of an aircraft was accurately simulated. Although not airborne, pilots could under expert instruction and with plotted performance fly a course and deal with situations and emergencies as if actually in the sky.

The Apollo astronauts were able to practice the whole of their journey to the moon, while remaining firmly on the ground in texas. This is not still widely used in business context as their value would not justify.

The reasons may be:-

(i) Cost

(ii) Not being able to provide full scale training facilities at the right level and in the right place.

(iii) A firm may wish to contract out much of the educational work and leave it instead to the professionals.

A Mathematical model can be constructed that simulates the operation of the real system by mathematically describing the behaviour of individual parts and the interactions between the parts.

A computer program can be developed which will cause the model to perform one cycle of operations. Common languages such as FORTRAN or BASIC, special purpose simulation languages such as GPSS, SIM SCRIPT or GASP are very effective in developing programs.

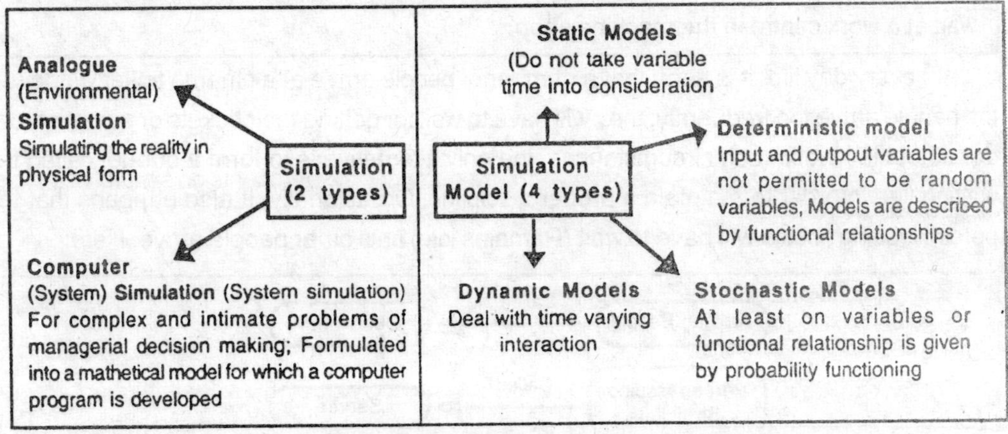

Fig. 3.17 Simulation and Simulation Model (Types)

Stochastic: One of the activities (Variable or functional relationship) in the model such as:

Time between variables, expected revenue, or tensile strength can be represented by probability distributions or frequency tables.

Deterministic: Models are described by functional relationships.

Queuing Theory

This deals with goods or people flowing through certain service points, the ways in which delays and bottle necks can be avoided, and the ways is which waiting time can be reduced to an absolute minimum.

The theory of queues was developed by a Dasing engineer called A.K. Erlang at the Copenhagen Telephone exchange in the 1910 s.

It deals with problems involving the flow of items through service facilities like.

- Toll Gate
- Traffic signal
- Petrol Bunk
- Directory enquiry
- Railway reservation counter
- Super market etc.

Using probability theory, the maximum waiting time and average waiting time can be computed and the number of facilities required to avoid excessive waiting time is determined.

Eg. This theory is useful for estimating the time the raw material or semifinished part to wait at a work centre in the machine shop.

In every day life, it is seen that a number of people arrive at a cinema ticket window. If the people arrive too frequently; they will have to wait for getting their tickets or sometimes to do without it. Under such circumstances, the only alternative is to form a queue, called the waiting line in order to maintain a proper discipline. Occasionally, it also happens that the person issuing tickets will have to wait (Remains idle) until other people arrive. Here:

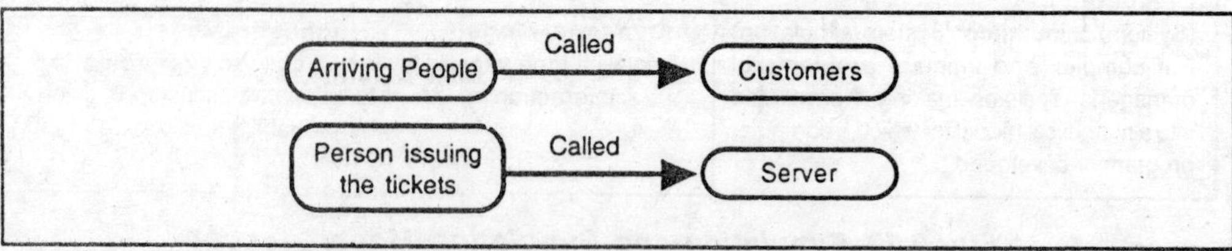

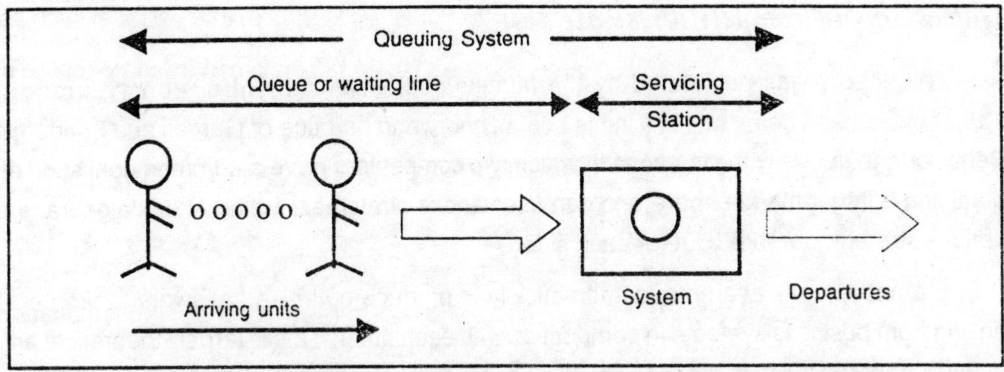

Fig. 3.18 Queuing system (with single service station)

(Consists of Input or arrival pattern, the service mechanism or service pattern, the queue discipline and customer's behaviour)

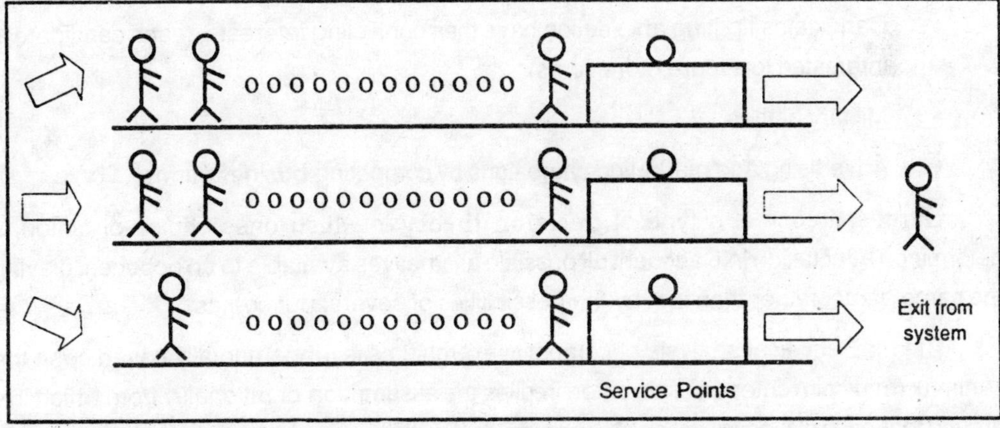

Fig. 3.19 A Queueing System with Several Queues and Several Service Stations.

Queuing theory is concerned with the statistical description of the behaviour of queues with finding Eg. the probability distribution of the number in the queue from which the mean and variance of queue length and the **probability distribution of waiting time** for a customer or the distribution of a **servers busy periods** can be found.

Main characteristics of a queuing system :

The problem is to determine the following:

- Probability distribution of queue length
- probability distribution of waiting time of customers.
- The busy period distribution.

Games Theory (competition strategies)

This theory was postulated by the famous mathematician **John Von Neumann,** Father of Games Theory in 1944 in his book 'Theory and practice of Games and Economic Behaviour, it details with situations in which two competitors have a common goal such as obtaining a larger market share and can use various strategies. Using Matrix algebra, the options strategy is worked out for each side.

Games theory attempts mathematically to produce optirnised answers to problems arising from business systems in competition with each other. This is largely theoretical and to that extent related to business games, used for educational purposes.

Life is full of struggle and competitions. A great variety of competitive situations is commonly seen in everyday life.

Eg:-

- Candidates fighting an election have their conflicting interests. (each candidate is interested to secure more votes)
- Military battles
- Advertising and marketing campaigns by competing business firms.

Games theory is a type of **decision theory** in which ones choice of action is determined after taking into account all possible alternatives available to an opponent playing the same game, rather than just by the possibilities of several out comes.

The mathematical analysis of competitive problems is fundamentally based upon the Minimax (maximin) critenon. This criteri implies the assumption of rationality from which it is argued that each player will act so as to maximise his minimum gain or minimise his maximum loss.

Political Application of Game Theory

Indian Strategy	Pakistan Strategy	
	Go Nuclear	**Sign Nuclear Fact**
Go Nuclear	Third Best for India Third Best for Pakistan	Worst for Pakistan Best for India
Sign Nuclear Fact	Worst for India Best for Pakistan	Second Best for India Second Best for Pakistan

The conflict between India and Pakistan it cites. The best overall solution may be the second best for each party would be signing of the nuclear pact by both with mutual trust. Still each country is having its own problems. That is why both the parties have settled for the third option resulting in nuclear race and ending in proliferation of nuclear weapons.

Computer Based Information System

Computer-based Information System is an information system that uses computer hardware and software to perform its information processing activities.

MIS is now considered as an **integrated user-machine system** and utilises computer hardware and software along with manual procedures; models for analysis, planning, control and decision-making; a data base.

Computer based information systems are information systems that include a computer. A **computer information system** consists of people, procedures, data, programs and computers. **Programs** are instructions for computers, just as **procedures** are instructions for people. The computer can serve several roles in the production of information. It can serve as a data storage and retrieval device. In this mode, the computer acts as a data librarian. Secondly, the computer can provide processing capabilities for the production of information. Thirdly, the computer can serve as a communication device to obtain data or information from other computers. Finally, the computer can present information by producing tables, reports, charts, graphs and formatted documents.

Computers, and humans act as partners in an information system. Work that the humans would have to do in a manual system is delegated to the computer. To make this possible, human procedures are translated into computer programs.

Computers can work at unbelievable speeds and at very high accuracies.

Computer based information systems (CBIS) rely on computer hard ware and software technology to process and disseminate information. There are formal organisational systems that rely on computer technology. The window on Technology describes some of the typical technologies used in computer based information systems today. Although CBIS use computer technology to process raw data into meaningful information, these is a sharp distinction between a computer and a computer program on the one hand and an information system on the other. Electronic computers and related software programs are the technical foundation, the tools and materials of modern Information systems. Computers provide the equipment for storing and processing information. Computer programs or software, are sets of operating instructions that direct and control computer processing. Knowing how computers and computer programs work is important in designing solutions to organisational problems, but computers are only part of an Information System. Computers and programs are the hammer, nails, and lumber of CBIS (just as what we use in house constructions) but alone they cannot produce the information a particular organisation needs. One must understand the problems they are designed to solve their architectural and design elements and the organisational processes that lead to these solutions.

Managements Information Systems (MIS)

MIS was the original type of information systems developed to support managerial decision making. An MIS produces information products that support many of the day-to-day decision making needs of managers and business professionals. Reports, displays and responses produced by MIS provide information that these decision makers have specified in advance as adequately meeting their information needs. Such predefined information products satisfy the information needs of decision makers at the operational and tactical levels of the organisation who are faced with more structured types of decision situations.

Eg:- Sales mangers rely on sales analysis reports to evaluate differences in performance among sales people who sell the same type of products to the same type of customers.

3.10 Meaning of Management Information Systems (MIS)

Management Information Systems is the study of information system focusing on their use in business and management. Davis and Olson in 1985 have mentioned that the study of MIS arose in the 1970s to focus on computer based information systems aimed at managers.

3.11 Contemporary Approaches Found in MIS

The two **contemporary approaches** found in MIS are **'technical approaches'** and **'behavioural approach'. Technical approach** involves computer science, management science and operations research with a practical orientation towards building systems and applications.

- **Computer science** is for establishing theories of computability methods of computation, methods of efficient data storage and access.
- **Management science** is for the development of models for decision making and management practices.
- **Operation research** is related to mathematical techniques for optimisation of selected parameters of organisations covering transportation, inventory control, transaction costs.

The second approach is **'behavioural approach'** which is concerned with behavioural issues that arise in the development of long term maintenance of information systems. The issues are raised by sociology, economics and psychology.

The two approaches found in MIS are shown in figure 3.20

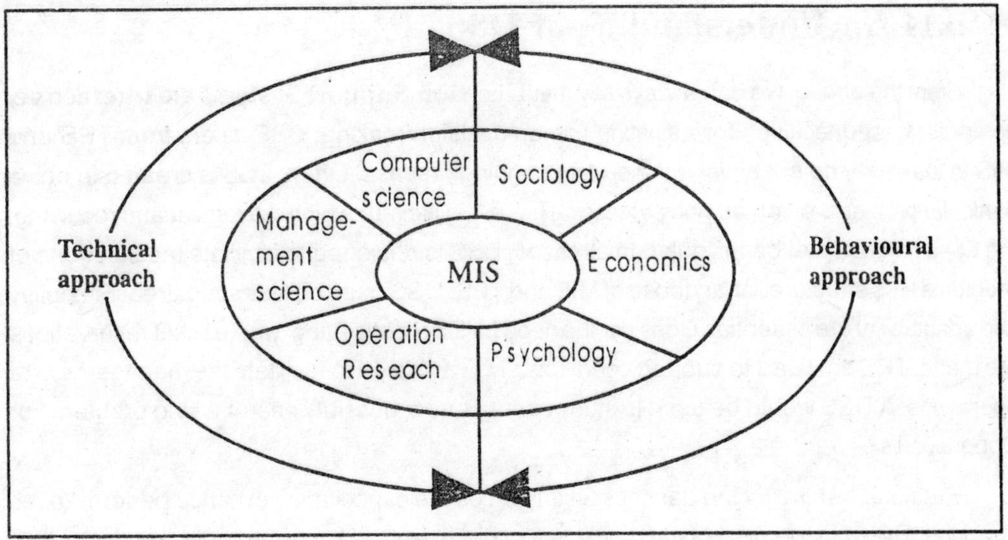

Fig. 3.20 Contemporary Approaches found in MIS

3.12 Management Information Systems for Decision Making

This shown in figure 3.21 below. The figure is self explanatory.

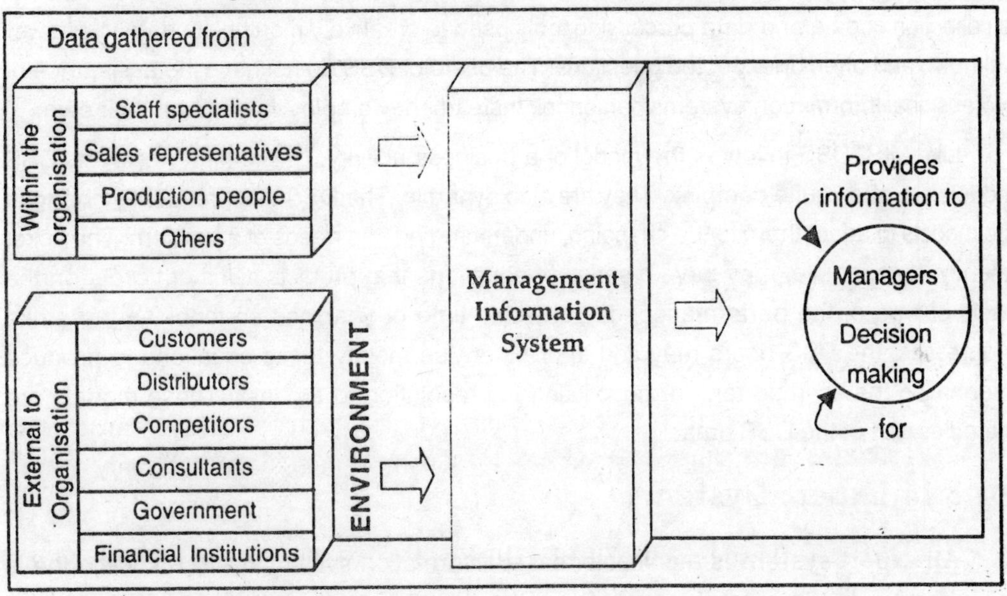

Fig. 3.21 Management Information System for Decision Making

3.13 Definitions of DSS

Scott Morton defined **Decision Support System (DSS)** as **Interactive computer based systems**, which help decision-makers utilise data and models to solve **unstructured** problems.

☛ 3.14 An Understanding of DSS

From the above, we can always say that **Decision Support Systems are interactive,** computer based facilities for assisting human decision-making. DSS differs from TPS and MIS in that, they do not always support an ongoing process. Often, DSS is created to solve particular problems on an ad hoc processing basis. Unlike MIS which are regular and recurring, the need for DSS can be irregular. In all cases, DSS is designed to facilitate the solutions of problems less structured than those of MIS and TPS. DSS must be less structured. Flexibility and adaptability are essential. Consider the need for DSS in a setting, where ticket reservations are made. TPS are used to support operations. MIS are used to facilitate the management of operations. A DSS would be used to study unstructured, possibly one-of-a kind problems or Opportunities.

Example, a strike by the dancer's union, forces the cancellation of dance performances arranged. The management of the dance association wants to know the impact on revenue of the cancellation of each performance. A DSS could be used to process the ticket agencies data to produce this information.

In some ways, the term *decision support facility* would be more accurate than the term decision support system. DSS is not structured, finished systems as TPS, and MIS are. DSS is collection of data and data processing tools used to creatively manipulate data to answer unknown and often unexpected questions. The users of DSS do not have the assistance of professional information systems personnel. Instead, they employ the tools on their own.

Like MIS, DSS involves the model of a business activity. Unlike MIS, however, DSS models are often quite complex. They are also dynamic. The DSS user frequently changes the models to adapt them to the changing, understanding and needs of a problem. The ticket agency, for example, may have a series of equations that predicts sales of tickets on the basis of type of the performance, day of week, time of year and so forth. As the strike progresses, the DSS users may add to or otherwise modify these equations to produce information that is important for negotiating the resolution to the task. These models are stored as part of the DSS data.

☛ 3.15 Expert System

An expert system is a computer based information system in which knowledge is represented in data, in which the processing of the knowledge is directed, primarily by computer programs. This system has the greatest degree of computer control of the three systems studied.

The development of systems that process the knowledge of a true human expert has proven to be difficult and expensive. The technology however, is useful in the solution of many smaller problems.

The term **expert system** originated because it was aimed, initially, at replicating the abilities of true human experts. The goal was to create a system that would be able, for example, to diagnose human diseases as well as or better than a human expert. Many of the expert systems, we encounter in business will not have the abilities of a true human expert.

One of the major branches of **Artificial Intelligence is expert system**.

Artificial Intelligence is science and technology based on disciplines such as computer science, biology, psychology, mathematics and engineering. The goal of AI is to develop a computer that can think as well as see, hear, walk, talk and feel. A major thrust of artificial intelligence is the development of computer functions normally associated with human intelligence such as reasoning, inference, learning and problem solving.

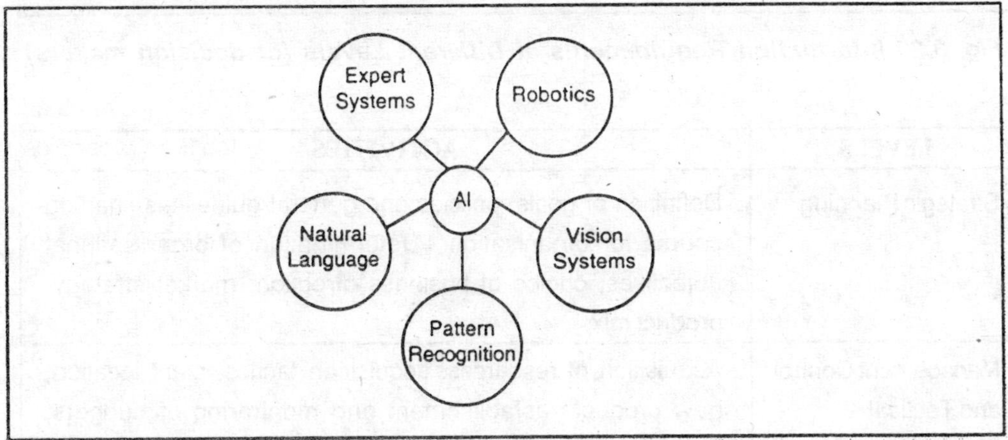

Fig. 3.22 Major branches of the artificial intelligence (AI) discipline.

Implementation

A decision is a choice which involves commitment of resources to a course of action. And at times, the decision might have far reaching consequences particularly so, if the decision is taken at the top of the organisation hierarchy.

The type of information needed by decision makers is related to:

- Level of management of decision making.
- Amount of structure in the decision situations they face.

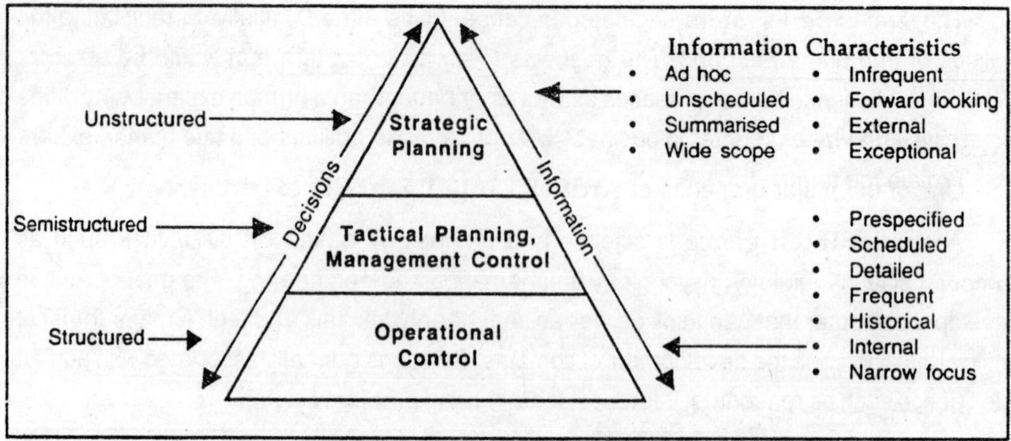

Fig. 3.23 Information Requirements at Different Levels (of decision makers)

LEVELS	ACTIVITIES
Strategic Planning	Definition of goals, policies and general guidelines charting course for organisation. Determination of organisational objectives, choice of business direction, market strategy, product mix.
Management Control and Tactical Planning	Acquisition of resources, acquisition tactics, plant location, new products establishment and monitoring of budgets, structuring of work, training of personnel.
Operational Planning and Control	Effective and efficient use of existing facilities and resources to carry out activities within budget constraints.

Fig. 3.24 Different Levels and Activities.

Questions

1. Define a decision.
2. What is the meaning of 'Decision'?
3. What is decision making?
4. What are the different forms of organisation?
5. Explain the decision making process with a sketch.
6. Classify Decision makers.
7. Explain the different types of decisions.
8. Differentiate objective Vs bounded rationality.

9. What is the meaning of rational decision making? What does it involve?
10. What do you mean by Rationality?
11. Explain bounded rationality.
12. Explain the terms problem space and search space with a sketch.
13. Which are the different categories of decision making?
14. Explain the terms 'Certainty', 'Risk', 'Uncertainty'.
15. What does Decision making under certainty involves?
16. Explain Linear programming and computer solution for the same.
17. What does Decision making under uncertainty involves?
18. Explain games Theory. Mention its applications.
19. What does Decision making under Risk involves?
20. Explain a decision tree. Mention its applications.
21. Explain Queuing theory. Mention its applications.
22. Explain Simulation. Mention its applications.
23. Compare and contrast Certainty, Risk and Uncertainty.
24. What do you mean by Scenario strategy?
25. Explain Basic risky decisions and model.
26. Explain Basic risky policy.
27. Explain Basic risky decision with multiple objectives.
28. Explain a Multiple objective, no risk decision model.
29. Discuss a decision tree. How it can be constructed? What are the rules?
30. Define an influence diagram.
31. How a decision tree is related with an influence diagram?
32. Explain simulation with a sketch.
33. Explain Monte Carlo Simulation technique.
34. What do you mean by simulation analysis?
35. What is Management Science?
36. Explain a mathematical Model. How it can be constructed?
37. Which are the common languages used in simulation.
38. Explain the different models under simulation.
39. What do you mean by Stochastic model?
40. What do you mean by Deterministic model ?

Organising

Chapter - 4

4.1 Preview

This chapter deals with:

- *Nature of organising*
  - Legal forms of organisation
  - Organising defined
  - Organising by key activities
- *Traditional organisational theory*
  - Patterns of departmentation
  - Significance of span of control
  - Factors determining effective spans.
- *Technology and organisation structure*
  - The wood word studies
  - The Aston studies
  - Perrows model
  - Impact of computer based technology
- *Modern organisational forms.*

4.2 Definition

As per louis A - Allen, organisation is the process of identifying and grouping the work to be performed, defining and delegating responsibility and authority and establishing relationships for the purpose of enabling people to work most effectively in accomplishing objectives.

Koontz and O'Donnel has defined the **organisation** as the one which involves the grouping of activities necessary to accomplish goals and plans, the assignment of these activities to appropriate departments and the provision for authority delegation and coordination.

4.3 Organising process

It involves taking a number of steps such as:

- determination of objectives.
- grouping of activities.
- assignment of duties to persons
- delegation of authority
- creating authority relationships
- leads to the creation of organisation structure.

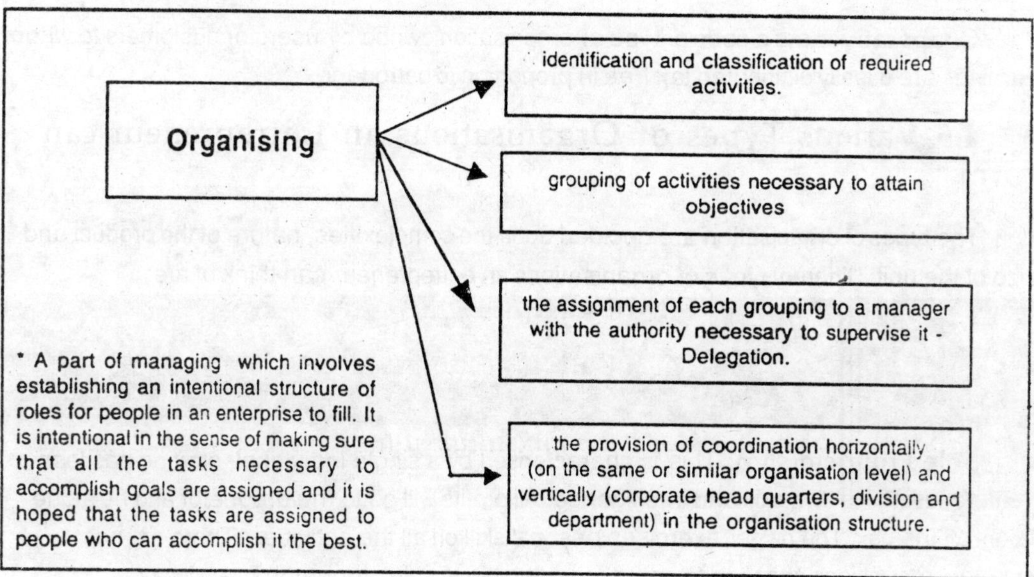

Fig. 4.1 Meaning of Organising

People working together in groups to achieve some goals must have roles to play much like the parts the actors play in a drama. A role implies that what people do has a definite purpose or objective, their activity is in an area where they know how their job fit into the overall group effort. Where they have the necessary authority to do the task and where they have the necessary tools and information to accomplish it.

Eg:- Purchase department in a company

- Purchase managers role was to study the material requirement of the company for a year.
- Develop suppliers who can supply the company
- The role of these assistants were to know the rates of each type of material and write the purchase orders.

4.4 Legal forms in which a business can be organised

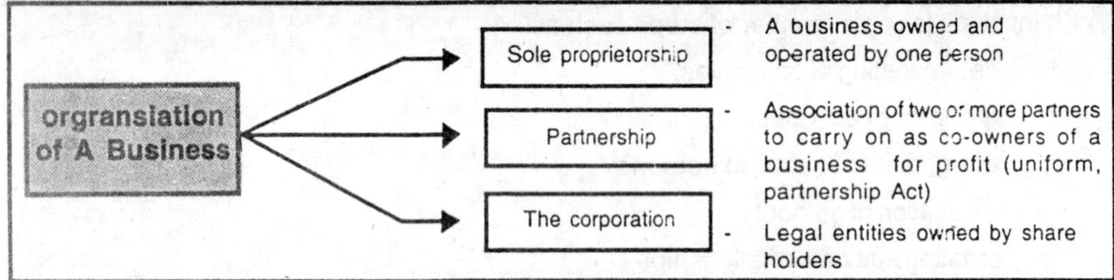

Fig. 4.2 Organisation of a A Business

Cooperatives are a special type of organisation owned by users or customers to whom earnings are usually distributed tax free in proportion to patronage.

4.5 Various Types of Organisations an Entrepreneur can form

The types of organisation are decided upon the complexities, nature of the product and size of the unit. Different types of organisations an entrepreneur can think of are:

- Proprietorship
- Partnership
- Companies

Sole Proprietorship: This is characterised by a single individual, starting has less venture, using his own skill and intelligence. All profits will go to the proprietor and he alone takes all the risk. The owner exercises pesonal skill on all the activities. There are no statutory regualtions attached to sole proprietorship. A sole proprietorship will have

- Limited capital
- Limited managerial skill
- Unlimited liability
- Uncertainty of continuity

Comparsion of Different Types of Organisations

Factors	Proprietorship	Partnership	Companies
1. Operation by	• Individual Eg. Majority of SSIs Tiny sector units Low capital investment SSUs.	Partners (embark upon a joint venture) Two persons minimum who are capable of entering into agreements (but not created with a minor, but limited to 20 persons as per section 11 of Companies Act, 1956 contravening the provisions of section 11 is an illegal association and is punishable with fine.	Seven or more persons where the company to be formed will be a private company (restricts the right to transfer its shares, limits the number of its members to fifty, prohibits any invitation to the public for subscription of shares in or debentures of the company
2. Setups	• Atomistic primitive type and no organisational structure.		
3. Run by	• Owner with assistance of family members and close friends.		
4. Hiring	- May hire one or two Journeymen - Adjusts employment levels according to fluctuations in business		
5. Business carried on	• In a personal way, accounting casual, business and personal funds mingled.		
6. Risk	• Bears the entire loss and his personal assets may be affected.	Every partner is jointly and severaly liable for any loss and personal assets may be brought into pay business debts., Partners bring capital or even property (may be also immovable) proportion to their share.	As per the Companies Act, 1956, incorporation, is the act of conferring judicial personality on a group of associated persons. The capital of the company with which the company is to be
7. Popular in	• Retailing, wholesaling, construction, real estate and traditional service.		
8. Money brought	• Individually money or even property (may be also immovable).		
9. Share	• Full share		

Factors	Proprietorship	Partnership	Companies
10. Agreement between partners		• In India, partnership organisations are governed by the Indian Partnership Act, 1932. Section 4 of the act defined a partnership as "The relation between persons who have agreed to share profits of a business carried on by all or any of them acting for all": **Conditions:** • Minimum 2 persons • An agreement should be there between persons • Persons should be legally competent to enter into a contract • Motive is to share profits • Business carried on by all or any of them acting for all • Contract between partners and the right during the subsistence of the partnership is to get share of profits from time to time as may be agreed upon. Partners are liable for the debts and liabilities of the firm; jointly liable for the sales tax and penalties due by the firm. It is not a matter of heritage status but purly one of contract, No heir of a deceased partner can Claim to have become a partner without the consent of others. • No introduction of partners into a firm without the consent of all the exiting partners.	registered and the division thereof is into shares of a fixed amount. The subscribers shall not take less than one share and each subscriber shall write opposite tohis name the number of shares he takes.
11. Responsibility of business loss and personal assets	By the Proprietor	• Jointly and severally responsible by every partner.	

Fig. 4.3 Comparison of Different Types of Organisations

Partnership: It is the relation between persons who agree to share profits of business, carried on by all or by any of them acting of all. The number of partners can be between 2 and 20. Profits are shared amongst the partners in an agreed proportion. As in case of proprietorship, the liabilities of partners are unlimited, which means creditor can realise dues from any or all the partners. Partnership deed, normally, is written indicating the nature of the firm and names of partners, amount of capital that each partner indicates to contribute.and ratio of sharing profits and losses. Partnership will be advantageous when the size of business is relativley small and the risk involved is not high.

Companies

(i) Private Limited

A private limited company is one, which by its Articles of Association,

- Limits the number of its members to 50 excluding those who are employees or were its employees in the past
- Prohibits an invitation to the public for subscription to its shares and debentures
- Restricts the transfer of its share
- The minimum number of members required is two
- The minimum number of directors is two

(ii) Public Limited

Any company which is not a private limited company is a **publ ic limited company.** The minimum number of members required to form a public limited company is 7 and there is no maximum limit. Here also the liability of members is limited to the extent of amount due on the shares, if any. In case of huge project outlay, public limited company is formed, the shares are offered to general public for subscription.

4.6 'Entrepreneur as a Dreamer'

Good entrepreneurs are those who always identify the business and build the same effectively. After developing the business initially, they try to sieze opportunities for further growth. Setting up of business and finally achieving the success of the venture is always difficult. Only few can succeed. It is difficult to have success in continuously dreams of all things possible and is determined to fend for himself because he is convinced if that no one else will fend for him. He builds up qualities like administrative capability, flair and ability for decision making, computation skill, delegation skill, organisational skill. He is good at communication, has sound technical knowledge, achievement motivation etc.

Entrepreneurship involves a few major decisions:

- Decision to become an entrepreneur
- Identification and selection of an opportunity
- Business plan formulation and its implementation
- Entrepreneurial continuum

Hence, he dreams of venturing into complex projects. He dreams of new ideas and opportunities. He would like to have innovatin for change. He would like to take calculated risks and has faith in his own capabilities. He would like to coordinate teh business management of the enterprise wihtout anybody's help and control the enterprise, motivate others. He would therefore dreams to be a successful entrepreneur by associating himself with many of the activities.

4.7 Key objectives organise first

While organising effectively, one should consider:

- Basic Mission
- Long - range objectives established for the organisation
- Strategy conceived to accomplish the above.

Peter Drucker used the word ' Load bearing parts of the structure' for the key activities

Key Activities to be worked out as per the questions posed by Peter Drucker

- Excellence in area required to obtain the company's objectives?
- Areas which lack performance and endanger the results, if not the survival of the enterprise?
- Values truly important to us in the company ?

Fig. 4.4 Key Activities to be Worked Out (Questions by Peter Drucker)

4.8 Peter Drucker also suggests the following:-

- An analysis of decisions
- An analysis of relations

Decision Stages Analysis

(i) Establish key activities

(ii) Analyse what decisions are needed to attain effectiveness in key activities ?

(iii) Nature of the decisions established in long term horizon?

(iv) Impact of this on other functions ?

(v) Frequency of decisions (recurrent decisions can be made ? at lower levels after establishing policies)

(vi) Extent to which their involvement in ethical, social and political considerations ?

Relations analysis Stage = Relations Analysis (asks the concerned activity manager to work and seek to assure " the crucial relations - the relationship on which success depends and the effectiveness of its contribution should be easy, accessible and central to the Unit")

4.9 Traditional organisation Theory

1) Patterns of Departmentation

Definition of Departmentation

The grouping of smaller activities of a business concern into small units for the purpose of facilitating administration is called **Departmentation.** Koontz and O' Donnell defines **Departmentation** as a process of dividing the large monolithic functional organisation into smaller and flexible administrative units.

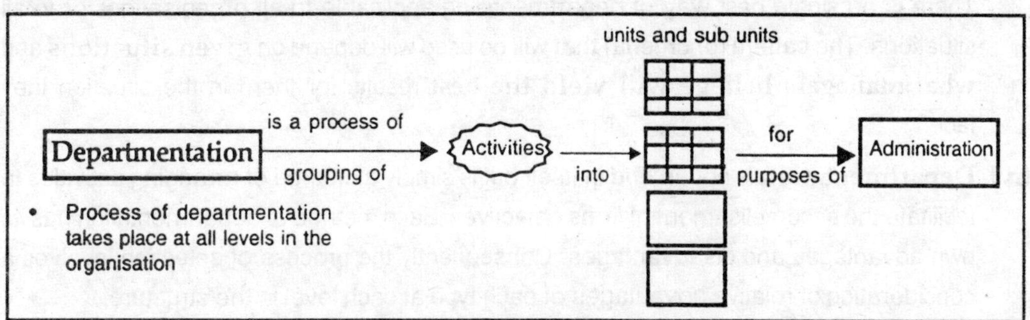

Fig. 4.5 Departmentation

The administrative units and subunits created may be designated as:

- Divisions
- Units
- Branches
- Sections
- Jobs

(ii) Need and Importance of Departmentation

The larger the size of the enterprise, the greater is the need for departmentation. Departmentation contributes to the success of the enterprise.

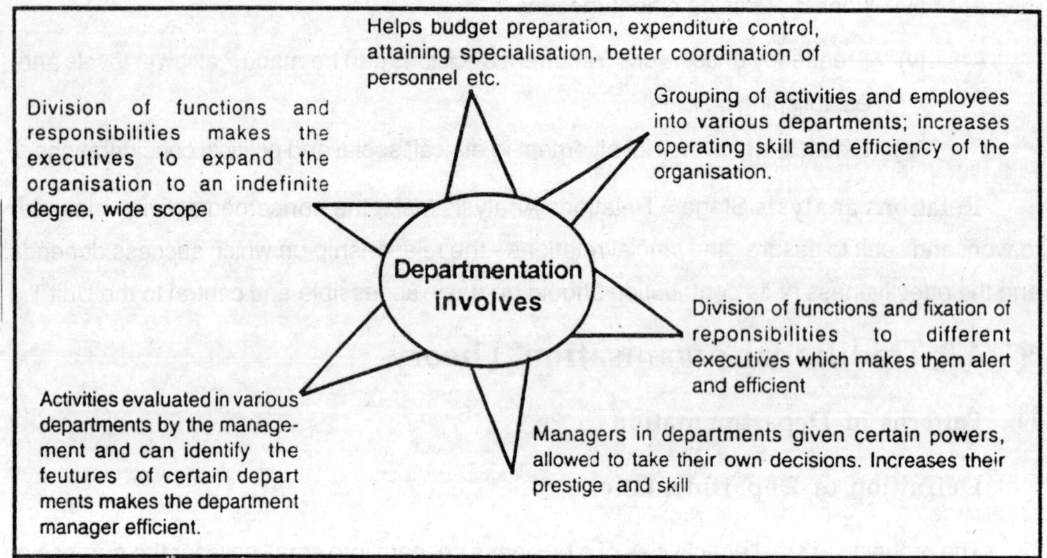

Fig. 4.6 Importance of Departmentation

(iii) Pattern of Departmentation

There is no single best way of departmentising applicable to all organisations or to all situations. The pattern (or criteria) that will be used will depend on **given situations** and **what managers believe will yield the best** results for them in the situation they face.

(iv) Departmentation is not an end in itself but is simply a method of arranging activities to facilitate the accomplishment of firms objectives. Each method of departmentation has its own advantages and disadvantages. Consequently the process of selection involves a consideration of relative advantages of each type at each level in the structure.

There are certain basic methods of dividing responsibilities within an organisation structure. They are by.

1) Enterprise Functions
2) By Time
3) By Simple numbers
4) By Regions or Territories
5) By Customers
6) By Process or Equipment
7) By Product or Service
8) By Marketing Oriented
9) Combination of Product and Functions (Matrix organisation)

Note: Organisational structures for 1 to 9 (except 2 and 3) are shown below in Fig: 4.7

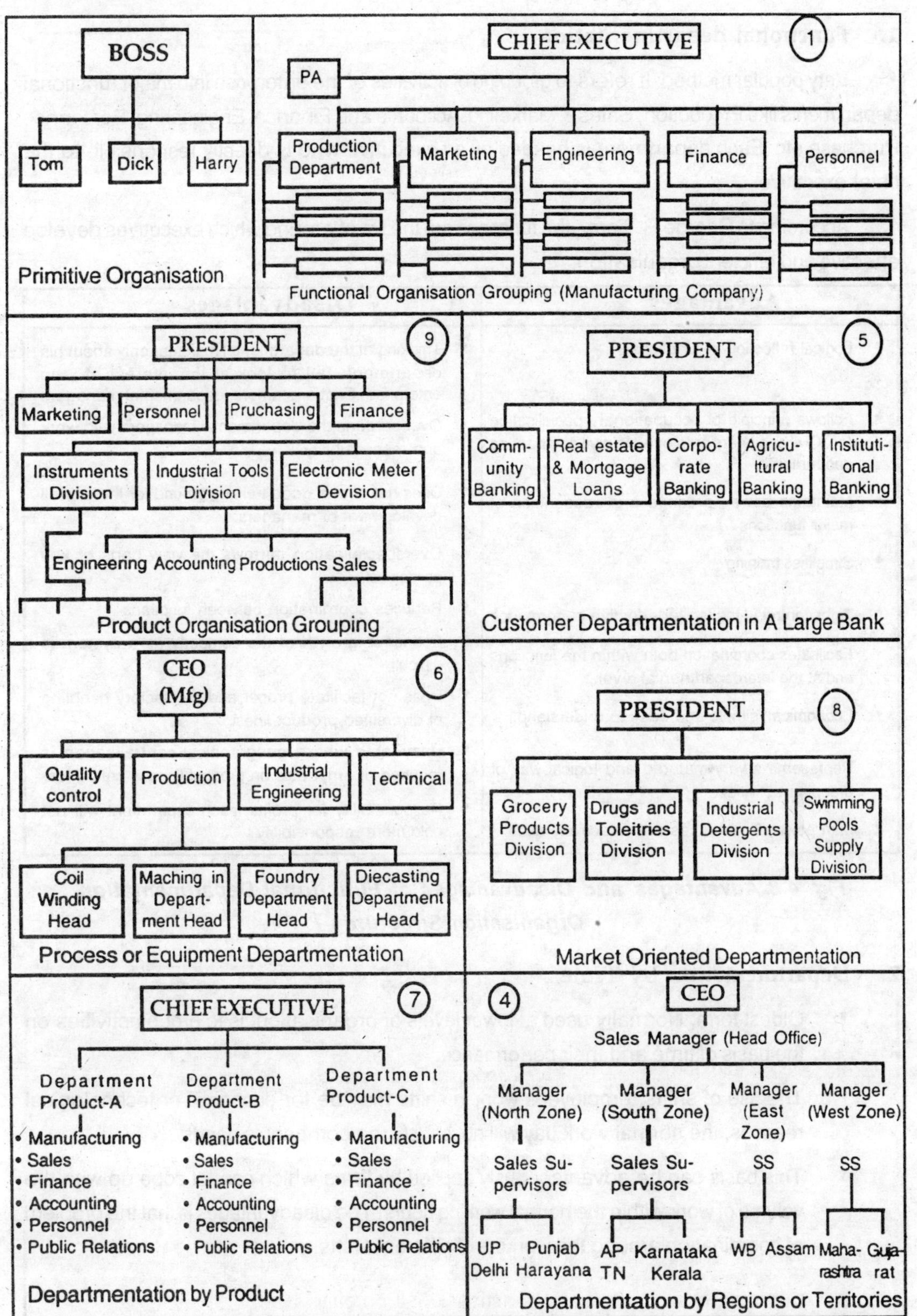

Fig. 4.7 Organisation Structure for 1 to 9 (Except for 2 & 3 responsibilities)

1. Functional departmentation

♦ Very popular method; It refers to grouping of activities of the enterprise into major functional depart ments like Production, Sales & Marketing, Accounts and Finance, Engineering, Personnel, Purchase etc. Each department is headed by an executive who is directly responsible to the chief executive.

♦ According to George R. Terry, the functions are the Pivot around which executives develop effective and efficient organisation.

Advantages	Disadvantages
♦ Logical reflection of functions	♦ Thinking of the departmental manager only about his department; fail to look at the interest of the enterprise; Frictions among departmental managers
♦ Follows principle of occupational specialisation (eg. Civil engineers employed in civil engineering department)	♦ Over burdens the departmental managers with work and responsibility
♦ Maintains power, prestige and recognition of major functions	♦ Does not offer a good training ground for the overall development of managers.
♦ Simplifies training	♦ Overspecialisation narrows the view parts of key personnel.
♦ Tight control at the top for effective performance	♦ Reduces coordination between functions
♦ Facilitates coordination both within the functions and at the interdepartmental level.	♦ Economic growth of the company as a system is difficult
♦ Economical, simple and easy to understand.	♦ Does not facilitate proper and satisfactory handling of diversified product lines.
♦ Represents a very matured and logical way of grouping activities.	♦ Unsuitable where geographical centralisation is required or emphasis on product lines is called for
♦ Man power & resources are effectively used.	♦ Responsibility for profits, each department will not hold more responsibility

Fig. 4.8 Advantages and Disadvantages of Functional Departmentation Organisation Structure

2. Departmentation by Time

♦ Oldest form; Normally used at lower levels of organisation, is to group activities on the basis of time and their performance.

♦ The use of shifts; employees work in shifts may be for economic or technological reasons, the normal work day will not satisfy the company's needs.

♦ This basis can be advantageously applied by firms which cannot cope up with the volume of work within the normal working hours. The disadvantages is that the problem of coordination among the workers of different shifts.

3. Departmentation by Numbers

Here, the persons who are to perform the same duties are divided into small groups and then each group is placed under the control of supervisor or officer

eg. In the army, troops are grouped into:

- Squads
- Batallions
- Brigades
- Regiments

On the basis of the number of men prescribed for each unit. In industries, this is not used.

4. Departmentation by Regions or Territories

- Common method for enterprises that operate over wide geographical areas; Activities in a given area or territory should by grouped and assigned to a manager; suitable for large scale firms where activites are physically or geographically spread.
- When similar operations are undertaken in different geographic areas as in Automobile assembly, chain retailing and whole saling and oil refining, Business firms resort to this method.
- Poor communication facilities are often advanced as a reason for preparing territorial departmentation ; This means that for day to day decision making, the different geographically dispersed units of the business need not communicate with each other. Hence separate departments based on Geography or Territory are needed.
- Another reason is the need for taking prompt and quick action in a given area.
- It is also proper when its purpose is to encourage local participation in decision making and to take advantage of a certain economies of localised operation.

Advantages	Disadvantages
♦ Encourages concentration on specific customers and their needs ♦ Gives the customer a feeling that they have a supplier who is fully organised to meet their needs ♦ Develops enterprise in customer area ♦ Helps the company to earn good will ♦ Promotes specialisation among the staff of the enterprise. ♦ Suitable where major emphasis placed on better service to specialised customers purchasing the company's products.	♦ Under utilisation of resources and facilities in some departments may take place ♦ Duplication activities. ♦ Difficulty in coordination ♦ As all the activities cannot be organised on this basis, its utility is limited. ♦ Difficult for coordinating operations between competing customer needs. ♦ Managers and staff to develop expertise in customer problems ♦ Not possible to departmentise customer groups clearly ♦ Possibility of underemployment of facilities and labour specialised workers in customer groups

Fig. 4.9 Advantages and Disadvantages of Departmentation by Regions or Territories Organisation Structure

5. Departmentation by customers

The grouping of activities to reflect a primary interest in customers is commonly found in a variety of enterprises. Customers are the key to the way the activities are grouped when the different activities an enterprise carries out are each managed by one department head. Business owners and mangers frequently arrange activities on this basis to cater to the requirements of clearly defined customer groups.

Advantages	Disadvantages
• Places responsibility at a lower level there by enabling development of talent even at lower levels. • Places emphasis and focases on local markets and problems and avoids, red tapism in problem solving • Improves coordination in a region • Takes advantages of economies of local operation. • Better face to face communications with local interest exists • Furnishes measurable training ground for general managers. Local markets exploited effectively • Provides opportunities to managers to improve their skills in various fields.	• Large number of executives, Hence increase in overhead costs. • May give rise to duplication of activities; many ... and service functions which are performed at the regional level could be carried out by Head office very economically. • Makes control from Head quarters less effective. • It is a costly system : small business concerns cannot afford it. • Increases problem of Top management control.

Fig. 4.10 Advantages and Disadvantages of Departmentation by Customers Organisational Structure

6. Processwise Departmentation

The enterprise is organised on the basis of process involved in the manufacture of the product.

Advantages	Disadvantages
• Facilitates the use of costlier equipment in an efficient manner. • For repairs and renewals, there is no need to interrupt the whole production process. Hence the maintenance of department is facilitated • There may be economy in operations • There is no duplication of activites • Follows the principle of specialisation • Enables effective performance control • Suitable for organisations which are engaged in the manufacture of such products involving a number of processes.	• Requlres more space and investment • Costly and hence small organisations cannot afford it. • Does not provide good training ground and opportunities for overall development of managerial talent.

Fig. 4.11 Advantages and Disadvantages of Process-wise Departmentation Organisation Structure

7. Departmentation by products

♦ Suited to large organisations; growing importance in multi product, large scale business enterprise; when companies started of, they adopted **function departmentation**. Here each major product manufactured by the enterprise, a separate department is created and department is put incharge of a manager.

Advantages	disadvantages
♦ Places attention and effort on a complete product line. The profitability growth and improvement program are focused. ♦ Places responsibility for profits at the divisional level. ♦ Improves coordination of functional activities. ♦ Furnishes measurable training ground for General Managers ♦ Permits growth and diversity of products and services ♦ Encourages healthy competition amongst different product lines.	♦ Require more persons with General Manager abilities ♦ Tends to make maintenance of economic central services difficult ♦ Presents increased problem of top management control.

Fig. 4.12 Advantages and Disadvantages of Departmentation by Products Organisation Structure

8 Market oriented Departmentation

Newer forms of basic departmentation involve organising an enterprise **around markets** served or **around marketing channels** used. While both these approaches to departmentation are designed to emphasise marketing and make it more effective, they do have some differences.

Organising around marketing channels require making an organisation structure reflect the ways company reaches an ultimate customer whether the route is through whole sale channels direct to grocery stores or direct to super markets, through channels designed to serve hardware stores or direct to drug stores.

Organising around markets groups activities to support marketing efforts in such key markets as Hospitals, Aerospace companies, Computer operations and Brokerage firms.

Both the above approaches may sound like customer departmentation and they are similar to it. The essential considerations in the market oriented departmentation are marketing channel and the market and not types of customers buying the product or services as in customer oriented departmentation.

Eg. A leading manufacturer of soaps, detergents, talcum powder and other related products in India found that neither product departmentation nor territorial departmentation patterns worked various soaps and detergents move to the ultimate customer through Grocery supermarkets as well as through Drug stores.

Advantages	Disadvantages
• Makes possible concentration on market place and marketing channels in each area. • Develops opportunites for more efficient marketing activities.	• Loss of concentration on product growth and profit. • Problems in training people to think in terms of markets rather than products • Problems in allocating products and charging costs of manufacture when the same product is marketed through two or more divisions but manufactured in one

Fig. 4.13 Advantages and Disadvantages of Market Oriented Departmentation Organisation Structure

Matrix organisation

Enterprises may combine several of all the above methods indicated in designing their organisation. We may see functional subdivision at the top level, product and process subdivision in manufacturing and geographical and customer departmentation in marketing.

4.10 Significance of span of control

When a new organisation starts growing to significant size, these is a requirements of subordinate managers to assist the top managers. This need was recognised as soon as large groups of people began working towards a common purpose.

The question would be how many managers are needed? (not whether immediate managers are needed). This is related to the number of people reporting directly to each manager, referred to as the "**span of management**" or "**span of control**".

Organisation Structure Defintion: Organisation structure results from the organising process is the basic frame work within which the decision-making behaviour of an executive takes place. It is a established pattern of relationships among the components of the organisation. Organisation structure consist simply of those aspects of pattern of behavior in the organisation that are relatively stable and change only slowly. It is the system of relationship that governs the activities of people who are dependent upon each other in achieving the common object.

An organisations authority structure may range from the highly centralised to decentralised.

A classical organisation is usually **pyramid shaped.**

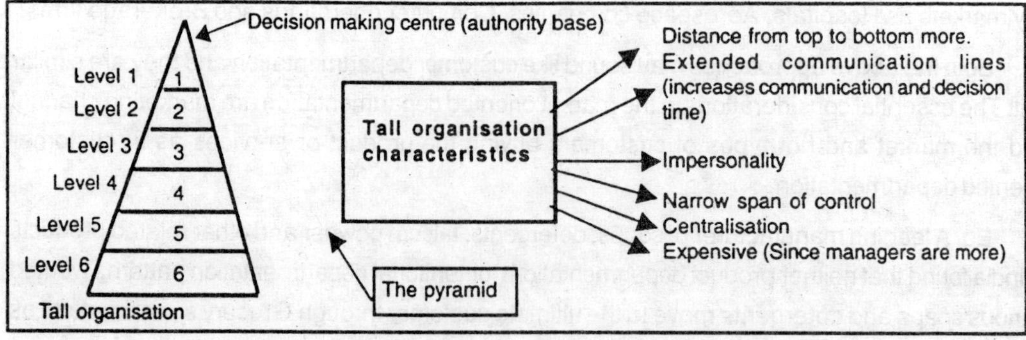

Fig 4.14 Tall Organisation and its Characteristics

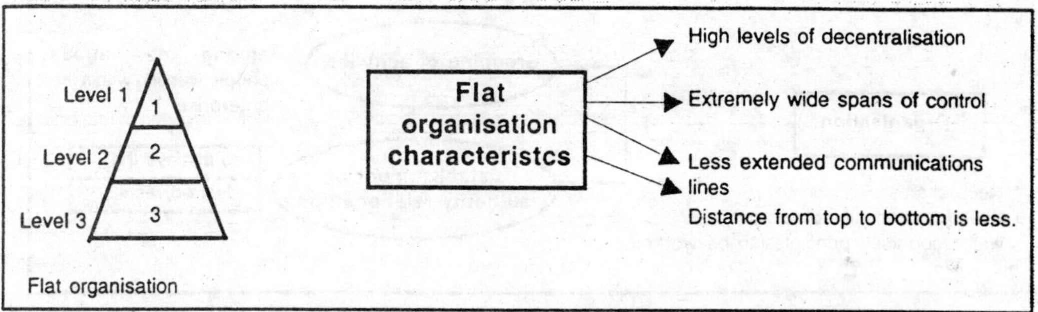

Fig. 4.15 Flat Organisation and its Characteristics

Wider spans of control are advocated by the behaviouralists which foster a flatter organisation structure, more general supervision, and more decentralisation; leaves managers with inadequate time to supervise the activities they are responsible for and leave subordinates with inadequate access to their busy supervisor.

4.11 How to Determine effective spans ?

This depends on:

Number of relationships that existed

- between manager and subordinates individually
- in combinations
- among the subordinates themselves

Graicunas worked out a formula $n [2^{n+1} + n - 1]$ for the number relationships for a manager with n subordinates. If 'n' is doubled, the number of relationships the manager has to be concerned with. Graicunas assumed, the difficulty of the job.

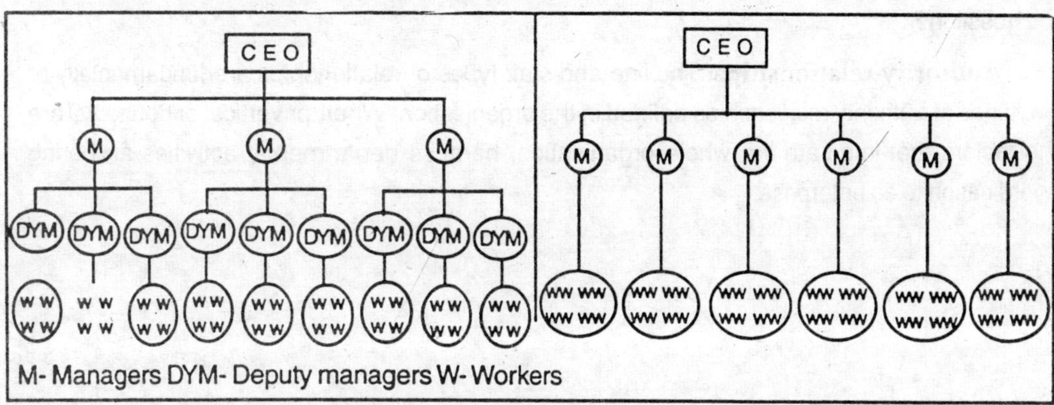

Fig. 4.16 Control Spans of Three and Six Managers Compared

Kimball and kimball says that the problem of the organisation is to select and combine the efforts of men of proper characteristics so as to produce the desired results.

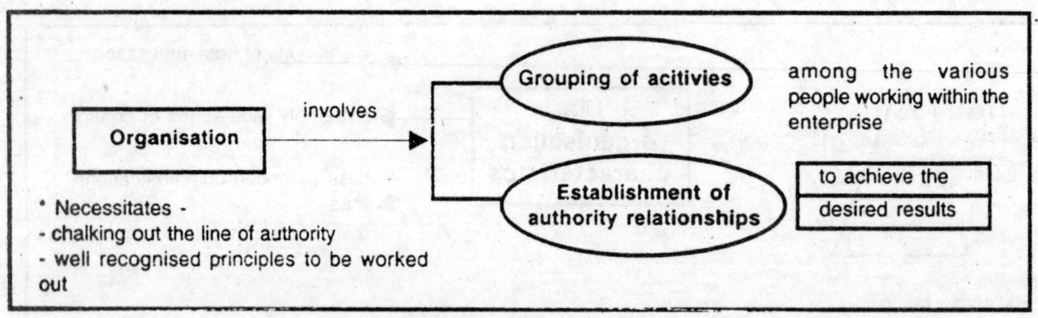

Fig. 4.17 Organisation Defined

Principles recognised for the purposes of establishing an internal organisation

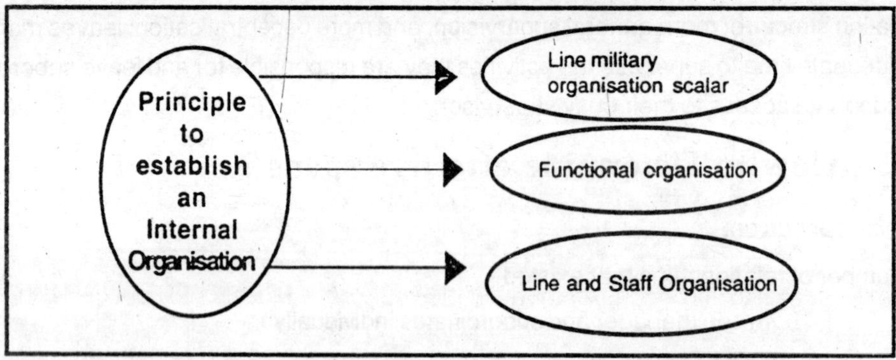

Fig. 4.18 Principles to Establish an Internal Organisation

Authority is the power to exercise discretion in making decisions. The various departments cannot become smoothly working units unless the department heads have some authority for taking decisions and run the departments. What kind of authority do we find in an organisation is the question?

Authority-relationships: The line and staff types of relationships are fundamentally of two types of authority relationships defined in the organisation. Whether vertical or horizontal are the factors that integrate the whole organisation, harness departmental activities and bring coordination to an enterprise.

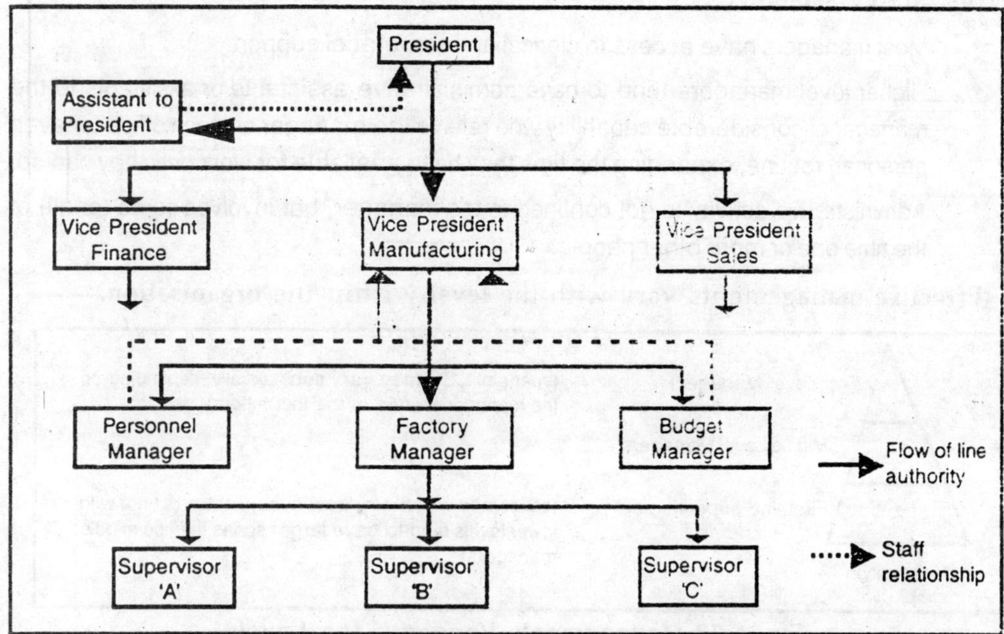

Fig 4.19 Line and Staff Authority Relationships

The conditions for increasing the number of people, a manager could effectively supervise after the study of the effective spans are as follows:

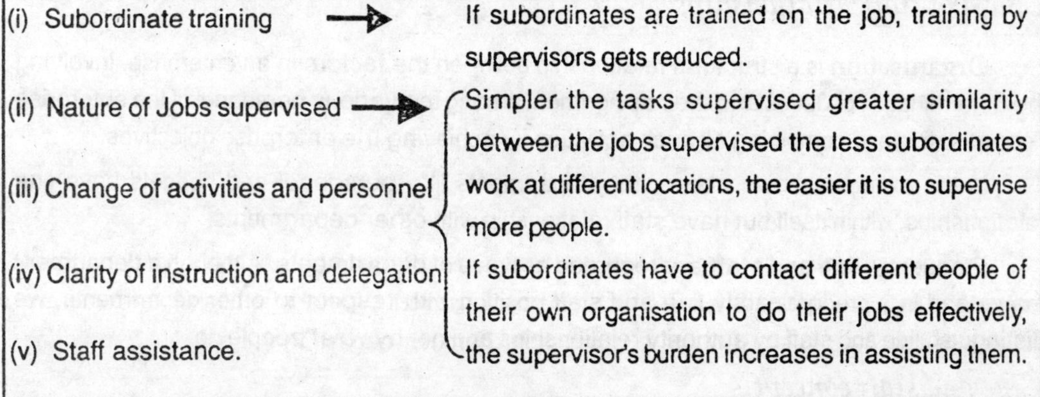

(i) Subordinate training →	If subordinates are trained on the job, training by supervisors gets reduced.
(ii) Nature of Jobs supervised →	Simpler the tasks supervised greater similarity between the jobs supervised the less subordinates work at different locations, the easier it is to supervise more people.
(iii) Change of activities and personnel	
(iv) Clarity of instruction and delegation	If subordinates have to contact different people of their own organisation to do their jobs effectively, the supervisor's burden increases in assisting them.
(v) Staff assistance.	

(iii) Change of activities and personnel

Activities change rapidly in some of the organisations for which the organisation should have more people for the rate of decision making.

(iv) Clarity of instruction and delegation

If the works to be done is very clear to the supervisor, he can interact and delegate to the subordinate, the right appropriate resources needed for this well defined job, The less subsequent supervision should be required.

(v) Staff Assistance

- Most managers have access to clerical and secretarial support.
- Higher level managers tend to have administrative assistants or assistants to the manager of considerable capability who releive the manager of much office (or even personal) routine, expanding the time they have available for work only they can do.
- Administrative activity is not confined to the manager, but involves some (or all) of the time one or more other people.

Effective managements vary with the level within the organisation:

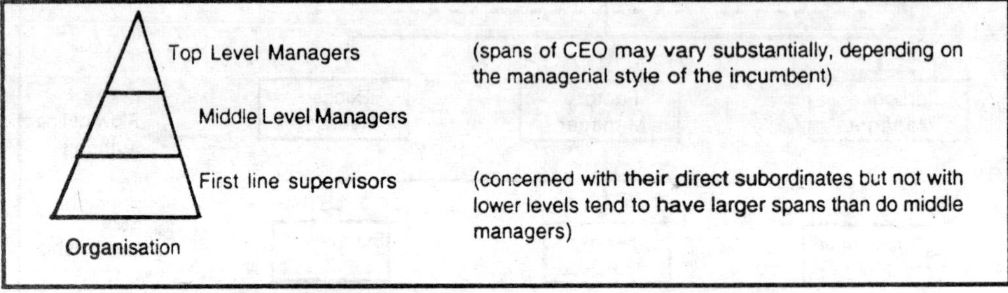

Fig. 4.20 Managements Vary with the Level

The skill and experience of the managers have an effect on:

- The number of people he/she supervises

Line and staff Relationships

Organisation is a structural relationship between the factors in an enterprise, involving the determination of duties and their assignment among the various personnel of the enterprise - coordinating and combining all such activities for achieving the enterprise objectives.

In the example shown above, the departments like personnel and budgets have line relationships, within itself but have staff relationship with other departments.

Frequently, **line and staff** are regarded as types of departments. Although a department may stand in a predominantly line and staff position with respect to other departments, we distinguish line and staff by authority relationships and not by what people do.

Line and staff concept:-

One widely held concept of line and staff type of authority relationships is that:

Line Functions	Staff Functions
• Those that have direct responsibility for accomplishing the objectives of the enterprise	• Help the line functions to be more effective in a accomplishing the primary objectives of an enterprise (such as expected

• For them of this opinion, they classify production and sales (sometimes finance) as **line functions**. Purchasing, accounting, personnel plant maintenance, industrial engineering and quality control as **staff functions**	**Is it Correct?**

Fig. 4.21 Line and Staff Concept

The confusion arising from such a concept is immediately apparent. It is argued that **purchasing** for example merely help in achieving the main objective of business because unlike the production departments, purchasing does not physically convert material into finished product. But is purchasing any less essential to the achievement of company's objectives?

And could not the same question be asked about other so called staff functions (or service departments) such as accounting, personal and plant maintenance ?

There is probably nothing that can support production of quality goods better than the staff department called **Quality Control Department.**

A more precise and logically valid concept of line and staff is that they are simply a matter of relationships. **Line authority** gives a superior (usually called as the boss) a line of authority over a subordinate. It exists in all organisations. Hence this arrangement is called scalar principle in organisation. The clearer the line of authority from the top management position in an enterprise to every subordinate position, the more effective will be decision making and organisational communication. Organisation structure involves the scalar principles of reporting and authority.

Line authority becomes apparent from the scalar principles being that relationship in which a superior exercises direct supervisor over a subordinate - **an authority relationship in direct line or steps.** The nature of **staff relationship** is advisory. The function of people in a pure staff capacity is to:

- investigate
- research
- give advice to line managers and line department

Comparison of Line / Staff / Functional / Service Relationships

Line	Staff	Functional	Service
♦ Superior / Subordinate ♦ Chain of command from CEO to the lowest worker	♦ Advisory in nature ♦ 4 types of staff relation ships - Providing advice on request - Reconnecting where the staff office deems appropriate - Consulting authority (managers consult staff in the area) - Concurring authority (staff specialist has a Veto authority on manager)	♦ Special type of staff authority on others not their line subordinates ♦ As binding as line authority. Does not carry the right for violation. ♦ Controls how to accomplish some action falling in the area of responsibility of the stage office, delegated to stage because of the need of uniformity Eg: Budget formats by the financial officer.	♦ Centralised facilitative activities for economy of scale, uniformity or special capability ♦ Supportive of the main or Eg Custodial Security Medical etc.

Fig. 4.22 Comparsion of Line/Staff/Functional/Service Relationships

Friction between line and staff personnel occurs frequently.

4.12 Technology and organisation structure

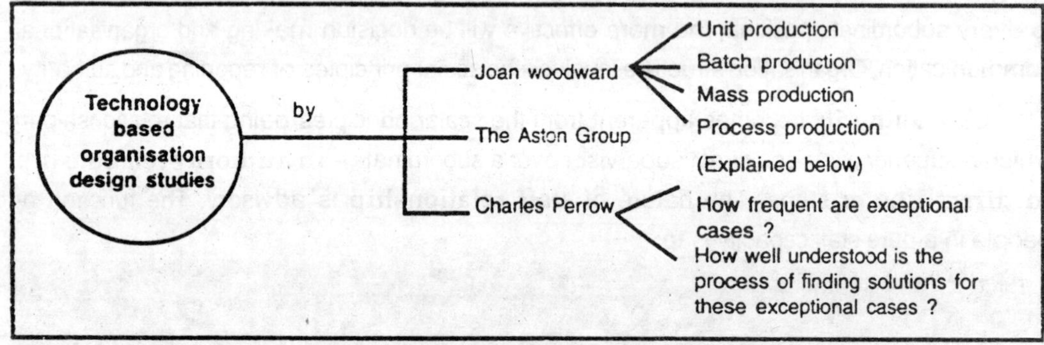

Fig. 4.23 Technology Based Organisation Design Studies

4.13 Woodwards observations were:

Characteristics	Production Technologies			
	Unit	Large batch	Mass	Process
(i) the number of levels of management (ii) the span of control for chief executives	Increases →			

Fig. 4.24 John Woodwards Observation Based on Techniques of Production

In many ways, the unit and process technologies at the low and high ends were similiar to each other and different from the large batch and mass production technologies in the middle of the scale. The former used were more likely to favour organic management systems, which are more decentralised with less rigidly defined jobs. less attention to rank and a great deal of lateral (as approved to vertical) communication. They also enjoyed a more pleasant and relaxed organisational climate, more reliance on verbal communication, and fewer people reporting to 1st line supervisors.

4.14 The Aston studies

A group of scholars at the university of **Aston, Birmingham, England** investigated number of firms and studied the **operations technology**. They agreed with woodward that **mass production firms has larger spans of control** for first line supervisors, with more staff specialists for control and greater distinctions between line and staff than did unit or process firms. They found that the size of the firm (number of employees) correlated better with other parameters than did the type of technology. The larger firms were more likely to have:

- high levels of specialisation
- standardisation
- formalisation
- cetralisation

} regardless of the type of technology

4.15 Perrows Model

Charles perrows classification of technologies is as under:

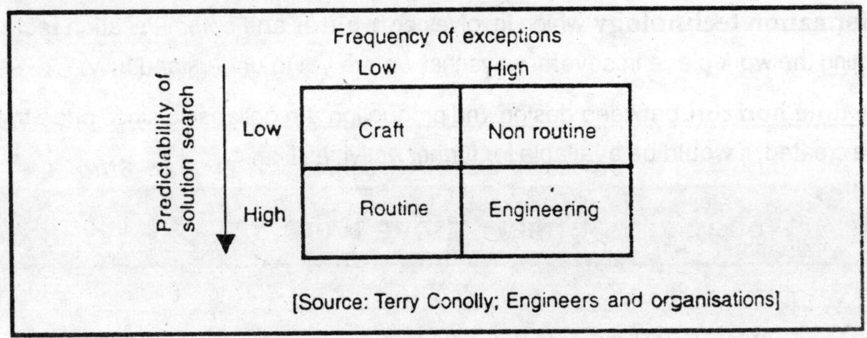

Fig. 4.25 Perrows Model

Conolly's scheme turn on 2 questions:-

- How frequent are exceptional cases ?
- How well understood is the process of finding solutions for these exceptional cases?

These questions suggest a 2 x 2 classification of technologies. Several different technologies many be found within a single organisation

Eg; Manufacture of electric motors - **Routine** (atleast for standard models)

Designing motors, though complex is pretty well understood - **engineering technology**.

- Dealing with customers may be **non-routine**
- Certain parts of building motors may require skilled workers whose expertise appears in no text book **(craft technology)**

All four of perrow's categories that is observed in a single plant

- **Nonroutine Organisation** Many variations from the routine; needs substantial creativity or judgement to resdve them ; works best as per **perrow** using a flexible, organic management style; allows the lowest level of management to exercise substantial discretion and power. Many management positions or R & D in new areas of technology seem to fit this model.
- **Routine organisation** Established principles and standards are applied to meet new specifications; encourage flexible yet cetralised mangement styles; involving few exceptions and clear methods for resolving them achieving greater efficiency with centrally developed plans and little delegations to lower levels.

4.16 Impact of computer based Technology

Information technology which involves **computer** and communication technologies are affecting the work place in several ways that we are yet to understand fully.

The **time horizon** between design and production are collapsing since once the design database created, it would be available for further activities like:

- Design analysis
- Evaluation
- Creating prototypes
- Control of ultimate production
- Planning and control of quality inspection

Time Horizon has already been explained in para 2.4.

The firms which are highly successful adopts, the principles of flexibility, adaptability and quick response which is possible only through computer based technologies since computers provide speed, accuracy, flexibility etc. Quicker start-ups, product changes reduce the optimal size of production runs, supplemented by resource reduction in inprocess and finished goods inventory. Product life cycle will be shortened in many industries for which industries would strive to become a successful one.

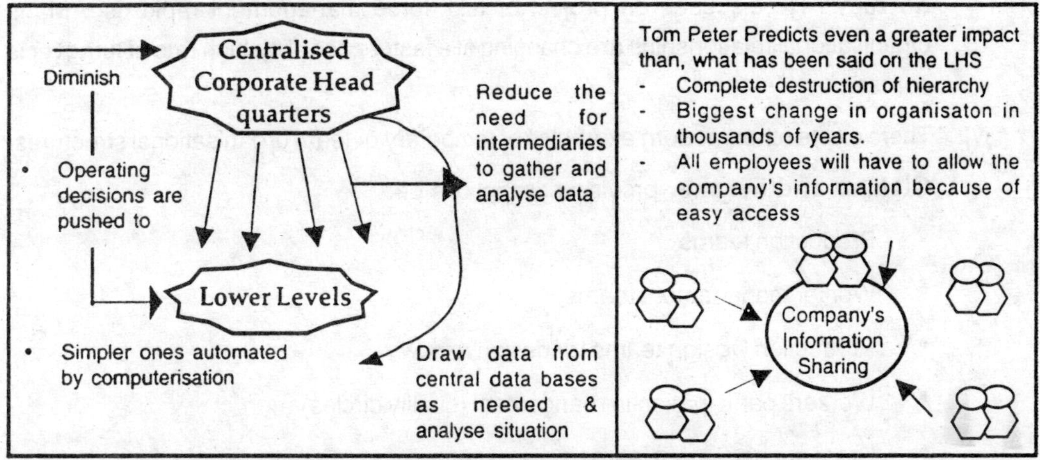

Fig. 4.26 Use of Computerbased Technology as per Experts

Computer based automation replaces conventional processes and reduces the number of workers (including supervisors) needed per unit of out put.

Skills needed by workers to monitor the production process:

- Visualisation
- Conceptual Thinking (abstract thinking)
- Study and Understand process (Not only machine, machine/material Interaction)
- Statistical conclusions (Trends, limits, data)
- Communication (oral-visual)
- Executives of command
- Responsibility (individual)

4.17 Modern Organisation forms

(i) **Maxwebers** described bureaucracy as formal, rather rigid organisational style still has value for carrying out highly structured, routine functions over long periods of time. Conventional bureaucracy can carry with it pressures to conform that it makes fool of innovation and growth.

(ii) **Whyte** has written in his book ' The organisation Man ' and has said that much more flexible structures are needed for many of tasks of today and tomorrow

(iii) **Toeffler** based on the above predicted ' **The breakdown of Bureaucracy**' in 1970 book; '**Future Shock**'. He said that the new organised system arrival has been witnessed to ensure challenge and this would ultimately supplant bureaucracy. **Toeffler** called it as the **organisation of the future** and named it as "**Ad-hocracy**". He discuses on project or task force management rapid rise. Mans organisational relationships are changing at a faster pace. The high rate of turnover is noticed.

iv) There exists other modern examples of temporary or team organisational structures. **Cleland and kerzner** provide descriptions of :-

- Production teams
- Worker management teams
- Production Design teams for design review
- Workers participation in mangement (quality circles)
- Cross-management teams
- Task Forces
- Configuration management* Production teams

Questions

1 Define organisation.
2 Explain an organising process.
3 Give the meaning of organisation. What does it involve ? Give an example.
4 Which are the legal forms in which a business can be organised ?
5 Explain the terms: Sole proprietorship, partnership, corporation and cooperatives.
6 While Organising, which are the key objectives ?
7 As per Peter Drucker, which are the key activites to be worked out and which are the questions involved ?
8 Explain the decision Analysis stage and relations analysis stage in organising.
9 What do you mean traditional organisation theory ?
10 What is departmentation ?
11 Discuss on the term 'Patterns of Departmentation'.
12 Discuss on the needs and importance of Departmentation.
13 Explain the patterns of departmentation.
14 Explain the various types of organisation structures dividing the responsibilities.

15 Explain **any two** of the following :

- Functional Departmentation
- Departmentation by Time
- Departmentation by number
- Departmentation by regions or territories
- Departmentation by customers
- Process wise departmentation
- Departmentation by products
- Market oriented departmention

16 What do you mean by matrix organisation ?

17 Define organisation structure.

18 Explain the significance of span of control.

19 Compare and contrast tall and flat organisation.

20 How do you decide effective spans ?

21 Define organisation.

22 What are the principles recognised for the purposes of establishing an internal organisation?

23 Define Authority. What do you mean by Authority relationship ?

24 Explain a line and staff authority relationship with a sketch.

25 Explain how managements vary with level.

26 Compare the line and staff relationship.

27 Compare Line, Staff, Functional and Service relationships.

28 What do you mean by technology based organisation studies ?

29 Explain the John woodword studies model.

30 Explain the Aston studies model.

31 Explain the Perrows model.

32 Compare all the three studies of John woodword, Aston and perrows model and give your views.

33 Distinguish routine and nonroutine organisations.

34 Explain Time Horizon.

35 Discuss the impact of computers based technology in organising function.

36 What does Land Hausen and Tom Peter say regarding the impact of computer based technology in organising function ?

37 What are the skills needed by workers to monitor the production process ?

38 According to the Woodword, Aston. studies, what conditions lead to a formalised. standardised organisational environment?

39 What changes in organisation structure. might you expect as a result of the computer revolution?

40 Explain the modem organisation forms one can think.

Some Human Aspects of Organisation

Chapter - 5

5.1 Preview:

The following topics are involved:

- *Staffing technical organisations*
  - Human Resource Planning (Hiring technical professionals, Hiring managers, job requisition/description) Here the type and number of people needed in the near future is established.
- *Process of personnel selection*
  - Effective resumes, employment application, campus interviews, reference checks, site (plant) visits, job offer
- *Process of orienting and training the new employee*
  - Appraising his/her performance
- *Nature of authority*
  - Formal authority, acceptance theory of authority
  - Sources of authority and power, the importance of status and culture.
- *Relationship of assignment, delegation and accountability*
  - Reasons for delegation, barriers to delegation for engineers, decentralisation
- *Discussion of committees and meetings*
  - Reasons for using committees, problems with committees, Making committees effective.

5.2 Staffing Technical Organisations

Keeping the jobs filled with right people is the staffing phase of the management job. It includes several functions.

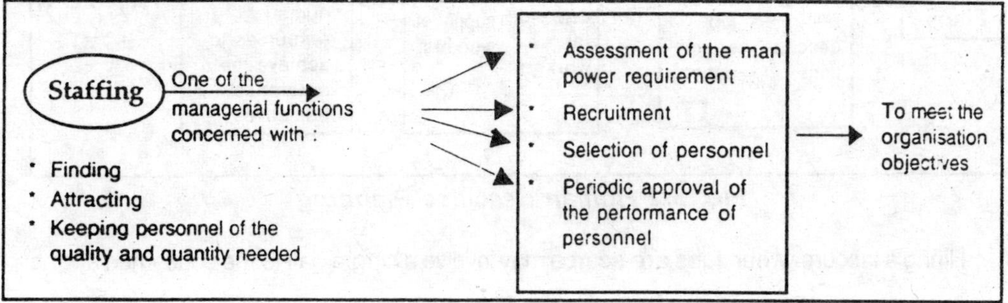

Fig. 5.1 Staffing Phase

S. Benjamin has defined **staffing** as the process involved in identifying, assessing, placing, evaluation and directing individuals at work. Staffing has to perform a number of subfunctions:

- Man power planning (short/long term-for immediate and future)
- Development (through training and development programme, performance appraisal)
- Determination of employment standards (Job specification, Job description)
- Determining the sources of personnel.
- Selection and placement
- Training (providing training to different types of personnel)
- Other functions (coordination, promotion, transfers, maintaining records etc.)

Human Resource planning:

Edwin Geisler states that man power planning is the process (including forecasting, implementing and controlling) by which a firm ensures that it has the:

- **right** number of people
- **right** kind of people
- at the **right** place
- at the **right** time
- doing things for which they are economically most useful.

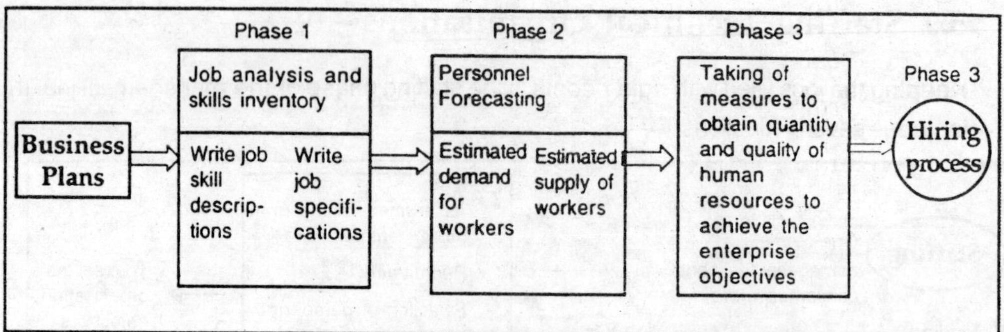

Fig. 5.2 Human Resource Planning

(I) Hiring a labourer when jobs are scarce may involve a single call to the concerned agency

(II) Hiring quantities of engineers and professionals requires planning ahead 6 months-1 year

(III) Hiring overall personnel for a large high technology firm is more complex and needs proper care

In the third case one may have to adopt the following method:-

a) Document the number of technical personnel of each classification at present on hand in the firm.

b) Estimate the number of professionals of each type needed in the future (say 6 months one year) to meet to firm contracts and likely potential business.

c) Estimate the attrition expected in the current staff.

- Resignations (may be demands of other companies, higher salary)
- Transfers
- Promotion to higher positions
- Retirements, deaths and leaves of absence.

d) Increased personnel is d) = c) - b) + a)

e) Work out different categories for hiring d) as under :

- From colleges
- From industries, experienced professionals, technicians
- From other sources

f) To meet temporary needs or for too short a duration of requirements, adopt methods like:

- Schedule overtime of the concerned existing staff.

- Hiring contract engineers (temporary)
- Borrow engineers from other company's sister concerns.
- Work itself can be contracted to other companies.

How do you hire managers? Here is an example. The figure is self explanatory.

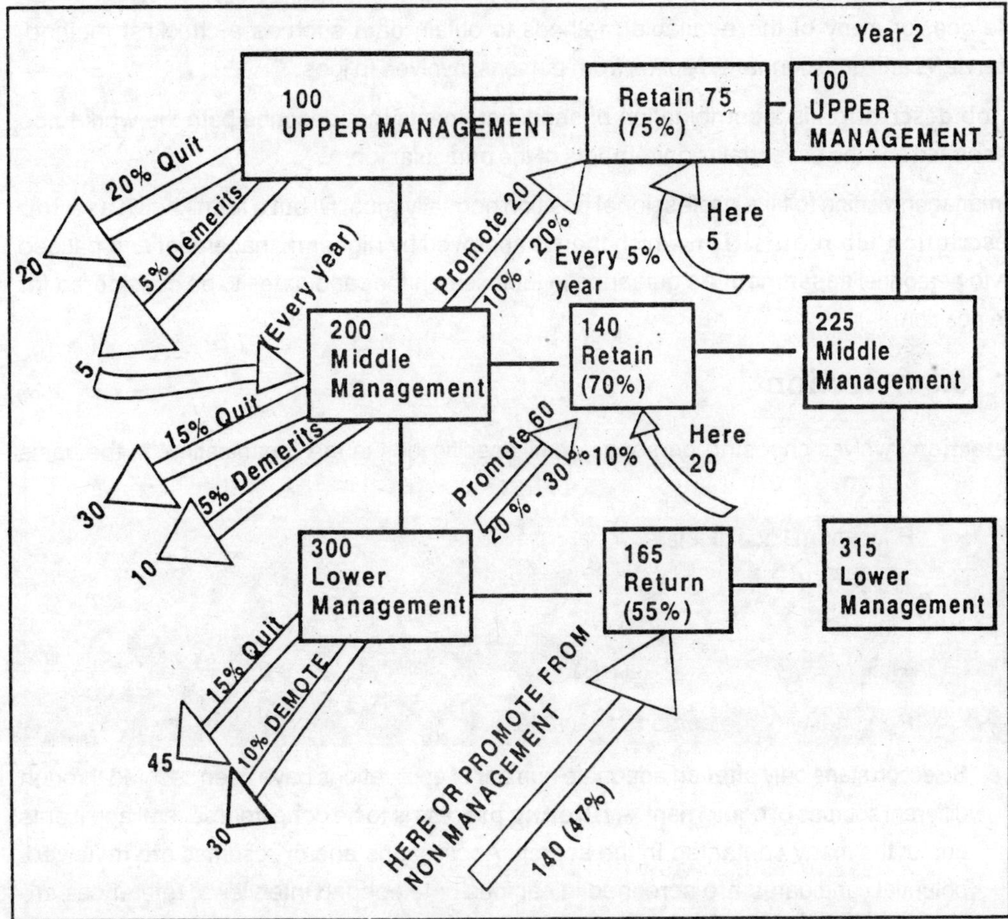

	Year 1		Year 2
Existing staff (Managers year 1)	Upper Management 100 Middle Management 200 Lower Management 300 Total 600	→ Needs of the Firm for (Managers year 2)	Upper Management 100 Middle Management 225 Lower Management 315 Total 640

Fig. 5.3 Hiring of Managers

Hiring is done from outside to have new skills (to infuse new blood who will bring new ideas and new technologies)

Job requisition/description

The most important aspect of any selection model is a description of various components of the job through job analysis. Those who are responsible for preparing a job description can use one or many of the available methods to obtain data such as a checklist method, interviews and questionnaire replies from persons involved in jobs.

A **job description** is a combination of short statements that describe both the work to be performed and the essential requirements of the particular job.

A manager wishing to fill a professional position normally must fill out a form known as a **job description/job requisition** which then is approved by higher management and passed on to personnel department as guidance in their search for candidates to be considered for the position.

5.3 Selection

Selection involves choosing personnel to fill specific jobs in the organisation on the basis of:

- Educational qualifications
- Training
- Skills
- Abilities
- Personality of the persons available for jobs

Selection starts only after an adequate number of applications have been secured through different sources of equipment. A **filtering process** is to be done from several applicants out of the many contacted in the search. Applications and/or resumes are reviewed, potential candidates are screened in campus or telephone interviews, references are checked and applicants who pass through these processes are invited to the company for interviews.

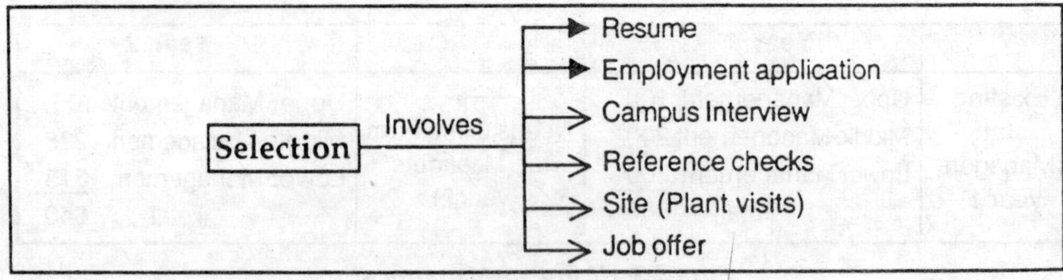

Fig. 5.4 Selection

Resume:- Most important; Forms the first impression. This has to be submitted along with a letter in response to an advertisement or as an inquiry. Resume normally contains:

Name, address, telephone number, current job position, status, current and long term objectives, educational qualifications, employment experience, publications, significant presentation, patents etc., significant honours and awards, professional affiliations etc.

Effective resume preparation is an important skill; Should not exceed 2 pages (exception in few cases like publications and presentation).

Resume should be:-
• Well organised • Concise • Attractively printed and reproduced • No grammatical and spelling mistakes • Highlighting the education and experience applicable to the position applied for

Many books have been written on the resumes writing and other aspects of job hunting (e.g. Lewis)

Employment application:

Interest will be created to the employer by going through a resume. Employee fills in mostly the same information in application arranged in a standard form familiar to interviews of that organisation. Race, religion, national origin, height, weight, age, marital status, age of children may not be asked in the application. The applicant may like to include these in resume along with photographs. The reason being antidiscrimination laws for the jobs in US.

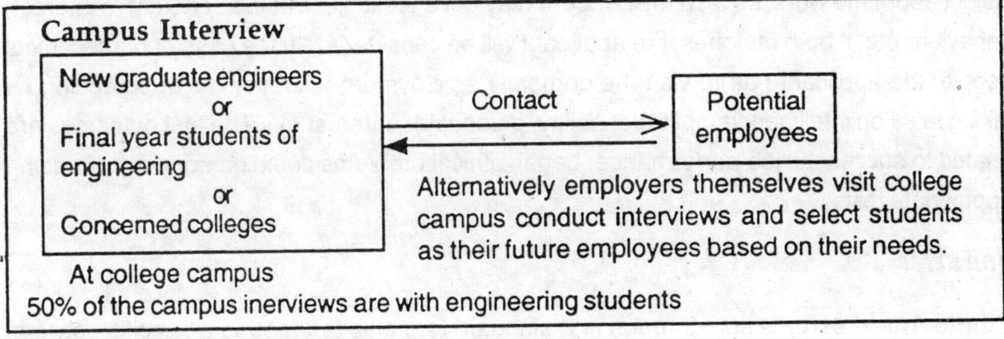

Fig. 5.5 Campus Interview

The applicant reads employee's placement brochure in advance and also about the company with the help of university reference library, discussion with classmates, professors who may be familiar with the company.

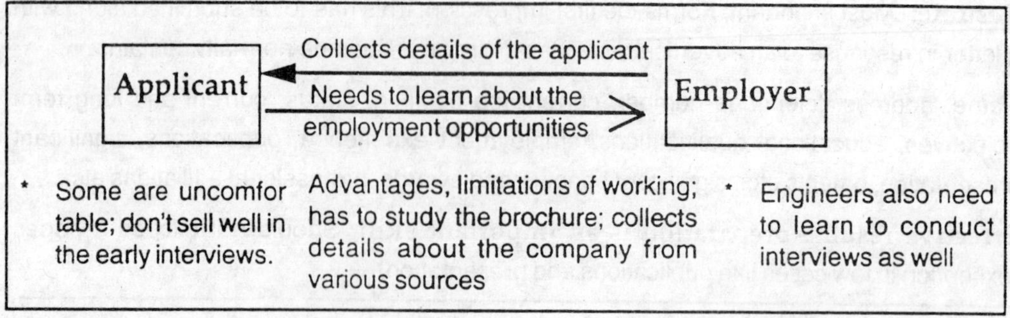

Fig. 5.6 Requirements of Employer and Applicant

Some colleges provide a chance for the students for mock interviews, often with television tapes to develop skill

Reference checks

References will be asked by the employer if the applicant has not provided the same. Candidates also take care to provide contain references in their application from professors and supervisors (part-time jobs), current supervisors and coworkers. It can be checked by the employer by mail or telephone. Mail is cheaper, slower, normally involve completion of a form. Employer will give more credence to references that have been written in confidence.

Site Visits

The company if it finds an applicant useful, he or she will be invited for a **visit to a particular location** of the company at company expense. Here the applicant will be interviewed by some people on the staff concerned where the applicant has to work. Candidate gets an insight about the work, so also the concern may get a feeling about the candidates interest, behaviour etc. If both matches, the applicant will be considered. In the case of nontechnical people, the applicant has to visit the company employment office for major screening by taking tests on intelligence, aptitude, ability, personality, interest etc. The test outcomes are related to successful job performance. Legal, ethical problems could be sorted out in using appropriate tests.

Job offer

Employment offer is sent through in a standard format letter offering a specific position, identifying salary, reporting date, position, title, to whom he should report?, Provisions about moving expenses. The letter is to be signed by a supervisor (under whom the candidate works) or by a personnel department manager who will be delegated with a responsibility for consistency. Fixing of starting salary is a difficult thing.

Figure below shows an example showing national averages for the year 1988 in US

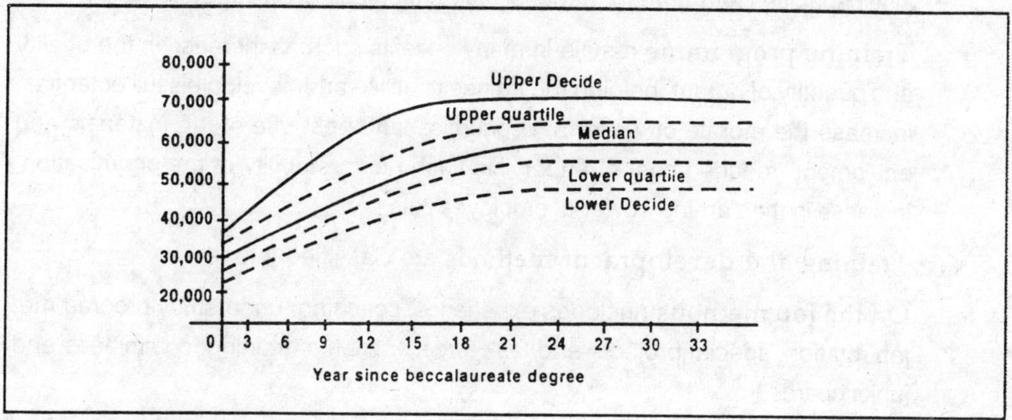

Fig. 5.7 Salary Curves for US Engineers in All Industries, All Degree Levels. (manufacturing and non manufacturing) (National average for 1988)

Inequalities in starting salary, inflation etc. will be adjusted slowly by companies.

5.4 Orientation

This involves making the new employee getting acquainted with the enterprise. During the period of orientation, he is informed about the people working by introducing to them, about the company, products. He is provided with many other things.

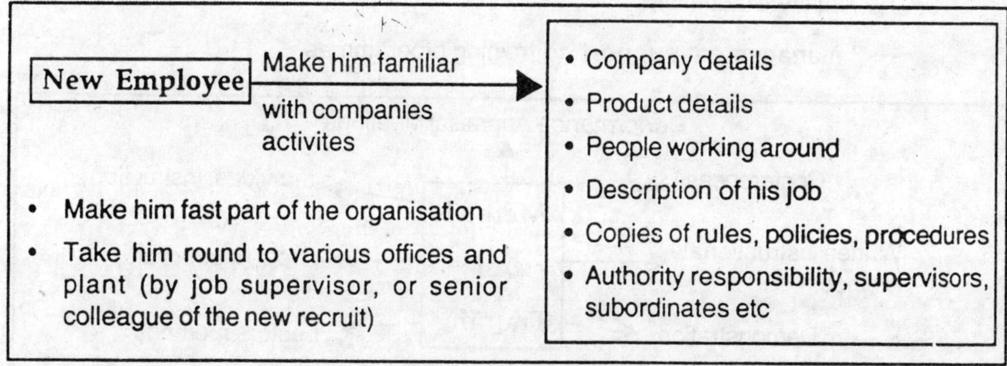

Fig. 5.8 Orientation

The **Total Socialisation** of the new employee to the environment and culture will be **Orientation + Training.** Effective socialisation results in order and consistency in behavior.

Training

- **Training** is an act of increasing the knowledge and skill of an employee for doing a particular job. Management development includes the process by which the managers and executives acquire not only skills and competence in their present jobs but also capacities for future managerial task of increasing difficulty and scope.

- **Training programme** results in many benefits such as increase in the quality and quantity of output, helping the trainee to utilise and develop his full potential , increase the morale of workers, economical and best use of the materials and equipment, reduced cost of supervision, long term stability of the organisation, increase in the earning power of employees etc.

- **Training and development methods** are classified into :-

- **On the job methods** (includes experience, coaching, understudy programme, job rotation, special projects and task force, vestibule, training, committees and junior boards.)

- **Off the job methods** (includes special courses and lectures, conferences. case studies, simulation and sensitivity analysis)

- **Effective training programme** involves certain principles. They are:
  - allowances for individual differences
  - relevance to job requirements
  - determination of training needs
  - result oriented training programmes
  - suitable incentives
  - **management support** to training programmes

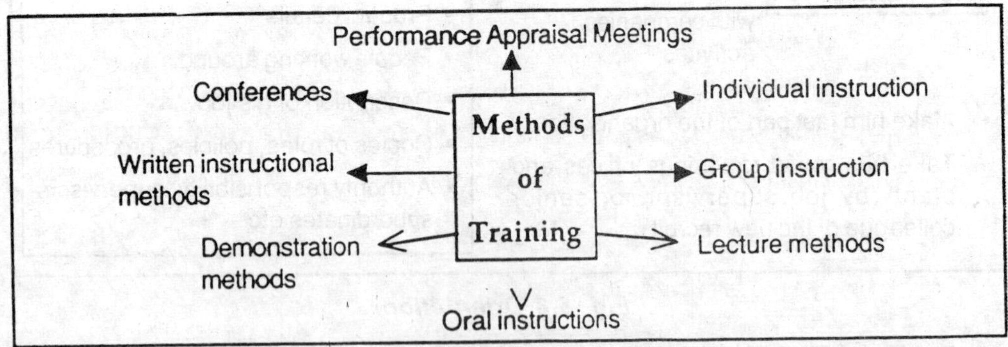

Fig. 5.9 Methods of Training

5.5 Performance Appraisal

Performance appraisal is a systematic, periodic, and so far as humanly possible, and impartial rating of an employees excellence in matters pertaining to his present job and to his potentialities for a better job. The personnel qualities that are appraised are:

- Leadership qualities
- Initiative
- Employee's knowledge of work
- Spirit of cooperation
- Punctuality or attendance
- Confidence
- Intelligence

Performance appraisal is used in business as a record of progress for apprentices and regular employees, as a guide in making promotions, transfers or demotions, as a guide in making lists for bonus distribution, for seniority consideration and for rates of pay, as an instrument for discovering hidden genius and as a source of information that makes conferences with employees helpful.

- **Limitations of performance appraisal methods** are unreliable, super fluous in small organisations, the supervisor may not follow uniform standards for appraising, inaccuracy in supervisors judgement of employee etc.
- **Popular methods of appraisal are:-**
  - Ranking Method
  - Forced Distribution Method
  - Check List Method
  - Critical Incident Methods
  - Forced Choice Method
  - Field Review Method
- **Requests of an effective performance appraisal programme are:**
  - Determination of objectives
  - Proper selection and training of appraisers
  - Establishing standards of performance
  - Deciding the correct frequency of appraisal
  - Designing suitable forms for the purpose of appraisal etc.

Ranking Method	Rating Scale Method	Forced Distribution Method
* Oldest, simplest • All the employees in a work group are ranked one against other. No. 1 No. 2 - - - No. 6 etc. • Useful if the no. of employees are small; for big companies not ideal • Does not evaluate the individual traits of employees • Easy and inexpensive • Reliability & validity doubtful • Size of the difference between individual also is not well defined	• Provides some kind of a scale for measuring absolute differences between individuals • **Discrete** - Exceptionally Good - Above average - Below average - Poor **Continuous on rating scale** - Numerical or alphabetical - descriptive adjective - man to man - behaviour sample • Compares individual performance to an absolute standard • Judgement about performance recorded on a scale • Widely used technique • Known as linear rating scale	• Forces the rater to distribute the ratings • Employees are rated for overall performance and not for each trait

Fig. 5.10 Comparison of Three Popular Methods of Appraisal

Users of Services/Customers: Employee performance in service organisations relating to behaviours, promptness, speed in doing the job and accuracy can be better judged by the customers or users of services.

For example, teacher's performance is better judged by students and the performance of a doctor is judged by the patients.

Consultants: Sometimes consultants may be engaged for appraisal when employees or employers do not trust supervisor appraisal and the management does not trust self-appraisal, peer appraisal or subordinate appraisal. In this situation, consultants are trained and they observe the employee at work for a sufficiently long time for the purpose of appraisal.

When to Appraise? Informal appraisals are conducted whenever the supervisor or personnel managers feel it necessary. However, systematic appraisals are conducted on a regular basis, say for example, every six months or annually.

5.6 PERFORMANCE APPRAISAL

A number of methods or techniques of performance appraisal have been developed. The important ones are:

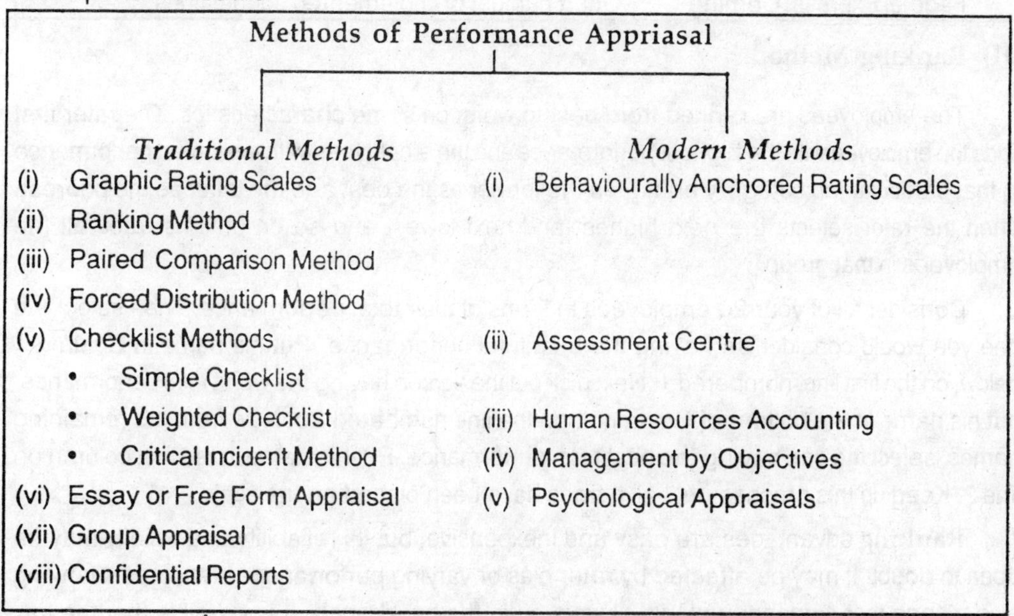

Fig. 5.11 Methods of Performance Appraisal

A. Traditional Methods

(I) Graphic Rating Scales: Graphic rating scales compare individual performance to an absolute standard. In this method, judgements about performance are recorded on a scale. This is the oldest and widely used technique, also known as **linear rating scale** or **simple rating scale.** The appraisers are supplied with printed forms, one for each employee. These forms contain a number of objectives, behaviour and trait-based qualities and characters to be rated like quality and volume of work, job knowledge, dependability, initiative, leadership qualities, emotional stability in the case of managerial personnel. These forms contain rating of scales. Rating scales are of two types viz. **continuous rating scale** and **discontinuous rating scales**. In continuous order like 0, 1, 2, 3, 4 and 5 and in discontinuous scale, the appraiser assigns the points to each degree. Performance regarding each character is known by the points given by the rater. The points given by the rater to each character are added up to find out the overall performance. Employees are ranked on the basis of total points assigned to each one of them.

Fibre Mark	Conduct frequent reviews of employee performance
Xerox Corporation	Promote manager-rep coaching sessions
Dupont	Monitor reps' calls periodically to facilitate coaching

Unilever	Design a scorecard to evaluate performance and target improvement opportunities
KPMG Peat Marwick	Identify key ratios to measure revenue per employee
Federal Express, Coming	Chart number of implemented suggestions

(II) Ranking Method

The employees are ranked from best to worst on some characteristics. The rater first finds the employee with the highest performance and the employees with the lowest performance in that particular job category and rates the former as the best and the latter as the poorest. Then the rater selects the next highest and next lowest and so on until he rates all the employees in that group.

Consider all of your 20 employees in terms of their total performance. Then select the one you would consider as having the best total performance. Put his name in Column 1 below, on the first line, numbered 1. Next pick out the person having the worst total performance, put his name at the bottom of Column II, on the line numbered 20. Now from the remaining names, select the one having the best total performance. Put his name in the first column on line 2. Keep up this process until all names have been placed on the scale.

Ranking advantages are easy and inexpensive, but its reliability and validity may be open to doubt. It may be affected by rater bias or varying performance standards. Ranking also means that somebody would always be in the backbench. It is possible that the low ranked individual in one group may turn out to be a superstar in another group. One important limitation of the ranking method is that the size of the difference between individuals is not well defined. For instance, there may be little difference in performance between individuals ranked second and third, but a big difference between those ranked third and fourth. Bajaj Tempo, SPIC and BASF follow this. E.g.5

- Elimination of Ratings as ratings seem to distract all efforts of organizational improvements.
- Focus on performance Improvements: Prime focal points of performance improvement programmes are to improve performance, standards, observable outcomes linked to business goals.
- Identification of constraints and eradicating them.
- Focus on expected and observable standards.
- Development of enablers.
- Align performance systems with strategies and goals.
- Create internal performance consultants. Performance consultants define performance, benchmarking and analyse performance.

(Source: Human Capital, August 2000, p.25)

Fig. 5.12 Current Trends in Performance Appraisal

(III) Paired Comparison Method

This method is relatively simple. Under this method, the appraiser ranks the employees by comparing one employee with all other employees in the group, one at a time. This pertains to assigning each employee's name a different capital letter on a separate sheet of paper. Example: A, B, C etc. Then follow strategies develop a chart such as one below and for each plotted pair, write in the letter of the employee who, in your opinion, has done the superior job over all given a positive comparison total and a certain percentage of the total positive evaluation. This percentage of positive comparison given in the paired comparison method has an advantage over other comparative methods (ranking and forced distribution).

Paired Comparison does not force distribution of employees in each department. For instance, if a department has two outstanding employees and six average employees and paired comparison is correctly utilised, then those two employees will get a much higher percentage of positive comparison than the other six. Paired comparison method could be employed fairly easily where the number of employees is less. The number of comparisons required equals N (N-1)/2. This means that where the number is fairly large (for instance for 20 employees, 190 comparisons would be necessary), the technique may be time consuming. Another limitation of this technique is that employees are simply compared to each other on total performance rather than specific job criteria. E.g.: Godrej Soaps, KOPRAN, NOCIL and OTIS.

(IV) Forced Distribution Method

The rater may rate his employees at the higher or at the lower end of the scale under the earlier methods. Forced distribution method is developed to prevent the raters from rating too high or too low. Under this method, the rater after assigning the points to the performance of each employee has to distribute his ratings in a pattern to conform to normal frequency distribution.

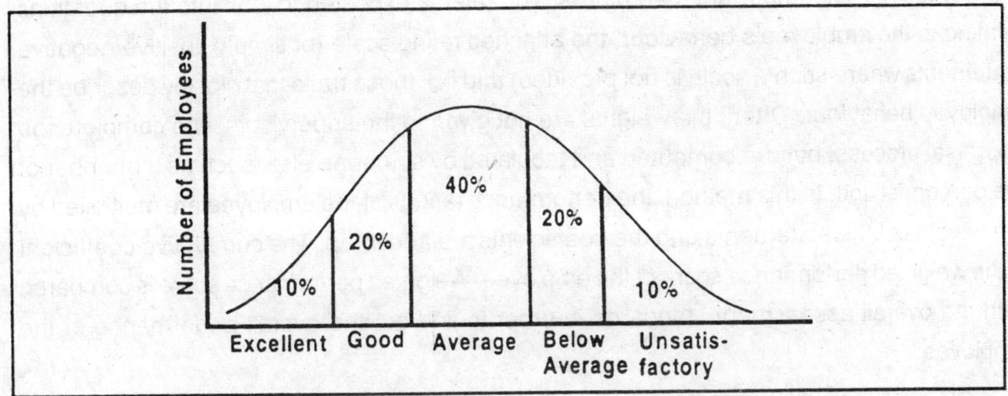

Fig. 5.13 Forced Distributions on a Bell-shaped Curve.

Thus, similar to the ranking technique, **forced distribution** requires the raters (supervisors) to spread their employee evaluations in a prescribed distribution. This method eliminates central tendency and leniency biases. However, in this method, employees are placed in certain ranked categories but not ranked within the categories. Quite often, work groups do not reflect a normal distribution of individual performance. This method is based on the rather questionable assumption that all groups of employees will have the same distribution of excellent, average and poor performers. If one department has all outstanding employees, the supervisor would find it extremely difficult to decide who should be placed in the lower categories. Difficulties can also arise when the rater must explain to the employee why he was placed in one grouping and other were placed in higher groupings E.g.. Usha, SPL and JCT.

(V) Checkiist Methods

The **checklist** is a **simple rating technique** in which the supervisor is given a list of statements or words and asked to check statements representing the characteristics and performance of each employee. There are three types of checklist methods, viz. simple checklist, weighted checklist and forced choice method.

(a) Simple Checklist Method: The checklist consists of a large number of statements concerning an employee behaviour.

The rater checks to indicate if the behaviour of an employee is positive or negative to each statement. Employee performance is rated on the basis of the number of positive checks. The negative checks are not considered in this method. A difficulty often arises because the statements may appear to be virtually identical to different raters in describing the employee. The word or statements may have different meanings.

(b) Weighted Checklist: The **weighted checklist method** involves weighting different items in the Checklist, having a series of statements about an individual, to indicate that some are more important than others. The rater is expected to look into the questions relating to the employee's behaviour, the attached rating scale (or simply positive/negative statements where such a scale is not provided) and tick those traits that closely describe the employee behaviour. Often, the weights are not given to the supervisors who complete the appraisal process, but are computed and tabulated by someone else, such as a member of the personnel unit. In this method, the performance ratings of the employee are multiplied by the weights of the statements and the coefficients are added up. The cumulative coefficient is the weighted performance score of the employee. Weighted performance score is compared with the overall assessment standards in order to find out the overall performance of the employee.

The weighted checklist, however, is expensive to design, since the checklist for each different job in the organisation must be produced. This may prove time consuming also in the end. Though the weighted checklist method is evaluative as well as developmental, it has the basic problem of the evaluator not knowing the items which contribute mostly to successful performance.

(c) Forced Choice Method: This method was developed at the close of World War II. Under this method, a large number of statements in groups are prepared. Each group consists of four descriptive statements (tetrad) concerning employee behaviour. Two statements are most descriptive (favourable) and two are least descriptive (un-favourable) of each tetrad. Sometimes, there may be five statements in each group out of which one would be neutral. The actual weightage of the statements are kept secret. The appraiser is asked to select one statement that mostly describes employee's behaviour out of the two favourable statements and one statement from the two unfavourable statements. The items are usually a mixture of positive and negative statements. The intent is to eliminate or greatly reduce the rater's personal bias, specifically the tendency to assign all high or low ratings. The items are designed to discriminate effective from ineffective workers as well as reflect valuable personal qualities.

Self review provides an opportunity to every employee to comment on his/her perceptions and views on achievements and targets as against each objective set six months earlier.

Performance review for new employees is conducted after six months of joining. This exercise conducted between the employee and the manager, helps in communicating business goals, achieving project goals, providing feedback to the employee and the manager, setting or revising objectives, improving the process, problem solving, establishing an going dialogue and developing employees.

It is difficult to construct and validate the statements under the forced-choice method, especially for relatively small organisations. For raters who are not properly trained, it may be difficult to choose among statements that are equally desirable or equally undesirable. Since they most often, do not know which of the statements in a given group have the discriminative power to draw the curtain between good and poor workers, they may fail to live up to the expectations and provide an objective evaluation. Further, it may be time consuming to prepare statements that suit the demands of a particular job or company. Finally, it may be unpalatable for the raters to believe that they cannot make an objective evaluation and hence their freedom curtailed to size. E.g.: WIDA, CEAT, Modern Threads and BOC.

(d) Critical Incident Method: Employees are rated discontinuously, i.e. once in a year or six months under the earlier methods. The performance rated may not reflect real and overall performance as the rater would be serious about appraisal just two or three weeks before the appraisal. Hence a **continuous appraisal method,** i.e. **the critical incident method** has been developed. Under this method, the supervisor continuously records the critical incidents of the employee performance or behaviour relating to all characteristics (both positive and negative) in a specially designed note book. The supervisor rates the performance of his subordinates on the basis of notes taken by him. Since the critical incident method does not necessarily have to be a separate rating system, it can be fruitfully employed as documentation of the reasons why an employee was rated in a certain way.

Continuing Duties	Targets	Critical Incident
Deposit Mobilisation	Rs. 10 lakhs in 1995	Mobilised Rs. 12 lakhs
	Rs 3 lakhs from business	Rs. 7 lakhs from business
	Rs 4 lakhs from Educational Institutes	Rs. 5 lakhs from Educational Institutes
	Rs.2 lakhs from individuals	Not mobilised
	Rs.1 lakh from Government Departments	Not mobilised
Customer Service	Prompt in disposing customers	Thrown the PassBook forcibly for enquiring about delay
	5 minutes for deposit	
	8 minutes for withdrawal	Abused the customer for enquiring about delay in withdrawal.

Fig. 5.14 Model of Recording Critical Incidents for a Bank Officer

The critical incident method has the advantage of being objective because the rater considers the records of performance rather than the subjective points of opinion, for example, mood, emotional balance, relationship between superior and subordinate. This certainly helps in reducing bias in the evaluation. However, the system is not without drawbacks. First, what constitutes a critical incident is not defined in the same manner by all raters. Next, recording events (critical) continually over a period of time may be resented by the raters. The question of discounting precious time of the executive is also involved here. Because of the time required to write complete profiles of critical incidents, managers can be asked instead to record sketchy notes of their observations noting the date and some other reminder of the event. Later, these could be transformed into detailed descriptions for completing a rating scale, of some kind. Associated with this method is the problem of decency or events. The decency or severity of events, sometimes may influence the opinion of raters. More often than the employee might have done something 'critically good and excellent' but the supervisor concerned may not be present and hence the concern was not recorded. Further, the method can result in employees becoming concerned about what the superior writes about them. Employee may being to fear the manager's "black book." E.g.: ITC Classic Finance, Voltas, VST Industries follow this.

(e) Essay or Free Form Appraisal: The manager has to write a short essay describing each employee's performance during the rating period. This format emphasises evaluation of overall performance, based on strengths/ weaknesses of employee performance rather than specific job dimensions. By asking supervisors to enumerate specific examples of employee behaviours, the essay technique minimises supervisory bias and the halo effect.

The time involved in writing separate essays about each employee can be formidable. Essays are not amenable for evaluation and analysis; fifty essays describing different employees' performance cannot be tied to merit increases and promotion possibilities because there is no common standard. Another inherent limitation of this method is that the evaluators may have unequal skills in writing than an awkward writer or supervisor. Thus, the quality of the ratings depends, not actually on employee performance, but on the writing ability of the rater. E.g.: BPL, Birla 3M, Wheels India and Bata follow this.

(f) Group Appraisal: An employee is appraised by a group of appraisers. This group consists of the immediate supervisor of the employee to other supervisors who have close contact with the employee's work, manager or head of the department and consultants. The head of the department or manager may be the Chairman of the group and the immediate supervisor may act as the Coordinator for the group activities. This group uses any one or multiple techniques discussed earlier. The immediate supervisor enlightens other members about the job characters, demands, standards of performance etc. Then the group appraises the performance of the employee, compares the actual performance with standards, finds out the deviations, discusses the reasons therefor, suggests ways for improvement of performance, prepares action plans, studies the need for change in the job analysis and recommends change if required.

This method is widely used for purposes of promotion, demotion and retrenchment appraisal. Kinetic Honda, Birla VXL and Blue Star follow this method.

(vii) Confidental Reports: Assessing the employee's performance confidentially is a traditional method of performance appraisal. Under this method, the superior appraises the performance of his subordinates based on his observations, judgement and intuitions. The superior keeps his judgement and report confidentially. In other words, the superior does not allow the employee to know the report and his performance. The superior writes the report about his subordinates' strengths, weaknesses, intelligence, attitude to work, sincerity, commitment, punctuality, attendance, conduct, character, friendlines etc.

Though confidential report is a traditional method, most of the public sector organisations still follow this method in appraising the employee's performance. This method suffers from a number of limitations.

B. MODERN METHODS

One of the modern methods is as explained below:-

Behaviourally Anchored Rating Scales (BARS)

The **Behaviourally Anchored Rating Scales (BARS) method** combines elements of the traditional rating scales and critical incident methods. Using BARS, job behaviours from critical incidents — effective and ineffective behaviours are described more objectively. The method employs individuals who are familiar with a particular job to identify its major components. They then rank and validate specific behaviours for each of the components.

Developing a BARS follows a general format which combines techniques employed in the critical incident method and weighted checklist ratings scales. Emphasis is pinpointed on pooling the thought process of people who will use the scales as both evaluators and evaluees.

Step I: Collect Critical Incidents: People with knowledge of the job to be probed such as job holders and supervisors, describe specific examples of effective and ineffective behaviour related to job performance.

Step II: Identify Performance Dimensions: The people were assigned the task of developing the instrument cluster pertaining to the incidents into a small set of key performance dimensions. Generally between five and ten dimensions account for most of the performance. Examples of performance dimensions include technical competence, relationships with customer handling or paperwork and meeting day-to-day deadlines. While developing varying levels of performance for each dimension (anchors), specific examples of behaviour should be used which could later be scaled in terms of good, average or below average performance.

Step III: Reclassification of Incidents: Another group of participations who are knowledgable about the job is instructed to retranslate or reclassify the critical incidents generated (in Step II) previously. They are given the definition of job dimension and told to assign each critical incident to the dimension that it best describer. At this stage, incidents for which there is not 75% agreement are discarded as being too subjective.

Step IV: Assigning Scale Value to the Incidents

Step V: Producing the Final Instrument

The other modern methods have not been discussed in this book such as Assessment Centre, Human resources accounting, Management by objectives and pyschological Appraisal.

☛ 5.7 Authority and power

One of the most important human considerations in any organisation is that it has to be:

- Adequately staffed and providing authority and power to them
- Provided with effective delegation

Authority is "legitimate power". **Delegation** is simply the concept of handing over to a subordinate, some part of the job that a superior is expected to carry out. On the face of it, this seems to be an easy way to reduce the administrative burden, but unfortunately some managers are constitutionally incapable of passing on work for others to perform. Among the usual reasons to be found are:

- Lethargy
- Undue concern for supposed loss of prestige
- Fear of being superseded
- Personnel interest in doing the job
- Lack of confidence in subordinates.

Often enough, the main reason is simply that the manager in his view is indispensible. Yet, the only way by which managers can hope to concentrate effectively on their major responsibilities is by unloading as much of the remaining work as possible.

An established guideline here is to delegate work down through the organisation to the point where it is just being done well enough without too many mistakes; at this point the staff concerned would be doing the utmost of which they were capable, costs thereby being kept to a minimum. Usually, too there is an increase in morale through enhanced job satisfaction. In addition, the work itself may be done much better than before simply because of the opportunity afforded for specialisation.

Delegation also requires someone suitable to whom the work can be handed over. This involves good staff selection, training etc. It is fundamental, of course that corresponding authority should be delegated with responsibility and that there should be full accountability to a superior for the actions that are taken.

Authority is the right based on one's position in an organisation to direct the work activities of subordinate.

Individuals invest their assets in corporate stock and elect a board of directors, delegating to them the right to manage their invested assets. The board in turn elects the executives of the officers of the corporation who will appoint subordinate managers, delegating authority to appoint lower managers. Thus the direction received by the lowest level employee from his foreman can be traced to the ownership authority of stock holders. Similarly authority over government workers stem from national and state constitutional authority conferred on the legislative and executive branches of the government, who in turn delegate authority and direction to the leaders of military and government agencies.

5.8 Assignment, Delegation and Accountability

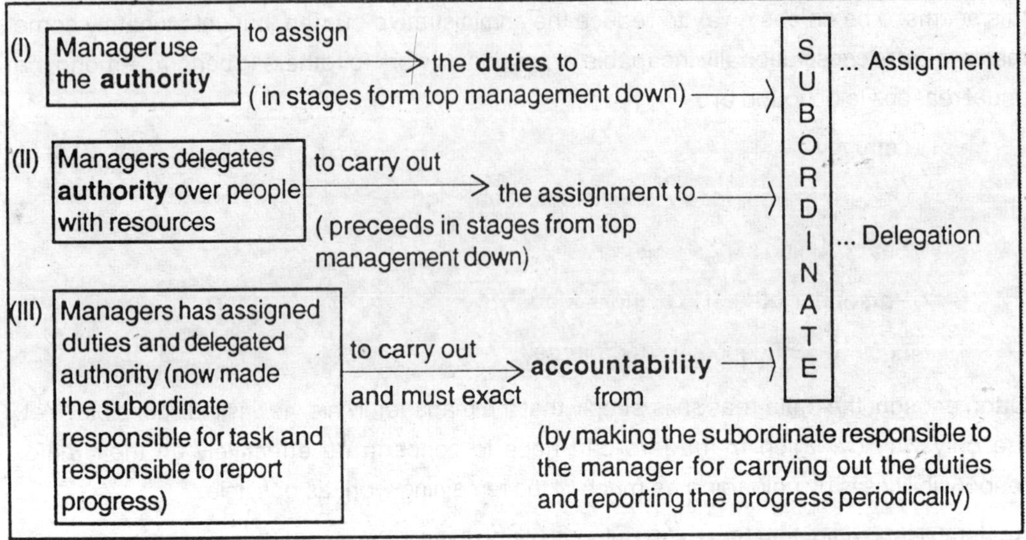

Fig. 5.15 Assignment, Delegation and Accountability.

The manager has now made the subordinate responsible in (III) above for the task and responsible to report progress accountable (responsible) to the next higher level of executive to assure that the task is effectively carried out.

5.9 Committees and Meetings

The **committee** is one of the most common forms of organisational structure. Milton Berle humorously point out that these are the group of men **who keep minutes and wastes hours**. The reason is since group of people are involved it is difficult for all the people to meet at one place and at the required time.

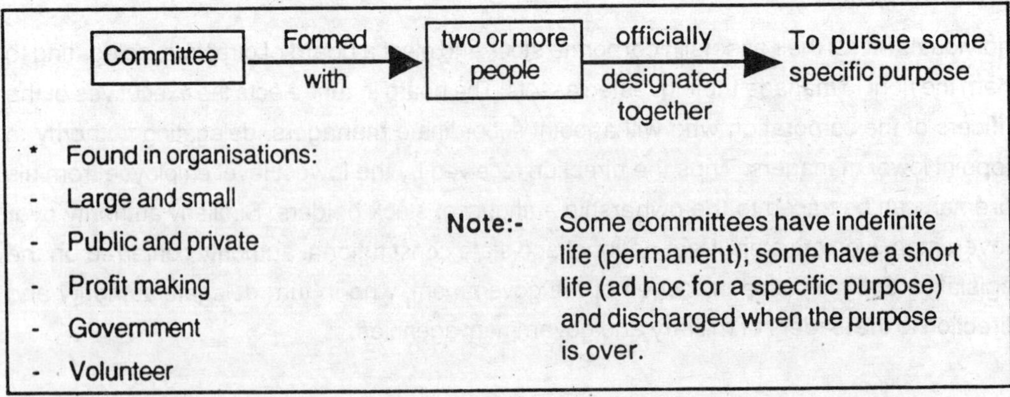

Fig. 5.16 Function of Committees

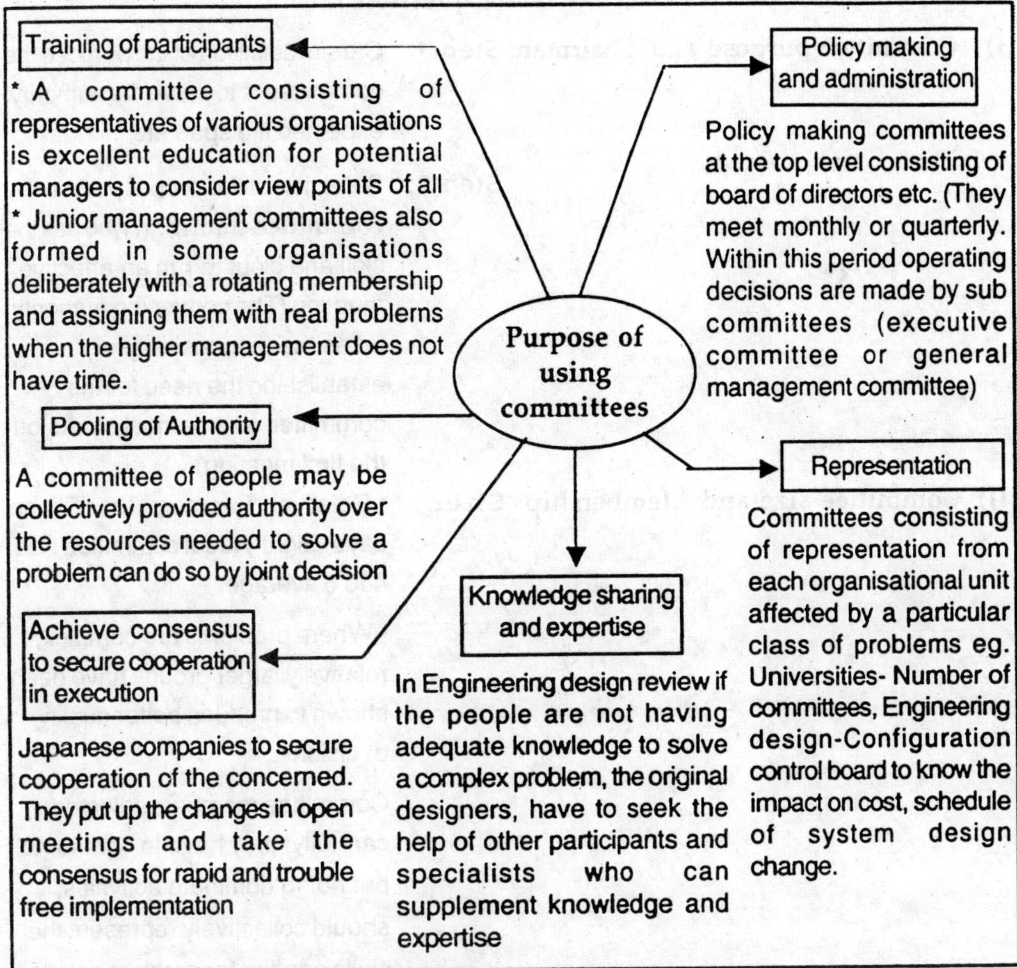

Fig: 5.17 Purpose of Using Committees

The problems with committees:-

- To produce compromise solutions (often solutions about which no one can be very enthusiastic) in order to expedite the committee decision and get back to work committee decisions are often inferior to the most complement group member; Problem can be resolved if the committee is an advisory group and the convening authority makes the final decision and shoulders the accountability for it.
- The delay often experienced in resolution of a problem by a committee.
- Japanese management may take more time in achieving consensus on a decision; when once an agreement is reached, implementation is rapid on the other hand. American model values, decisive executive decision making, lack of cooperation, or opposition when the executive tries to impose the solution on managers who had no part in the decision is found.

How to make committees effective is the question ?

(I) Committee purpose and Chairman: Step 1: Careful definition of the purpose the committee is to serve, its authority; expected life span etc.

Step 2: Selection of the proper person as **committee chairman** who has the skill and clout to run an effective meeting (The convening authority takes the responsibility of establishing the need for the committee and normally kicks off the first meeting)

(II) Committee size and Membership: Size:

- Relatively few members (Tilman says "Eight") Ideal committee size: 4 to 6 average
- Where problems are complex, relatively larger groups have been shown to produce better quality decisions.

Committee members selected carefully; they have to contribute but not to dominate activities; should collectively represent the skills needed for problem solution and/or the organisations whole resources needed to solve the problem faced and whose cooperation in implementing the solution is essential

(III) Preparing for the meeting: Committee chairman heads the activity; He publishes the date and time of the meeting. These are noted down by the concerned. An agenda prepared sent to members earlier (few days in advance), should include any back ground material that needs to be read in advance and identification of specific information numbers; effective interaction by chairman should be there; (pad, pencils, latest handouts, coffee etc. to be given)

(IV) Conduct the meeting: Every group leader has 2 functions (As per Benne and Sheaths)

Task functions:- To get the work done as under:-

- Initiating (tasks, goals, ideas etc.)
- Information or opinion seeking/opinion giving clarifying (status of discussion)
- Summarizing
- Testing for consensus

Group relations functions:- To maintain constructive relations among the members to facilitate attaining group objectives:

- Encouraging (the other contribution)
- Expressing relations functions
- Harmonizing
- Modifying
- Gate keeping (to keep communication channels open)
- Evaluating (group function, production, commitment, and results)
- Groups are effective when members assist chairman in the above

(V) Meeting Following: Chairman should assure concise readable minutes are given to all attendees and other persons interested, on the same day after the meeting. Minutes identify the action items and the responsible for the same deadline dates, time and venue of next meeting. Even the dissolution of the committee on the basis of its failure to be recommended to the convening authority by the chairman of an ad hoc committee if the committee outlived its usefulness.

Questions

1. Define Staffing.
2. Give the meaning of Staffing.
3. How do you staff technical organisations?
4. State the subfunctions of staffing.
5. Explain Human Resource Planning. Mention the phases involved in it.
6. How do you hire a manager ? Explain the process.
7. Define Job regulation and job description.
8. Define selection. What steps are found in selection? Explain each one of the steps.
9. What is orientation?
10. Explain the purposes of training an employee. Discuss on the training programming, training and development methods.
11. Define performance appraisal. Mention the purpose of having performance appraisal used in a business.
12. What are the limitations of performance appraisal methods?
13. Mention the popular methods of performance appraisal. What are the requests of an effective performance appraisal programme?
14. Compare and contrast some of the important performance appraisal methods.
15. Define Authority. Discuss on authority, power and delegation.
16. Distinguish Assignment, Delegation and Accountability.
17. Define committee. Explain the functions of committees.
18. Explain the purpose of using committees.
19. Mention the problems faced by committees.
20. How to make the committees effective?
21. Mention the purposes of meeting and the way it should be conducted.
22. Explain how the methods of performance appraisal can be classified.
23. Explain Ranking method of performance appraisal.
24. Explain Paired comparison method of performance appraisal.
25. Explain Forced distribution method of performance appraisal.
26. Explain simple checklist method and weighted checklist method of performance appraisal.
27. Explain Forced choice method of performance appraisal.

Chapter - 6

Motivating and Leading Technical people

6.1 Preview

Following topics have been considered in this chapter:

❖ *The two theories in understanding motivation*

- Content theories: based on human needs (Maslow's need hierarchy, Mc Gragors Theory X and Y Models, Herzberg's two factor theory, Mcclelland's acquired need theory
- Four process theories: Adam's equity theory, vroom's expectancy theory, the portex lawler extension, skinner's behaviour modification

❖ *Nature of leadership*

- Traditional trait theory
- Its application to the engineering manager

❖ *Several related approaches*

- Concerned with talks
- Concerned with people

} Includes the Managerial Grid, the Michigan and Ohio state studies, Life cycle theory.

❖ *Two Situational Approaches*

- The leadership continuum
- Fiedler's contingency model

❖ *The nature and motivations of technical professionals. Some observations on their successful leadership.*

☛ 6.2 Motivation

We will first understand the word 'motivation'. The word **motivation** is derived from the word 'Motive'. A **motive** is an inner state that energises, activates or moves and directs or channels behaviour towards goals (Definition from Berelson and Steiner)

The dictionary meaning of **motivation** is to cause a person to act in a particular way or stimulate the interest of a person in an activity.

Motivation is a general term applying for the entire class of drives, desires, needs, wishes and similar forces which are responsible for human beings to behave in a manner. It represents an unsatisfied need which creates a state of tension, or disequilibrium, causing the individual to move in a goal directed pattern towards restoring a state of equilibrium by satisfying the need.

Encyclopedia of Management says '**Motivation** refers to the degree of readiness of an organisation to pursue some designation goal and implies the determination of the nature and locus of the forces, including the degree of readiness'

To say that managers motivate their subordinates is to say that they do those things which they hope will satisfy these desires and induce the subordinates to act in a desired manner.

Campbell defines motivation in terms of three measures of the resulting behaviour.

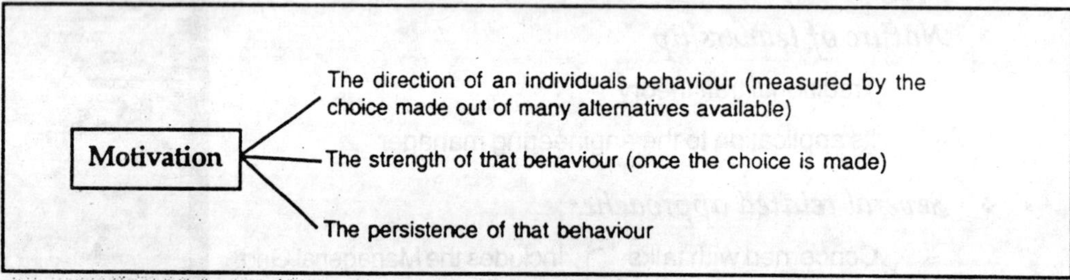

Fig. 6.1 Motivation

☛ 6.3 The Basic Motivation process

Motivation is a process that starts with a physiological or psychological deficiency or need that activates behaviour or a drive that is armed at a goal or 'incentive'

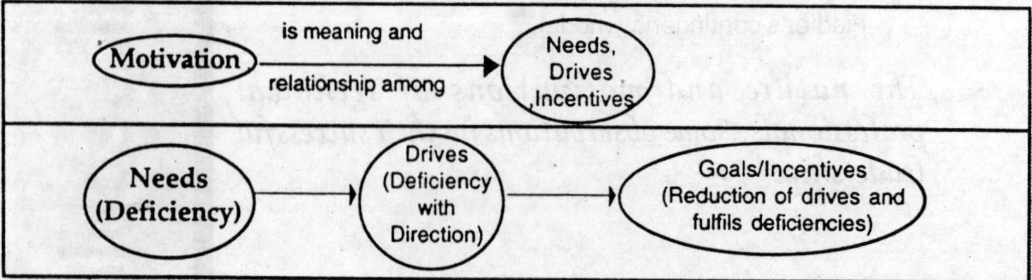

Fig. 6.2 Motivation process

Objective of Motivation:- We use a small portion of our mental and physical abilities. To exploit the unused potential, people are to be motivated. Exploitation results in greater efficiency, higher production, better standard of living of the people

Types of Motivation:- Two types.

(i) **Positive approach** - pull mechanism

(ii) **Negative approach** - push mechanism

(i) **Positive Motivation**

- People are said to be motivated **positively** when they are shown a reward and the way to achieve it - This may be **financial** or **nonfinancial.** It creates an optimistic atmosphere in the enterprise.
- **Monetary Motivation**: includes differentive incentives, wage plans, productive, bonus schemes etc (Provides a better standard of life)
- **Non Monetary Motivation** includes Praise for the work or appreciation, participation in management, social recognition etc (Satisfy the ego of a man, societal status may improve)

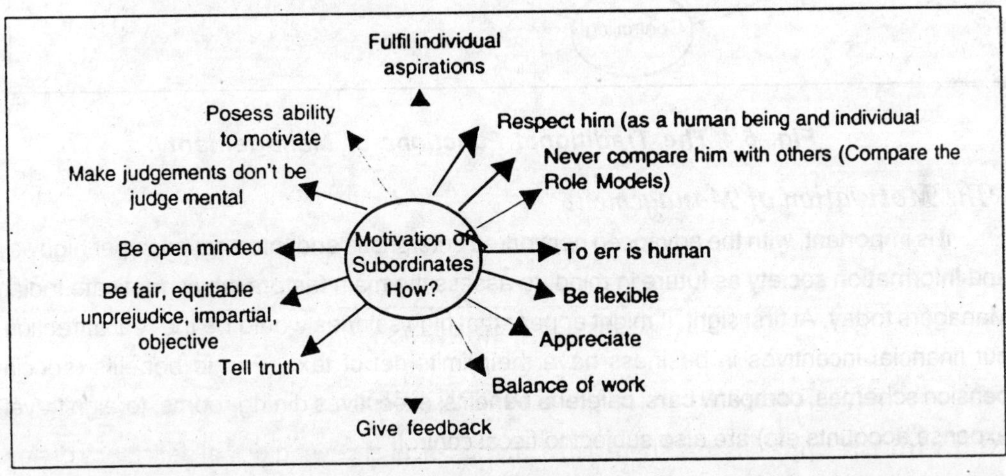

Fig. 6.3 Motivation of Subordinates (Source:- Human capital July 21, P.50)

ii) **Negative Motivation** This is by instaling fear in the minds of the people, one can get the desired work done. This method has limitations as fear creates frustration, a hostile state of mind and an unfavourable attitude towards the job affecting efficiency and production. It should be restricted.

6.4 Where does motivation positions in the traditional functions of Management?

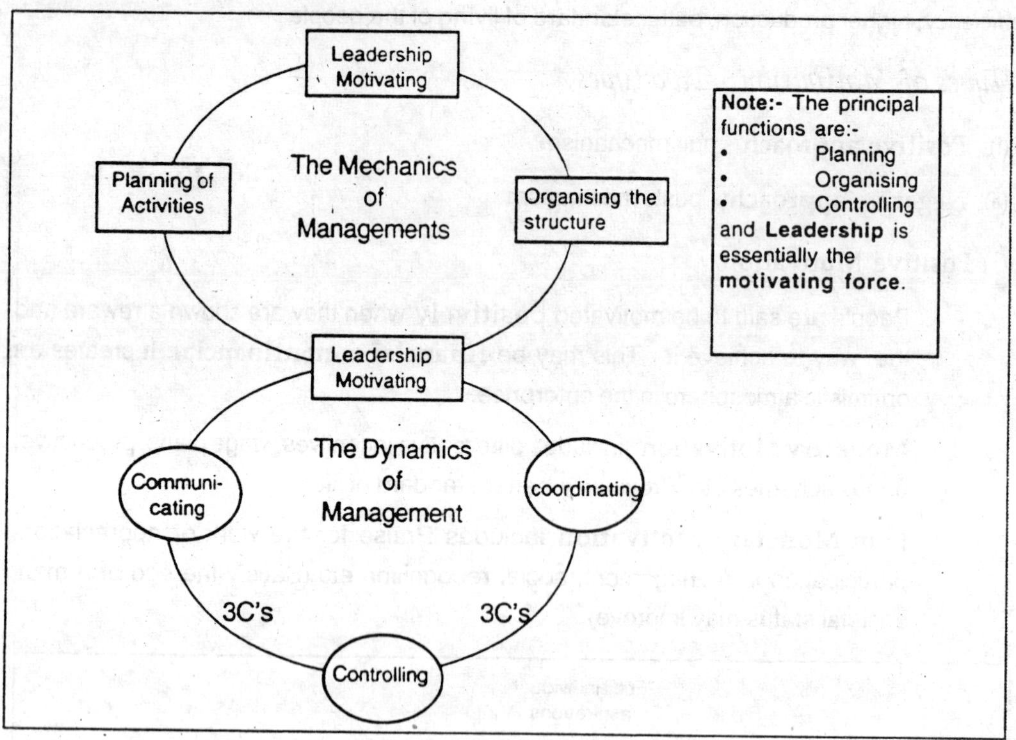

Fig. 6.4 The Traditional Functions of Management

The Motivation of Management

It is important, with the advanced networked enterprises and Information super highway and Information society as future in mind, to assess the main factors which motivate Indian Managers today. At first sight, it might appear that high salaries would be the real attraction, but financial incentives in business have their limits net of tax - Fringe benefits (special pension schemes, company cars, cafeteria benefits, executives dining rooms, foreign travel, expense accounts etc) are also subject to fiscal control.

Nevertheless, with promotion through the hierarchy, it is still posisble to achieve an increasing standard of living, subject, of course to inflation and government increasing policies. One certain acceptable standards have been achieved, however, every effort will usually be made to keep them.

Disincentives:- Promotions within the firm or by joining another firm, usually cause domestic disturbance (more travel, increased expenses plus additional worry). Money alone then seems hardly the best way to stimulate managerial performance or motivate mobility.

Financial incentives tend to be well down the list in order of importance (In questionnaries put to the respondents)

(II) **Non Financial Incentives:-** Top rating in given to personal achievements measured against naturally acceptable company targets and the recognition given to those achievements.

(III) **Rewards and penalties:** Recognition of achievements and productivity shake out (demotion, inspired resignation, straight dismissal) to weed out costly passengers.

(IV) **Motivating Future Managers**

☛ 6.5 Theories of Motivation

There are several theories of motivation significant are:

- Maslow's Hierarchy of needs
- M\C Gregors Theory X and Y
- Herzberg's Two-factor Theory
- Vrooms Expectancy Theory
- Alderfer's ERG Theory
- Porter and Lawler's Expectancy Theory
- Adams Equity theory of work Motivation
- Behaviour Modification
- Mc Clellands trio of needs - Content theory

Process Theories treat human needs as just one part of the mechanism that people use in choosing their behaviour and place greater emphasis on the expectation of favourable consequences or rewards.

Content versus process theories: How people are motivated are explained in two categories of theories; **Content theories** are based on human needs and people's (often unconscious) efforts to satisfy them. **Process theories** assume that behaviour choices are made more rationally, based on the expected outcomes.

A. Maslows Theory of Hierarchy of Needs

As per Abraham H. Maslow, human needs form a hierarchy, starting at the bottom with physiological needs and going to the top to the higher need of self-actualisation as shown below in figure. He says when one set of needs are satisfied, they no longer work as motivators as a man seeks to satisfy the next higher level needs

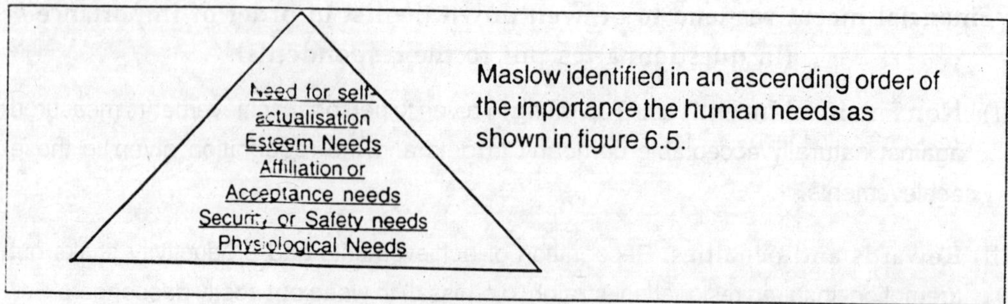

Fig. 6.5 Maslows Hierarchy of Needs

(i) **Physiological Needs**:- These are the basic needs of sustaining human life such as food, water, warmth, shelter, sleep and sexual satisfaction. Maslow says until these needs are satisfied to the required level, man does not aim for the satisfaction of the next higher level needs. As far as work organisation is concerned, these needs include basic needs like, pay, allowance and benefits

Motivators

Monetary	Non-monetary
• Pay in conformity with market trend	• Awards: Trophies, Plaques, Citations
• Skill based reward system	• Tokens: vacations trips, watches, tiepins
• Merit pay	• Clubs memberships
• Employee stock option	• Cafeteria or menu for salary; Salary breakup according to employee's choice
• Performance bonus	• Medical benefits, Group life insurance Retirement benefits

Fig. 6.6 Comparison of Moentary and Non-monetary Motivators

(ii) **Security/Safety Needs**:- These are the needs to be free of physical danger and the fear of loss of a job, property, food or shelter. This implies secured life and safety of belongings of a person. When the psysiological needs are satisfied, man starts thinking of the way by which he can continue to satisfy these physiological needs. Security needs spring up the momen the makes an effort in the direction of providing himself the source of continutiy of physiological needs. This is exactly the reason why attitude towards security is an important consideration in choosing a job. These include conformity, security plans, membership in unions, severance pay job tenure, medical, unemployment and disability insurance and pension provisions.

(iii) **Affiliation or Acceptance Needs** (Social Needs or Love Needs): As people are social beings, they need to belong, to be accepted by others. This is the need which people have to be associated with a particular class or group in the society (affectionate relations with friends, family and people in general, and group acceptance people looks for the association of other human beings and strives hard to be accepted by its group. Social needs at the work place include: human relations, formal and informal work groups.

(iv) **Esteem Needs** Once people begin to satisfy their need of affiliation they would want themselves to be in an esteem position. This kind of need produces such satisfactions as power, prestige, states and selfconfidence. These needs for employees include status symbols, awards, promotions, titles etc.

(v) **Need for selfactualisation**: This is the highest need in Maslow's hierarchy. It is the desire to become what one is capable of becoming to maximise one's potential and to accomplish something. Maslow's concept of hierarchy of needs has been subjected to considerable research. There have been researchers who have surveyed Practicing managers to infer the existence of hierarchy of needs.

i) Maslow's inference that the human being always aims at the lowest level of needs, in the hierarchy and only on the satisfaction of the lower level needs, he will move on to achieving the highest level of needs, has been put to practice by managers worldwide. Hence needs follow hierarchy.

(ii) Managers advance in an organisation, their physiological and safety needs tend to decrease in importance and their needs for affiliation, esteem and self-actualisation tend to increase. They insisted however that the upward career changes and not from the satisfaction of lower order needs. Needs do not necessarily follow the same hierarchy among all people at all times. It depends on the cultural values and personality of the individuals and their environment. The higher order needs can be fulfilled either at work or in society self actualisation for example: can be achieved through hobbies, education and personal growth and charitable or religious activities in the community as well as through achievement at work. The challenge to effective management is to find ways in which the higher order needs of the individual can be satisfied in the process of achieving the objectives of the organisation.

B. Herzberg's-Two Factor theory

Maslow's need approach has been considerably modified by Fredrick Herzberg and his associates. Their research reveals a two factor theory of motivation

(I) Maintenance Factors or Dissatisfiers or Hygiene Factors

• Company policy and administration	• Salary	• Relation with Supervisors
• Supervision	• Status	• Quality of Supervion
• Working conditions	• Job security	• Relations with subordinates
• Extrinsic Factor	• Personal life	• Inter personal relations

These needs were classified by Herzberg and his associates to be only dissatisfiers and not motivators, which means if they exist in a work environment in high quality and quantity, they yield no dissatisfaction. However, their existence does not in itself motivate people to contribute better, but lack of existence would result in dissatisfaction. These needs were reffered to as Hygiene factors by Herzberg indicating that these needs give a clean working environment but in any case does not induce people to work harder.

(II) Motivational Factors or Satisfiers or job content factors

• Job content	• Growth in the job
• Achievement	• Intrinsic factors
• Recognition	• Work itself
• Challenging work	• Responsibility
• Advancement	

Their existence will yield feelings of satisfaction and lack of it will motivate people to acquire them.

The **first group** of factors (Hygienic Factors) will not motivate people in an organisation, yet they must be present otherwise dissatisfaction arises.

The **second group** are found to be the real motivators, because they have the potential of yielding a sense of satisfaction. If this theory of motivation is found, managers must give considerable attention to upgrading job content of the subordinates.

Example

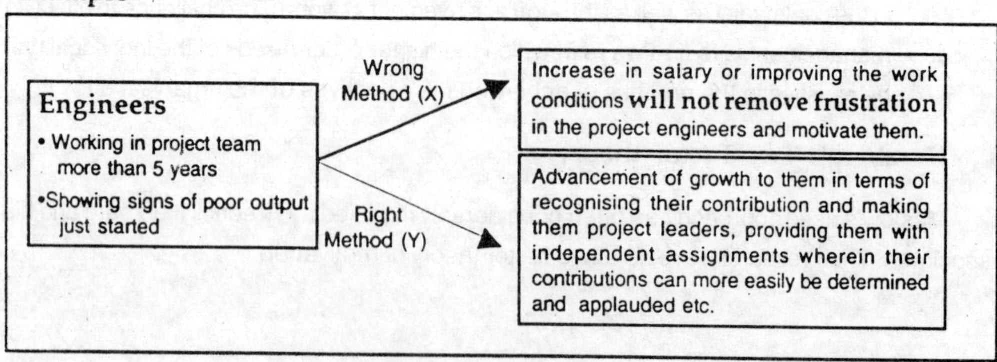

Fig. 6.7 Right Method of Motivation

Maslow Vs Herzberg Models

- Both the theories are not of much difference
- Most of the maintenance factors of Herzberg come under lower levels of Maslow.
- Maslow emphasises that any unsatisfied need, whether of lower or higher level will motivate people; Herzberg clearly identifies certain needs and calls them as maintenance factors which can never be motivators

C. Vroom's Expectancy Theory of Motivation

This was formulated by victor vroom in 1964. Vroom felt that content models were inadequate explanations of the complex process of work motivation. He developed a relatively new theory of motivation. As per him, motivation of any individual depends on the derived goal and the strengthof his expectation of achieving the goal. His model was built in three **concepts:-**

- Valance
- Instrumentality
- Expectancy

Valance :- It is the strength of an individual preference for a particular outcome. It can be taken as equivalent of value, incentive, attitude and expected utility

	Outcome		
Valence	Positive	Zero	Negative
Person must (I) Prefer Attaining the outcome to not attaining	✓	-	-
(II) Indifferents towards the outcome	-	✓	-
(III) Prefers not attaining outcome to attaining it	-	-	✓

Fig. 6.8 Valance

Instrumentality:- An another major input into the valence is the instrumentality of the first level outcome in obtaining the desired second level of outcome eg., Assume that an individual desires promotion and feels that superior performance is a very strong factor in achieving that goal. His **first outcomes** are then superior, average or of poor performance. His **second**

level outcome is promotion. The first level outcome of high performance thus acquired a positive valance by virtue of its expected relationship to the prefered outcome of second level promotion. In this case, the person is motivated to achieve superior performance (First level outcome) is seen as being instrumentation in obtaining promotion (Second level outcome)

Expectancy Though the expectancy and the instrumentality appears to be one and the same at the first glance, they are different. **Expectancy** is a probability (ranging from 0 to 1) or strength of a belief that a particular action or effort will leave a particular first level outcome. **Instrumentality** refers to the degree to which a first level outcome will lead to the 2nd level outcome:- Vroom says the sum of these variables is **motivation.**

Broadly, **Expectany theory** invoolves a combination of two expectations

- Effort to performance expectancy
- Performance to outcome expectancy

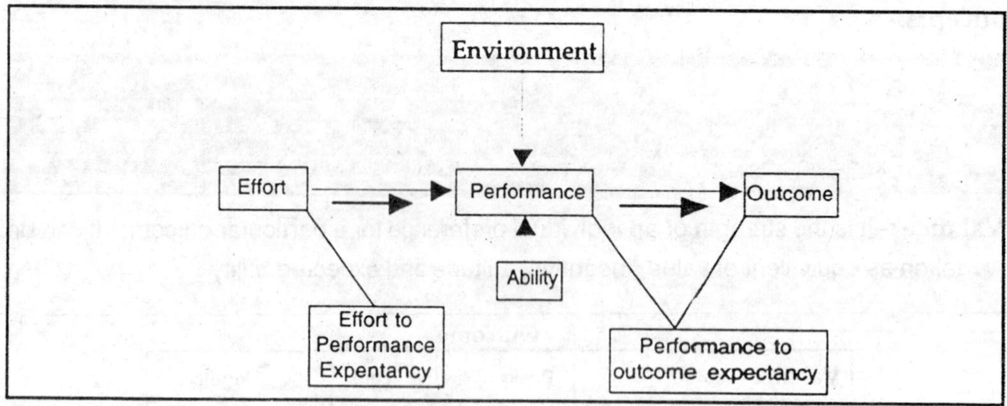

Fig. 6.9 Expectancy (2 Types)

Effort to performance expectancy

A person's perception of the probability that his effort will lead to **high performance**, usually in meeting an organisationally desired goal. Here high performance is 1st level outcome. The ability to achieve high performance is considered a function of individual ability and the environment (tools, resources and opportunity), in addition to the effort applied.

Performance to outcome expectancy is also known as **instrumentality**. It is the person's perception that attaining the performance described in figure will lead to intrinsic and extrinsic rewards (2nd level income). **Intrinsic rewards** are intangibles such as a feeling of accomplishment or sense of achievement; **extrinsic rewards** are tangible outcomes such as pay or promotion. Both the efforts to performance and the performance to outcome expectancy may be rated on a scale from 0.0 (no relationship) to 1.0 (certainty).

Valence may be positive or negative measures the strength of a person's desire for these outcomes.

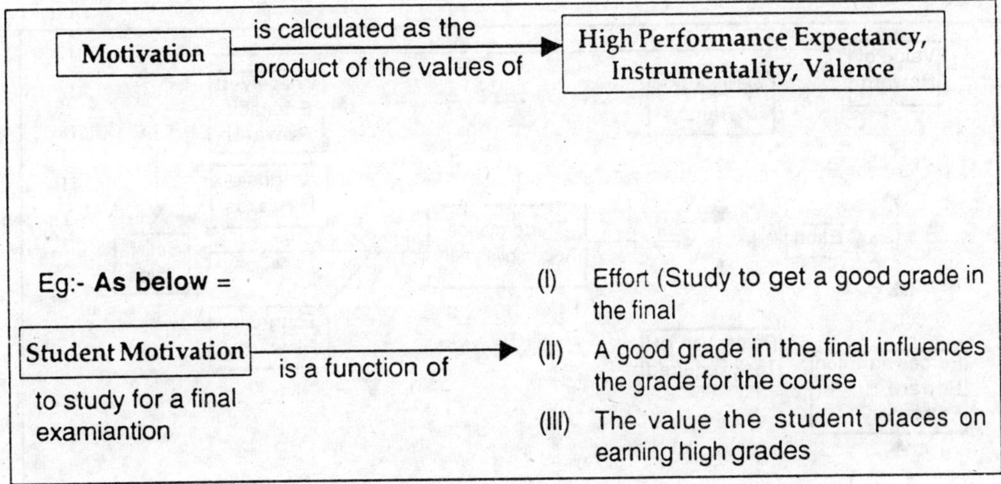

Fig. 6.10 Motivation

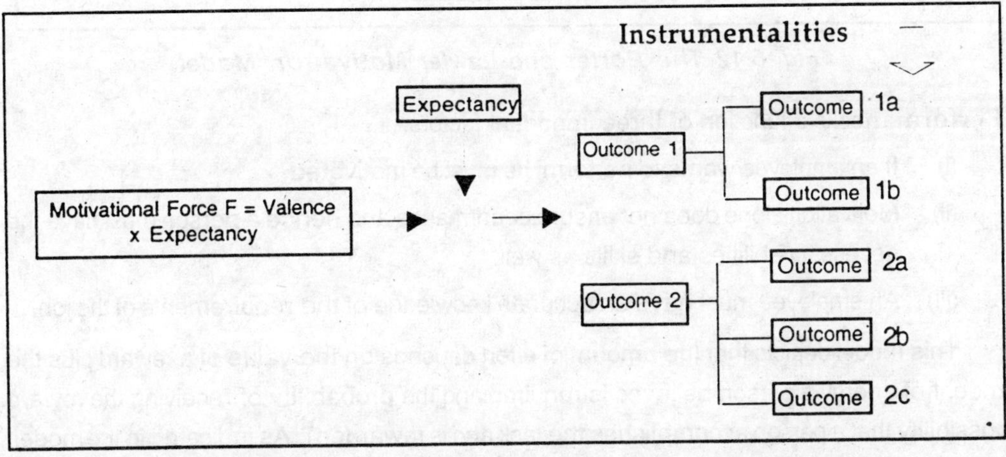

Fig. 6.11 The Vroom's Expectancy Theory of Work Motivation

D. The Porter and Lawler Model on Motivation:

Lyman W. Porter and Edward. E. Lawler exploded the complex relation between motivation, satisfaction and performance (complete model of motivation). This was applied primarily to managers.

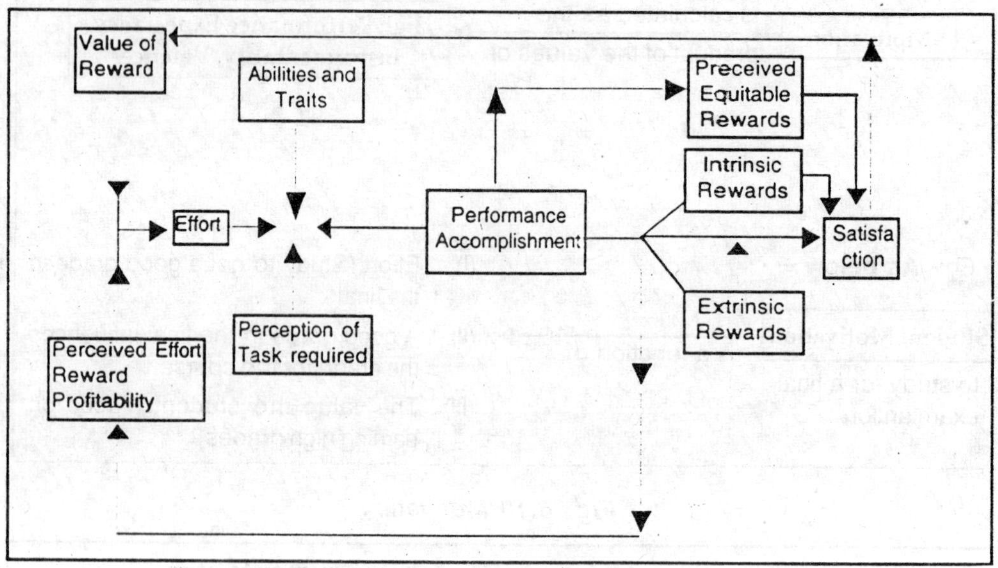

Fig. 6.12 The Porter and Lawler Motivation Model

Performance is a function of three important factors:-

(I) If an employee wants to perform, he must be motivated

(II) Motivation alone does not ensure performance and hence a person must have the necessary abilities and skills as well.

(III) An employee must have an accurate knowledge of the requirements of the job.

This model depicts that the amount of effort depends on the value of a reward plus the amount of energy a person believes is required and the probability of receiving the reward (possibility that a person accomplishes the task and is rewarded). As indicated in the model, the perceived effort and the probability of actually getting a reward are, inturn, influenced by the record of actual performance. Clearly, they have a better appreciation of the effort required and know better the probability of rewards.

Following are the key variables in this model:-

Motivation:- Satisfaction and performance

Effort:- Effort does not directly lead to specific levels of performance. Efforts is only the amount of energy exerted by an individual to achieve a specific task. It is only the result of the attractiveness of the reward and how he perceives a relation between effort and pay off. The individual will exert greater effort if he perceives that there is a greater probabilitty that his effort will lead to the reward. So motivation is seen as a force on the employee to expect effort.

Performance :- Effort is not enough, as performance results only when the effort is combined with the ability. Effort and performance are not same.

Reward :- A person gets intrinsic reward himself by performing a task well, which will be a feeling of accomplishment. Extrinsic rewards like pay, promotion and status are offered by the organisation.

Satisfaction:- The satisfaction depends on the perceived rewards and the actual rewards. If an individual feels that he should have received more for what he has done, it results in dissatisfaction and vice versa

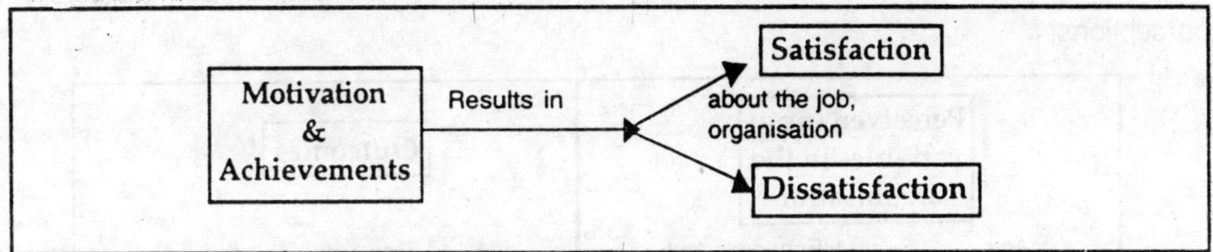

Fig. 6.13 Motivation and Achievements

Actual performances in a job (the doing of jobs or meeting of goals) is determined principally by effort expended. But it is also greatly influenced by an individual's ability (knowledge and skills) to do the job and his or her perception of what the required task is (the extent to which the persons under-stand the goals, required activities and other elements of a task). Performance, in term, is seen as leading to intrinsic rewards (such as sense of accomplishment or self actualisation) and extrinsic rewards (such as working conditions and status). These rewards, as tempered by what the individual sees as equitable, lead to satisfaction. But performance also influences sensed equitable rewards (what the persons feels the rewards should be). As one can understand, what the individual sees as a fair reward for effort will necessarily effect the satisfaction desired. Likewise, the actual value of rewards will be influenced by satisfaction

E. Equity theory of Work Motivation

J. Stacy Adams developed this theory on the basis of a simple belief that people want to be treated fairly relative to the treatment of others. He describes this comparison in terms of input/outcome ratios. This theory argues that a major input into job performance and satisfaction is the degree of equity or inequity that people perceive in their work situation.

Inequity occurs when a person perceives that the ratio of his or her outcomes to inputs are unequal: Schematically, this is represented as follows:

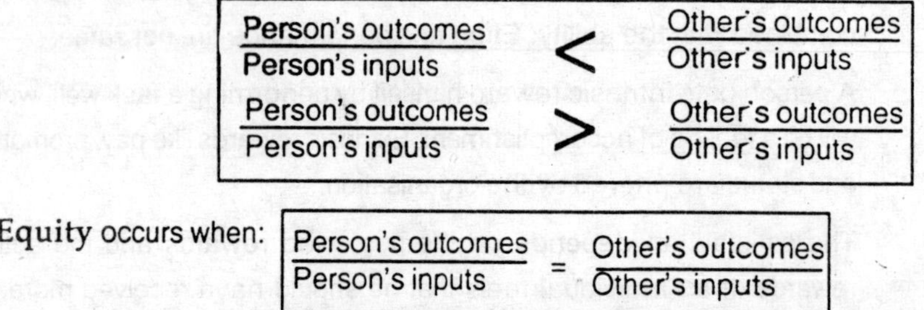

Equity occurs when:

$$\frac{\text{Person's outcomes}}{\text{Person's inputs}} = \frac{\text{Other's outcomes}}{\text{Other's inputs}}$$

Both the inputs and the outputs of a person and others are based upon the person's perceptions:

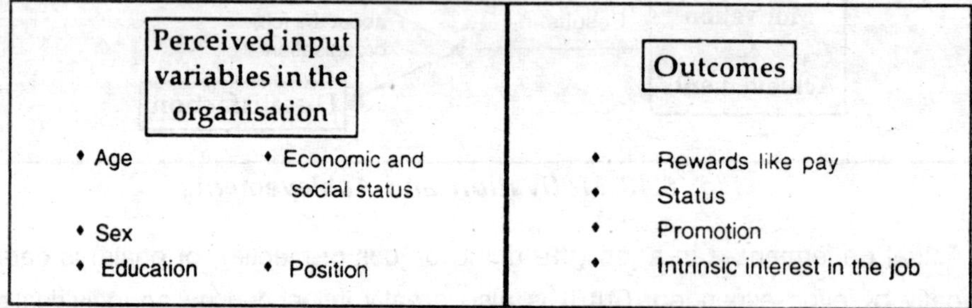

If the perceived ratio of a person is not equal to the others, he or she will strive to restore the ratio to equity. Thus the work motivation of oneself depends upon other's imputs,output and one's perceived output.

F. Mc Clelland's trio of needs

Mc Clelland's and others have proposed that there are three major motives or needs in work situations:

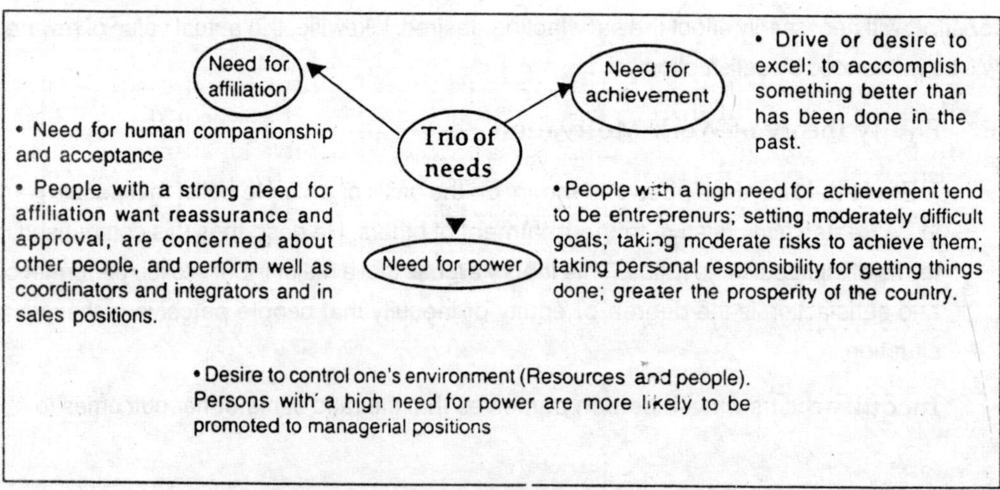

Fig. 6.14 Mc Clelland's Trio of Needs

Civilisations and nations that expect a lot from their youth have high achieving societies.

The need for affiliation might be compared with Maslo's thirtd level (Love); the need for power with his fourth level ego or esteem; the need for achievement with the 5th level (self actualisation)

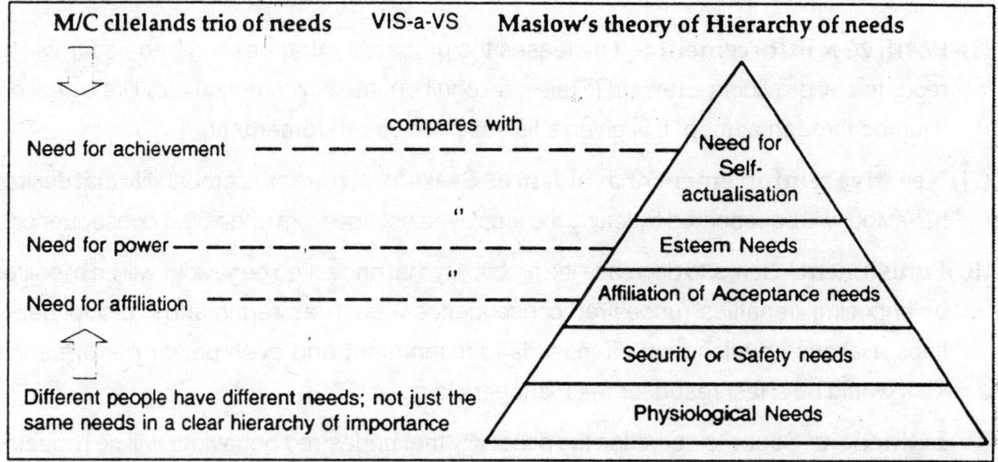

Fig. 6.15 Comparison of Mc Cllelands Trio of Needs with Maslow's theory.

G. Alderfer's ERG Theory :- Alderfer also feel that needs should be categorised and there is basic distinction between lower order needs and higher order needs. He identifies three groups of needs VIZ

- **Existence needs:-** Concerned with survival or physiological well-being
- **Relatedness needs:-** Speaks about the importance of interpersonal and social relationships
- **Growth needs:-** Concerned with the individuals intrinsic desire for personal development.

Maslow's Model	Alderfer's Model	M/c Clelands Trio of Needs	Herzberg's Model (2 Factor theory)
5 Need for Self Actualisation	Growth	Need for achievements	**Motivating:-** Challenging work; Achievement.
4 Esteem Needs	Relatedness	Need for power Need for affiliation	**Growth in the job Responsibility:** Advancement, • Recognition; Status
3 Affiliation or Acceptance Needs			**Maintenance Factors** Interpersonal relations; Company policy; Quality of Supervision
2 Security or Safety Needs	Existence		• Working conditions • Job Security
1 Physiological Needs			• Salary • Personal life

Fig 6.16 Comparison of Some of the Models

H. Behaviour Modification or Reinforcement Theory or Operant Conditioning

BF Skimmer worked in this. Behaviour is followed by an event (Reinforcement) that affects the Probability that the behaviour is repeated. Four types of reinforcements are availble to the manager.

(I) **Positive reinforcement :-** It increases the probability that desired behaviour will be repeated by providing a reward (Praise, recognition, raise, promotion etc) like a sealion. It jumps through a hoop. It is given a fish as positive reinforcement

(II) **Negative reinforcement or avoidance:-** Seeks to increase the probability that desired behaviour will be repeated by letting the employee escape from undesired consequences.

(III) **Punishment:-** Seeks to decrease the probability that undesired behaviour will be repeated by imposing penalties (undesired consequences) such as reprimands, discipline, or fines. Because punishment often leads to resentment and even power performance. This would be a last resort for the managers to try.

(IV) **Extinction:-** Seeks to decrease the pobability that undesired behaviour will be repeated by ignoring it and withholding positive reinforcement

6.6 Leadership

Definition

- **Leadership** is the knack of getting other people to follow you and to do willingly the things you want to do.
- **Leadership** means inspiring confidence and trust so that there is maximum cooperation from the employees within the control of a manager
- **Leadership** is the mixture of persuasion, compulsion and example that makes men do what you want them to do (Sir William Slim)
- **Leadership** is the ability to pursuade others so that the people work enthusiastically to meet the organisations objectives.
- **Leadership** may also be defined as the process of influencing a group in a particular situation at a given point of time and in a speccific set of circumstances that stimulate people to strive willingly to attain company objectives.
- **Leadership** is the ability to get men to do what they don't want to do and like it (Trueman)

From these definitions it is obvious that leading is the process of influencing people so that they strive willingly and enthusiastically towards the achievement of the goals of the organisation. No matter how effectively a manager plans, organises, staffs and controls the manager must supplement these activities by giving people guidance, communicating well and leading.

Leading must be based on an understanding what motivates people and what brings them satisfaction as they contribute to organisational goals. Management and leadership are often regarded as the same activity. It is true that the most effective manager will almost certainly be an effective leader and that leading is an essential function of managers.

Managing involves:-

- Planning carefully
- Setting up organisation structure that will aid people in achieving plans
- Staffing the organisation structure with people who are as competent as possible
- Devising effective control system to follow up the process of the planned activities

For all these managerial functions to deliver results and for the company to prosper, manager should influence the people working under them, guide them and ensure that people wholeheartedly contribute to the upliftment of the company's profile and profits. For all these, managers should understand the human factors in their operations and know how to lead people in such a way to produce desired results. Leadership is also followship and the managers who want to be leaders as well should discover why people follow. Basically, people tend to follow those in whom they see a means of satisfying their own desires and needs.

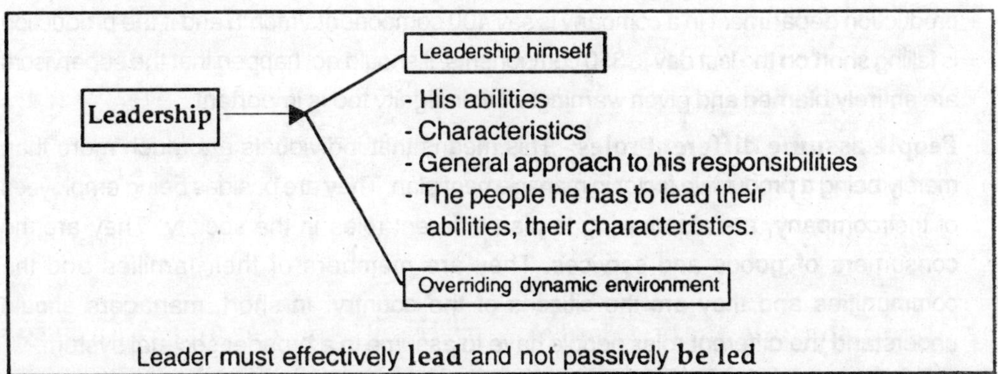

Fig. 6.17 Leadership

Eg. The managing director as a leader (like all other executive directors) has to wear two different hats;

- one as a director making policy
- other as a manager carrying out that policy.

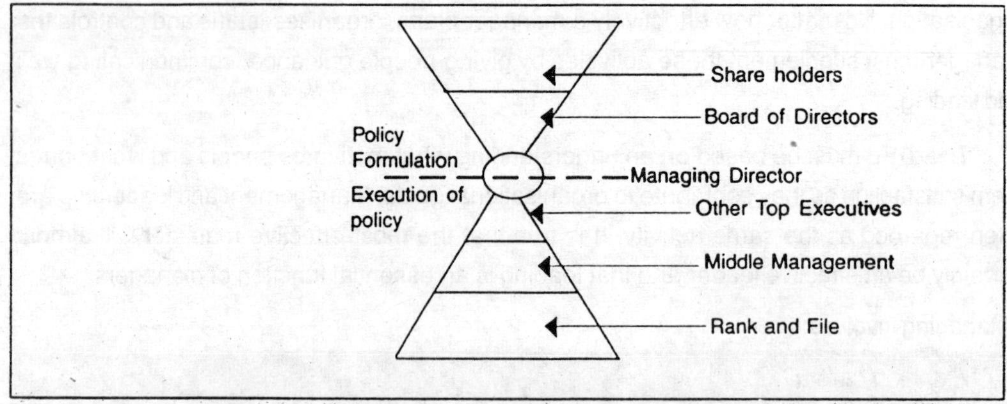

Fig. 6.18 The Managing Director as a Focal Point

Leadership traits For carrying out an important function as leading, the managers need to understand the following principles of human behaviour which will enable the managers to have an influence on the subordinates. Important ones are:

- **There is no average person who can represent the entire community of the group.**

  Each person has different attitudes, different desires for responsibility, different levels of knowledge and skills and different potentials.

- **People always try to uphold their dignity** i.e. Managers in their drive to achieve results should never violate the dignity of the people. For example, if the target of production department in a company is say 400 components/month and if the production is falling short on the last day to 350 components, it should not happen that the supervisors are entirely blamed and given warnings. Their dignity too is important.
- **People assume different roles**:- This means that individuals are much more than merely being a productive factor in management plan. They are besides being employees of theircompany, are also having to plan different roles in the society. They are the consumers of goods and services. They are members of their families and the communities and they are the citizens of the country. In short, managers should understand the different roles people have to assume in a broader societal system.
- **Emphasise others**:- Managers should always act after considering the question how it should have effected if they themselves were in the posistion of their subordinates.

  Thus Managers should understand the reality of the people's behaviour and design the management systems accordingly. If successfully done, a manager can also be a leader.

We had great leaders in India like Mahatma Gandhiji, Subahs Chandra Bose, Sardar Vallabhai Patel, Lokamanya Tilak, and even in business, like Jemshedji Tata, Russi modi, Sri Jamanlal Bajaj etc. have effected if they themselves were in the position of their subordinates.

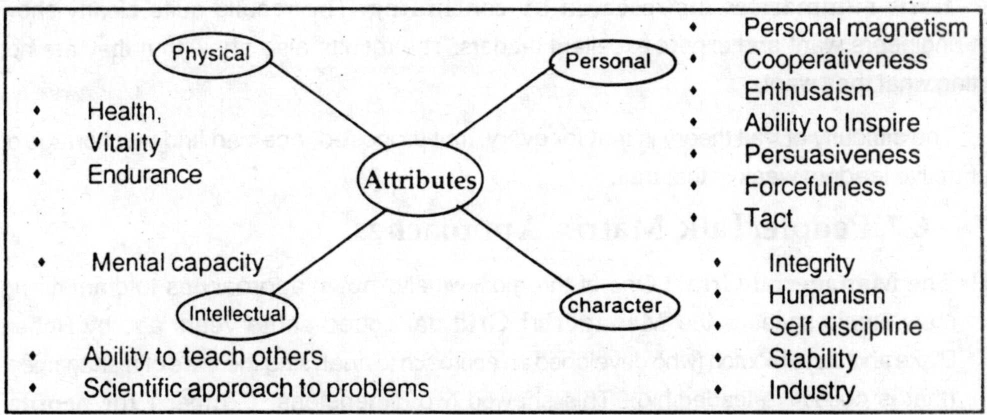

Fig. 6.19 Eighteen Attributes Needed for a Leader

Haris had 18 qualities and attributes for engineering Managers 1 Ability to inspire 2 Enthusiasm 3 Integrity 4 Tact 5 Self discipline 6 Stability 7 Cooperativeness 8 Mental capacity 9 Industry 10 Persuasiveness 11 Ability to teach 12 Health 13 Forcefulness 14 Personal magnetism 15 Vitality 16 Endurance, 17 Scientific approach to problems 18 Humanism

How the study made	Highest ranked Qualities & attributes			Lowest ranked Qualities & attributes		
	Gr1	GrII	GrIII	GrI	GrII	GrIII
Study made by E. Douglas Haris on a total of 176 engineers (mostly mechanical, electrical & aerospace) working for high technology firms at different places of USA Ist phase 130 engineers divided based on their experience (Group I) 0-5 years (Group II) 6-15 years >15 years (Group III)	1 11 8 5 2 4 6 3 7	2 6 5 1 3 8 10 7 11	3 1 4 6 5 10 9 2 8	12 13 14 8 15 16 9 17 11	12 15 13 14 19 17 9 17 4	12 13 11 14 18 7 15 17 16
	Note:- The number given above as per the list of qualities and number given above					
IInd phase 46 engineers repeated the evaluation above to rate their current engineering managers, on the same scale	Haris then calculated the difference between the mean ranking of the perceived quality or attribute with the mean rating of current engineering managers. He found that engineering managers most exceeded the perceived need in the following categories:- 6.95 for Health 4.12 for Endurance 3.79 for Scientific approach to problems 3.69 for Vitality 3.67 for Forcefulness Engineering managers most failed to meet expectations in the following categories: 9.16 Ability to inspire 5.36 Tact 4.82 Persuasivenss 4.17 Stability 2.88 Enthuasiasm					

Fig. 6.20 Eighteen Qualities and Attributes for Engineering Managers-Study by Douglas Haris.

Haris summarises his research by concluding: The results quite clearly show that engineers want and expect excellent leaders. The results also show that they are not getting what they want.

The difficulty of trait theory is that for every, trait proposed, one can find no shortage of -- effective leaders weak in that trait.

6.7 People/Talk Matrix Approaches

(I) **The Managerial Grid** : One of the most widely known approaches to dramatising leeadership styles is the **Managerial Grid** developed some years ago by Robert Blake and Jane Mouton (who developed an approach to analysing the style of management (that is collective leadership). This showed two dimensions: **Concern for people; Concern for production**. The grid shown in figure 6.21 below has been used throughtout the world as a means of managerial training and identifying various combinations of leadership styles.

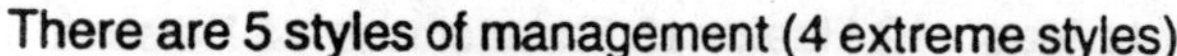

There are 5 styles of management (4 extreme styles)

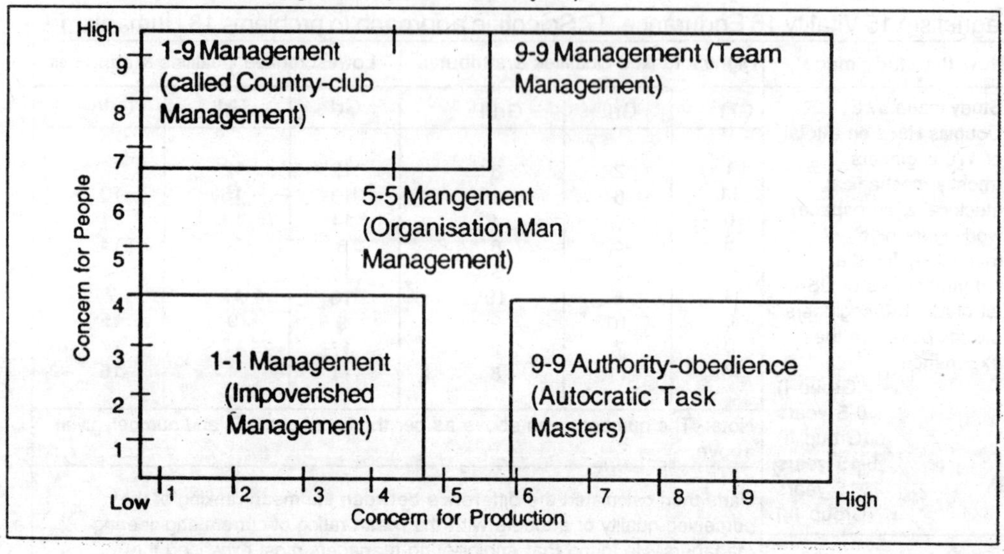

Fig. 6.21 The Managerial Grid (From Robert R. Blake and Jane S. Mouton)

(I) **9-9 Team Management:** Management work accomplishment is from commited people, managers are highly but equally concerned for both performance and human relations. Here individual objectives are achieved in the process of achieving organisational goals is the ultimate in effective mangement. A set of exercises carried out to achieve organisational development by helping the management of client organisations identify their current managenment style and then work towards the recommended 9-9 style.

(II) **1-9 Management:** Concern only for people (1-9) leads to a work place that is enjoyable but not productive. Managers have little or no concern for production but are concerned only with people. They promote an environment where everyone is relaxed, friendly and happy and none is concerned about putting forth coordinated effort to acccomplish enterprise goals. Here people do not take seriously their work and gain importance by the extent of informal personality

(III) **9-1 Management-Autocratic Task Masters** is another extreme in the grid who are concerned only with developing an efficient operation - no concern for people; and who are autocratic in their style of leadership. Human elements interfere to a minimum degree.

(IV) **1-1 Management:** Exertion of Minimum effort to get required work done is appropriate to sustain organisation membership (inpoverished management). Managers concern themselves very little with other people and production and have minimum involvement in their job and only mark time or act as messengers communicating information from superior to subordinates.

Using these four extremes, every managerial technique, approach or style can be placed somewhere in the grid. Clearly 5-5 managers have medium concern for production and for people. They obtain adequate, but not outstanding, morales and production. They do not set goals too high but still maintain strict control and supervision for achieving targets of performance. It does not tell us why a manager fails in one part or another of the grid.

(II) Michigan and Ohio state studies

- **Rensis Likert and åssociates of Michigan Institute for Social Research** included a series of studies comparing ther effectiveness of job-centered and employee-centred provision.

  - **Job centred Supervision** Emphasises the work to be performed.

  - **Employee-centred Supervision :** Emphasises development of effective work groups.

- In a related effort, Researchers at ohio state university studied the four possible combinations of high or low initiating structure with high or low considertation.

(III) Ohio State Leadership Styles

Initiating structure (IS)	Consideration (C)	
	Low	High
High	High IS Low C	High IS High C
Low	Low IS Low C	Low IS High C

Initiating structure (IS) refers to the task actions of the leader to define who does what and how

Consideration (C) refers to the measure of the leader's concern for followers. Intuitively, one would expect the high-high leadership style in each of these cases to be the most attractive but this does not always prove true. Structuring behaviour helps only if the task is unstructured consideration helps satisfaction oniy there is no adequate alternative source of satisfaction (such as interesting work). Providing either structure or consideration when not needed is unhelpful and may actually hinder.

(IV) Hersey and Blanchard Life cycle Theory

These two people proposed an extension of the model (under the name **life cycle** or **maturity** theory). in which the most effective leadership progresses with time through these four quadrants. An example

Quadrant 4	Quandrant 1
- Talk has been ungained - Parent need not pay attention(LOW IS, LOW) - Attention can be shifted to more advanced tasks	**Teach a child to put on a dress** - Parent initially concentrates on details of the task - Child will not do (High IS, Low C) much and tries to put on, but fails
Quadrant 3	**Quadrant 2**
- Less work by the parent after the child leams - Continuues to praise the child after it learns the task (Low IS,High C)	- Parent continues to correct take errors of the child - Parent praises the child for success (High IS, High C)

Fig. 6.22 Model Based on 'Life cycle' and 'Maturity Theory' (An example)

6.8 Situational Approaches

The leadership models described in two dimentional approaches above imply that only two factors (one dealing with people and the other with task or production) are important, There is one best combination of the two for effective leadership.

Tannebaum and Schmidt argued that there was a **leadership continuum** of availble technology leadership styles; one's choice within this continiuam should be contingent on the situation. **Boone and Bowen** asses the significance of this work.

Contingency theory says that there is no one right way to manage. The manager should develop the following:

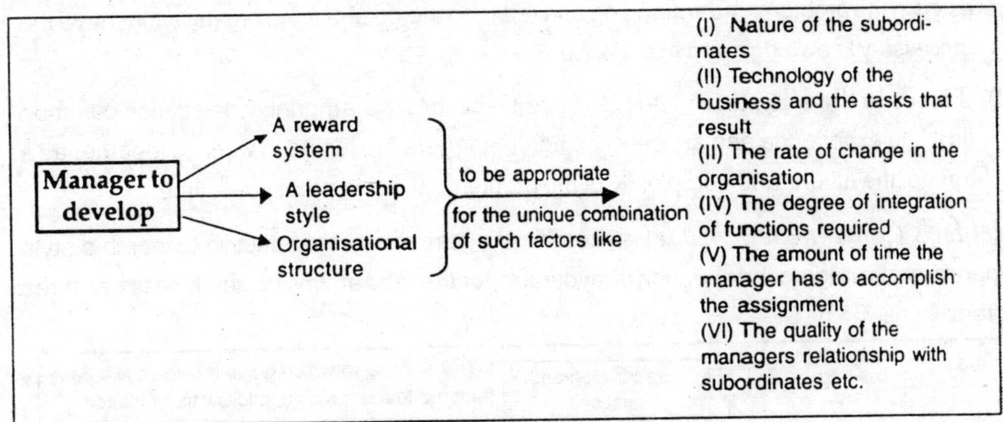

Fig. 6.23 Situational Approach

Leadership Continuum by Tannebaum and Schmidt : The two proposed a continuum of leadership style as under:-

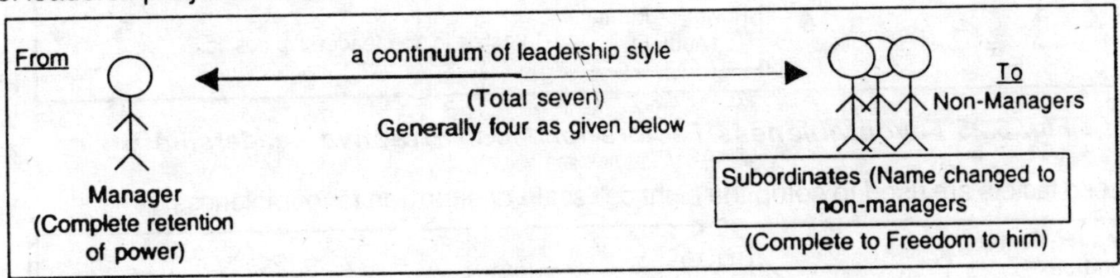

Fig. 6.24 A Continuum of Leadership Style

Four styles of Leadership : Managers work in the following ways:

(I) **Autocratic :** Makes decisions with little or no involvement of non-managers.

(II) **Diplomatic or Authorisation :** Makes decisions without consultation but attempts to persuade non-managers to accept the decisions (Modifications made if it creates too much objection by non-managers)

(III) **Consulative:** Obtain non-manager's idea and uses them in decision making

(IV) **Participative or Democratic :** Involves non-managers heavily on the decision.

Tannenbaum and Schmidit suggested ***Three Types of Forces*** for the manager to decide on the management style to be adopted by the later.

(I) **Forces in the manager:** Value system regarding leadership; his own leader inclination, confidence in non-managers, his feelings of security (or tolerance for ambuity) in an uncertain situation.

(II) **Forces in the Non-manager:** Greater delegation provided to non-managers if they have a need for independence, ready to assume responsibility, can tolerate ambiguity, interested in the problem understanding and relate to the goals of the organisation, have the necessary knowledge and experience

(III) **Forces in the situation:** The type of organisation, the amount of delegation common in it, the experience and success the non-managers have had in working together as a group, the nature and complexity of the problem, and the pressure of time.

Fielder's Contingency Model : According to him, the most effective leadership style depends on the degree the situation is favourable for the leader, this favourablness has three factors:

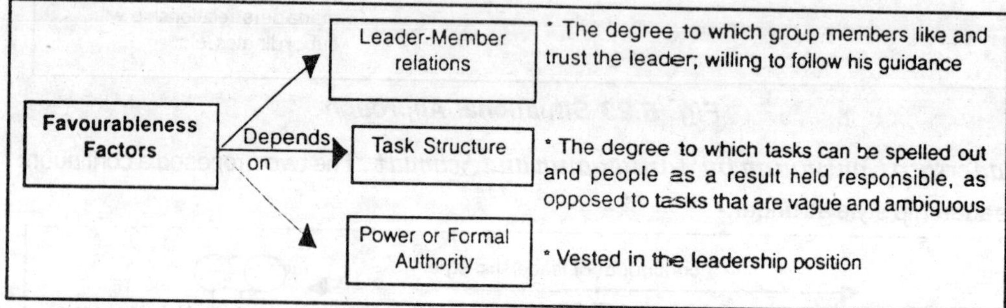

Fig. 6.25 Favourableness Factors for Most Effective Leadership Style

These factors are used to setup the eight cell scale of situation favourableness

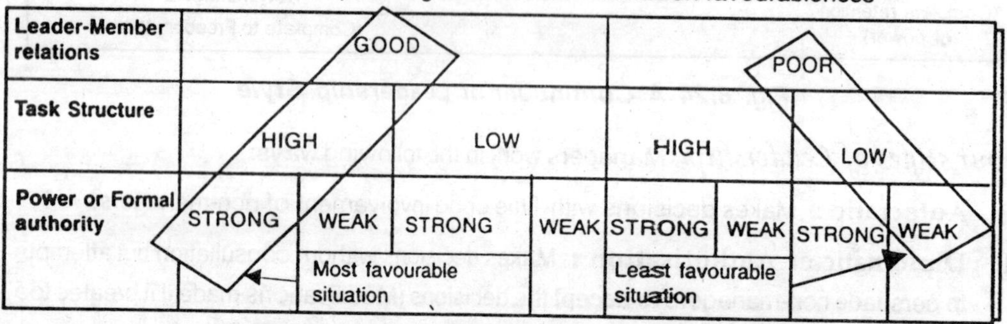

Fig. 6.26 Fiedler's Eight GROUP SITUATIONS

The most favourable situation for the leader offers good member relations; high task structure and strong position power; opposite is the least favourable.

Fiedler also developed a **least preferred coworker** (LPC) scale. He proposes measures whether the leader is task or relationships oriented. An individual is asked to think of the person with whom you could work least will of all those with whom you have ever worked; categorise that person on a scale of 1 to 8 for each of 18 pairs of adjectives. (8x18=144 range total). Examples include scales from hostile (1) to suppostive (8), quarrel some (i) to harmonious (8) and nasty (1) to nice (8). A total score of atleast 64 of a possible range of 18 to 144) designates a 'high LPC' leader and one of 57 or less , a low LPC leader.

Fiedler used this scale in a number of applications where the favourableness of the situaiton, an LPC score, and some measure of leadership effectiveness could be estimated.

LOW LPC (Task oriented) leader was **more effective in highly favourable situations** (cells 1, 2 &3) or in highly unfavourable situations (cells 7, 8)

High LPC (Relations oriented) leader was more effective in intermediate favourableness (cells 4, 5, 6)

Since you cannot change how you feel about a co-worker, which determines your LPC score, this implies that it is difficult for a leader to change leadership style.

Fiedler suggests finding a match of leader and situation View points by others:

Most of the other authors have tried to characterise leaders in complex ways. Eribbin has identified 14 types of executives by their behaviour; Eight are merely successful (they would have been more effective if they were not of some serious weaknesses)

Other 6 types like the enterpreneur, corporateur, developer, craftsmen integrator and gamesman are effective leaders in appropriate situations.

Differences betweeen Engineers and Scientists

Scientists	Engineers
• Science students place higher value on independence and learning even as undergraudates.	• Concerned with professional preparation success and family life
• Commonly assumed to have a doctorate	• Begins professional practice with BE and take up ME later on.
• Puts a high value on professional autonomy and publication of results • Desires career development and advancement • Depends on reputation with peers outside the company • Science grows through evolutionary additions to the literature.	• A team workers; places little value on publication Same as scientist • Motivated more by organisational goals; comfortable with more applied assignments; more likely to seek tangible rewards within the organisation • More likely to be working with the developments that are considerred proprietary information by the organisation; less opportunity to publish results

Fig. 6.27 Engineers VS Scientists

6.9 Motivations of Technical Professionals

A survey conducted and authored in 1960 by **Raudsepp** in which 3000 emginers associated, categorised by their occupation, weighed the importance of factors in choosing a new positioin. The result was interesting as reported by majority. Diversified work was more important than salary & specially inportant to R & D engineers who placed a higher value on **opportunity to learn.** Engineers seeking Management, sales and production functions put a higher value on **opportunity for promotion.**

6.10 Leadership of professional Groups

Mc call evaluated a number of studies of the relationship between: A formal leader and a follower group of professionals (generally in R & D). M/c call concludes that effective supervisory leadership is more orchestration than direct application of authority. The supervisor in not the only factor determining group effectivenss. Mc call identifies four general areas where the leader can make difference:

1. **Technical competence:** The supervisor's technical competence is related both to scientific productivity and the scientists willingness to comply with management directives.

   Leaders (of productive group) serve many roles pertaining to technical expertise like:

   - recognising good ideas emerging inside / outside the group.
   - defining significant problems.
   - influencing work goals on the basis of expertise
   - providing technical simulation

2 **Controlled Freedom:** Leaders of productive groups create controlled freedom in general. A condition in which decision making is shared but not given away; Autonomy is partially preserved.

3 **Leader as metronome :** The job of project manager as an example as one that:

- widens/narrows limits
- adds or subtracts weights where trade offs are to be made
- speeds up or slows down actions
- increases emphasis on some activities; decreases emphasis on others.

4 **Work Challenge :** Challenging work is the most important thing for a professional, the technical manager is measured by the extent to which he can provide challenging assignments. The professional's view of this challenging must be reconciled with:

- needs of the organisation
- the challenge to the supervisor is not just making wise assignment
- structure them as much as possible to provide the desired challenge
- persuading the individual of their importance

Use of Motivational Theories

After studying 408 engineering managers with a survey, **Utley and Wester Brook** studied to determine which motivational theories the former are familiar and which theories they were using. It was found that they were familiar with three related concepts: not discussed in this chapter:

- Management by objectives (MBO)
- Quality circles (QC)
- Findings of Peter and Waterman (In search of excellence)

But, they were also familiar with:

- Motivational concepts (More familiar by toplevel managers)

Motivational concepts were more in high technology companies.

Questions

1. Define Motivation.
2. What is the meaning of Motivation?
3. Explain the basic motivation process.
4. What do you mean by objective motivation?
5. Explain the different types of motivation.
6. Explain the motivation of subordinates.
7. Differentiate:
   - Positive motivation, negative motivation
   - Monetary motivation, non-monetary motivation
8. Explain theories of motivation.
9. Explain content and process theories.
10. Explain where does motivation positions in the traditional functions of management.
11. Discuss on the motivation of Management.

12. Explain Maslows theory of hieraracy of needs with a sketch.
13. Discuss the various needs coming under Maslows theory and explain each one of them.
14. Explain Herzberg's two factor theory.
15. Explain the right and wrong methods of motivation for engineers.
16. Compare Maslows theory with Herzberg models.
17. Explain Victor vroom's expectancy theory of motivation.
18. What do you mean by valance? Explain.
19. Explain the terms: Instrumentality, Expectancy.
20. Distinguish the terms Valence, Instrumentally, Expectancy.
21. Explain the Porter and Lawler model on motivaiton with a sketch.
22. Define performance. Explain performance with motivation relationship.
23. What does motivation and achievements results in?
24. Explain equity theory of work motivation. When does equity and inequity occurs?
25. Explain Mc chellands trio of needs.
26. Compare Mc Clellands trio of needs with Maslow's theory of hierarchy of needs.
27. Explain Alderfer's ERG theory.
28. Explain Skinner's Behaviour modification or reinforcement theory or operant conditioning.
29. Define Leadership.
30. Give the meaning of leadership.
31. Explain the managing director as a leader (as a focal point).
32. Explain the leadership traits the managers needs to understand the principles of human behaviour. Which are the importance ones?
33. Explain the eighteen attribute needed for a leader under different categories studied by Douglas Haris.
34. Discuss the Managerial Grid explaining the 5 styles of management.
35. Explain Michigan and Ohio State studies.
36. Explain Hersey and Blachard's life cycle theory.
37. Discuss on situational approaches.
38. Explain leadership continuum explained by Tannenbaum and schmidt.
39. Explain the four styles of leadership and three types of forces.
40. Explain Fiedler's contingency model. Which are the three factors for favourableness?

Chapter - 7

7.1 Preview

This chapter has the following subdivisions:-

- *The process of Control*
  - Nature of the Control process
  - Closed loop versus Open loop control
  - Three time perspective on control (Feedback control, Screening or Concurrent control, Feed forward control)
  - Characteristics of effective control systems.
- *Financial Controls:-*
  - Financial statements
  - Ratio Analysis
  - Budgets (Budgeting process)
  - Audits of Financial data
- *Non Financial controls*
  - Human resource controls (Management audits, Human Resources Accounting, Social Controls)
  - Other non-financial controls.

7.2 Definition

Controlling is the measurement and correction of performance in order to make sure that enterprise objectives and the plans devised to attain them are being accomplished. This is one of the important management function. **Controlling** is the function of everyone in the organisation starting from top most executive to the lowest manager (president to supervisor). Managers at the lower levels often think that this is not their function. The exercise of control rests with every manager charged with the execution of plans. However, the scope of control varies among managers.

Control in the case of a system involves monitoring and evaluating feedback to determine whether a system is moving towards the achievement of its goal. The control function makes necessary adjustments to a systems input and processing components to ensure that it produces proper output. For example: A sales manager exercises control when reassigning sales persons to new sales territories after evaluating feedback about their sales performance. B.E-Goetz & other authors say that:

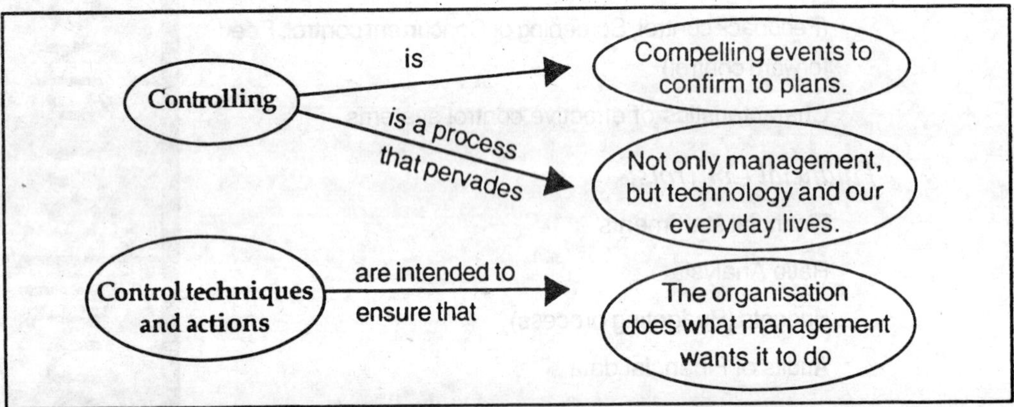

Fig. 7.1 Controlling and Control Techniques

Control commences with planning in whichever function of business (be it production or material or financial control) involves 3 steps:

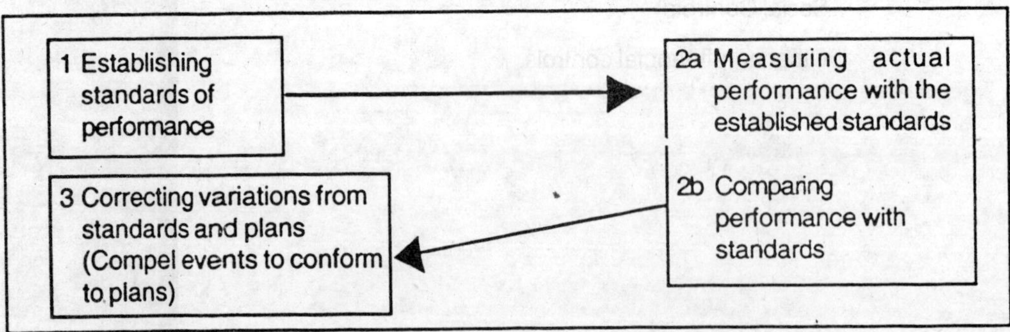

Fig. 7.2 Three Steps of Control

On the whole, **control** is a management function that involves:

- observing;
- measuring organisational performance and environmental activities,
- modifying the plans and activities of the organisation when necessary.

Example If the production is planned to achieve 100 pieces per hour, periodic review of production achieved every hour reveals that the required rate of production is not being achieved, then the variations from standards can be rectified probably by correcting the input or the efficiency of the labour etc. The corrective action is taken as required to **'compel events to conform to plans'.**

☛ 7.3 Two types of control are:

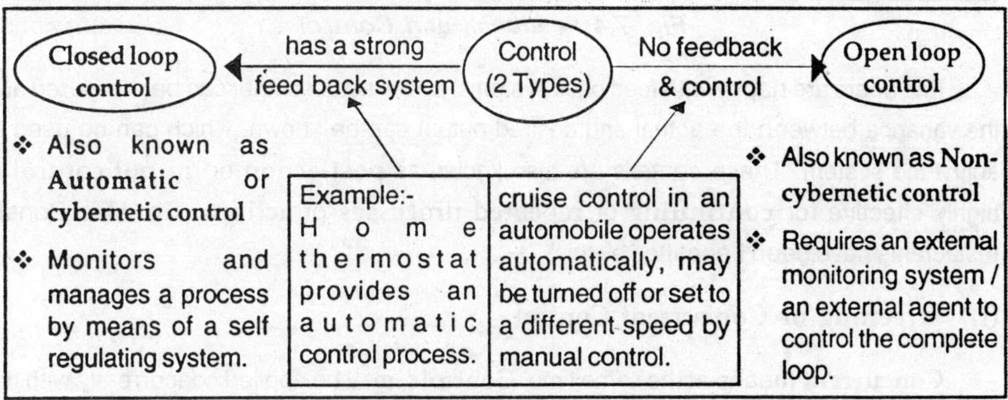

Fig. 7.3 Types of Control

In engineering, corrective action requires human judgement. The action required when a machining process fails to meet the desired tolerance may be due to:

❖ Old machine (worn out - do not maintain such a close tolerance)

❖ Operator not skilled enough to achieve the desired results (he needs training)

❖ tolerance is too close to achieve on the material (so the designer relaxes the specification or choose a more tolerant design easily achievable on material)

The decision maker has to make a choice among various solutions by using the information to the problem brought by the control system.

Three time perspectives on control:-

They are:

(I) Feedback control:

(II) Screening or concurrent control:

(III) Feed forward control:

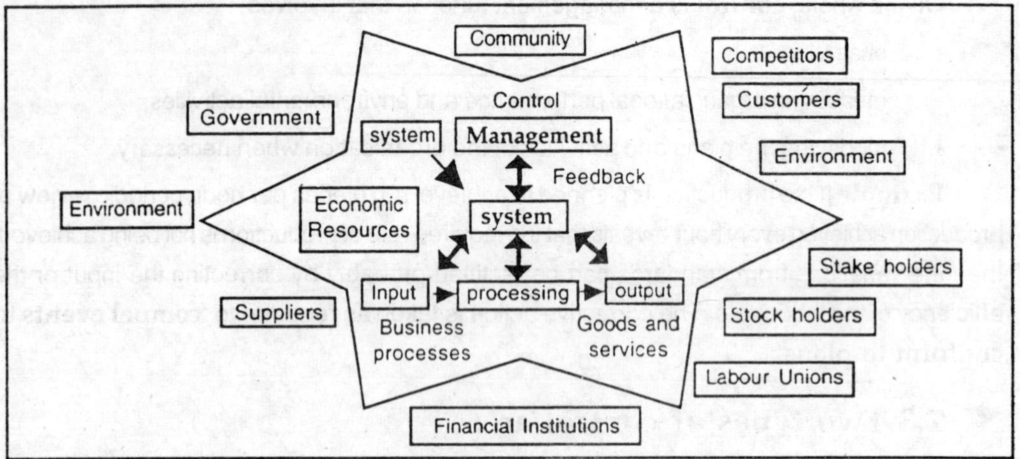

Fig. 7.4 Feedback and Control

Engineers are happy with feed back systems, as the actual output can be measured and the variance between the actual and desired output can be known, which can be used to adjust the system. These controls are also known as **post-action** or **output control** is highly effective for **continuing** or **repeated processes** or **actions.** Eg: Mac Donald restaurants have been benefitted by this.

(II) Screening or Concurrent Control

Concurrent means at the same time. **Controls**, may be applied concurrently with the effort being controlled.

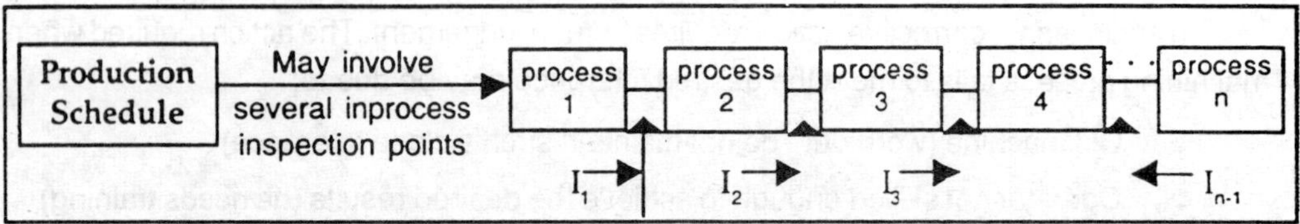

Fig. 7.5 Production Schedule Involves Inspection Points

- Inspection points are: -I_1, I_2, I_3 - - - - - I n-1
- Further investment in defective parts can be avoided by a series of inspections one after another.

So also, an engineer takes the job first time, (with a series of steps) is checked by the superior at every step.

This control is expensive, stifling of initiative, and lead to inactivity while awaiting the next inspection.

(III) Feed forward control:-

This is also known as **preliminary or steering control.** Here, the system can predict the impact of current actions or events on failure outcomes, to enable the current decisions can be adjusted to assure that future goals will be met. The controls could be applied in the early phases of a project or program to enable the latter to be completed on time with minimum resources. There are several management tools like work break down structures and network systems like (PERT or CPM)-**The Programme Evaluation Review Technique** or **Critical Path Method**. PERT identifies the longest path known as the 'critical path' of tasks that must be completed in sequence to complete the project, control over the early tasks in this system gives us 'Feed forward' control over the total project duration. Gantt control chart is also one of the methods adopted for controlling the activities of the project.

Example: Production problems can be reduced with feed forward control in manufacturing like:-

- careful sequencing of machine operations.
- inspection of raw materials.
- preventive maintenance of machines etc.

Another example is to forecast the next periods revenue and sales by the controller of a firm so that the cash will be ready when needed and will be deployed in the proper way by him. Similarly the tax payer can work out in advances his tax liability for the preview year.

Feed Back Loop of Management Control can be shown as under:-

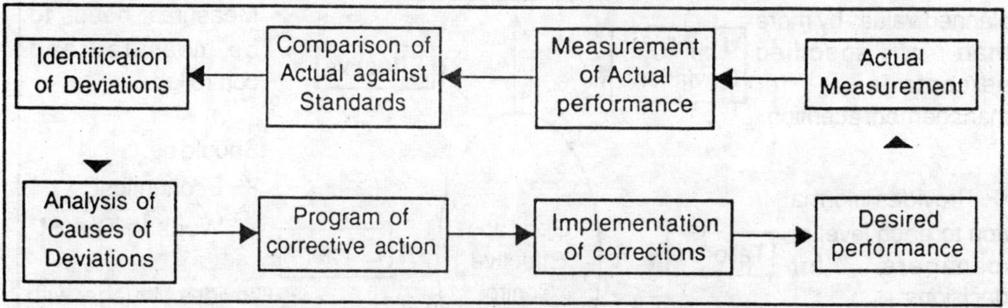

Fig. 7.6 Feed Back Loop of Management Control

7.4 Common Types of Standards used in Control Process:

Every objective, every goal of the many programs, activities carried out in a business enterprise become standards against which actual or expected performance might be measured. The various types of standards are:-

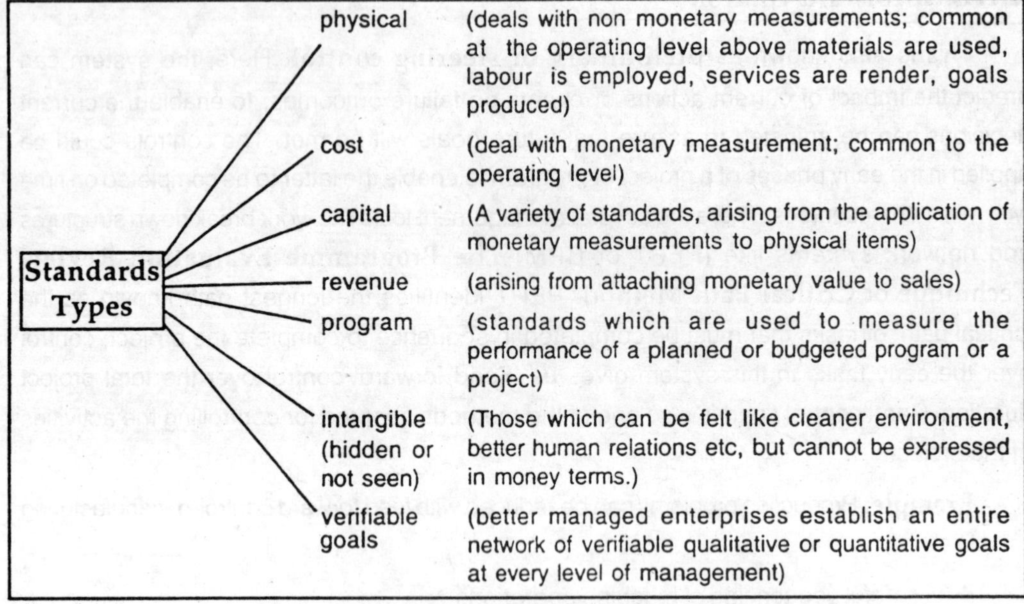

Fig. 7.7 Standards Used in Control Process

7.5 Characteristics of Effective Control Systems:

A good and effective control system should satisfy the following criteria.

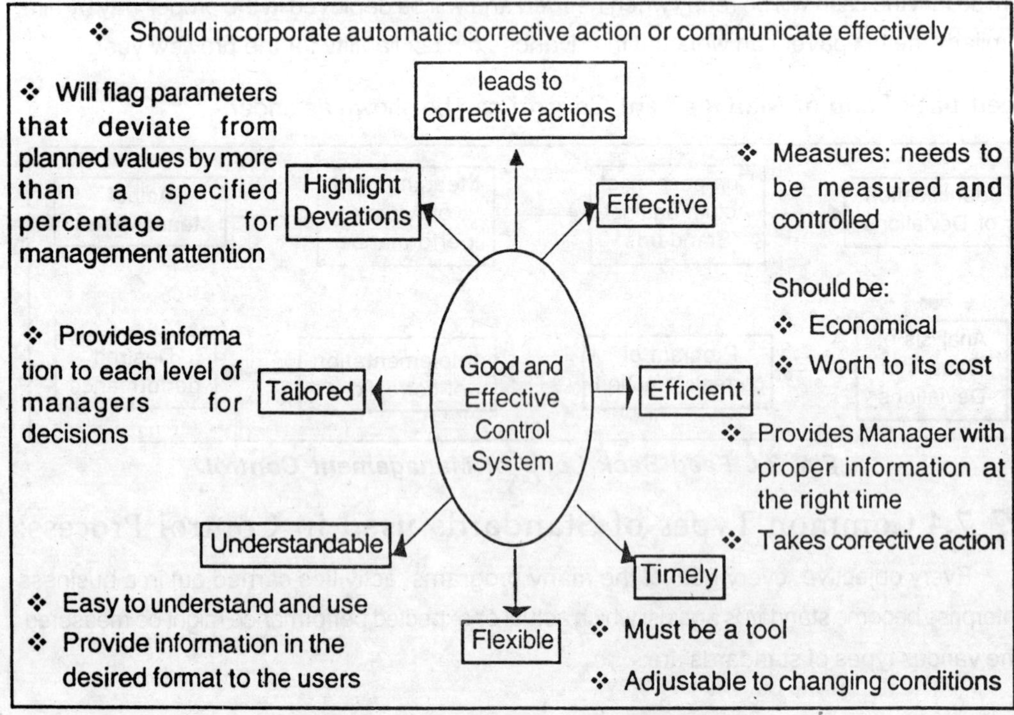

Fig. 7.8 Good and Effective Control System

☛ 7.6 Delegation

Delegation requires effective control systems to assure that delegated power is to be used wisely.

Delegation requires clear assignments of a specific task, clear definition of the expected results and a dead line. The subordinate to whom the talk is delegated should keep the boss well informed about the task; The subordinate also has to alert the boss immediately if the former notices any possible surprises - rather than try to 'project' the boss against surprises.

☛ 7.7 Control

The controls could be grouped as:-

- ❖ Financial Controls
- ❖ Non Financial Controls

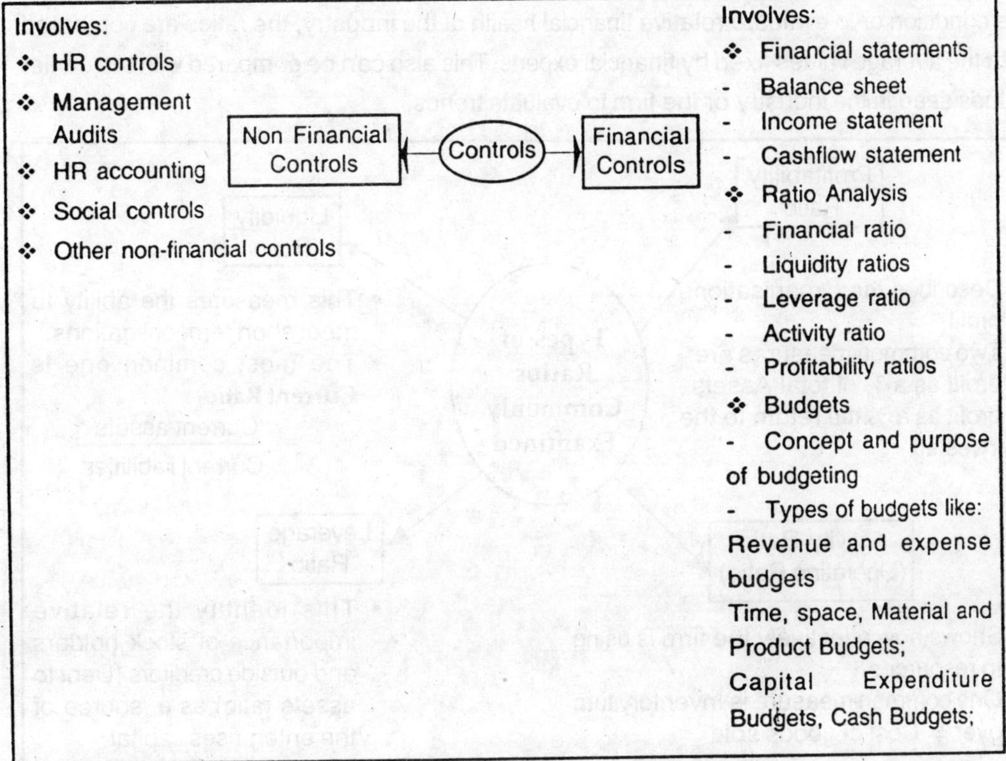

Fig. 7.9 Classification of Controls

(i) Financial Statements

These provide the basic information for the control of cash and credit which are vital for the survival of a company.

Financial Statement involves three types:-

- ❖ **Balance Sheet:-** It shows the firms financial position at a particular instance in time.
- ❖ **Income statement:-** This is also called a **profit and loss** or **revenue and expenditure statement**, shows the financial performance of the firm over a period of time (three months or a year).
- ❖ The **cash flow or source** and **uses of funds statement** shows above funds come from and what they are used for. Like the income statement, it concerns financial activities overtime.

(See figures 7.12 to 7.14)

(II) Ratio Analysis:

These are ratios of any two financial numbers taken from the balance sheet or income statement. The average values for any type of industry is fixed by financial experts. To know the condition or to evaluate relative financial health of the industry, the ratios are compared with the average values fixed by financial experts. This also can be compared with the earlier values seen in the industry or the firm to evaluate trends.

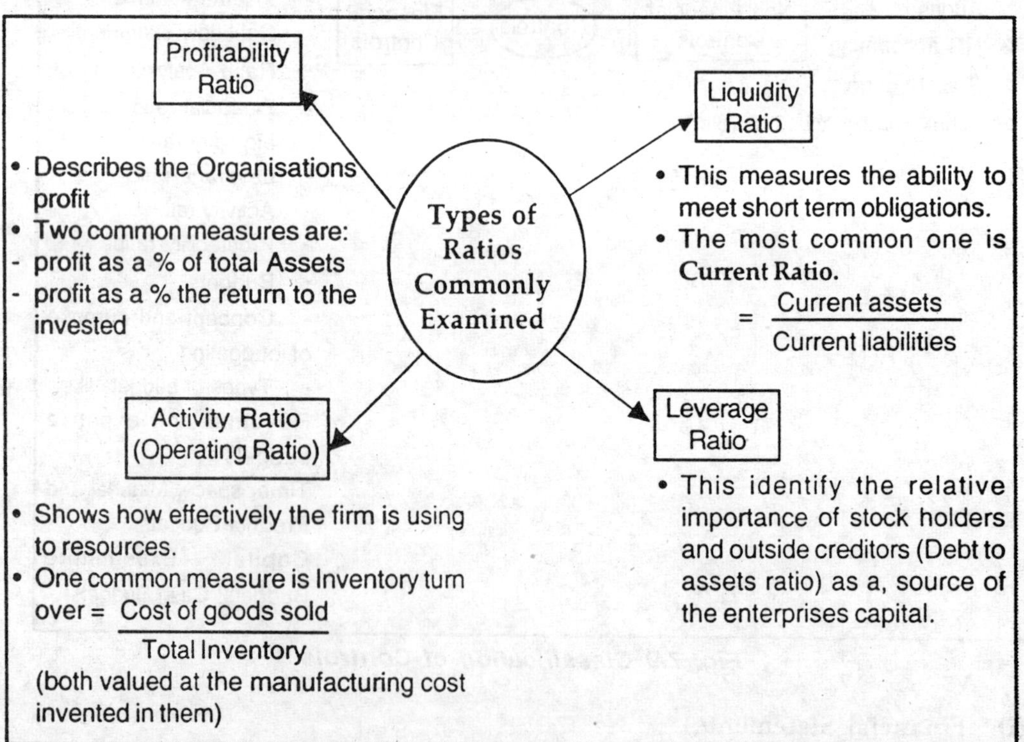

Fig. 7.10(a) Types of Ratios Which are Commonly Examined

Different types of Ratios	Formula	Remarks
1. Liquidity Ratio - Current Ratio = -- - - Acid Test Ratio - -	**Current Assets %** Current Liabilities **Current Assets-Inventory %** Current Liabilities	Analysts take current ratio 2.0 as minimum, will vary industry to industry; If it is 10, considered as high; indicated that assets are not efficiently employed. Acid test ratio over 1.0 is prudent.
2. Leverage Ratio - Debt to Assets ratio -	**Total Debt %** Total Assets	Debt as a fraction of the sum of debt plus stock holders equity.
- Debt equity ratio ---	**Total Debt %** Total Equity	Higher the leverage ratio accepted in Japanese culture and economy
3. Activity Ratio (Operating ratios) - Inventory turnover ---	**Cost of goods sold %** Inventory	Retail forms might have much lower debt ratios.
- Assets turnover or sales/assets	Net sales % Total Assets	Also books say it is sales % inventory.
- Accounts receivable turn over	Net sales % Accounts receivable	
4. Profitability Ratios - Profit margins - Return on Total assets	Net income % Net sales Net income % Total assets	A measure of how well the firm is using its assets to produce sales
- Earnings per share of common stock	Net income less preferred stock dividends % shares of common stock outstanding.	Here the stock market investor can compare to the current market price

Fig. 7.10(b) Types of Ratios which are Commonly Examined.

COMPANY: XYZ

Consolidated Balance Sheet as at 30 November 2005

	Schedule	Rupees in lakhs 3-11-2005	30-11-2004
SOURCES OF FUNDS			
Share holder's funds			
Share Capital	A		
Reserves and surplus	B		
Loan funds			
Secured loans	C		
Unsecured loans	D		
Deferred tax liability			
Total			
APPLICATION OF FUNDS			
Fixed assets	E		
Gross block, at cost			
Less: Depreciation			
Net block			
Advances on capital account and capital work in progress, at cost			
Investments	F		
Current assets, loans and advances	G		
Inventories			
Sundry debtors			
Cash and bank balances			
Loans and advances			
Less:			
Current liabilities and provisions	H		
Current liabilities			
Provisions			
Net current assets			
Miscellaneous expenditure			
(To the extent not written off or adjusted			
Deferred revenue expenditure			
Total			
Notes	K		

Per our report attached

For and on behalf of the Board of Directors

For - - - - - - - - -

Chartered Accountants

- - - - - - - -

Partner

- - - - - - - - -

Sr. Vice President - Finance

- - - - - - - - - -

- - - - - - - - - -

- - - - - - - - - -

- - - - - - - - - -

- - - - - - - - - -

Directors

1st December 2005

- - - - - - - - -

Company Secretary

- - - - - - - - - -

Managing Director

Fig. 7.11 Balance Sheet

Consolidated Cash Flow Statement for the year ended 30 November 2005

Rupees in lakhs

	Current Year	Previous Year
A. Cash Flow from operating activities		
Net Profit before tax		
Adjustments for :		
- Depreciation / Amortisation		
- Provision for doubtful advances		
- Unrealised Exchange difference		
- Financial lease payments		
- Loss / (profit) on sale of fixed assets (net)		
- Loss / (profit) on sale Investments (net)		
- Provision for doubtful debts		
- Interest expense		
- Bad debts written off		
- Translation adjustment on consolidation		
- Operating profit before working capital changes		
Adjustments for :		
- (Increase) / Decrease in sundry debtors		
- (Increase) / Decrease in inventories		
- (Increase) / Decrease) in loans and advances		
- (Increase) / (Decrease) in current liabilities and provisions		
- (Increase) / (Decrease) in miscellaneous expenditure		
Cash generated from operations		
- Direct taxes paid		
Net cash from / (used in) operating activities (A)		
B. Cash flow investing activities		
Additions to fixed assets (including capital) work in progress and advances on capital account)		
Proceeds from sale of fixed assets		
Proceeds from sale of Investments - subsidiary company		
Proceeds from sale of Investments - others		
Purchase of investments - others		
Purchase of investments - subsidiary company		
Dividend received		
Interest received		
Net cash from / (Used in) investing activities (B)		
C. Cash flow from financing activities		
Proceeds from issue of preference share capital		
Redemption of preference share capital		
Proceeds from borrowings		
Repayment of borrowings		
Financial lease payments		
Dividends paid		
Tax on Dividends paid		
Interest paid		
Net cash from / (used in) financing activities (C)		
Net cash flows during the year (A+B+C)		
Cash and cash equivalents (opening balance)		
Add: On conversion of an associate into subsidiary company		
Cash and cash equivalents (closing balance)		

Notes

1. Cash and cash equivalents exclude unrealised exchange gain of Rs. lakhs (2004 : loss lakhs)
2. The figures for the previous year have been regrouped / recast, where necessary.

Per our report attached
For
Character Accounts
---------------Partner
1st December 2005

For and on behalf of the Board of Directors,

Sr. Vice President Finance --------------------------- Directors
----

Company Secretary --------------------------- Managing Director

Fig. 7.12 Cash Flow Statement

Consolidated Profit and Loss Account for the year ended 30 November 2005

	Schedule	Rupees in lakhs Current Year	Previous Year
INCOME			
Sales..			
Less : Excise Duty			
Net Sales Income			
Other income			
Total			
EXPENDITURE			
Operating and other expenses			
Depreciation / Amortisation			
Interest			
Total			
PROFIT BEFORE TAXES AND EXCEPTIONAL ITEMS			
EXCEPTIONAL ITEMS :			
Provision for doubtful loans and advances			
Income taxes - Current			
- Deferred			
PROFIT AFTER TAXES FOR THE YEAR			
Less : Income tax of earlier years			
Share of profits less losses of associates ...			
Less : Amortisation of goodwill on consolidation			
NET PROFIT			
Details of movement in retained earnings			
Notes			
Earnings per share - Basic and diluted (Rs.)			

Per our report attached

Directors,

For and on behalf of the Board of

For

---------------- ---------

Sr. Vice President - Finance- --------- } Directors

Directors

1st December 2005

Company Secretary   Managing Director

Fig. 7.13 Profit and Loss Account

The above financial ratios vary with the industry, economy, culture and the on going company history. However, they are valuable tool for financial management.

Controlling techniques

Two major control techniques are: The **Budget and Return on Investment**

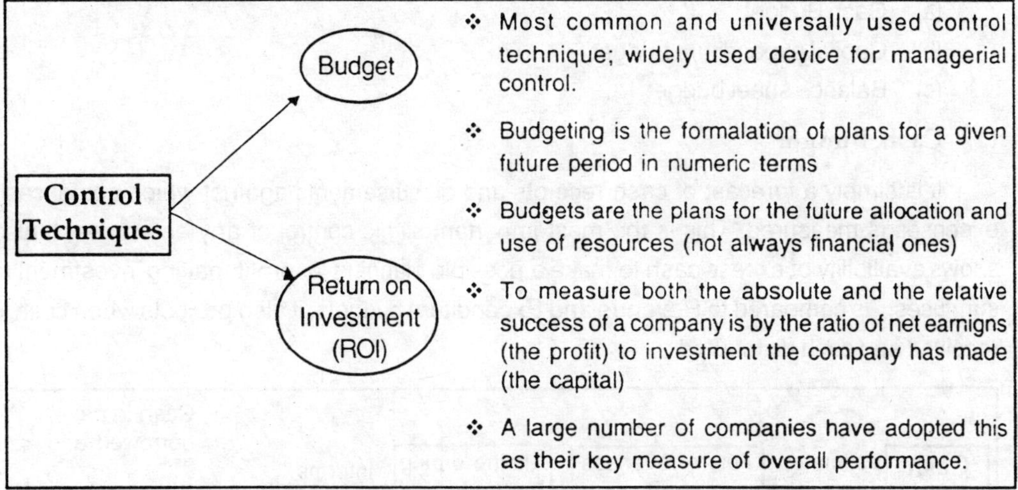

Fig. 7.14 Two Major Control Techniques

The budgeting process makes the managers to think about:

- ❖ The future operations in quantitative terms:
- ❖ Obtain approval of the planned scope of operations
- ❖ Provides a standard of comparison for judging actual performance in the control process.

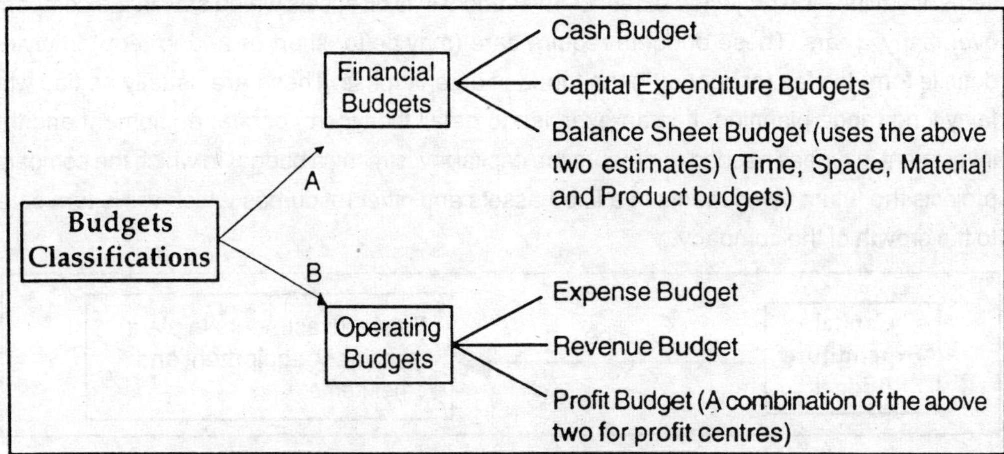

Fig. 7.15 Budgets Classifications

The budgets classification is indicated as above in Fig. 7.15

A **Financial budgets** describe:

- From where the firm intends to get its cash for the coming period?
- How it intends to use it?

Financial budget has three components as shown in figure 7.16

(a) Cash Budget
(b) Capital expenditure budget
(c) Balance sheet budget

(a) Cash Budget

It is simply a forecast of cash receipts and disbursements against which actual cash expenses is measured. This is the most important single control of any enterprise. It also shows availibility of excess cash to make a possible planning for profit making investment of surpluses. As compared to Revenue and Expenditure budgets, it also projects when cash is received and cash distributed.

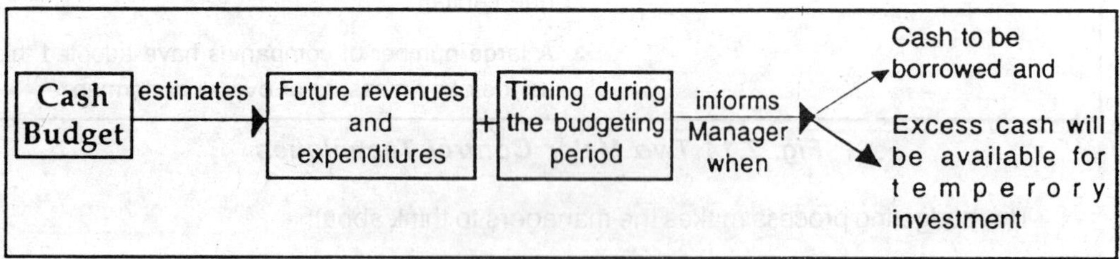

Fig. 7.16 Cash Budget

(b) Capital Expenditure Budgets

These outline specifically capital expenditures for plant, machinery, equipment and other items. It outlines the projected extent of Investment in fixed assets which stay in the company over many years. These budgets require care (may be for short or a long term) in giving definite form to plan for spending the funds of an enterprise. These are usually be tied with fairly long range planning. It is an exercise to detail the type of capital equipment and the investment in rupees needed to procure the capital investment; a budget in which the company projects the future investments in a fixed assets and other resources which will is turn cater to the growth of the company.

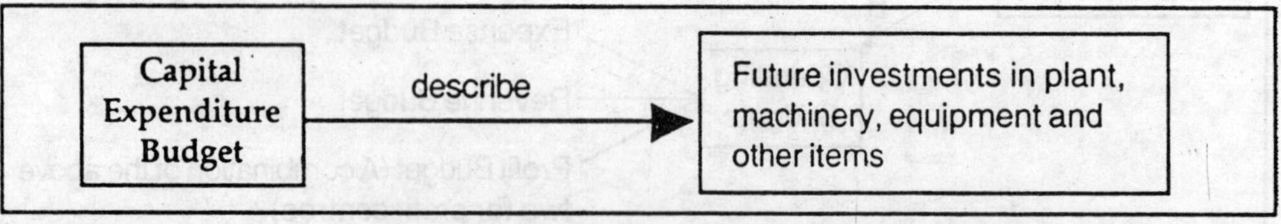

Fig. 7.17 Capital Expenditure Budget

Expenditures for fixed assets require for their long term use for to recover the investment, capital expenditures usually are scrutinised by top level management carefully than are operating expenditures.

(C) A Balance Sheet Budget uses the previous (I) and (II) estimates to predict how the balance sheet will look at the end of the budgeting period.

For closer control: Organisations are divided as under:

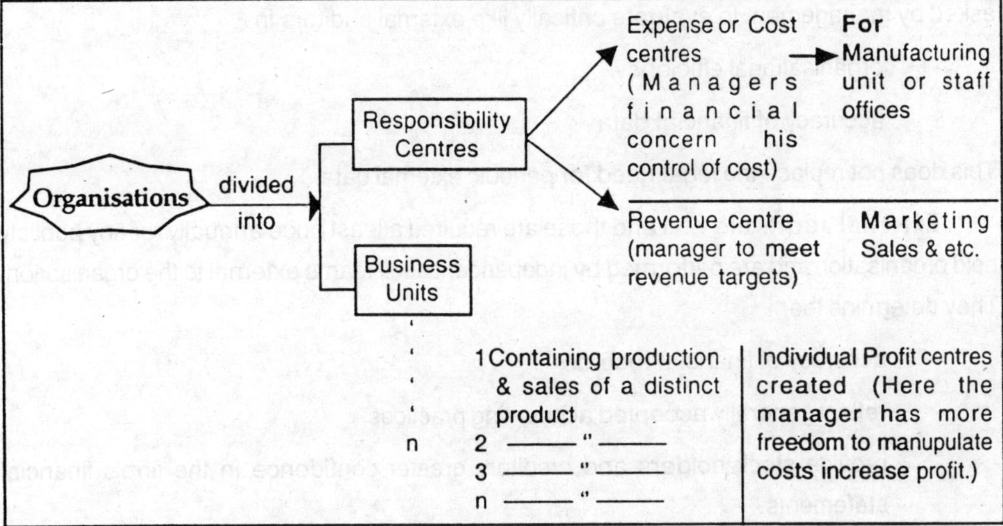

Fig. 7.18 Organisations for Closer Control

- Packages and supplemental additions are then ranked on a cost benefit basis at each management level.
- Top management allocates resources to meet organisational goals which may require expansion of some units or shrinking/elimination of others.

Budgets should act like a tool; Management should have flexibility in adapting them as conditions change in their organisation. A **Variable budget** is needed when the level of output varies as many budgets are valid only for the level of production and sales on which they were based.

(III) Audits of Financial Data

In any business, the audit of the business records and documents are conducted periodically or at the end of the year. The auditors study documents like ledgers, balance sheets etc to see whether the documents have been prepared correctly and the entire lot of transactions have been accounted properly. In accounting, a **financial transaction** is the basic entity. **Audits** are investigations of an organisation's activities to verify their correctness and identify any need for improvement.

The types of audits are carried out:-

- ❖ Internal
- ❖ External

Internal audits are carried out by their internal auditing staff who spend their time auditing the several subunits of their organisation. The concerned people who conducts the unit study have a good knowledge of their organisations accounting systems and may be asked by management to evaluate critically like external auditors in:

- organisational efficiency
- accuracy of financial data

This does not replace the legal need for periodic external data.

External audits are vital and those are required atleast once annually for any publicly held organisation and are performed by independent audit teams external to the organisation. They determine the:

- accuracy of financial records
- reflect generally accepted accounting practices
- provide stock holders and creditors greater confidence in the firm's financial statements.

❖ However, in the case of companies where:

Unit 1 ⟶ has a primary customer as Unit 2 of the same company, the transfer price credited to one profit centre and debited to the other must be established, where there is no accurate market price for the product exists.

(IV) Time, Space, Material and Product Budgets:

Many budgets are better expressed in physical terms than in monetary terms. Although such budgets are usually translated into monetary quantities which are easily measurable and verifiable. More common of these are the budgets for:

- Direct labour hours
- Machine hours
- Units of materials
- Square feet allocated
- Units produced

Most firms budget product output and most production departments budgets their share of the output of components of the final product. It is common to budget labour either in labour hours or labour days. Such budgets cannot be well expressed in monetary terms since the Rupees cost would not accurately measure the resources used or the results intended.

Budgeting process Methods: Following are the methods adopted.

	Method 1	Method 2	Method 3 (a combi -nation of 1 & 2)
Preparation by:	Central Staff group	Responsibility centre level	Top Management provides guide lines for budget process; Middle Management provides more detail; Various responsibility centres prepare proposed revenue and expense budgets; These are merged, modified and negotiated at each middle management level, approved at top. Passed back down as operating guide lines for the coming period.
Imposed by:	Top Management		
Imposed on:	Everyone (down the line)		
Method:	Top down approach		
Disadvantages of this method:	❖ Information from lower management levels ignored that might improve the budget process ❖ Does not foster commitment from lower level mangers to confirm to the budget	❖ Such budget tends to be inflated ❖ Do not consider adequately upper management goals and objective for the near future period	

Fig. 7.19 Budgeting Process Methods

- ❖ Budgets are frequently proposed and approved as % increases order or decreases in current levels. This makes it difficult to change priorities in resource use quickly to meet new priorities. The technique of Zero half budgeting was developed to overcome this.
- ❖ Each responsibility centre develops a budget package with a core of resources expenditure that is absolutely necessary to meet next years objectives. One or more additions required to the job more effectively are considered.

☛ 7.9 Non-Financial controls

Just as actual financial performance conforms to plans, so also there is human and organisational performance conform to expectations. Even management by objectives, by its very nature is a control system.

Two tools used in non-financial controls to evaluate collective human and organisational performance are:

- ❖ Management Audit
- ❖ Human resource accounting

One should consider **social controls** also through group values and self control.

(I) Management audits

The financial data audit definition can be applied to other areas including the audit of the entire system of managing an enterprise. Management service staffs have been developed to conduct management audits or firms may seek many of the objectives through an enterprise self-audit.

(II) Human resource accounting

A major asset of an enterprise is its people. Investments in acquiring outstanding people and an extensive training program to them represent capital investments in the future, purchase of new machinery. Quantifying the value of human resource investment is rather difficult, but a number of approaches are being evaluated.

(Costs for R & D and inprocess improvement are treated as current expense and written off. It has to be more appropriately recognised as capital investments).

(III) Social controls:

Organisations will not be effective if they rely only on formal controls. Two things are important: Group Values and self control.

The excellent companies seem to have developed cultures that have incorporated the values and practices of the great leaders; These shared values can be seen to survive for decades, even after several years after the death of guru. eg Nonahimsa of Gandhiji. The real role of the chief executive is to manage the values of the organisation.

For values imbued in the corporate culture to be effective make the employes in general to exercise self control over their actions.

Like other controlling systems, self control in human involves:

- The existence of standards (General workers knowledge about the organisation's objectives & values)
- Comparison with actual outcomes (Feedback of performance to the individual, not to management or a quality control group)
- Corrective action (individuals to have the tools, autonomy and motivation to make corrections)

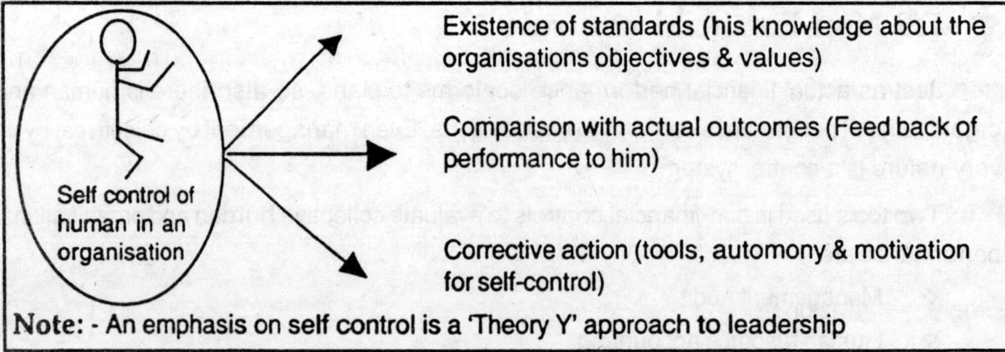

Fig. 7.20 Self - Control of Human in an Organisation

Other non-financial Controls:-
These could be:

- ❖ Methods of evaluating the effectiveness of Research activities
- ❖ Control systems for drawing release and for engineering design changes (configuration management)
- ❖ Effective production management requires inventory control and quality control among other control systems.
- ❖ Project management requires control systems monitoring of all its key variables like schedule, cost and the performance of the resulting product.

7.10 Useful hints in designing a control system

Knowing the basic process and the fundamentals of control which is understood properly by all the practicing managers, the actual system requires special design. If controls are to work, they must be specially tailored:

- ❖ to plans and positions of the company
- ❖ to the individual managers and their personalities
- ❖ to the needs of efficiency and effectiveness.

Hints or Requirements of a control system

- ❖ Control should be tailored to plans.
- ❖ Controls must be tailored to individual managers.
- ❖ Controls should point up expectations at critical points.
- ❖ Controls should be objective.
- ❖ Controls should be flexible.
- ❖ Controls system should fit into the organisational climate.
- ❖ Controls should lead to corrective action.

Return on Investment (ROI)

❖ One of the most successfully used control technique of measuring both the **absolute** and **relative** success of a company is by the ratio of:

Net Earnings (the profit) to the Investment the company has made (the capital).

This is known as ROI (Return on Investment) - the core of the control system.

In both Indian and companies abroad, a large number of companies have adopted ROI as their key measure of overall performance. ROI in effect means the rate of return that a company or division earns on the capital allocated to it.

The better company is one which makes more profit on a lower investment (or the company will have higher rate on investment)

- One of the principal advantages of using ROI to control overall performance is that it, like profit and loss focuses management attention to central objectives of the business to make the best profit on the capital available.
- It measures the efficiency of the company as a whole and of its major divisions or department, its products and its planning. It takes attention away from mere increase in sales volume or asset size or even from the level of costs and draws attention to the combination of factors making for successful operation.
- Another advantage is that it is effective where authority is decentralised. It offers the possibility of comparing the efficiency in the use of capital within the company and with other enterprises.
- Lastly, it is complete and indicates all the factors bearing upon the return. It enables managers to locate weakness Eg; if inventories are rising, the effect will be shown in lower rate of return.

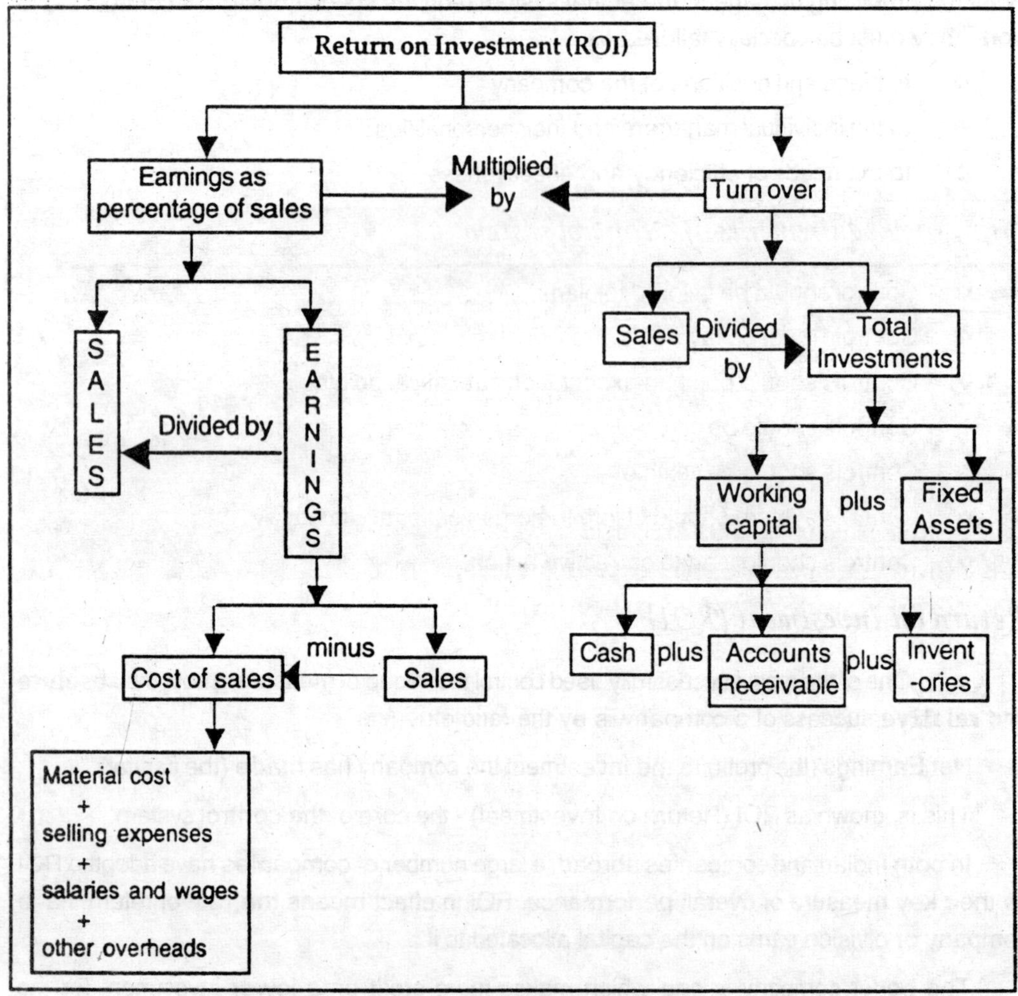

Fig. 7.21 Factors Affecting Calculation of ROI

Questions

1. Define Control.
2. What is the meaning of controlling?
3. Explain controlling and control techniques.
4. Explain the three steps of control.
5. Mention the two *Controlling* types of control.
6. Differentiate closed loop control with open loop control.
7. What do you mean by cybernetic control?
8. Mention three type perspectives on control. Explain each one of them.
9. What do you mean by feedback control?
10. What do you mean by screening or concurrent control?
11. What do you mean by feed forward control?
12. Explain feedback loop of management control.
13. Mention the common type of standards used in control process.
14. Explain the characteristics of effective control systems.
15. What is delegation? What are its requirements?
16. Mention the groups of controls. Explain the classification of controls.
17. What does Financial statements involve?
18. Explain Ratio analysis. What are the benefits from this?
19. Show a simple Balance sheet for any company.
20. Show a sample of consolidated cash flow statement for any company.
21. Show a consolidated profit and loss account for any company.
22. Explain two major control techniques.
23. Distinguish Budget and Return on Investment (ROI).
24. What are the different classification of Budgets?
25. Explain Financial Budget.
26. Explain Operating Budget.
27. Give the meaning of Cash Budget.
28. Give the meaning of capital expenditure budget.
29. Give the meaning of balance sheet budget.
30. Explain an organisation for closer control.
31. Explain different types of Financial data.
32. Distinguish time, space, material and product budgets.
33. Explain non-financial controls.
34. What are management audits?
35. What do you mean by human source accounting?
36. Explain Social controls.
37. Explain Self control of human in an organisation.
38. Give a list of useful hints in designing a control system.
39. What are the hints or requirements of a control system?
40. Describe factors affecting calculation of Return on Investment (ROI)..

Managing Technology through the Product Life Cycle

Chapter - 8

8.1 Preview

The eighth chapter covers:-

- *Product and Technology life cycle*
- *Nature of Research and Development*
  - R & D defined
  - Distribution by Funding and Performance
- *Research strategy and organisation*
  - New Product strategies.
  - Corporate Research organisations
- *Selecting R & D projects*
  - Need for selection
  - Initial screening
  - Quantitative approaches
- *Protection of ideas*
  - Patents
  - (Establishing patent rights)
  - Trade marks and other marks
  - Trade secrets
  - Companion of Protecting ideas
- *Creativity*
  - Nature of creativity
  - The creative process
  - Encouraging creativity (Providing the environment, Brainstorming and other creativity techniques)
  - Creating and the Innovation process
  - Evaluating R & D effectiveness (individual effectiveness)
  - Support for R & D

8.2 Managing the Research Function

Management of technology plays an ever increasing role in management and engineering. Management of technology for competitive advantage begins with R & D (Research and Development). R & D efforts must be directed towards technologies that are most likely to impact company's primary markets. R & D project selection and evaluation must keep customer desired and market dynamics in view far better than has traditionally been the case everywhere in the world. The technological progress function can help access the remaining potential to be mined in a given technological areas.

New technologies emanating from R & D must work their way through design and manufacturing to energy in the form of beneficial innovation. The USA is a leader in invention, but not in moving inventions through to innovation and diffusion. Too often the transition of new inventions from R & D into products or processes has been left to serendipity; It needs to be managed. The*Controlling* thrust towards concurrent engineering usefully provides firms into considering manufactureability, marketing and maintenance -- throughout the design process - by including representatives of those functions on the design team from the beginning.

The **dictionary meaning of research** is systematic investigation and study of materials, sources etc. In order to establish facts and reach conclusions. **Research and development** are commonly lumped together under the term "R & D"

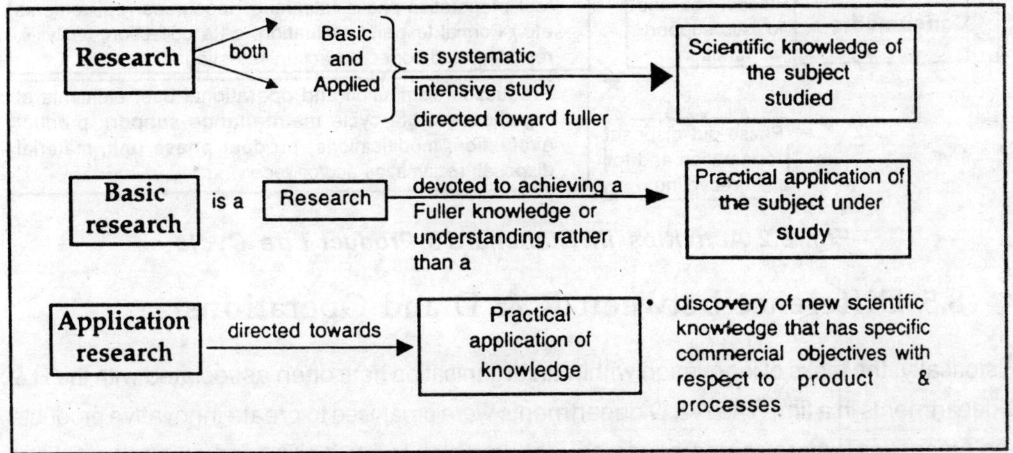

Fig. 8.1 Research, Basic research, Application research

Development is the systematic use of scientific knowledge directed towards the production of useful materials, devices, systems, or methods including design and development of prototypes and processes.

8.3 Research and Development is a work directed towards the innovation, introduction and improvement of products and processes.

8.4 Product Life Cycle

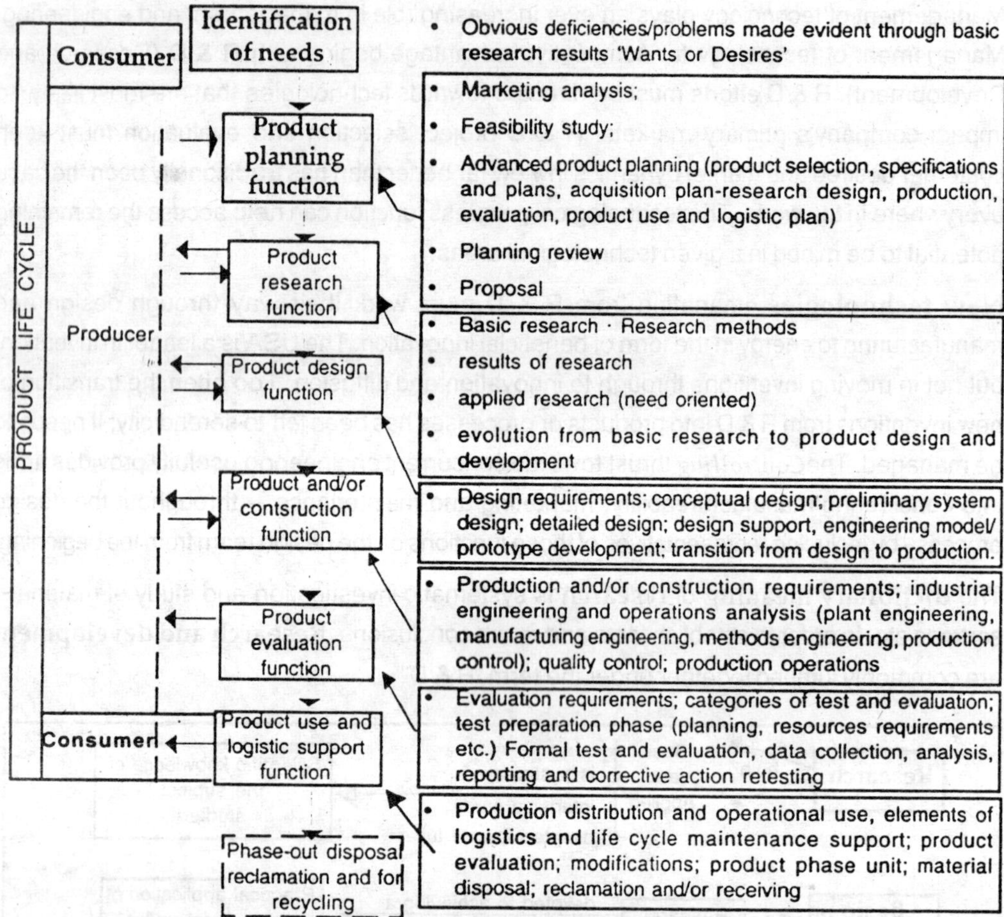

Fig. 8.2 Activities in Blanchard's Product Life Cycle

8.5 Difference between R & D and Operations

Historically, the tasks of innovation within an organisation here often associated with the R & D departments in a firm. The R & D departments were organised to create innovative products and processes, where as operations sought predictability, reliability and efficiency. One of the earliest insights in organising for innovation was that the **talks for innovation and operations differed** considerably along three dimensions: -

- Nature of feed back
- Goal operation
- Interpersonal orientation.

(I) Nature of Feedback: In traditional marketing environments, employees performed more or less clearly defined talks. The outcomes of their activities were clearly visible to them and the results of their efforts were available within a short span of time.

- Unlike manufacturing environments, the individuals who were engaged in R & D activities performed tasks that were not clearly specificable. The feed back-outcome of the activities performed by individuals was ambiguous at best. Further there was significant delay in the feed back because of the project might have taken several months or years.

(ii) Goal orientation: As the tasks were clearly specified and the feed back was clear and quick, the appropriate goal orientation for operating environments was shorter. Individuals were likely to set relatively short term goals that served their purposes.

- In contrast, for R & D, the appropriate time horizon tended to be much longer, because the nature of the path and the quality of the feed back were considerably ambiguous

(iii) Interpersonal orientation:

- Here both R & D and manufacturing departments resemble each other. The interpersonal orientation appropriate for employees working in these two departments tended to be impersonal. In operating environment, individuals located on opinions where as in R & D departments, they focussed on written information. For the appropriate performance of activities in each of these departments, the information needed to be objective. Hence the interpersonal relationships in most of these departments tend to be characterised by impersonality : based on objective, quantifiable or verifiable information.

Dimensions	R & D	Operations	
		Manufacturing	Sales
Formalisation	• Low Basic Research Lowest	High	• High (Lower than manufacturing)
Interpersonal orientation	• Moderate task and relationship • Applied Research Lower on task	High task orientation	High relationship orientation
Time Horizon	Long term Basic research Longest	Short term	• Short term (Longer than manufacturing)

Fig. 8.3 Difference between R & D and Operations

Two broad generalisations emerged in the last two decades.

	Dimension	R & D	Operating Environment
1	Formality Levels	Not much and high formality levels not required	Greater or High (Greater formality of structure written policies, procedure and regulations needed)
2	Leadership styles	• Participative leadership more effective • Authoritative style likely to be dysfunctational	Authoritarian, command-and-control leader may be successful

Fig. 8.4 Formality and Leadership Styles

8.6 Multistage Decisions (options) embedded in R & D in various stages

There are three stages:

1. Research – stage 1
2. Technical construction/Development- stage2
3. Implementation/commercialisation – stage 3

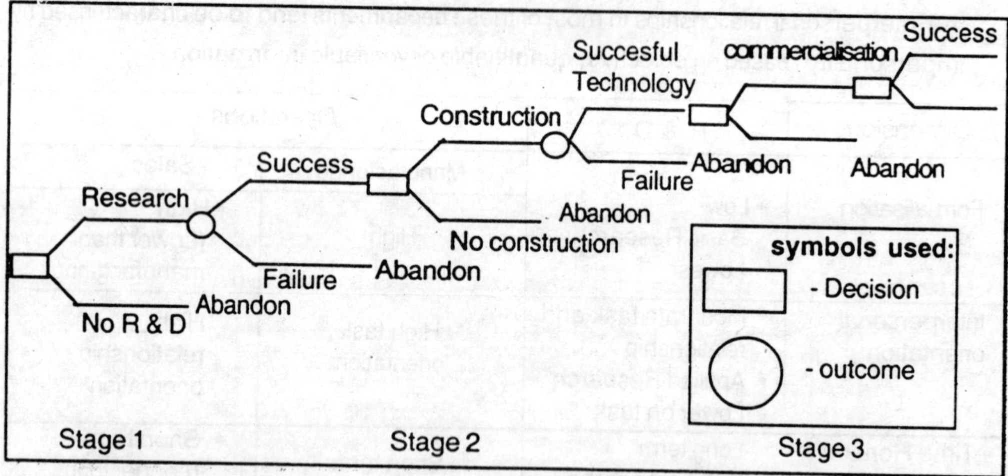

Fig. 8.5 Multistage Decisions Embedded in R & D at 3 Stages

Stage 1- Research:

Management has to decide whether to engage in research for the discovery of a new product or technology. This often depends on whether the management finds such an investment of strategic importance for the company's future growth. Success in many industries (in high technology) demands a steady flow of new and innovative processes or products. Research has become an **increasingly costly** and **time consuming.**

Stage 2- Technical Construction / Development:

Once the research stage is proven to be a success, management may decide to start the technical construction resource and development phase. Technical construction requires considerable capital as well as human resources to be committed. Technical knowledge for the construction is not only difficult to find, but also costly. New information that arrives may prove that such an investment is not profitable enough for the firm to justify its research and construction expenses. Management will eventually decide what is the best from this new information. If these problems are surpassed and technical construction and subsequent commercialisation are seen to be essential for the competitiveness of the firm, construction will commence.

Stage 3. Implementation/ Commercialisation:

The final stage is this activity of the new technology in the market. Management considers the possibility that the new product cr technology might be successfully launched in the market place. At these phase, the new product or technology typically faces competition from substitutes and management has to make sure that it has properly anticipated competitive reaction and its impact on profit value before launching the product into the market.\

The basic structure of multistage decision making is not unique to R & D. It is prevalent in many (if not most) strategic situations.

8.7 Technology Life Cycle

Technology life cycle portrayed by Frederick Betz is as shown below:-

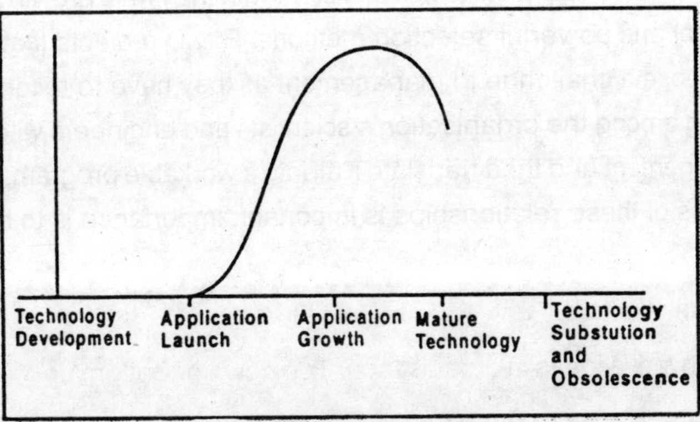

Fig. 8.6 Technology Life Cycle

When the application is launched, there occurs a fast growth in the penetration of technology into markets (or in creating new markets). After some time, the innovation rate comes down and market creation will be peak, known as **maturity technológy stage.** Finally when competing or substituting technologies emerge, the mature technology begins to slide down in competition with the competing technologies. Obsolescence stage will reach.

8.8 R & D Projects

Complex R & D projects require the mobilisation of substantial resources and the coordination of activities in different laboratories and sometimes in different countries. The management of such projects constitutes a formidable task that demands considerable skill. Comparable challenges exist when a new product is designed, developed and marketeq. The entire process involves people from several departments and disciplines in one or more laboratories, firms, and/or institutions. Scientists, specialists and engineers must collaborate to carry the product from 'concept' to 'launch'. Yet organisationally they belong to separate parts of the enterprises or even to another organisation. In large projects, where several firms and institutions are involved, the project manager's difficulties are obviously compounded.

R & D and engineering projects have other characteristics. Projects are carried by a highly trained, highly motivated professional staff. Mostly, they are one-of-a-kind undertakings involving considerable uncertainty and risk. Project managers therefore need tools and techniques that will help them better grasp the intricacies of the relationship among various components and will also equip them with capabilities for skillfully handling human problems. The mechanics of project management involving the scheduling of tasks and the allocation of resources are well explored; many software systems are available to help project managers. However, there should be a mechanism that provides them with a rapid feedback about the process, particularly about early warning signals regarding potential failures.

One of the important tasks of organisations is to select only R & D projects that may **have some potential for future exploitation** consistent with the firm's growth strategy. There is a need for practical and powerful selection methods. R & D projects that are part of the innovative process pose a challenge to management as they have to reconcile the visions and ideas originating among the organisation's scientists and engineers with the views and plans of upper management and then translate it all into a workable program. Understanding the internal dynamics of these relationships is important. Importance is to be given for the following:-

- Project portfolio selection.
- Initiation of innovative ideas in organisation: Top down or Bottom up.
- Human problems in project management
- Postmortem analysis of projects.

Project Portfolio selection

Organisations may have some sort of a project. Many organisations have several and occasionally a large number of ongoing projects. These projects are to be monitored constantly and evaluated for their potential usefulness to be organisation. Their utility must also be compared with new opportunities. The re-examination and revaluation of priorities are thus an important part of the management of R & D. Easy-to-use decision support systems for managers can be developed for the purpose.

Initiation of innovative ideas in organizations:

Organisations having long term business strategies will be expecting that strategic decisions and operational plans when communicated from top management will be translated into focused programs and projects. Such instructions may not fit well with the ideas and aspirations of scientists and engineers in the innovation chain. Consideration must be given to:-

- Creating a balance between the divergent views
- Understanding the dynamics of this balance
- Finding and evaluating existing patterns and identifying their impact on organisational performance.

Human problems in project management:

Project management is continuously growing in importance, -- and internationally, in both public and private organisations. Many capabilities have been developed for scheduling and monitoring. Much needs to be done to help project managers in selecting personnel and in coping with the problems created by the multidisciplinary and multicultural background of the professional project staff.

Post-mortem analysis of projects:

It is important to conduct post-mortem analysis of projects, both those with successful and those with unsuccessful outcomes. Understanding the commonalities and divergences among projects with similar outcome can be helpful to decision makers. It is also necessary to understand the interfaces between a project and the rest of the organisation and between the project and the external environment and their effects on the success or failure of the project.

8.9 Selecting R & D projects

Technology based manufacturing firms will have more ideas for successful research projects, than its capability of investing in resources.

Booz, Allen and Hamilton Inc has suggested the following ratios.

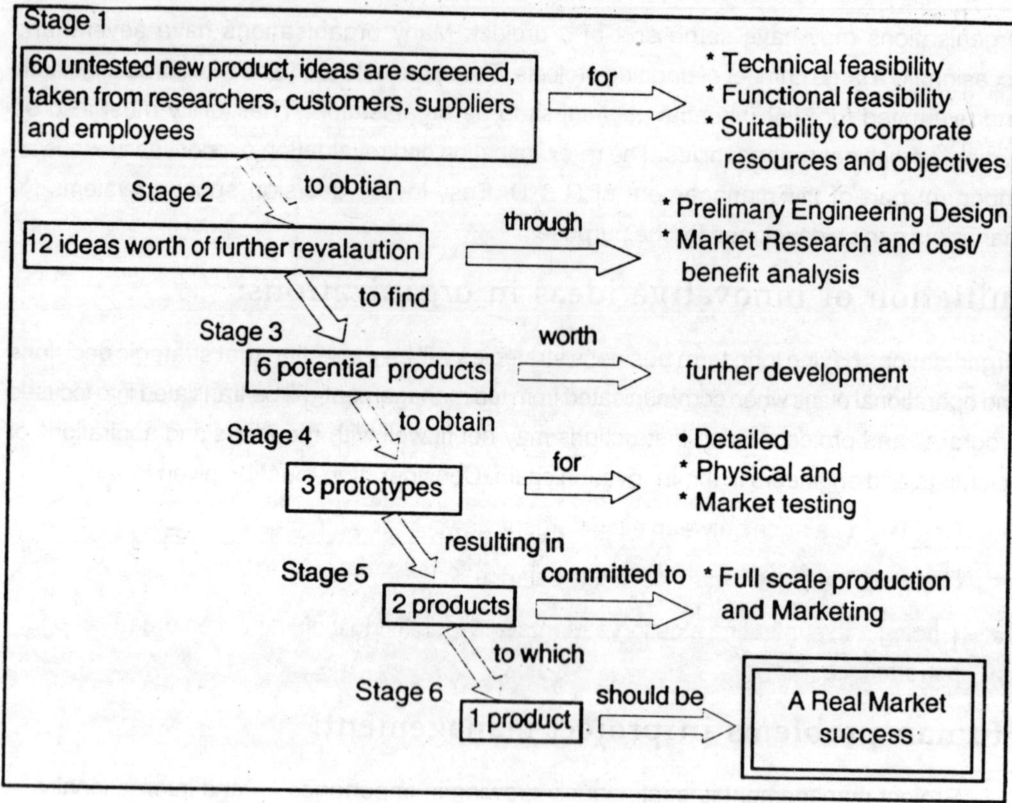

Fig. 8.7 Screening of Research Project Ideas

(II) Initial Screening:

Stage 1 to Stage 2 → requires a method that is quick/inexpensive.A common method is use of a checklist, in which the proposed product is given a simple judgemental rating like (poor, fair, good, excellent) or scores like (-2, -1, +1, +2) for each of a number of characteristics.

The various factors to be considered according to seiler are:-

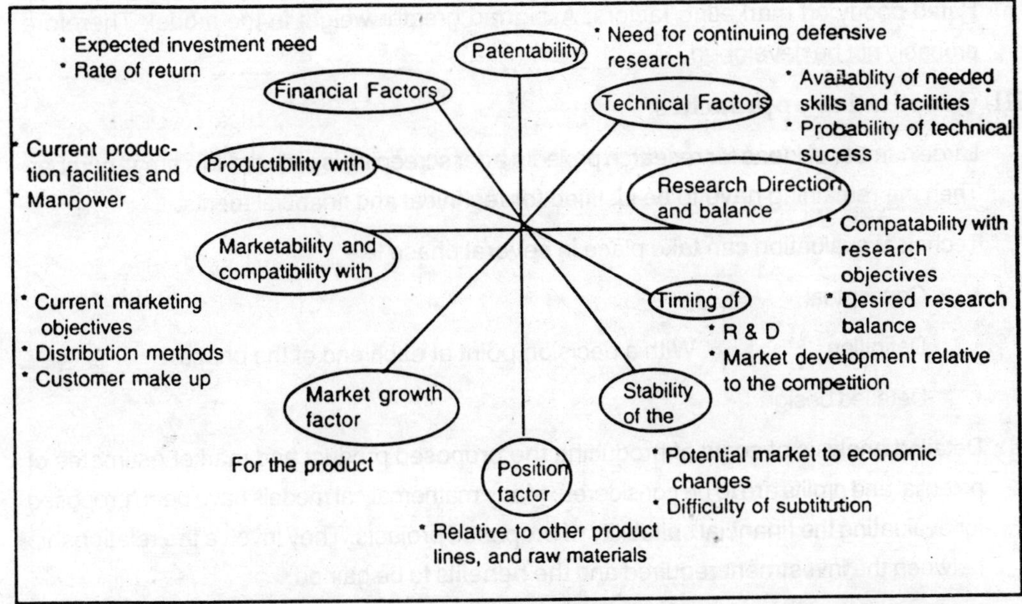

Fig. 8.8 Factors Considered for Scoring Needed or Initial Screening

Weighted checklist or scoring model

Here every factor is scored on a scale 1 to 10. A relative weight representing the importance of that factor is then multiplied and the weighted score for all factors added.

Example of a weighted score model

criteria	weight (say)	score	weightedscore
Technical Factors			
① — —	2	8	16
② — —	2	7	14
③ — —	1	9	9
Marketing Factors			
①	4	5	20
②	4	4	16
③	2	6	12
Total		39	87

(I) Raw Score of 39 (65%) – out of 60

(II) Weighted score of 87 (58%) – out of 150

* The product was judged very favourably on technical factors could be developed with such confidence of technical success.

* Rated poorly on marketing factors; Assigned greater weight in the model; Therefore probably not be developed.

(III) Quantitative approaches

Large number of ideas for research projects after screening is reduced to a small number. Then the remaining have to be justified for technical and financial merits.

Technical evaluation can take place in several phase like:

- Conceptual
- Definition
- Detailed design

} With a decision point at each end of the phase

Detailed analysis of costs of producing the proposed product and market estimates of potential and profits are to be considered. Many mathematical models have been proposed for evaluating the financial suitability of proposed projects. They involve the relationship between the investment required and the benefits to be gained.

- Simple pay back time is often used to justify investments that need to be recovered quickly because of uncertainties; but unsuitable for long term investments because it ignore profits expected beyond the point of pay back and does not consider the time value of money.

Any sum p today placed at an annually compounded interest would compound to:

$A_1 = p(1+i)$ in one year; $A_2 = p(1+i)^2$ in years---; $An = p(1+i)^n$ in n years.

(I) The present worth of any future sum Aj can be calculated as under $P = \frac{Aj}{(1+i)j}$

(II) $P = \sum_{j=1}^{n} \frac{Aj}{(1+i)j}$ where p = present worth of n years.

(III) Maximum expenditure justified Em_j based on the estimated probabilities of success:

$$Em_j = Fc \times Ft \times p$$

Where Fc is the probability of commercial success.

Ft is the probability of technical success

8.9 Protection of Ideas

Introduction

Before studying the patents, trademarks and copyrights, let us understand the design first.

Design

A **design** means only the features of shape, configuration, pattern or ornament applied to any article by any industrial process, or means, whether manual, or chemical, separate or combined, which in the finished article appeal to and are judged solely by the eye; but does not include mode or principle or construction or anything which is in substance a mere mechanical device, and does not include any trademark.

In simple terms, the dictionary meaning of **design** is art of producing; sketch or plan for product; lines of shapes as decoration; layout; established form of product; mental plan; purpose etc.

A design is registered only if it is new or original. The Controller General of patents and Designs will not register a design if the same is already registered or published in India in respect of the same or any other article prior to the application of registration. The registration of a design confers on its proprietor valuable rights to use the registered design exclusively by him. Article with registered design shall be marked 'Registered' along with the Registration number.

Trademarks, Patents and Copyrights

Trademarks, patents and copyrights affect the growth and prosperity of every industry and more so with the following industries.

- Chemicals and pharmaceutical industries, boilers, valves, regulators etc.
- Printing, publishing, entertainment industries like the files and recording industries.
- Computer software industry.

It is essential to be familiar with the law relating to the above subjects as these are fundamental to business strategy. It is significant to know the rights and options as well as the legal formalities and requirements necessary for protecting the products and ideas in the present day's competitive markets.

The above are governed by separate laws and they have to be studied separately.

A comparison of the above is as given in the Fig. 8.9

Copyright protection is explicit and clear cut. It protects against copying of entire programs or their part. Damages and relief are readily obtained for infringement.

The central ethical issue posed to individual concerned are:

- Should you copy for your own use a product protected by trade secret, copyright and/or patent law? If every one copies product, very little new products would be produced because creators could not benefit from the results or their work.

Does Your Work Involve Intellectual Property Rights?

Intellectual Property (IP), a creation of the mind, is an asset, and as such it can be bought , sold, licensed, exchanged, or gratuitously given away like any other form of property. Further, the IP owner has the right to prevent the unauthorised use or sale of the property. The most noticeable difference between IP and other forms of property, however, is that IP is intangible, that is, it cannot be defined or identified by its own physical parameters.

Educational institutes deal mainly with copyrights, though some of them do sometimes deal with other IP including trademarks and patents. **Copyright** is an exclusive right to reproduce an original work of authorship fixed in any tangible medium of expression, to prepare derivative works based upon the original work, and to perform or display the work in the case of musical, dramatic, choreographic, and sculptural works. Copyrights are protected in India, by the Copyright Act of 1957 along with the Copyright Rules, 1958 several subsequent amending Acts, and the latest Copyright (Amendment) Act of 1999.

Copyrightable Work

Works of authorship that fall within the definition of copyrightable work include:

- Literary works (books and other writings, musical compositions, paintings, sculpture, computer programmes and films);
- Musical works and accompanying lyrics;
- Dramatic works.
- Pictorial, graphic, and sculptural works;
- Sound recordings; and
- Cinematograph films

Copyright protection comes into existence from the moment the work is fixed in a tangible expression. Copyright registration is not mandatory. However, it is advisable to register because in India copyright registration constitutes prima facie evidence of the validity and ownership of the copyright.

The **US patent system** is governed by the Patent Act first established in 1970 although it has been amended on numerous occasions. It is an exclusive property right to an invention issued by the commissioner of patents and trade marks, US department of commerce. There are three classifications of patents.

(i) Utility – may be obtained for a process, machine article of manufacture, composition of material, or any improvement there of for 17 years. It cannot be obtained on laws of nature, methods of doing business, scientific principles or printed matters.

(ii) Design – granted in new, original, and ornamental design of an article of manufacture for a term of 3 1/2 years, 7 years, or 14 years, as the applicant may elect. It is not concerned with how the article of manufacture was made and how it was constituted, but with how it looks.

(iii) Plant – are granted for 17 years for plants when asexually reproduced with the exception of tuber propogated plants or plants found in the uncultivated state.(periods mentioned above are in US)

US Intellectual property system:

Form of protection	What it protects	Standard for protection	Length of protection
Patents - Utility	Inventions	Useful, Novel, Nonobvious	17 years after patent issues
- Designs	Designs	Ornamental, Novel, Nonobvious	14 years after patent issues
Trade Secret	Information	Secret, valuable	Unlimited
Copy right	Expression in tangible media	Original	Life of author plus 50 years
Trade mark	Identifying symbols	Capable of distinguishing sources of goods	Unlimited

The **patent act** entitles a person to a patent for an invention that if invention is novel, nonobvious and a proper subject for protection. It is given to the creators of innovations or the originators of novel and nonobvious ornamental designs. During the life of the patent, the details of the invention are fully disclosed to the public for scrutiny, thus increasing the likelihood that competitive improvement will hit the market either immediately or on the expiration of protection (or sooner) if the invention is approved.

Three tests to be met for a product or design to be patentable.

i) novelty ii) nonobviousness iii) proper subject.

In contrast to copyrights and trade secrets an inventor must undertake an arduous examination and approval process to receive a patent application.

The invention process includes i) conception and ii) reduction to practice. To the extent that the first to conceive made a reasonable, diligent effort to reduce the invention to practice, he will receive the patent, even though he was not the first to reduce to practice. It is critical that the inventor maintains good records to establish the date of conception and diligence in reduction to practice in case of any later interference. A written disclosure of the invention should be made as soon as after conception as possible. To demonstrate diligence to 'reduce to practice', a written record of developmental activities should be maintained in a bound note book. Daily entries are encouraged with signature on each page and with witness.

Details	Patents	Trademarks	Copyrights
1. Definition	It is a monopoly right grandted to a person who has invented a new and useful article, or new process of making an article. It consists of an exclusive right to manufacture the new article invented or manufacture an article according to the invented process for a limited period. After the expiry of the duration of patent, anybody can make use of the invention.	It is a visual symbol in the form of a word, device, name, letter, numerical, brand, heading, signature or label, or combination of these, applied or used in relation to goods so as to indicate a connection, in the course of trade between the goods any some person who is the proprietor or registered user of that trademark. The identity of that person may or may not be disclosed.	It is a negative right which prevents the appropriation of the fruits of man's work, labour or skill by another person. This protection is given by making any infringement of copyright as unlawful; copyright probihits any person from reproducing or copying any "literary, dramatic, musical or artistic work" without the consent of the owner of the copyright in that work.
2. Dictionary meaning (Little Oxford dictionary)	Document conferring right, title etc., to sell some invention or process so protected.	Device or name legally registered to represent a company or a product, distinctive ch...acteristic.	Exclusive right to print, publish, perform etc., material.
3. Benefits	They encourage inventions on a commercial scale and ensure that ultimately the patented article or process is utilised for the general good of the people at large.	It distinguishes the goods as regards their manufacture or quality, dealt by a particular person, company or firm, from similar goods manufactured or dealt by oher persons, companies or firms.	It ensures that any intellectual or artistic work, which often is immeasurable in terms of money, belongs to its rightful owner or author, and none else is able to derive any benefits by annexation of its fruits.
4. Governing Act	**The Indian Patents Act, 1970,** contains the law governing patents. This Act extends to the whole of India.	**The trade and Merchandise Marks Act1958,** provides for the registration and better protection of trademarks and for the prevention of the the use of fraudulent marks on merchandise. It extends to the whole of India and came into force on 25th Nov.1959.	**The Copy Right Act 1957,** contains the law relating to copyright. It extends to the whiole of India and came into force from 21st Jan.1958. It set up a copyright office under the control of the registered officer for the registration of copyrights. Important amendments were made in the Acts in 1984 and 1992. The copyright 1992 which is pending before parliament, seeks to extend more than effective protection to owners of copyright in the context of technolological developements, affecting the reproduction of musical compostions, videotapes of films and various computer programs and computer generated works.
5. Registration	Section 134 provides that where any country does not accord to citizens of India the same rights in respect of the grant of patents and its protection	A register of trademarks is kept at the head office of the trademarks registry in which all trademark, registered are entered with the relevant particulars. This register is	A register of copyright will be in copyright office in which the names or titles of the works, the names and addresses of authors, publishers and owners of copyright and certain other

- Continued in next page -

	as it accords to its own nationals, then no national of such c ountry shall be entitled to apply for the grant of patent or be registered as assignee of the proprietor or other privileges granted by the Act. Subject to the above provision, an application for a patent for an invention may be made by: Any person claiming to be the true and first inventor of the invention by any person bneing the assignee of the person mentioned above. By the legal representative of any deceased person who immediately before his death was entitled to make suchan application.	divided into two parts. Part A and B. The qualification for registraation in Part B is less stringent than Part A registration. The validity of Part A cannot normally be challenged after the expiry of 7 years from the date of registration. Contents: 1. The name of a company individual or film represented in a special or particular manner. 2. The signature of the applicant for registration or some predecessor in his business. 3. One or more invented words. 4. One or more words having no direct reference to the character or quality of the goods, niot being a geographical name or a surname or a personal name or the name of a sect, caste or tribe in India. 5. Any other distinctive mark.	particulars are entered on making an application to the regis trar. Such registration is however, optional and is not a condition for acquiring copyright. The advantage of registration is a certified copy of an entry in the registrar of copyrights as a primafacie evidence of the particulars entered there in all courts without further proof of production of the original. The registrar publishes in the official gazette all entries made in the register of copyrights. The author of a work has the right to claim authorship of the work as well as the right to restrain or claim damages in respect of (a) any distortion, mutilation or other modification of his work, or (b) any other action in relation to his work which would be prejudicial to his honour or reputation.
6. Terms	Every patent granted under this Act shall be in respect of the process of manufacture of food or a medicine or drug, 5 years from the date of sealing of the patent, whichever is shorter. In respect of any oher invention, 14 years from the date of the patent. A patent shall cease to have effect on the expiration of the aforesaid period, unless it is renewed.	On registration of a trademark, the registrar will issue a certificate of registration in the prescribed form, with a seal of trademarks registry. The registration will be for a period of 7 years but may be renewed from time to time on payment of the, prescribed renewal fee. A trademark removed from the register for failure to pay the renewal fee can be restored on application.	In published leterary, dramatic, musical and artistic work (other than a photograph). Sixty years from the beginning of the calendar year next following the year in which the authro dies. In case of work of a joint authorship, the reference to the author shall be construed as to that author who dies last. In case of a photograph the copyright shall subsist for 50 years from the beginning of the calender year following the year of publicatin. In case of cinematograph films and records, this shall subsist until to years from the beginning of the calendar year next following the year in which the film or the record, as the case may be, is published.

Fig. 8.9 Companies of Patents, Trade Marks and Copyrights

8.10 The creative process

a) **Creativity** means the ability to produce new and useful ideas with the combination of **known principle** and **components** in **novel** and **non-obvious** ways. We find creativity throughout the population, largely independent of :

* sex
* education
* age

There are a number of **models for problem solving.**

(i) **Simple trial and error:-** This method is inefficient

(ii) **Planning/decision making process:-** involves problem definition – identification of alternatives, evaluation alternatives against objectives. Its major thrust is analytical reasoning; its success is enhanced by some creativity in selection of alternatives to be evaluated.

b) Steps identified in the creative process:

- **Preparation** – A period of conscious direct, mental effort devoted to the accumulation and information pertinent to the problem
- **Frustration and incubation**
- **Inspiration and illumination**
- **Verification**
- **Preparation:-** The problem is solved generally at the preparation stage itself as one submerges oneself in the problem while trying to:
- structure the problem
- collect all available information
- understand relations and effects
- solve sub-problems
- explore all possible solutions and combinations that may lead to a satisfactory solution
- **Frustration an incubation:** If the problem is not solved satisfactorily by the analytical process above it will lead, to frustration and the decision to set it aside and get on with some thing else. The problem fortified with all facts gathered about

it 'stews' or incubulates in the subconscious mind.

- **Inspiration or illumination**:- Problem may be solved with a possible solution, occur as a spontaneous insight, when the conscious mind is at rest during relaxation or sleep. Many creative individuals are never without a notepad and pen on their person or bedside table, to write down these flashes of insight.
- **Verification:**- Intuition or insight is not generally correct. The solution revealed in a flash of insight is to be examined by tests and evaluation to ensure a satisfactory solution to a problem.

c) *Characteristics of creative people can be grouped as under:-*

* **Self confidence and Independence**- (Self confident, self sufficient emotionally stable, able to tolerate ambiguity, independent in thoughts).
* **Curiosity** – good observers, good memories drive for knowledge
* **Approach to problems** – open minded, uncritical in the early stages of problem solving, generating large numbers of ideas.
* **Some personal attributes** – More comfortable with things than people, have fewer closer friends, not joiners; have broad intellectual interests – enjoy intellectual games, practical jokes, creative writing, almost always attracted by complexity

d) *Encouraging creativity*

(i) Providing the environment

Creative people tend to be independent, non-comformist, and to work intensively for long periods but with disregard for conventional work hours. People doing routine work and those doing creative work should be separated where possible.

Creative people value working on problems of interests to themselves and working on their own schedule.

(ii) Brainstorming and other creativity techniques.

Brain storming is a process in which members of value analysis team throwout ideas as they occur during the group sessions. It attempts to elicit creative thinking. Suggestions are not evaluated on the spot but are written down as felt as they are made. The emphasis is on '**stimulation**' or '**hitch hiking**'.

This modern method for '**organised ideation**' was first employed in the west by **Alex Osborne** in 1938. A similar procedure was asked in India for more than 400 years. The essence of brainstorming is creative inference for the purpose of developing a long list of ideas. Brainstorming is used as a technique in a product development could also be classified as Consultative and Advisory.

Dhillon describes eight creativity techniques designed for one, two or dozen or more people, including several versions of **brain storming.**

e) *Creativity and Innovation*

Creativity is the engine of innovation. The essence of creativity is combining two or more ideas to arrive at an entirely new one.

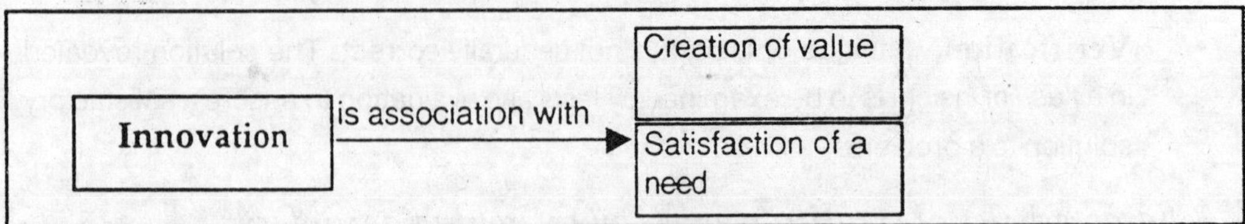

Fig. 8.10 Innovation

Example:- Henry Ford's assembly line was based on combining the production of standard parts; Eli whitney - a concept with idea of bringing the parts to the worker rather than moving the worker for the parts.

Johannes Guntenberg invented the printing press by combining three existing ideas:

(i) **A press** - as used in wine making.

(ii) **Movable type** - as used in minting coins.

(iii) **Wood blocks** - as used in printing calendars and playing cards.

Creativity favours the prepared mind and is often inspired sense of dissatisfaction with existing practice. Creativity depends both people and environment.

According to Jain and Triandis in 1990, a creative environment has the following characteristics.

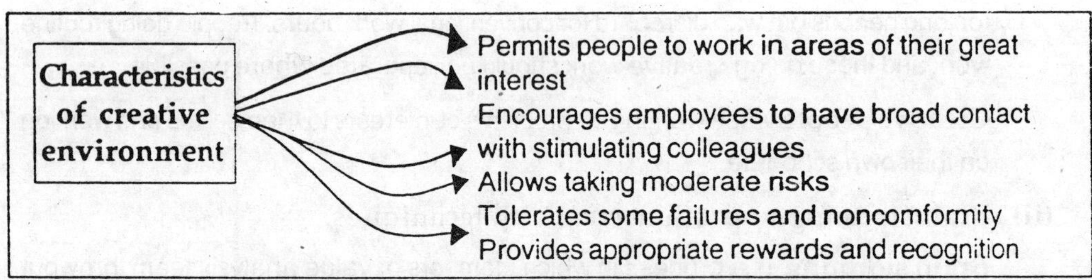

Fig. 8.11 Characteristics of Creative Environment

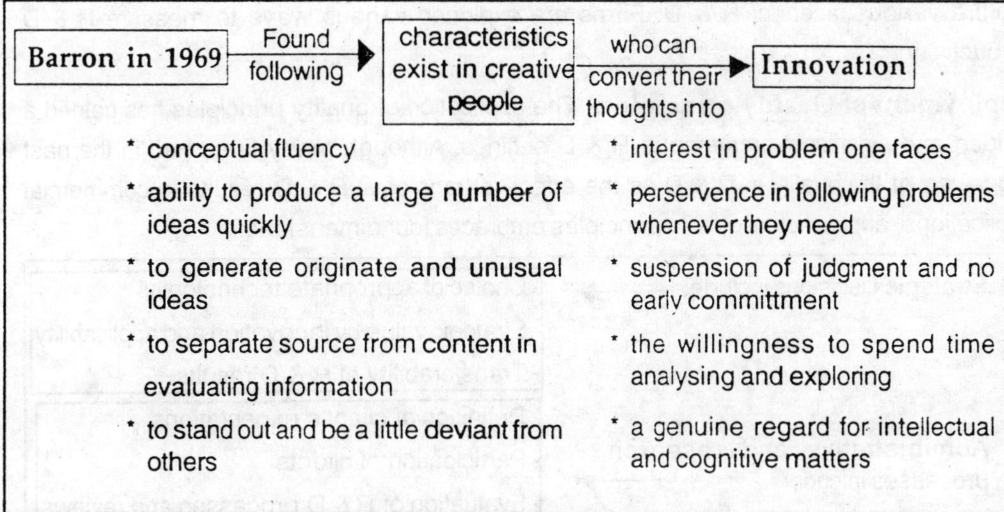

Fig. 8.12 Innovation

Invention (the creative process) only produce "ideas; they are not useful while they are reduced to practice and use, which is the process of innovation. Roberts and wainer have identified five types of people who are needed for technological innovation.

- **Idea generator** – Individual who creates
- **Enterpreneur** – the person who carries 'the ball'
- **Gate keepers** – Researches who maintain a broad network of outside contacts, both with people outside the organisation and the technical literature; they are not appointed people but the wise research manger recognise them and their function
- **Program managers**
- **Sponsor** - the senior managerial person also provides financial and moral support

e) *How to make R & D organisation successful?*

(i) Productivity of In-house R & D:- In recent years, with the shift towards third generation principles and the pressure of the capital markets, firms have been focused on the productivity of the in-house R & D function. This search for productivity has proceeded in two aspects:-

- Bench marking
- Deployment of Quality principles

Bench Marking : A number of firms have begun to benchmark their activities with the R & D function against those of their competitors as well as against those of the best performing firms. One consequence of these has been the development of matrices or measures to capture various facets of R & D. Firms are exploring various ways to measure R & D productivity.

Deployment of Quality principles:- The application of quality principles has gained a sudden and significant presence in R & D settings. Although many firms had in the past conceived of the quality in R & D as the effective transfer of R & D results to commercial applications, application of quality principles embraces four dimensions:-

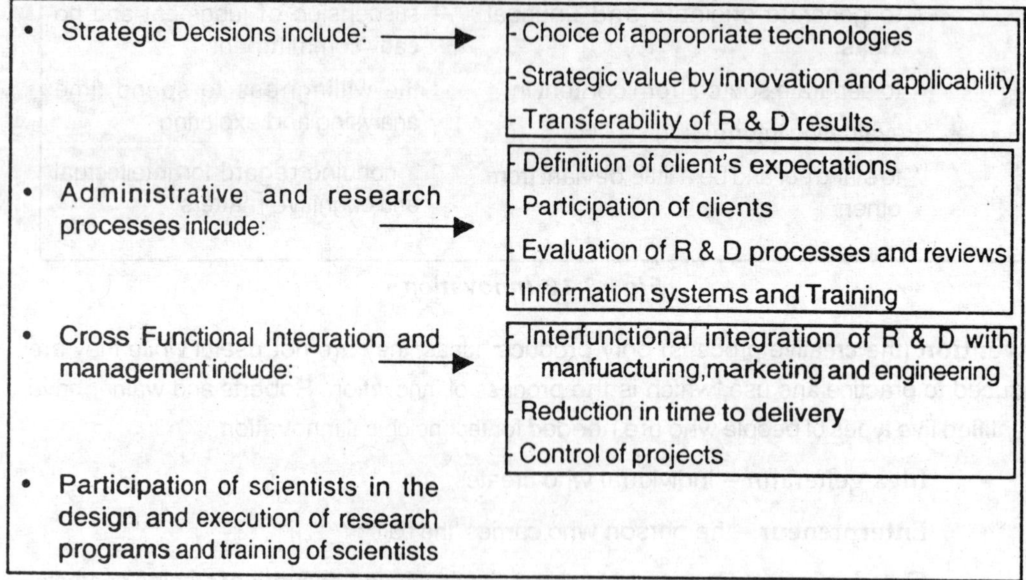

Fig. 8.13 Deployment of Quality Principles

It is found that the productivity of R & D has been enhanced in many organisations by the adoption of quality principles

f) *Evaluating R & D effectiveness.*

A Organisation Effectiveness : Balderston suggest the following eleven criteria for business enterprise R & D

- Ratio of research costs to profits
- Percentage of total earnings due to new products
- Share of market due to new products
- Research costs related to increase in sales
- Research costs to ratio of new and old sales
- Research costs per employee
- Ratio of research costs to overhead expenses (administrative and selling expenses)
- Cash flows (for research expense – Both outflow and inflow)

- Research audit (including indicators of administrative and technical objectives such as costs, time, completion dates, probability of the success/ commercial success, expected market share/profits - ROI, design and development
- Weighted averages of costs and objectives
- Project profiles (a more complex weighted scoring of each project using criteria as those in the research audits)

Individual Effectiveness:

Individual researchers effectiveness can be evaluated by the normal techniques:

- Performance appraisal
- Management by objectives (MBO), emphasising research objectives
- Few quantitative measures, like:
  - number of patents and publications
  - citations by other of those publications

This gives limited insight into research effectiveness.

g) *Support for R & D*

Quality supporting services for the highly trained scientists and engineers to make them work more efficient and productive. The assistance of special types needed in research and engineering are:-

- Technician support (to carry out repetitive testing and other functions)
- Technical library
- Shop support of mechanics, carpenters, glass blowers to produce test and research equipment based on researcher's sketches.
- Technical publication support (including typing, editing and graphical support to simplify researcher's production of reports, technical papers and presentations)
- A flexible, responsive system (for approving and acquiring equipment as needed by researchers)
- Ample computer facilities (available to researchers)

8.11 Influence of environmental Trends on R & D.

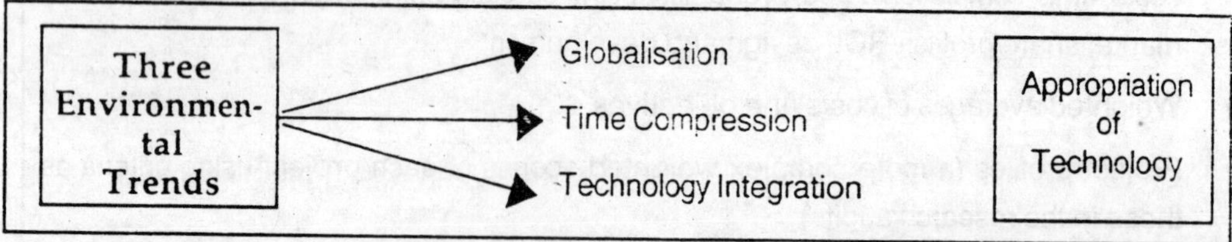

Fig. 8.14 Influence of Environmental Trends on R & D

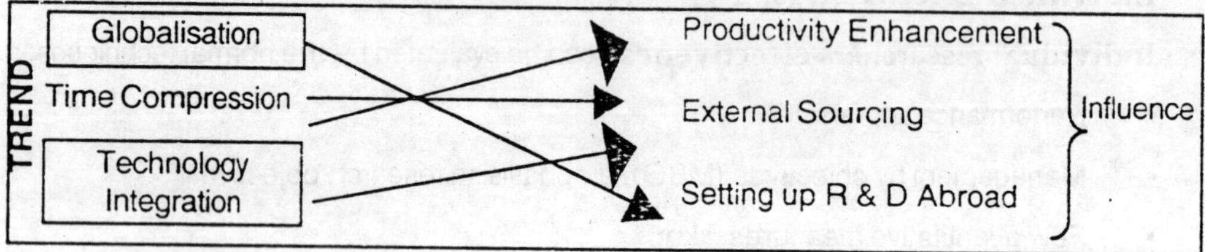

Fig. 8.15 Influence of Environmental Trends and Influence

Globalisation is becoming a global enterprise by expanding into global markets, using global production facilities, forming alliance with global partners, and so on.

From the figure 8.14 you can observe that both **time compression** and the potential for **technology integration** have intensified **search for collaborative arrangements** to appropriate technology.

Time compression, especially the influence of capital markets, has induced firms to apply quality principles and bench marking to **shorten the development time** and enhance the productivity of the in-house R & D function.

Consistent with the environmental trends, nowadays it is seen that firms are increasingly globalizing their R & D activities. Foreign investment to local market need, as well as improved leverage from accessing multiregional resources for technology strategy, US firms and Japanese firms have been increasing the scope of their R & D operations abroad.

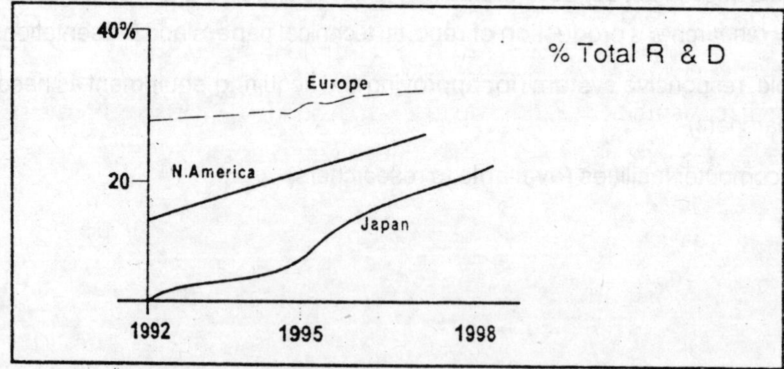

Fig. 8.16 R & D patterns in Europe, Japan and North America

Why do companies establish R & D operations in foreign countries?

Five different reasons motivate firms to invest in global R & D

- To be responsive to national markets:
- To establish an R & D base in the region eg IBM's operations in Asian markets.
- To cooperate with host country laboratories (Japanese firms in US)
- To employ host country R & D personnel.
- To serve as a window on the development in the respective region.

Relative to both Europe and US, the Japanese tend to engage in joint R & D cooperative arrangements with other organisations.

One Example:

Intel is continuing to bet on India's talent pool for high research and development of a wide range of country specific products like **community PC** for the computing needs of rural and farming communities. Intel also has taken up a premier pilot project in India for **WIMAX.**

Questions

1. Define Research.
2. Define development.
3. Explain how technology plays an important role in management and engineering ?
4. Discuss on new technologies emerging from R & D.
5. Distinguish Research, Basic research and applied research.
6. Define Research and Development. How it is useful for organisation and to the nation?
7. Explain steps or functions found in Blanchard's product life cycle with a sketch.
8. What is the difference between R & D and operations? Explain with dimensions.
9. How does the innovations and operations differ along three dimensions 1) Nature of feedback ii) Goal orientation and iii) Interpersonal orientation?
10. Explain the formality levels and leadership lines as applicable to R & D and operating environment.
11. Discuss about multistage decisions (options) embedded in R & D in various stages.
12. Explain a technology life cycle with a sketch.
13. How do you select R & D projects? What is the need for selection ?
14. Analyse the various issues found in the selection of R & D projects.
15. How do you screen research project ideas? Explain with a sketch.
16. Discuss on quantitative approach.
17. Which are the factors considered for rating in the case of initial screening ?
18. Explain a weighted, check list or scoring model.

19. Discuss on protection of ideas with regard to patent rights, trade marks and other marks.
20. Explain US intellectual property system.
21. What does the patent act involves?
22. What does the invention process includes?
23. Which are the three tests conduct to meet for a product or design to be patentable?
24. Define creativity.
25. Explain the creative process.
26. Which are the problem solving models?
27. What are the characteristics of creative people?
28. Explain how creativity is encouraged.
29. What do you mean by brain storming?
30. Distinguish creativity and innovation.
31. Explain the characteristics of creative environment.
32. Differentiate invention and innovation.
33. How to make R & D organisations successful? Explain the criteria involved in this.
34. Explain Bench Marking.
35. How to evaluate R & D effectiveness.?
36. Explain the deployment of quality principles to R & D.
37. Discuss on the effectiveness of individual researches.
38. Mention some of the special types of support needed for research and engineering.
39. Discuss in the environmental trends on R & D.
40. What do you mean by the terms:- Globalisation, Technology integration, Time compression?
41. Discuss on the R & D patterns in Europe, Japan and North America.
42. Why do companies establish R & D operations in Foreign countries?
43. What are the three different regimes that protect intellectual property rights?
44. What do you mean by intellectual property rights? Explain.
45. What is design? Explain.
46. Define design.
47. Define Trademark.
48. Define patents.
49. Make a comparison of trademarks, patents and copyrights.

Chapter - 9

Managing Engineering Design

9.1 Preview

This chapter covers the following topics:

- *Engineering design process*
- *Phases in Engineering design*
  - Conceptual or Feasibility phase
  - Preliminary design or definition phase
  - Final design and verification phase
- *Simultaneous Engineering*
- *Control Systems in Design*
- *Product Liability and Safety*
- *Designing for Reliability*
- *Other 'Ilitis' in Design*

9.2 Designing and Engineering are closely associated. **Designing** is to create something that has never existed before - a solution to a new problem or a better solution to a problem solved previously in a different way.

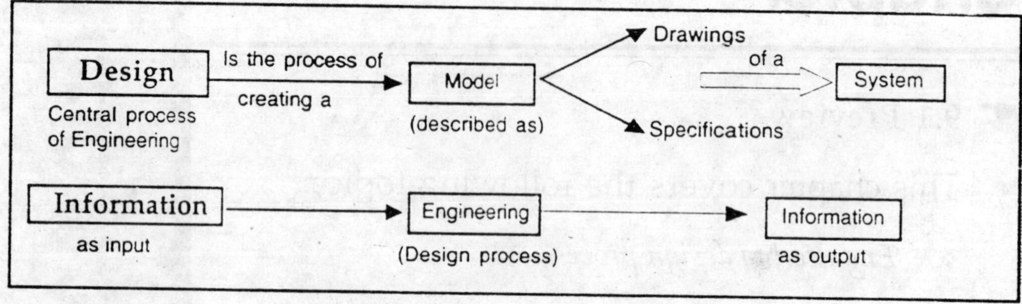

Fig. 9.1 Designing and Engineering

Engineering design is a process of transforming information (input) to obtain information (output). The information provides the input to the process in terms of :

- **Statement of the problem to be solved**
- **Design standards**
- **Design methods**

In the process stage, the engineer performs some logical sequence of activities, decisions and analyses to develop a solution to the problem. This solution will gain importance only when the engineer communicates the solution in the form of:

- Drawings
- Specifications
- Financial Estimates
- Written reports
- Oral presentation

The above will explain and promote the solution. The engineers have to realize the importance of this last step of communication without which all work done would be useless.

9.3 Typical phase in the Systems Engineering phase.

- Each phase starts with an approval to use the resources needed by that phase; agreement on the work to be accomplished in that phase. This is shown at **'Activities of phase'.**

- Accomplishment of the work of the phase – a modest or an amount of work. The results of that phase (Output of phase) are then compiled in terms of:
  - Designs and Specifications; Analysis of reports; A proposed plan for conducting the next phase.

At this point, a conscious and formal review to decide whether the expense of the next phase is to be done to know that there would a substantial increase in resource commitment and that is justified.

Any one of the three types of decisions should come out of this review.

i) **Cancel the development** – if the development cannot be justified

ii) **To go back (recycling)** – Do more work in the present phase if still uncertainties exit.

iii) **To proceed with the next phase**–for increased resourse expenditure with confidence.

The names and number of phases in the systems engineering process vary considerably depending on the industry. The sequence of:

- Concept development / Feasibility Study
- Preliminary design/definition (System level design)
- Detailed Design
- Testing and refinement.

Shown in figure is representative of more lists:-

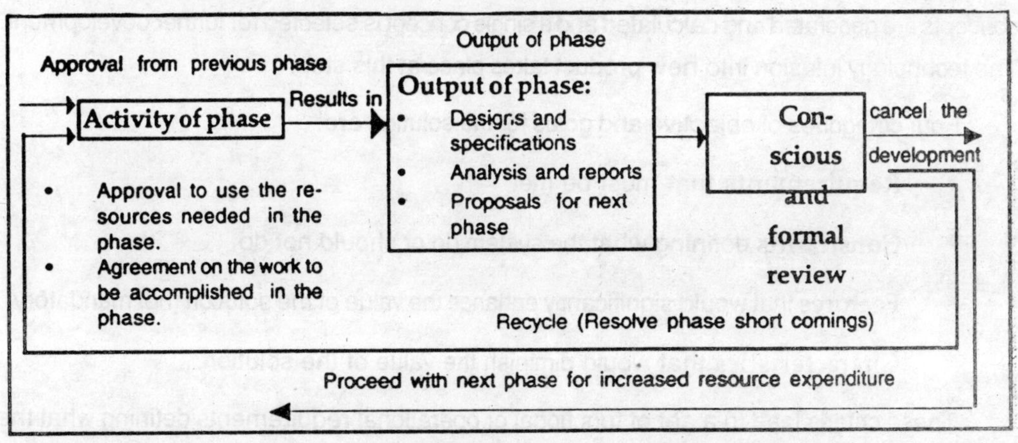

Fig. 9.2 Systems Engineering Process Phases

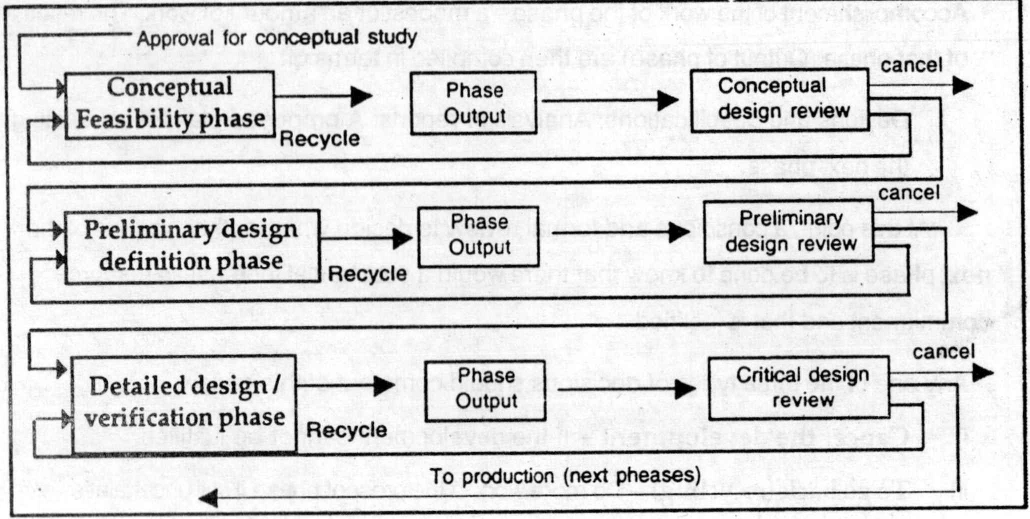

Fig. 9.3 Systems Engineering Design Phase

I) Conceptual or Feasibility phase

During this phase, an analysis of the need of the system for its validity is examined. The careful statement of the design problem, with a clear definition of the design intended for its accomplishment, the performance characteristics it is expected to meet, any possible constraints limiting the solution and the criteria used to judge the quality of the design solution are all examined.

Product concept is a description of the form, function, and features of the product. During concept development, the needs of the target market are identified, alternative product concepts are generated and calculated and a single concept is selected for further development. The technology infusion into new product takes place at this step.

Four categories of objective and goals for the solution are:-

- **Requirements** that must be met
- **Constraints** defining what the system do or should not do.
- Features that would significantly enhance the value of the solution (not mandatory).
- Characteristics that would diminish the value of the solution.

These criteria lead to a set of functional or operational requirements defining what the required solution must / should be able to achieve. Then only the synthesis of possible design can start. It is the synthesis step which most characterise the project as a design undertaking. Creating is a very essential ingredient of engineering design.

The **operational phase** can be broken down into 5 major steps.

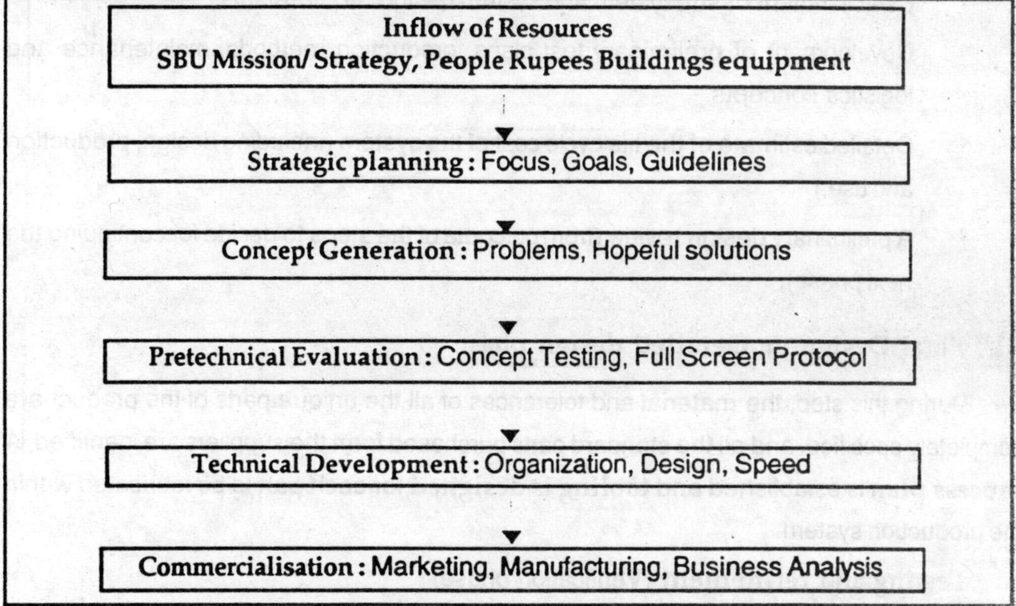

Fig. 9.4 Stages of New product Development.

The concepts are to be screened for:

- Physical realisability (can they be made with the available state-of-the-art).
- Economic worthwhileness (Do they generate a sufficient market to make a profit ?)
- Financial Feasibility.

The best of the solutions is selected for further development in the next phase.

(II) Preliminary design (system level design)

This step consists of the definition of the product architecture and the division of the product into components and subsystems (building blocks are identified). The final assembly scheme for the production system is also usually defined during this step. This phase is to be settled on single system design concept, subsystems needed, designing design requirements and reconfirm the desirability of creating the system. It involves :

- Subsystem identification
- Trade off studies
- System integration.
- Interface design.

- Testing of only components or concepts where uncertainty exists.
- Establishment of subsystem and system design requirements.
- Development of preliminary test plans, production methods, maintenance and logistics concepts.
- Detailed estimate of the life cycle cost of the system (including design, production and use.)
- A preliminary design review (from outcome of the steps to decide for continuing the next phase).

(III) Final Design or Detailed design phase

During this step, the material and tolerances of all the unique parts of the product are completely specified, and all the standard parts purchased form the suppliers are identified. A **process plan** is established and **tooling is designed** for each part to be fabricated within the production system.

Testing and refinement (Verification phase)

Effective design normally requires that design and testing proceed in parallel in an interactive manner. Testing and refinement involve the construction and evaluation of multiple preproduction versions of the product. Early prototypes of the product are usually built with production parts (parts with the same properties are those intended for the production version of the product). Two types of prototypes are:-

- **Alpha prototypes:** Tested to determine whether or not the product will work as designed.
- **Beta prototypes:** Usually built with parts supplied by the intended production processes but may not be assembled using the intended final assembly process. Customers in their own environment often tested beta prototypes.

Testing may begin with a sequence of **mockups** updated as the design proceeds, experimental modes of different kinds and **bread board tests** (in which components similar to the ones being designed are mounted in approximate relationships and tested). Later tests are of the final materials, components, subsystems, and the prototype system. As preliminary tests are being carried out, the design is defined in more and more detail and revised to accommodate problems discovered in testing.

Production ramp-up: In this phase, the product is made using the intended production systems. The purpose of the rampup is to train the workforce and to work out any remaining problems in the production process. The transition from production rampup to ongoing production is usually gradual and continuous. At some part in this transition, the product is launched and becomes available for widespread distribution.

Internal Organizational Mechanisms:

9.4_ Simultaneous Engineering

The **operational phase** consists of several steps starting from:

- Concept development
- System-level design
- Detailed design
- Testing and refinement
- Culminating in production ramp-up.

Fig. 9.5 Operational Phase

In the traditional product development process, these steps were viewed as sequential, with various functional from develop to manufacturing being involved in different steps in the process.

e.g: The design is thrown back between design and manufacturing. The result of a such process has often been:

♦ Extended lead times	♦ Extensive paperwork	♦ Antagonism between design
♦ High reject rates	♦ High warranty costs	♦ Design and manufacturing.
♦ High cost of the products	♦ Quality reduction	♦ Maintainance/and repair difficult

These are very common in industries like automobile manufcturing, product completed the design process described above and was then thrown over the wall to a separate manufacturing engineering department and to the engineering deprtments of suppliers, who would then figure out how to make what has been designed. One mechanism to avoid these pit falls often used everywhere is **'concurrent engineering'**. In this, concept and process design stages are allowed to overlap, thus making the steps in the operational phase parallel instead of sequential. Usually, this is done by **cross functionl teams with manufacturing engineering** being represented in the product design team. It is expected that the use of cross functional teams with representation from manufacturing engineering will lead to three benefits:

- Manufacturing can inform design about its manufacturing capabilities so that design can take these capabilities into account during the design.

- Manufacturing can also suggest ways to design the product for ease of manufacturability.
- Manufacturing can learn enough about the product to design the manufacturing process while the product is being developed.

Here designers (stylists), product planners, design engineers, manufacturing engineers, supplier representatives work together from the beginning to assure that parts are designed well and produced economically with good quality to save time and to prevent problems. It requires that each team member contribute from his side and have a tough understanding with other, by proper communication. We find this approach in many automobile and other industries for the advantages it provides.

Inhouse	Off the Shelf technology utilising technologies	• QFD/concurrent engineering • EMI/Design for manufacturing • Cross Functional Teams
Collaborative	Inward Technology Licensing	Joint development with: - Suppliers - Customers

EMI= Early manufacturing Involvement

QFD- Quality Function Deployment

Fig. 9.6 Speeding Time to Market

(II) Quality Function Deployment (QFD)

QFD is a formal management process currently being implemented in many US companies to improve product development eg:- Mitsubhishi's Kobe Shipyards developed QFD in 1972. Several firms now have adopted QFD thereafter like Toyota in 1978, Fuji Xerox in 1983, Ford in 1983. Since 1983, many US firms like cummins engines, DEC, GM, Hewlett - Packard (HP), Proctor and Gamble, Poleroid adopted QFD. It is applied in many firms in India also.

QFD objective:-

- To reduce the development time
- To enhance the success of new product launches

Concept

- To capture and convert the voice of the customer into the product and process requirements throughout the development process.
- Employs fully empowered cross-functional teams to more product development activities from a sequential to a parallel mode.
- Provides a coherent process to encourage integration across individual functional aspects of new product development, say marketing research and engineering design.

- Emphasizes the need to anchor development activities on systematically collected and ordered data.

QFD allows:

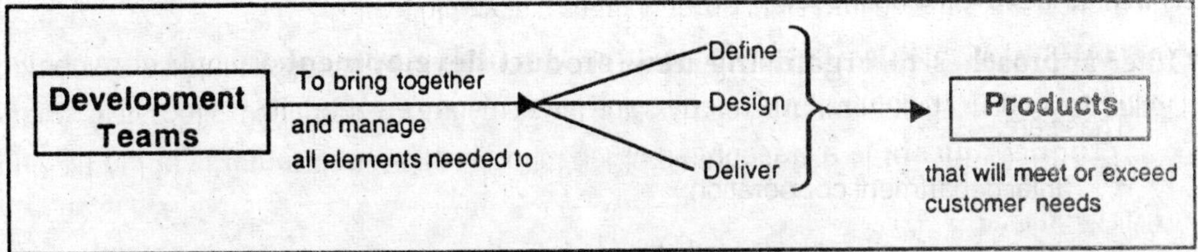

Fig. 9.7 Development Teams.

Unique Feature of QFD

- Visual data presentation format (but engineers and marketing personnel find easy to use)
- Invokes the House of quality which consists of 4 houses.

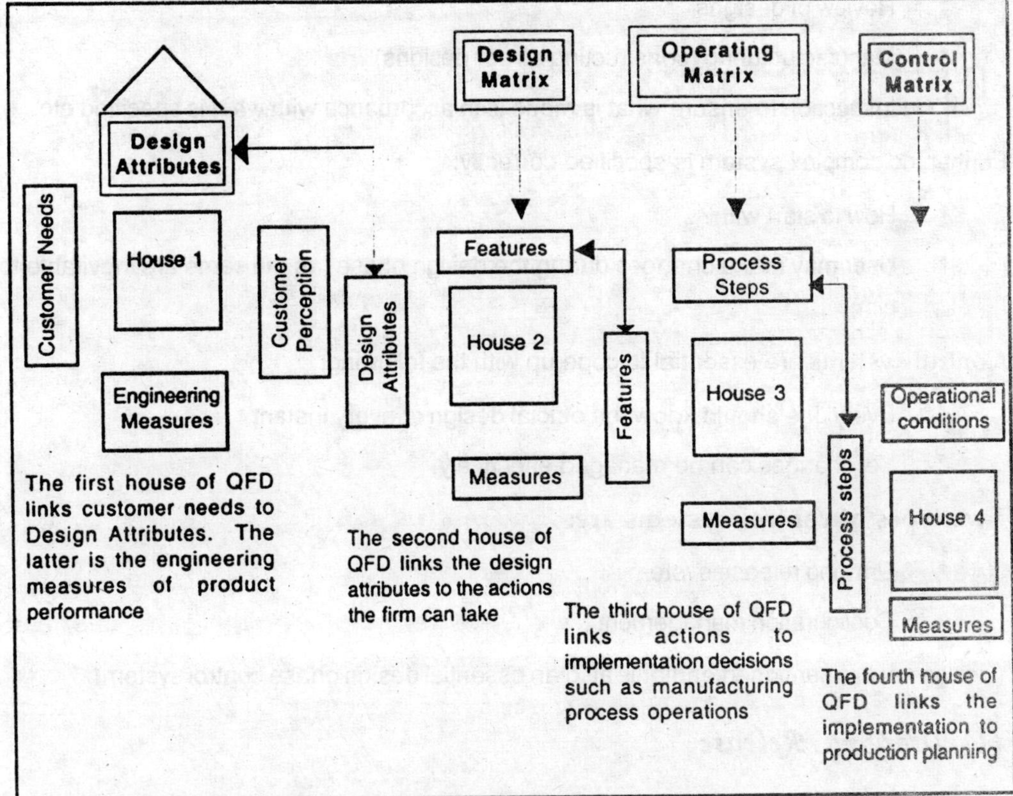

Fig. 9.8 Quality Function Deployment

The **cross functionality developed matrix:** Nature of QFD is expected to lead several specific process-related benefits.

Both QFD and concurrent engineering aim to speed the new product development process as well as improve its success.

Other approaches to organising new product development

These are:-

- Inter department cooperation
- Inter organisational cooperation

This has not been discussed in this book.

Control Systems in Design

Imgine a complex systems where thousands of engineers, technicians, workers are involved in:

- Creating designs
- Review of designs
- Manufactucturing (constructing as per designs)
- Inspection to ensure what is made is in accordance with what is specified etc.

Further, no complex system is specified correctly:

- How to start with?
- User may make changes during the design phase (as the same are inevitable to him)

Control systems are essential to cope up with the following:

- Every one should know the official design at every instant.
- Yet changes can be managed effectively.

Two types of control systems are:

- Drawing release system
- Configuration management

(Design review mentioned earlier is also an essential design phase control system)

(I) Drawing Release

It is the process of identifying when a particular design drawing or change has been officially accepted. The steps of preparing a drawing or release are:-

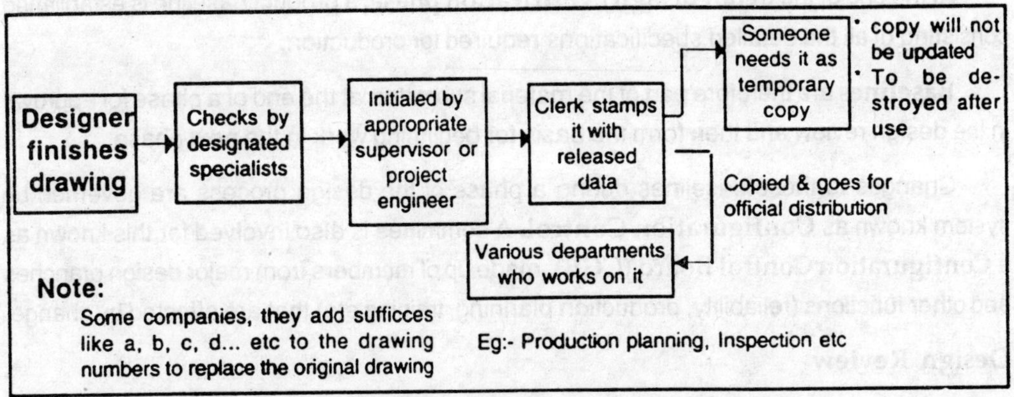

Fig. 9.9 Drawing / Release

Many companies allow use of temporary devices such as the engineering order for minor changes or an engineering stop order, if there is a major change to stop production. These orders are attached to the original drawing and are late superseded by recording their information on the next lettered revision of the drawing.

Now a days, the whole process is computerised and has become easy and simplified. Designs are being created, analysed and reviewed on the computer which will be accessible by everyone as soon as the design change is released.

Configuration Management

The design of a complex system makes design specialists often find some need for advantage in changing the design in one way or another.

The designer cannot tell what the impact of the change will be on other parts of the complex system being developed. A design change in one area may require engineers in a second discipline to change many things including test equipment and training manuals. Unless everyone knows the design criteria, their design neighbours are working towards, they may be investing substantial effort in designing a system that no longer exists. Therefore, there must be agreement as to the current design criteria (or configuration), and there must be a control system to define this configuration and to control changes to it rigorously.

At the end of the **conceptual phase**, a **functional base line** is developed to identify the functional characteristics and design contraints that must be satisfied by the design.

At the end of the **system definition** or **validation phase**, an allocated base line is prepared which describes the performance characteristics each subsystem and component must meet.

At the end of the **detail design / verification phase,** a product baseline is established consisting of all the detailed specifications required for production.

Baselines are therefore part of the material submitted at the end of a phase for approval in the design review and then form the basis for beginning work in the next phase.

Changes to these baselines during a phase of the design process are governed by system known as **Configuration Control.** A committee is also involved for this known as a **Configuration Control Board (CCB),** made up of members from major design branches and other functions (reliability, production planning, training etc) that are affected by change.

Design Review

After completion of every phase, it is desirable to come to an explicit decision. These may be:

- The work of that phase has progressed for enough to justify going on to the next phase at greatly increased resource cost.
- The project should be scrapped at that point
- Further work needs to be done in that phase before proceeding

This is accomplished by a design review board (DRB), consisting of engineering managers not directly involved in the design but with the general type of system and client representative if there is one. All major design groups present their design concept. Other affected 'ilites' (such as reliab<u>ility</u>, maintainab<u>ility</u>, producib<u>ility</u> and safety engineers asseses the design from their view points. The DRB convening authority then makes a decision to proceed with the next phase of the system design, to delay decision pending remedial work or to cancel the project.

9.5 Product liability and safety

Development of Product Liability

From a long time, the relationship between buyer & seller is existing. The Roman philosophy of **caveat emptor** persisted in western thinking. Caveat emptor means let the **buyer beware.**

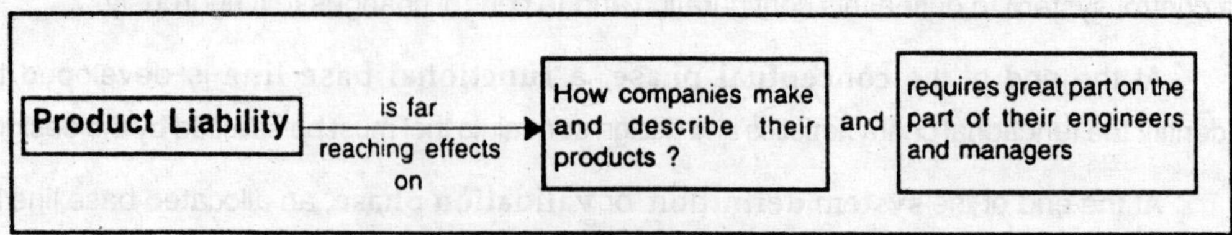

Fig. 9.10 Product Liability

The plaintiff (or the injured party) had to prove manufacturers negligence; he has to show that the manufactuerer omitted doing something that:

- A 'reasonable man' guided by the 'ordinary considerations' that regulate human affairs, would have done.
- Did something that a 'reasonable and prudent man' would not have done?

Alternatively

The **manufacturer,** on the other hand, could defend by showing that the plaintiff did not use the product as a ' reasonable person' would (and was therefore guilty of contributory negligence)

Absolute Liability is the worst threat where a manufcturer could be held strictly liable for failure to warn on a product hazard, even if the hazard was scientifically unknowable at the time of manufacture and sale of the product.

Liability problems are to be tackled prudently and repidly for they can destroy even large companies. One of the companies in USA was forced to bankruptcy in 1982 because of the claims of tens of thousands of workers exposed to asbestos. Some of the companies took extra care withdrawing some of the products after knowing that it would create problems like Johnson and Johnson in Tylenol product. Similarly in India, HMT, a public sector, withdrew the milk separators from all the customers after the lid is blown off at one of their customers end to prevent further accidents.

Liability awards in American courts to reach very high levels of compensation to be paid. Plaintiffs attorneys receive a third or more of the award on contingency basis. The damages claimed are very high.

How to reduce liability?

Designers must foresee such unlikely conditions to protect against product liability. Some of the toy manufacturers had to pay heavy compenstion as the children who used toys had serious injuries in throat, tongue etc. There are several cases which were considered severe in the court of law and the manufacturers liability was considered as the cause.

How can the designers reduce the threat of product liability?

Designers and managers have to anticipate liability problems

- Include safety as an improtant specification for product design
- To use always standard, proven materials and components

- Subject the design to thorough analysis and testing
- Employ a formal design review process where in safety is the main consideration
- Deploy proven manufacturing methods
- Assure an effective independent quality control and inspection process (Never sacrifice quality)
- Be sure that there are warning labels on the product whereever safety is the criteria.
- Supply clear and unambiguous instructions for installation and use
- Establlish a traceable system of distribution to avoid disputes with warranty cards, against the possibility of product recall
- Provide an effective failure reporting and analysis system with timely redesign and retrofit as appropriate.
- Document all product safety precautions, actions and decisions through the product life cycle.

In the recent days, several engineers are involved in product liability work as it has reached primary importance. There are many organisations who are providing supports and services such as system safety society and seeking certification as certified safety professionals. They will be working for manufacturers, goverments or consumer groups. Some will even serve as 'expert witnesses' before courts of law. Ethical codes of the engineering professional require placing the public interest and safety paramount. To summarise, **product safety** is the only one and important way an engineer can meet his or her professional obligations.

9.6 Designing for Reliability

Definition of Reliability

Reliability is:

- the **probability** that a product, piece of equipment or system
- **perform** its intended function
- for a stated period of **time**
- under specified **operating conditions**

This definition has four important elements:

Probability; time;; performance and operating conditions.

Like quality, **reliability** is often defined in a similar 'transcedent' manner as a sense of trust in a product's ability to perform satisfactorily or resist failure. Reliability is an issue that requires a more objective, qualitative statement.

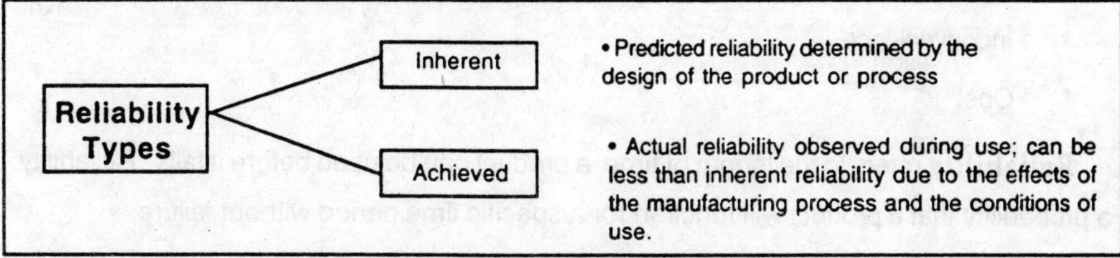

Fig. 9.11 Reliability Types

(I) **Reliability** is defined as probability- that is a value between 0 and 1

(II) **Reliability** is defined as time. Clearly a device having a reliability of 0.95 for 100 hours of operation is inferior to one having the same reliability for 5000 hours of operation, assuming that the device is expected to have a long service life.

(III) **Performance** refers to the objective for which the product or system was made.

Failure is used when expectations of performance of the intended functions are not met.

Two types of failure can occur I) functional failure at the start of the product life due to manufacturing or material defects such as a missing connection or faulty component, and (II) reliability failure after some period of use.

Example of reliability failure are:

- a device that does not work at all (car will not start)
- the operation of a device is unstable (car idles rough)
- the performance of a device deteriorates (gear shifting becomes difficult)

The final component of a reliability definition is operating conditons which involves the type and mount of usage and the environment in which the product is used. Reliability must include extreme environments and conditions as well as the normal usage condition.

Reliability and Risk

Reliability and Risk are closely related. Risks of poor quality are of concern to both producer and the consumer. Some aspects of risk from the producers point of view are:-

- Competition
- Customers requirements

- Warranty and service costs
- Liability costs

Some of the risks of poor reliability borne by the consumers are:-

- Safety
- Inconvenience
- Cost

Reliability refers to the length of time a product can be used before it fails. Reliability is a probability that a product will function for a specific time period without failure.

Risk may be defined as the chance (probability) of injury, damage or loss. We need a basic feeling for probability and statistics for making good decisions in a technological age.

Why to study reliability?

We need to understand the probability laws governing failure patterns in order to better design processes to build reliable systems. Incorrect analysis of failure can lead to disastrous consequences. Reliability is an issue of concern from two perspectives.

(I) To implement total quality management one has to understand the reasons of failure of products- how and why? Designing an effective quality delivery system will require clear understanding of the randomness of failure patterns.

(II) One has to understand the failure patterns of the equipment used in the manufcturing process. With this effective maintenance policies for the equipment can be developed.

Reliability must be an integral part of all organisational functions like marketing, design, purchasing, manufacturing and field service.

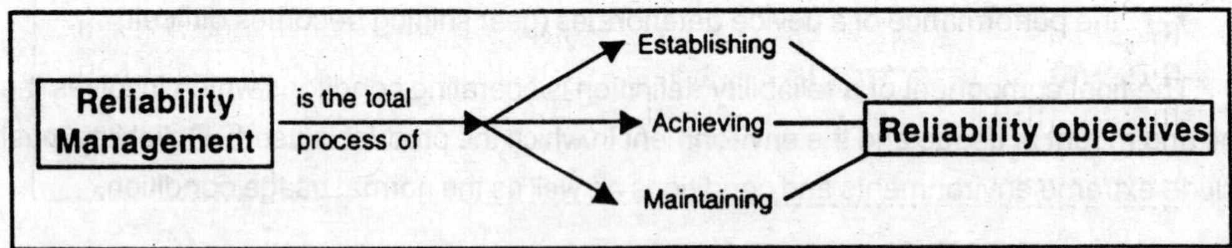

Fig. 9.12 Reliability Management

Reliability Measurement

Reliability is measured/determined by the number of failures occur per unit time during the duration under considertaion (called the failure rate). The reciprocal of the failure rate is used as an alternative measure. Some products must be scrapped and replaced upon failure others can be repaired. For items that must be replaced when a failure occurs, the reciprocal of the failure rate expressed as time limits per failure is called the mean time to failure (MTTF). For repairable items, the mean time **between** failures (MTBF) is used. Every part of the product is designed for a given level of component reliability. The **component reliability** is defined as the probability that a type of part will not fail in a given time period or number of trails under ordinary conditions of use.

Component reliability is usually measured by:

(I) reliability(CR)

(II) failure rates (FR and FRn)

(III) mean time between failures (MTBF)

Component reliability (CR) = (1-FR)

Where $FR = \text{Failure rate} = \dfrac{\text{Number of failures}}{\text{Number tested}}$

$$FRn = \frac{\text{Number of failures}}{\text{Unit hours of operation}} \quad \text{and}$$

$$MTBF = \frac{\text{Unit hours of operations}}{\text{Number of failures}} = \frac{1}{FRn}$$

9.7 System Reliability/Product Reliablity

This is the product of the reliabilities of the parts or components of which the product is composed.

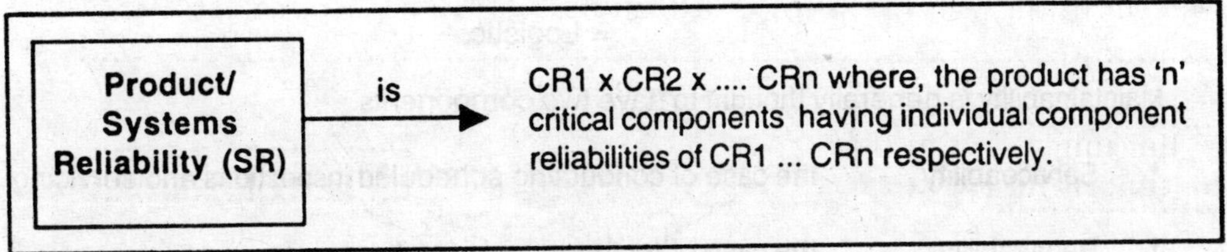

Fig. 9.13 Product/Systems Reliability

The more components in a product or process, the more complete is the system and thus gretear is the risk of failure or unreliability.

Reliability of a product over a given time period is also expressed by the negative exponential distribution as

$e^{\frac{-t}{m}}$ where R= Probability of failure free operation for a time period equal to or exceeding 't'

R = natural algorithm = 2.7183

t = specified period of time

μ =mean time between failures

Eg: If the expected product life is exponential with a mean of five years, the probability of failure free operation for three or more years is $2.7183\left(\frac{-3}{5}\right)$ or about 55%

Maintainability: refers to the restoration of a product or service once it has failed. Since all customers consider maintenance or repairs as undesirable activities, a high degree of maintainability is desired so that a product can be restored to use quickly. Maintanability can be measured by the mean time to repair (MTTR) of the product, mean preventive maintenance time and mean down time.

Product availability is defined as the continuity of service to the customer. A product is available if it is in operational state and not down for repair or maintenance.

Availability is a combination of reliability and maintainability. If a product is higher in both reliability and maintainability, it will also be high in availability.

$$\text{Availability} = \frac{\text{MTBF}}{\text{MTBF+MDT}} = \frac{\text{MTBF}}{\text{MTBF+MTTR+PM+L}} = \frac{\text{MTBF}}{\text{MTBF + MTTR}}$$

(where PM and L are negligible) MTBF = Meantime Between Failure

MTTR = Mean Time To Repair

MDT = Mean Down Time

PM = Preventive Maintenance Time Logistics

L = Logistics

Maintainability is generally thought to have two components.

- Serviceability - the case of conducting scheduled inspections and servicing
- Repairability - the case of restoring service after failure.

☛ 9.9 Designing for Reliability

Designing for Reliability includes considerations of component reliability, system reliability and some of the ways of increasing the reliability of the products at the design stage itself. The three practical approaches are:

- Over design
- Design simplification
- Providing redundancy

Before discussing these, it is desirable to know how the component reliability affects the system reliability in

- Series systems
- Back up or parallel systems

Components and reliability in a series system

The more components in a product or process, the more complex is the system and thus the greater is the risk of failure or unreliability.

(I) Components in Series

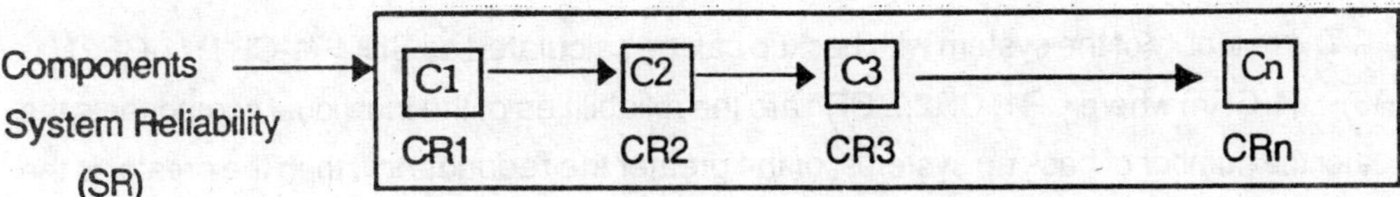

This is a basic structure of a system which contains 'n' components in series SR=CR1xCR2x...CRn

n = number of interacting parts or components in a joint probability relationship

Eg:- If a product has 4 critical components; component reliability of each component = 0.9 (or 90%), then

Reliability of the system (or the product) is SR= 0.9x0.9x0.9x0.9=0.656

System Reliability versus Number of components/Parts

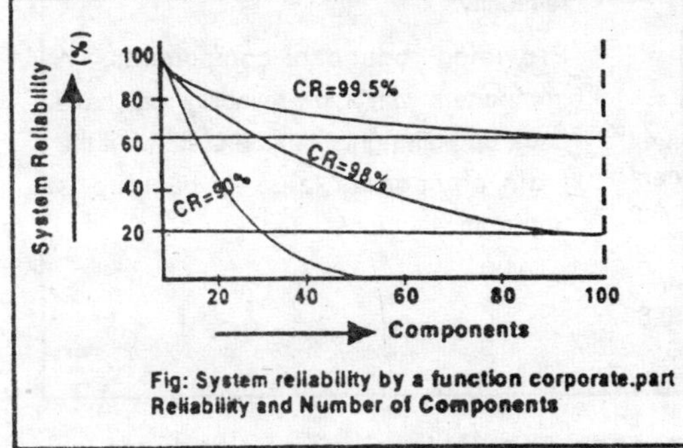

Fig: System reliability by a function corporate.part Reliability and Number of Components

From the figure, we can interpret that if there are 50 critical parts/components in a product (system) each having a component/part reliability of 0.9 (90%) then the reliability of the product as Zero. Similarly, when the components/parts have reliability parts of 99.5% then the system reliability is 66% when there are 100 critical components or parts.

Fig. 9.14 System Relibility as Function of Component/Part

(II) Back up or parallel systems:-

In situations where the failure of a component or system would be problematic, dangerous or catastrophic, then back up systems would be in place to operate in eventual failure of the principal system. The components would be in parallel

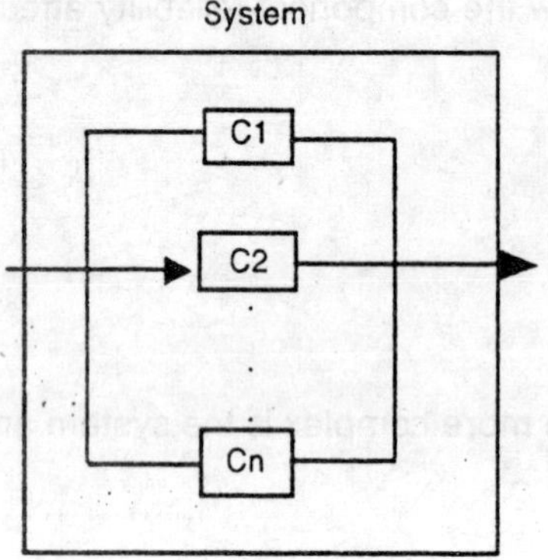

Hospitals have backup energy systems (diesel generators) in case of failure or principal power supply. Banks have back up computer systems containing client data should one system fail. When backup systems are in place, this implies redundancy when the back up units are not normally operational

Fig. 9.15 Parallel Systems

The reliability of the system with backup can be calculated as Sr= 1-(1-CR1) (1-CR2) (1-CR3) ....(1-CRn) where CR1, CR2,...CRn are the reliabilities of the individual components the greater the number of back up systems, or the greater the redundancy, then the greater is the reliability of the system.

Eg:- CR1= 0.99; CR2=0.95, then the system reliability is

SR=1-(1-0.99) (1-0.95)=0.9995=99.95%

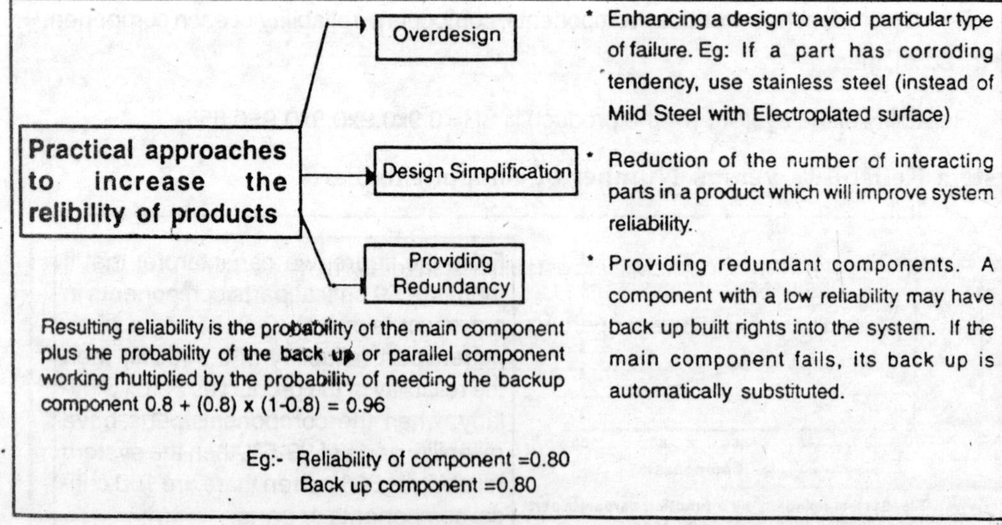

Fig. 9.16 Practical Approaches to Increase the Reliability of Products.

Thus the system reliability is greater than with a single component when the back up components of quantity n have the same reliability (CR1), then the system reliability would be:

SR= 1-(1-CR)n

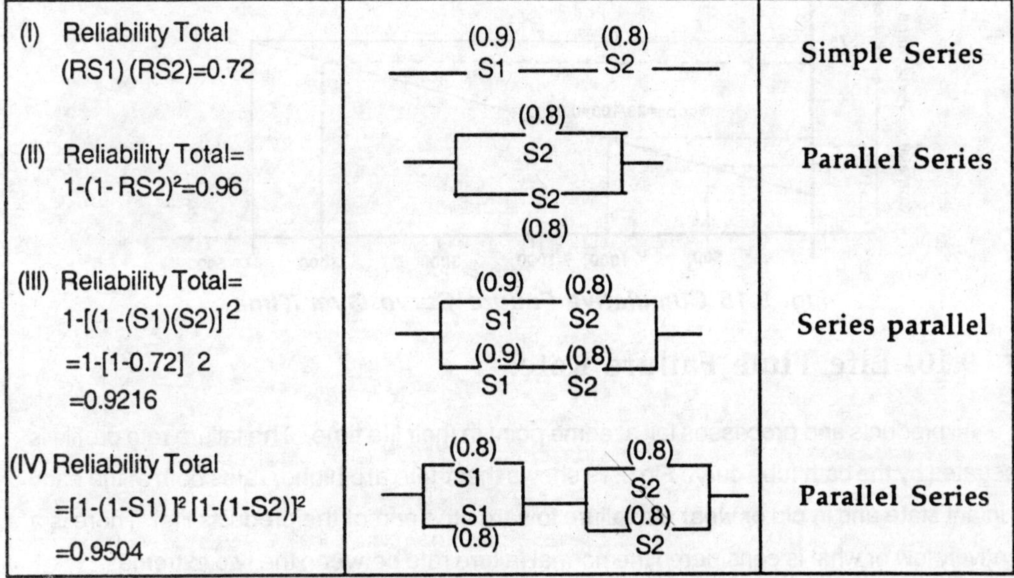

Fig. 9.17 Relationship Models I) Series II) Simple parallel III) Series in parallel IV) Parallel in Series

9.8 Developing Reliability over the product life cycle

Reliability is a continuing concern throughout:

- Design
- Manufacture
- Initial use

} of complex system

First step in planning for reliability is establishing a reliability goal.

- a probability of successful operation and its complement
- the acceptable failure rate for the system

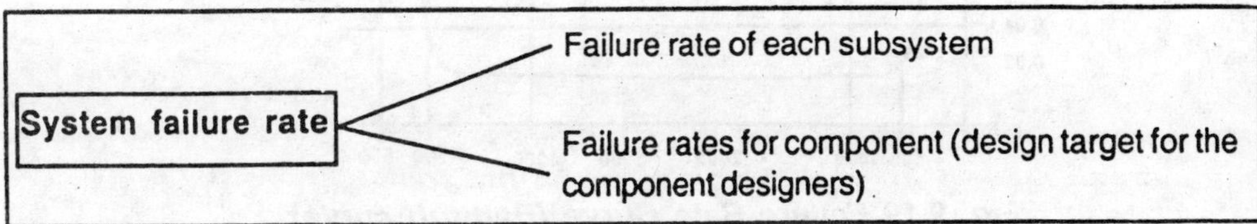

9.9 Failure rate and product life characteristics curve

In considering the failure rate of a product, suppose that a large group of items is tested or used until all fail and that the time of failure is recorded for each item. Plotting the cumulative percentage of failures against time results in a curve shown below.

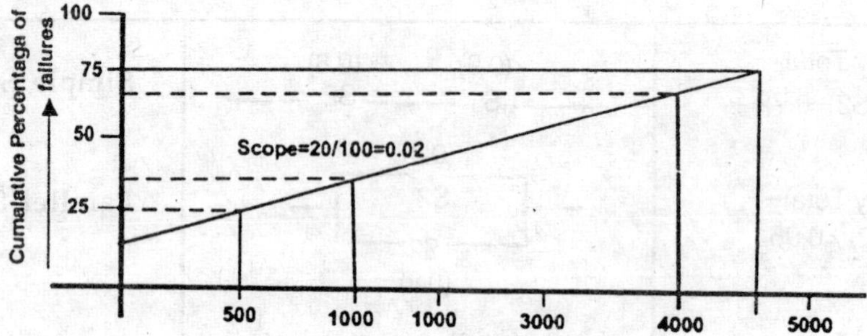

Fig. 9.18 Cumulative Failure Curve Over Time

9.10 Life Time Failure Rate:

All products and processes fail at some point in their life time. The failure rate profile is illustrated by the bath tube curve Fig 9.19 shows that there are higher rates both at the early or infant state and in old or wear out failure towards the end of the products life. There is a relatively low or what is considered the normal failure rate between the two extremes.

9.11 Infant mortality

At the early stage of the product life, components may be fragile as they have not been 'run in' or conversely operators are not familiar with equipment and because of bad use, the equipment break down eg washing mchines or power lawn movers. Some firms may 'run in' or 'burn in' a product before it is released in the market to ensure that all the teething (start up) problems has been overcome. To cover the possibility of failure in the early days of a products life certain firms provide a 90 day warranty for their products. The term 'infant mortality' is obviously used because young children are fragile at this point of their life.

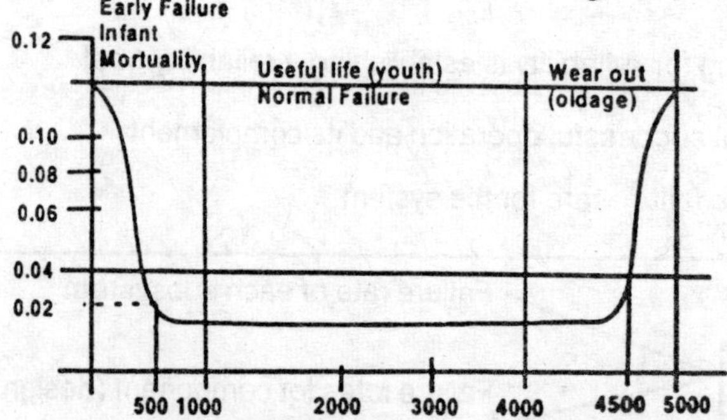

Fig. 9.19 Failure Rate Curve (Bathtub curve)

Normal Failure: Once a product line has been used for some time, it is normally pretty robust and with correct preventive maintenance, will last throughout its expected life time. During this period, the failure rate is pretty constant and low. This period can be considered as **'youth'**

Wearout Failure: Towards the end of the life of a product or process, the failure rate starts to increase rapidly again as parts become used or worn out and eventually fail. This period is like **'old age'** of human. If limited data are available, the failure rate is computed among the following formula.

$$\text{Failure rate (Fn) or } \lambda = \frac{\text{Number of failures}}{\text{Total unit operating hours}}$$

$$\text{or alternatively Fn or } \lambda = \frac{\text{Number of failures}}{(\text{Unit tested}) \times (\text{Number of hours tested})}$$

Techniques used in designing components and subsystems are many.

- One is to 'start with the best' to specify and use parts of known high quality.
- Providing redundancy, using components in parallel as previously modeled. (A Jet airliner will have two, three or four independent hydraulic lines or electrical wires to control a critical function routed through different paths. Single incident will not affect them)
- Reliability is enhanced by assuring a comfortable factor of safety which is the ratio of minimum strength provided by the design to the maximum stress anticipated in use.

9.12 Other "Ilities" in Design

'Ilities' is casual term in aero-space industries for a loosely defined set of specialist disciplined ended in the suffix **"Ility"** that enhance effective design in some effect.

Eg:- Availa**bility**, Maintaina**bility**, producti**bility** etc.

Human factors engineering, standardisation and engineering is also studied along with **ility.**

Maintainability:- It is already defined in para No 9.8.

It is an inherent design characteristic of a system or product

Maintainability:- It is pertaining to the performnce of maintainence to have easy, accuracy, safety and economy actions.

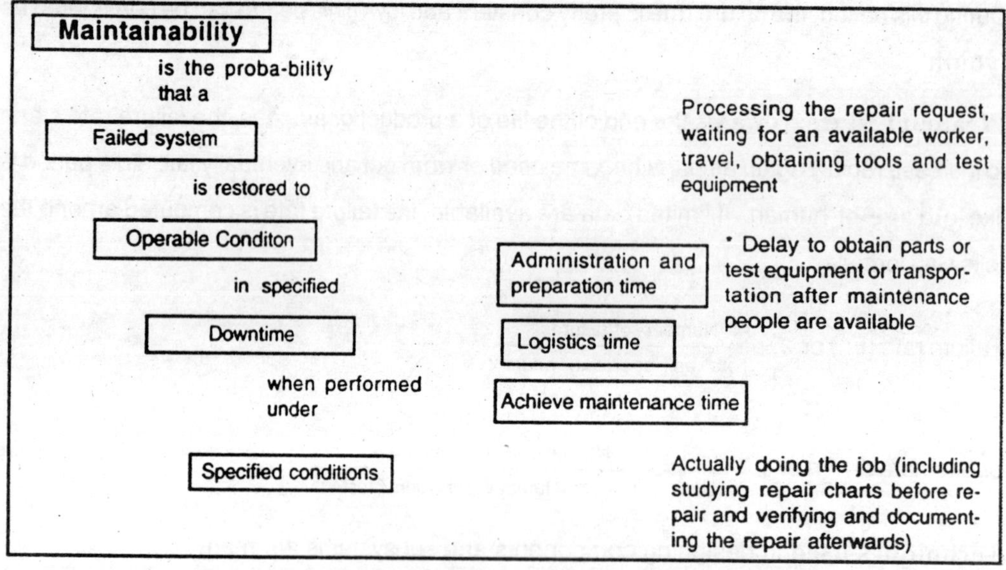

Fig. 9.20 An Understanding of Maintainability

Two types of Maintenance are:

- Corrective Maintenance (Made necessary by failures)
- Preventive Maintenance (Designed to prevent failures)
- Predictive Maintenance (is also sometime used to predictive in advance the positive failures)

9.14 Human Factors Engineering:-

(Also known as Erogonomics). This is concerned with ways of designing machines, operations and work environments to match human capacities and limitations.

Ergonomics

Ergonomics, also known as **worksite design,** or **human factors engineering** or **biomechanics** or **engineering psychology** is one of the important topics under **Methods Engeneering.** It explains how human beings physically interfacw with their work and deals with designing of jobs and equipment to suit the physical abilities of individuals (senses, movement etc). Physical aspects of the workplace which influences employees productivity and morale are of great concern in Ergonomics.

Ergonomics deals with the following:

- To make the workplace pleasant, by using pleasing colours on the walls, roof; create private offices, work spaces; provide gtood lighting, interesting pictures, gardening etc.
- Work flow improvement, reduction of unnecessary motions causing fatigue, economy in human efforts, development of better working conditions, placing team members close for interaction, creation of lounges for rest breaks, etc.
- Provide elegant, suitable office furniture to fit one and all etc.

9.14 Standardisation

- A standard is defined as:-

  - a set of specifications for parts

  - materials

  - processes intended to achieve uniformity

  - a specified quality
- Important purpose of a standard is to place limit on the number of items in the specifications so as to provide a reasonable inventory of tooling, sizes, shapes and varieties.
- In the earlier days, there were no standards for bolts, nuts screw threads etc. Varieties were also too many. One size of nut would not fit the other size of bolt. Hence confusions existed. Now the standardisation of all types of raw materials and components are existing.

Standardisation and Variety Reduction

A separate group is organised in most of the large industrial undertaking to study material standardisation, variety reduction, rationalisation and codification. In some cases, this department is known as **standards department** which may come under designs and development activity. A number system is used to reduce the number of sizes or ratings to which a family of products should be produced to cover the full range and at the same time to satisfy the customers. Preferred numbers are arranged in geometric progression. e.g., 1,3,9,27,... etc. It is found customers tend to be content with geometric progression, geometric progression leads to greater variety. For example, Electric motros between 10 HP to 1000 HP can be considered as 10, 33, 100, 330, 1000 HP, in 5 sizes, instead of having all the sizes (10 x 3.3, 33 x 3.3., 100 x 3.3, 330 x 3.3).

Indian Standard Institution

Indian Standard Institution (ISI), now known as **Bureau of Indian Standards** (BIS) was established in January 1947 to formulate Indian standards in almost all sectors of the economy. The work of standards formulation is done through a large number of technical committees.

Standards are authoritative statements of the criteria necessary to ensure that the material, product or procedure is used for its intended purpose. Product standards generally prescribe optimum levels of quality, safety and performance as well as sampling and methods of practical evaluation.

National standard bodies, vested with the task of standardisation are established all over the world. Bureau of Indian Standards is the National Standards body in India.

BIS has a central office at New Delhi and 5 regional offices in different zones like central, eastern, northern, southern and western. It has offices all over India, in mostly all the capital cities of the states and inspection offices at many places.

More than 1600 Indian standards have been formulated so far; of these almost 60% are product specifications, in which basic aspects of quality are laid down in quantifiable terms as far as possible. The remaining 40% standards are no methods of testing, codes of practice, glossary of terms, sampling etc.

For the common man, it is normally not possible to assess the quality of the product purchased, at its face value i.e. by merely looking at it, touching or smelling it. Standards may be used as the basis to assess the quality of the product to be purchased.

9.15 Producibility

After the design of the product, careful attention is needed to produce the product most economically and efficiently for competing in the market. The engineers who are familiar with manufacturing techniques, production capabilities should be involved in reviewing components designed for tolerances, materials and shapes that are more producible.

- manufacturing preferences
- performance consequences if certain critical specifications and tolerances are relaxed.
- manufacturing method is to be simplified, ultimate product is produced most economically and at the needed time.

9.16 Value Engineering Analysis

Cost reduction can start with the products by having a 'brain storming' session using a technique known as **'value analysis.'** Representatives of several departments like R&D, purchasing, production, sales and accounts get together at regular meetings to compare the cost of a product with the value being obtained from it, and in the event decide as against possible alternatives, whether the expenditure involved in making it is really justified. This analysis should periodically be applied to innovations as well as having a hard new look at all existing products.

9.17 Value Engineering

When the above technique aims at preventing, instead of identifying, unnecessary cost, it is more usual to refer to **'value engineering'**. But the team approach in same, with a full scale attack on design and development right through to some basic questions may be asked:

(i) What exactly does the product/component/part do?

(ii) Is the part really needed?

(iii) How much does the product or part cost?

(iv) Could some alternative do the job equally well and be produced more cheaply?

The team may be able to recommend after thought, substantial cost-saving changes in design, material or process. A typical cost break down shows that more than 40% of that cost could be made up of raw materials and bought in components, 10% direct labour. Hence, there remains considerable scope for economy.

It is essential that the right attitude to cost savings should percolate from the top downwards.

Questions

1. Define design.
2. Explain Engineering Design.
3. Discuss the typical phase in the systems engineering phase.
4. What do you mean by activities of phase?
5. Which are the three types of decisions we arrive at while the review is made in the systems engineering phase?
6. Explain system engineering process phases.

7. Explain system engineering design phase.
8. Explain Conceptual or Feasibility phase pertaining to systems engineering design phase.
9. Explain the preliminary design stage.
10. Explain the final design or detailed design stage.
11. Explain the verification (Testing and refinement) phase.
12. What do you mean by production ramp up?
13. Explain the 5 steps of operational phase.
14. Define concurrent engineering.
15. Define Quality Function Deployment (QFD).
16. What are the objectives and concepts of QFD?
17. What is the unique features of QFD?
18. Explain the control system in Designs.
19. What do you mean by configuration management?
20. Define Product Liability. Explain the development of product liability.
21. Which are the ways of anticipting liability problems by designers and managers?
22. Define Reliability. How to design reliability? Which are the diferent types of reliability? Give some examples of reliability failure.
23. Why to study reliability? Give the meaning of reliability management. Explain how the reliability is measured.
24. Define the terms: Maintainability, Availability, Serviceability, Repairability.
25. Explain the components and reliability in a series system or back up or parallel system.
26. Explain how to develop reliability over the product life cycle.
27. Explain the failure rate and product life cycle characteristic curve.
28. Describe a failure rate curve or a bath tub curve.
29. Which are the techniques used in designing the components or subsystems?
30. Explain all the 'ilities' in design.
31. Define maintainability. Explain what do you understand by this term.
32. Explain the tems: Human Factors Engineering, Standardisation, Producibility and Value Engineering Analysis.
33. Explain Standardisation.
34. Explain Value Analysis.
35. Explain Value Engeneering.

The Engineer's Role in Production Activity

Chapter - 10

10.1 Preview

This chapter covers the following topics:

- *Introduction to Planning Production Activity*
  - Vital Nature of Production
  - The Engineer in Production activity
  - Intensity of use of engineers
- *Planning manufacturing facilities*
  - Plant location
  - Plant design
  - Plant layout
- *Quantitative tools in production planning*
  - Inventory control
    (Types of inventory, Economic order quantity, Problems with EOQ analysis)
  - Break even charts
  - Learning curves
- *Production planning and control*
  - Introduction
  - Steps in production planning
  - Current production planning and control systems (Material requirement planning (MRP), Manufacturing resource planning (MRP - II), Just-in-time (JIT), Synchronised manufacturing.
- *Flexible Manufacturing Systems (FMS)*
  - Need for FMS
  - Some definitions
  - Advantages of an FMS

10.2 The Engineer's Role in Production Activity

Production is the conversion of raw materials to end product by using processes, machines, men, tools and so on. It is the process by which goods and services are created. Production implies the creation of goods and service to satisfy human needs. **Production** is considered as a system. This view is known as '**Systems Concept of Production**'. **Production** is considered as a crucial function which creates goods and services where as **marketing function** generates demand for products or obtain customers orders, **finance function** keeps track of how well the organisation performs by taking care of cash inflows and cash outflows, **human resources function** looks into the people's aspect of the organisation and the best utilisation of the people in the organisation. **Production function** is having a central role in achieving the objectives of any business organisation.

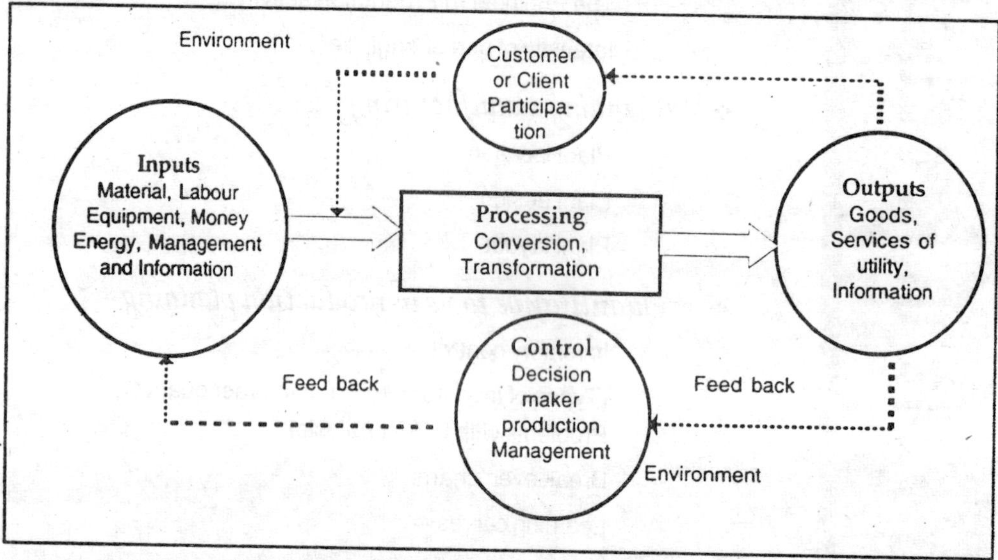

Fig. 10.1 Production Function as a System

Production organisations vary with :

- The industry involved
- Size of the organisation
- Type of production (Mass Production of standard items or small quantities of special items)
- Other factors

It would be better to explain a typical manufacturing plant based on a model, which we can generate the functions needed in the organisation and the way the managers can fit into such organisations.

10.3 Organisation Structure (Sample)

One of the structures of the organisation is shown below in figure 10.2, producing products researched, designed, financed and marketed at the corporate office seperate from the plant.

In the example shown below, the **General Manager** or the **Plant Manager** is considered as the chief.

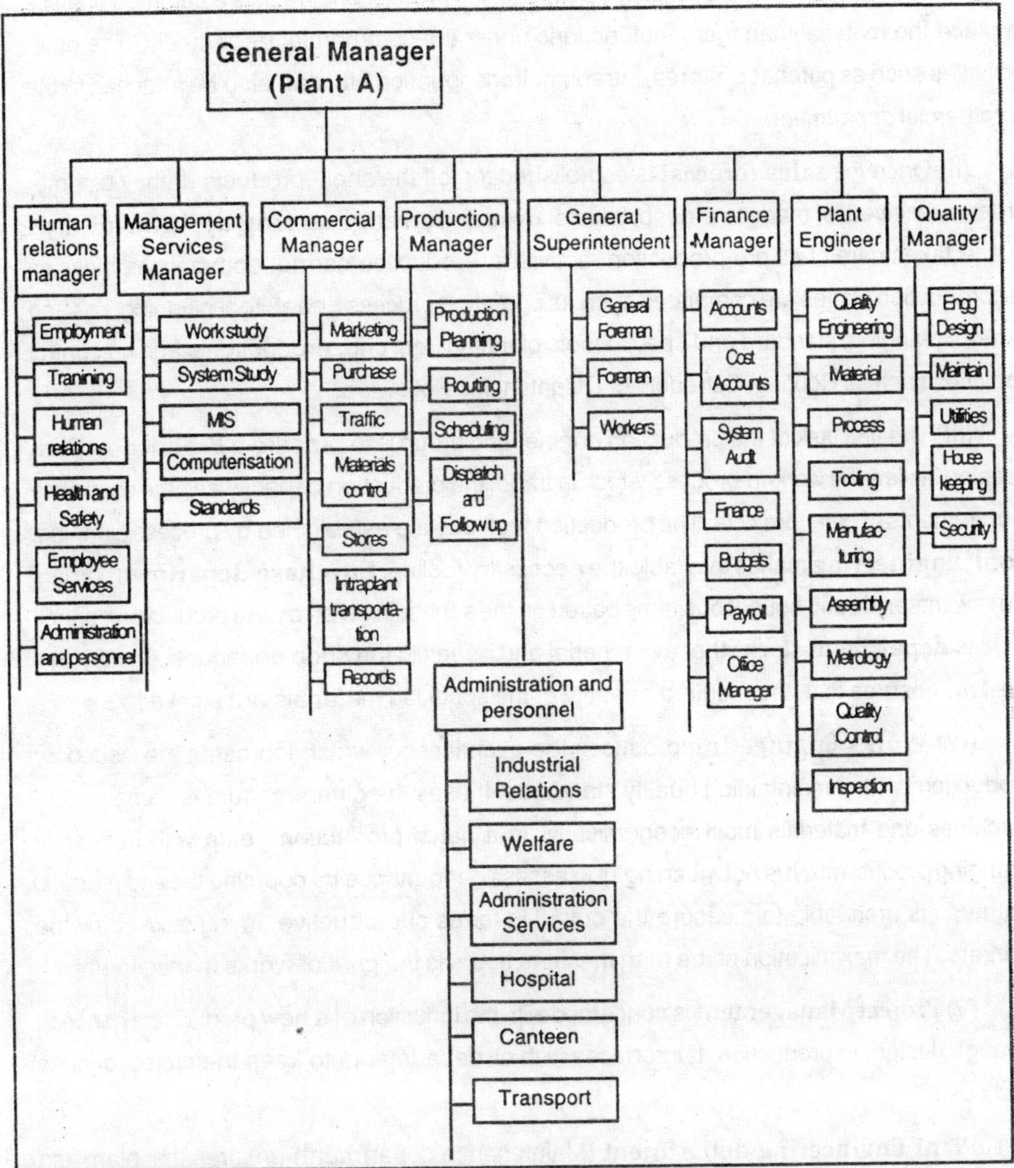

Fig. 10.2 A Sample Organisation Chart for One Plant of a Multiplant Company

In a manufacturing company, undoubtedly the pride of place is occupied by **Production Management**, but at the same time it is not to be considered that other functions are less important. The department under each head are also shown on the chart and their roles are briefly explained in the subsequent paragraphs.

(I) **Production** starts with **marketing.** Commercial department handles all marketing activities such as market forecast, sales planning and product pricing. It is a common practice to place the material management functions under the commercial department. The other activities such as purchase, stores, intraplant transportation etc. can also be attached to the commercial department.

(II) Once the **sales forecast** is established for 'off the shelf' products or the customer order is received for made to order products, **production engineering department** steps in and takes care of all pre-production activities. Production cannot commence unless all preproduction stages are completed such as operation process sheet, tool planning, jigs and fixtures planning, standard and special tools planning, tool crib, production planning control activities such as Routing, Scheduling, Dispatch and Follow up.

(III) The first task of the production engineering group is to prepare a **Production Plan** keeping in view the work-in-process, stock in trade, the production capacity and the conflicting requirements of other projects. The production methods are established by process planning. **Tool Engineering** makes available the necessary tooling. **Purchase department** orders the raw materials and bought out items based on the schedule given by the production control. **Stores department** stocks the raw material and issues to the shop on request. **Inventory control** ensures that the required quantity of the specified materials are stocked.

(IV) **Works Engineering** produces the quantities for which job cards are issued by production control maintaining quality standards. It uses the given resources namely men, machines and materials most economically. In a batch production setup with frequently changing product mix, it is not meaningful to assess performance by counting the end product. Rather, it is preferable to measure the output in terms of productive timing clocked by the workers. The maximisation of the man machine hours is the goal of works management.

(V) **Project Management** is concerned with the induction of a new product firm concept, through design, to production. It interfaces with all departments to keep the project on time and cost.

Plant Engineering department (Maintenance department) ensures that plant and machinery are available in good running order for production as per schedules released by production control. It takes care of the servicing, repair and overhaul of all production facilities. **Factory construction** and **safety engineering** are also placed under this department.

(VII) **Inspection and quality** control ensures that the product is as per specifications and the material, men, machines and processes employed in the factory are right for meeting the desired quality standards. This includes **metrology area** (Calibration of instruments)

(VIII) **Management Services department** has grown out of the old **industrial engineering** department. It renders system and decision making support to all other departments in a factory. Its main functions are :

- Support for long range planning
- Capacity planning and plant balancing
- Man power planning
- Work study
- Systems Study
- Design and management of incentive schemes.
- Design and implementation of Management Information Systems including computerisation.

(IX) Finance

This manages the following departments and activities :

Finance	Budgets	Accounts	System Audit
Financial Forecasting, Financial planning, Funds management Scrutiny and Concurrence of:- - Project Reports - Proposals for manpower, Consultancy - Training works and services - Draft contracts - Purchase proposals - Purchase orders	Preparation of Production, Capital, Revenue, Cash, purchase Manpower and Departmental budgets linking Performance to expenditure	Preparation of profit and loss statement and balance sheet	Physical verification of assets and audit of procedures and transactions

First line production management positions such as foreman or assistant foreman provide an excellent opportunity to learn production problems and to test one's wing as a leader. Most such positions will be filled by non-engineers but they provide a good starting place for the engineer interested in manufacturing management. Positions as general foreman and superintendent or production manager are natural steps up the promotional ladder. Several other positions may call for engineers in larger plants

eg. :-
- The safety engineer
- Materials control engineer
- Purchasing (where the technology of the item being purchased is paramount)

More often the above posts and others (technical employment for eg) will be staffed by technical people at the corporate level, with nonengineers implementing their recommendations at the plant level.

10.4 Comparison of Japanese Companies with US Companies

It is observed from a study at US that with extensive automation in production that the technological literacy of a company workers' is critical.

Japanese Companies	US Companies	
> 40% of work force was made up of college educated engineers, all trained in the use of CNC (Computer Numerically Controlled Machines) Japanese factories had an average of 2 1/2 times CNC machines, 4 times as many engineers, and 4 times as many people trained to use the machines compared to US.	8% of workers are engineers < 25% have been trained on CNC machines . US industry is not ready to employ engineers as intensively as will be neccessary in manufacturing.	• It may be concluded that in US in the beginning of new millenium, it is faced with new challenges in the form of : • An environment ofexploding scope (more product sophistication variation, a global manufacturing environment and extensive local and economic challenges). • Engineer to perform multiple roles.

Fig. 10.3 Comparison of Japanese Companies with US Companies

- **Multiple** roles are in the form of manufacturing engineers, operations integrator and manufacturing strategist and as technical specialist.
- Engineer has to use **advanced tools** (including more powerful computer hardware, larger databases, great choice of software and expert systems and advanced CAD/CAM).
- **Changed work emphasis** (Focussing on teams, not individuals, with a more human, less technical orientation and the use of more outside services - **outsourcing**).

10.5 Plant location and plant selection

10.5.1 Definition of Plant Location

Location of plant is the function of determining where the plant is to be located, for maximum operating economy and effectiveness. The plant location once decided, must be permanent, and to be into consideration factors like the raw material, supplies, labour and markets.

10.5.2 Steps in Choosing a Location for the Plant

Step 1. Selection of the region: The entrepreneur must look for a suitable region or state where he can find raw materials, nearby markets, power, transport, and climate. He can meet the competition between different states by producing the product in a most economical way, in a particular region.

Step 2. Selection of appropriate place within the region: After selecting the region or state, the entrepreneur has to find a suitable place within the region. For example, the State is Karnataka, the place may be Bangalore or Mysore, where the skilled labour at a cheaper rate, water, civic amenities, etc. are found. Finance should be easily available. He should get research facilities. Local taxes and restrictions should be minimum. Start-up activities should proceed fast.

Step 3. Selection of various sites within the selected place: After deciding the place, the entrepreneur has to decide on various sites and work out the costs. The factors to be considered are:

Availability of cheap land to build and to expand the plant, soil, size and topography, low cost of construction in leveling of land and foundations, facilities for transportion of goods and materials, facilities for housing of the workers and their transportation to the work-site, cost of installation of electricity, gas and other facilities, cheap means of disposing of factory waste, minimum government restrictions, facilities for the upkeep and general maintenance, availability of qualified and experienced sub-contractors, cost of laying the water supply, sewage and disposal work, low noise, pollution.

Step 4. Decide optimum site: After considering all the factors as mentioned in Step 3, the entrepreneur has to work out the costs for different sites and finally select the 'optimum site' where he would get the maximum benefit.

The four steps for selecting an optimum site are explained above.

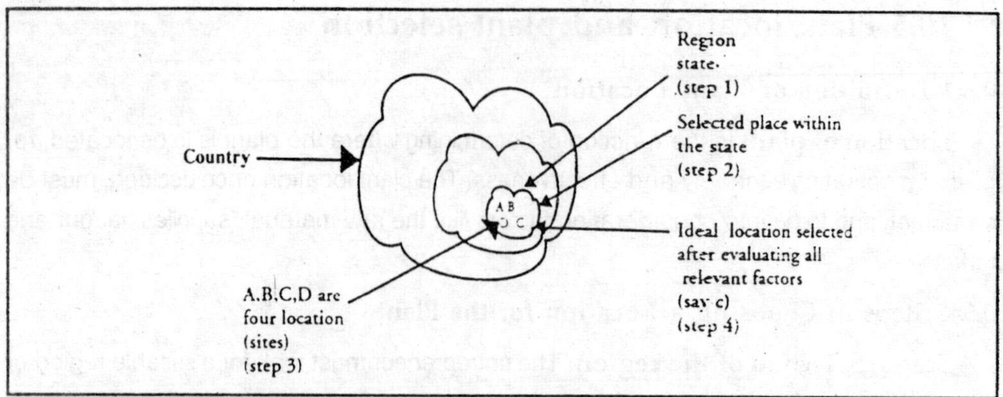

Fig. 10.4 Selection of Optimum Site

10.5.3 Factors affecting the Location of a Plant

The following factors affect the location of a plant:

Nearness to markets; Availability of power; Transportation facilities; Communication facilities; Road, Rail, Water connections; Civic amenities for workers. Easy availability of finance, including working capital; Skilled labour, Research facilities; Local taxes and restrictions; Fast start-up activities. Availability of cheap land: Soil, size and topography considerations. Low cost of construction; Facilities for housing of workers, their transportation to work site; Cost of installation of electricity, availability of gas and other facilities; Cheap means of disposing factory waste; Minimum government restrictions; Facilities for the upkeep and general maintenance, Availability of qualified and experienced subcontractors; Nearness to the industrial area, industrial sheds for offloading purpose and procurement; Cost of laying the water supply; Sewage disposal provision, less noise pollution; Nearness to government organisations who render help to entrepreneurs; Suitability of climate; Personal factors like on enterprising merchant or businessman who wants to start an industry in a particular area. A few of these factors are discussed below:

Raw materials

Manufacturing units use raw materials and convert them into finished products. Raw materials generally form 40 to 70% of the product cost and hence have to be procured at a low price with minimum transportation cost. Even 1% savings in material would increase profit by 10%. Raw materials depend on the type of products produced. Not all the industries can be started at any place, since raw materials are available only at certain places. For example,

Cotton textile industry: It is located in Kerala, AP, Karnataka, Tamil Nadu, Mumbai, West Bengal, Sholapur, Kanpur, Gujarat, MR

The reasons for choosing these places for cotton textile industries are: (i) Availability of raw cotton (ii) Excellent transport facilities (iii) Humid climate (iv) Presence of enterprising merchants (v) Suitability of these places to trade with other countries (vi) Important financial and commercial centers.

Sugar industry: It is localised, based on the availability of raw materials like sugarcane and chukander. Sugar mills are mainly situated in UP, Bihar, MP, Maharastra, Tamil Nadu, Mandya in Karnataka.

The reasons for choosing these places for sugar industry are: (i) Availability of fresh sugarcane and chukander (ii) Tropical climates and rainfall (It is also grown in sub tropical regions) (iii) Transportation facilities (iv) Waste disposal provision.

Iron and steel industry: Raw material and power are the most important factors, for this industry. The raw materials are available in large quantities in Bihar, Orissa, MP, West Bengal, Karnataka and UP. TISCO Jamshedpur; Indian Iron & Steel Co., West Bengal; Visveswariah Iron & Steel Works, Badravathi; Rourkella Steel Plant, Orissa; Bhilai Steel Plant, MP; Durgapur Steel Plant, Bengal; Bokaro Steel Plant, Bihar; Salem Steel Plant, TN; Vijayanagar Steel Plant, Karnataka; Vishakapatnam Steel Plant, AP; are some of the iron and steel plants.

The raw materials needed are iron ore, coal, limestone, manganese, dolomite and refractory material. Excellent transport facilities are also required, preferably with rail sidings. As it is a capital intensive unit, most of the iron and steel companies are set up by government and public undertakings.

Cement industry: Raw materials like limestone, chalk clay, and gypsum are important in the cement industry. There are located in Bihar, TN, Gujarat, MR AP UP Assam, HP and Orissa.

The factors influencing the setting up of the cement industry are (i) Nearness to raw materials (ii) Transportation facilities (iii) Because of pollution, factories will be situated outside the cities and towns. Hence, Transport arrangement for the workers or a township is required.

Jute industry: There are situated on the banks of Hoogly river, West Bengal. The reasons for the concentration of the Jute industry exclusively at Bengal are: (i) The availability of raw materials (ii) Network of waterways for connection to the important jute growing belts in West Bengal (iii) The availability of cheap thermal power (iv) Scottish enterprise.

Paper industry: Raw materials like bamboo, grass, wood, sugarcane, are important in the paper industry. It is situated at WB, Orissa, UP, Nagaland, Kerala, Assam, Bhadravati in Karnataka.

The reasons for the location of paper industry in the above places are: (i) Availability of raw material (ii) Climate (iii) Provision for waste disposal.

Coal industry: Coal mines are situated at Raniganj, West Bengal, Bihar, Orissa, MR TN, Assam, Gujarat, Rajastan and Kashmir.

The reasons for the location of coal industry in these places are: (i) Availability of raw material (ii) Transportation facilities (iii) Availability of cheap labour.

Information technology industry: Raw materials are not important in this industry. It is situated at Bangalore, Hyderabad, Poona, Madras, Delhi and other major cities.

The reasons for the location of Information Technology industry in these places are: (i) Availability of educated technical personnel (ii) Power (iii) Satellite link (iv) Telecommunication (v) Transportation facilities etc.

Factors influence plant location for a software industry are:

1. Satellite link and tele communication facilities and speed of services.
2. Availability of information workers (Computer Engineers and Telecommunication Engineers).
3. Whether the state welcomes, foreign technology and investment.
4. Recognistion of the importance and the key role of the private sector in accelerating growth.
5. Availability of modern technology and equipment like networks, computer hardware, software, communication equipment, communication software etc.
6. Availability of power and transportation facilities.
7. Existence of complementer and competing industry.
8. Finance and research facilities.
9. Appropriate site with good, soil, size, topography and good climate.

Bangalore is known as silicon valley of India in view of the above advantages for software industry. Many of big foreign companies have also setup their units in Bangalore like IBM, Microsoft, Siemens, SAP, People Soft, Baan, Oracle, JB Edwards etc, apart from the big ones like Infosys, Wipro, Satyam, etc.

Transportation: Industries using heavy materials depend on transportation for procuring raw materials as well as for transporting finished products. The cost of transportation depends on the classification of raw materials, into (i) Non-Weight losing materials (Eg. Cotton & Wollen production (ii) Weight losing materials (Eg. Machine tools, Engineering products etc.). The transportation cost in the case of weight losing material is higher for the raw materials than the product, since the materials lose weight in the course of manufacture. In the case of non weight losing materials, the transport cost is higher for the product than for the raw materials.

Transportation includes not only transportation of material but also transportation of men to the factory. A place which is well connected by rail, road and water transport is ideai for plant location. A hilly place may be selected for light industries like manufacture of watches where surface transportation is not heavy. Such locations are choosen to create employment opportunities.

Availability of power:

Power is an important resource for many industries. Coal, electricity, oil and natural gas are the sources of power.

Suitability of climate and nearness to market are other important factors for the location of the plant.

10.5.4 Various Factors involved in the Location of a Sugar Plant

As explained earlier, sugar industries need raw materials like sugarcane and chukander. Hence the availability of these raw materials is important in selecting the location of a sugar plant. Transportation of raw materials and finished product (i.e. Sugar) is also another important factor. Sugarcane grows mostly in tropical climate. Hence climate is another consideration. Nowadays, sugarcane is grown even in non-tropical climates. Provision for waste disposal is another factor. Power is not a dominant factor to determine the location of a sugar industry because bagasse obtained as a bye product is more than enough to meet the entire requirements of the mills for generating power. Market is not a problem as sugar is an essential commodity. Government policies and programmes influence plant location. In the name of balanced regional development, many backward regions in India are sometimes selected for the location of an industry, even ignoring the essential factors.

10.5.5 Various factors involved in the location of a Cement Plant

In the case of cement industry, the raw materials are lime stone, chalk clay and gypsum. Hence, the proposed factory should be close to the place where raw material is available. Transport facilities should be adequate. Material handling should be arranged. Because of pollution (dust and smoke), such industries cannot be set up within the city limits. Market is not a constraint in the case of cement, as it is required everywhere in construction works. Transportation of cement bags to cities needs a good network of transport carriers.

10.5.6 Advantages and Disadvantages of Selecting a Site in a big city, a suburban or a village.

	Aspects	Big City	Suburban	Village
(i)	Cost of Land	High	Medium	Low ✓
(ii)	Single Storey buildup	Uneconomical	Normal	Most economical ✓
(iii)	Spacious layout	Not possible	Possible	Highly possible ✓
(iv)	Open Spaces	Not possible to provide or minimum	Normal	Plenty ✓
(v)	Skilled Workers	Available in large numbers ✓	Available	Not available
(vi)	Transport facilities for travelling	Available in plenty ✓	Available	Insufficient
(vii)	Labour Problems (Labour unions, Labour unrest)	More	Normal	Fewer ✓
(viii)	Wages	Normal for Skilled Workers, High for unskilled (higher than village) ✓	In between	High for skilled workers ✓ Low for unskilled workers
(ix)	Fire hazards from nearby industries or neighbouring units	High	Less	Nil ✓
(x)	Civic amenties for employees	More ✓	Normal	Nil
(xi)	Educational and amusement advantages	High ✓	Normal	Less
(xii)	Police Protection	Satisfactory ✓	Normal	Not Satisfactory
(xiii)	Undersirable neighbours	Plenty	Normal	Do not exist ✓
(xiv)	Municipal Service for Water, Sewage, disposal Public health, Education	Good ✓	Not so good	Bad
(xv)	Large Local market	Exists ✓	Patially exists	Does not exist
(xvi)	Shape of Buildings	Awkwardly shaped, Ill lighted, Poor ventilation	Normal	Can plan properly, ✓ Good ventilation, Good lighting
(xvii)	High advertising value other related services	Available ✓ available ✓	Partly available available	Not available available
(xviii)	Restrictions on smoke and the dispoal of effluents	More	Normal	Nil ✓
(xix)	House rent for workers	High	Normal	Low ✓
(xx)	House taxes, water tax, sanitation taxes and other similar taxes	High	Normal	Low ✓
(xxi)	Training Institutions & Training facilities	Available ✓	Normal	Not available
(xxii)	Sub-contracting of work (Opportunity)	Plenty ✓	Normal	Not available
(xxiii)	Off-loading of opeations	Plenty ✓	Normal	Not available
(xxiv)	Employer Employee relations	Not always friendly	Better relationship	Comparatively better ✓
(xxv)	Availability of consultants/Technical advisors	Available ✓	Not available so much	Not available
(xxvi)	Scope for consulting other firms, scope for improving techonology	High ✓	Not high/low	Low
(xxvii)	Communication facilities	Excellent ✓	Fairly Good	Bad

Note: Ticked ones (✓) are the advantages in the 1st and 3rd columns. Suburban sites offer a compromise between the city and the villages; they have the advantages of both. They can draw the labour from nearby villages or cities; they can provide facilities like parks, schools and clubs; Rail and Road transport facilities are also available. Hence, they prove to be better; than the village or city sites. However, entrepreneurs often and it difficult in choosing one of the above three. In general, a city location is preferable for small plants.

10.6 Definition of Plant Layout

Plant Layout is referred to as the arrangement and location of different departments and of the machinery within a department so than an optimum utilisation of space available can be made with a view to enabling the plant to function in an effective manner. It involves the allocation of space and arrangement of equipment in such a manner that overall operating costs are minimised. The efficiency of any manufacturing unit depends largely on the planning of the layout and the design of the factory.

10.6.1 Objectives of Plant Layout

The **principal objective** of a good plant layout is to maximise the production, at the minimum cost. It should accommodate the changes in management policies and processes and techniques of production. It should satisfy the needs of all those associated with the production system like workers, supervisors and managers.

The layout should therefore be planned keeping the following features in mind.

- Economy in handling of materials, work in process, and finished stock.
- Optimum utilisation of all resources like men, materials, equipment and space.
- Minimising work-in-process and maximising inventory turnover (Materials within the plant should move fast and congestion eliminated).
- Ensuring flexibility of layout for varying needs of the enterprise.
- Ensuring efficient supervision and production control.
- Reduced damage and wastage of materials.
- Ease of working, greater safety and reduced health hazards for workers.
- Flexibility with regard to changing conditions.
- Minimising delays and bottle-necks in production systems.
- Avoiding frequent changes so that production programme is not upset.
- Boosting employee morale by providing employee comforts and satisfaction.
- Convenient service centers.
- Utilisation of the three dimensions of the space available, floor space, vertical roof space, known as cubical space.

10.6.2 Factors Influencing Plant Layout

Each industry decides on its own layout. Primarily, the layout of a plant is influenced by the relationship among materials, machinery and men.

The following are some of the factors which influence the layout.

Materials: Design and specifications of materials, physical and chemical properties of the materials, quantity and quality of materials etc. are the most important factors in planning a layout. Material handling and materials storage should be given due consideration.

The materials storage factors are:

- rate of consumption of raw materials
- type of raw materials (solid, liquid, light or heavy, small or large)
- space, weight, volume of raw materials
- availability of raw materials (seasonal variation materials)
- floor capacity
- ceiling height
- method of storing etc.

Material handling equipment depends on:

- type of raw materials
- availability of raw materials

The material handling equipments used are cranes, trolleys, pipelines, roller conveyors, belt conveyors, chain conveyors.

Normally, while working out the plant layout, material flow charts are made to visualise the path of material flow or movements. The movements should be straight, should not crisscross, should be in the short path and there should be no back trackings.

Nature of the product: This affects the plant layout significantly. Fixed position layout is ideal for heavy products, while the line layout is best suited for manufacture of light products, because these can be moved from machine to machine easily.

A product like a ship or an aircraft cannot be taken from machine to machine, and therefore needs a fixed position layout, whereas, watch assembling needs line layout.

Volume of production and standardisation of the product: If standard products are to be manufactured on a large scale, the product type of layout may be adopted. Alternatively, if the production is to be made on the basis of customers orders, a functional layout may be alright.

The demand for a product determines the volume of production, the area of the storage space and other facilities, which in turn determine the type of the layout.

Nature of plant location: The size, shape and topography of the site at which the plant is located affects the type of layout. For example, if the site is near the railway line. If the space is narrow and the product process is lengthy, the layout may have to take a letter-shape like U or S.

Type of Industry Process

The industry processes influence the layout of the plant. Depending on the processes, Industries can be classified as:

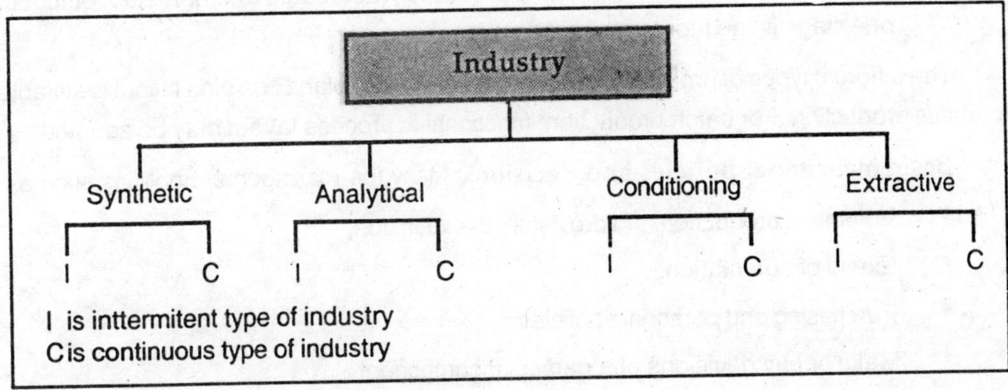

Fig. 10.5 Type of Industry Process

- **Synthetic industry** (Assembly Industry) involves the production of a product by the use of various elements Eg. Chemical, cement, automobile, light and heavy engineering, watch making etc.
- **Analytical industry** breaks the raw materials into various elements or parts Eg. Oil refinery yields naphtha, gasoline, paraffin, etc. sugar mill gives sugar, bagasse and molasses.
- **Conditioning Industry** involves a change in form or physical properties Eg. Foundaries, metal working industry, leather tanning concerns.
- **Extractive industries** involve the separation of one element from another Eg. Metal from the ore.

In each of the above industries, processes can be either intermittent on continuous:

- Intermittent type industry - This manufactures different components on different machines. They manufacture the parts and store them, and then assemble these into a product based on the market needs. Eg. Machine tool plant, cycle manufacturing plant, ship building plant, electrical goods manufacturing plant etc. Functional layout is the best for this type of industry.
- Continuous type industry - Raw materials are fed from one end and finished goods are received at the other end. This may be either analytical or synthetic. Product layout is the best for continuous industry.

Types or methods of production: The different methods of production are already explained in pages 3 to 5.

- Job order production (production is based on the orders of customers)
- Batch production (the production of goods is done in batches, it is standardised and made in anticipation of sales)
- Mass production (standardised goods, produced in large quantities)
- Process production or continuous production (automatic and non-stop, output of one stage is the input of the next stage)

The different types of production would affect the layout plan E.g., Line layout is suitable for mass production. For batch production, functional or process layout may be adopted.

Basic managerial policies and decisions: Many top management policies such as:

- Volume of production and provision for expansion;
- Extent of automation;
- Purchasing and personnel policies
- Make or buy decisions of a particular component
- Desire for quick delivery of goods etc.

determine the plant layout and the scope of the plant activities.

Nature of the machines: If machines are heavy in weight or are noisy, they have to be grouted onto the floor; ample space should be provided around the machines for complicated and dangerous machines to avoid accidents. Various alternatives are available to determine which ones are to be moved.

(i) Product + workers $\xrightarrow{\text{to move}}$ Machines stationary

(ii) Product $\xrightarrow{\text{to move}}$ Machines and workers stationary

(iii) Worker and machines $\xrightarrow{\text{to move}}$ Product stationary

The layout or arrangement of machines should be planned to suit the alternatives used in a plant.

Human factors and working conditions: Man's safety and comforts should be given priority while planning a layout. The following factors may be considered:

- Employee facilities such as health and related services
- Obstruction - free floor
- Exit provisions
- Hazard free work atmosphere

- Rest rooms
- Drinking water
- Lavatory etc.

Provisions of Factories Act should be followed strictly.

Characteristics of the building:

- Shape of the building
- Covered and open area
- Number of storeys
- Facilities of elevators
- Parking Area
- Storing place etc. influence the layout plan.

10.6.3 Principles of Plant Layout

The basic principles of a good plant layout are:

- **Principle of overall integration:** Men, materials, machinery, supporting activities and other relevant factors should be interpreted to make the final layout look integrated and compact.
- **Principle of minimum distance:** If all other things are equal, the movement of materials and men is the factor to be considered. It should be minimum, for the best layout.

Minimum movement of material is possible in the case of product layout as the machines are arranged in a sequence. A similar exercise has to be done in the case of process layout, to achieve the principle of minimum distance to the extent.

- **Principle of flexibility:** The best layout is the one which can be adjusted and re-arranged at a minimum cost and without much inconvenience.
- **Principle of satisfaction and safety:** The best layout is the one which makes work satisfying and safe for workers.
- **Principle of cubic space:** The best layout is that in which all available space, both vertical and horizontal is used most economically and effectively.
- **Principle of economy:** The layout ultimately should result in fixed minimum capital investment.

The plant layouts differ from plant to plant, location to location, industry to industry. (Eg. A watch industry, job industry, small sized factory, big industry would have different layouts). The layout once prepared may not hold good for all the times. Whenever there is a change in management or takeover of the industry, the layout may be changed by the new management.

Changes in product design, production techniques, increase in size of the plant invariably call for revision in layout. The basic principles, however, remain the same.

10.6.4 Types of Layouts

The different types of layouts or methods of grouping are:

- **Process layout** (Functional layout)
- **Product layout** (Straight line layout)
- **Combination of process and product layout** (Hybrid Layout)
- **Fixed position layout**

10.6.5 Process Layout

Process layout, also known as **functional layout,** is based on the functions performed by a department. Under this system of layout, machines or equipment of the same functional types are grouped together in a particular department e.g., All lathes are grouped in the turning section. Separate departments are established for each production operation. If drilling is to be done on a component, it should go to drilling department. Thus, there are different departments like painting department, heat treatment department etc. (not shown below in figure 4.2) where particular operations are to be carried out. To start with, the raw material goes to the first machine, i.e., a lathe in the turning section from the receiving section. Then, if drilling is the next operation, it will go to the drilling department.

Receiving	Milling Machines (5 Nos)	Drilling (9 Nos) Machines	Grinding (5 Nos) Machines
Cutting (3 Nos)	Turning (9 Nos)	Great Cutting (1 No)	Plating (2 Nos)

Fig. 10.6 Different Departments Grouped Together in Process Layout (As an Example)

The same sketch is redrawn below, showing the flow of components across departments. Three components flow from department to department. The material moves over long distances and cris-cross.

In this type of layout, for each of the operations, raw materials have to travel from department to department (departments may not be close to each other). The materials may have to be taken sometimes to the same department back from a different department by retracing the path or to a separate building and brought back to the same building. This is known as back tracking.

Process layout is the arrangement of a facility so that work centres or departments are grouped together according to their functional type. Process layout is also called **Functional layout** or **Job shop layout.**

10.6.6 Product layout or Straight Line Layout (Line Processing Layout or Flow Line Layout)

Product Layout involves the arrangement of machines in one line, depending upon the sequence of operations. Each of the components skip some of the machines not required. Machines are arranged serially, to machine similar components. Materials are worked out into finished components through a series of integrated operations. Back tracing is avoided.

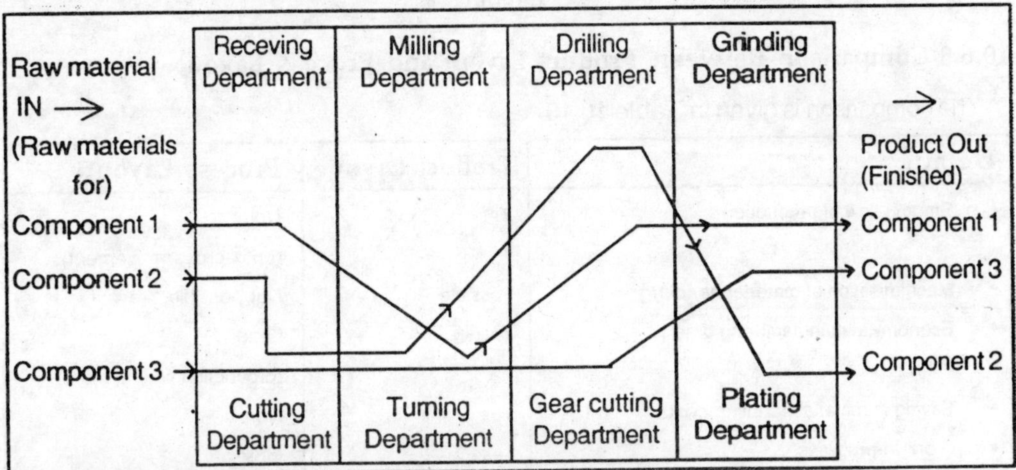

Fig. 10.7 Components Flow in the Process Layout

Components	Operations to be done
1	Turning, Drilling, Plating
2	Turning, Drilling, Grinding
3	Cutting, Turning, Gearcutting, Grinding

Fig. 10.8 Operations to be Done in Components 1,2,3, (as shown in figure 10.7)

The machines can be arranged either:

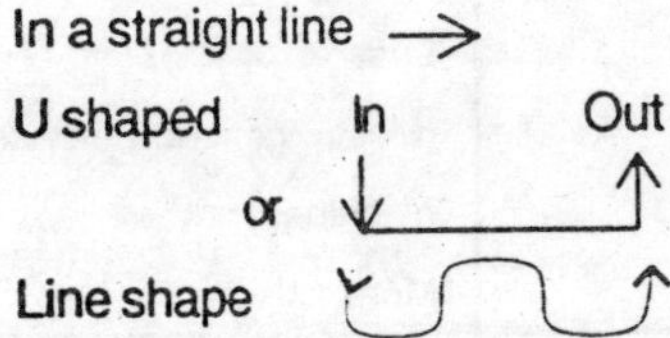

10.6.7 Principles for Grouping Machines into Product Layout and Process Layout

Factors	Product Layout	Process Layout
(i) Placement of machine tools	At the points demanded by the sequence of operations	In the respective departments at convenient places. Department should also be suitably located in a sequence.
(ii) Travel of materials and components	No criss crossing	Less criss-crossing and back tracking.
(iii) Inspection and supervision	At points of Convenience	At points of convenience within each of the departments
(iv) Material feeding to machines	Only at the time of requirement in assembling	Any time to suit convenience

Table 10.9 Principles for Grouping Machines into Product Layout and Process Layout

10.6.8 Comparison Between Product Layout and Process Layout

The comparison is given in Table 10.10

Details	Product Layout	Process Layout
• Smooth flow of production	Yes ✓	No (criss-cross movement)
• Mechanisation of material handling	Possible ✓	Not possible
• Economy in manufacturing time	Yes ✓	Less (production time is more)
• Saving in material handling costs	Yes ✓	No
• Work-in-progress	Less ✓	More
• Inspection	Easy ✓	Difficult
• Control Production	Better ✓	Difficult
• Maximum utilisation of available space	Yes ✓	No
• Effective utilisation of available resources	Yes ✓	No
• Floor area per unit production	Less ✓	More
• Detection of mistakes or badly produced	Early ✓	No quick
item	Higher ✓	Lower
• Incentive to group of workers to increase their performance	Yes	No
• Avoidance of bottlenecks	More	Less ✓
• Investment on machines		(Mostly general purpose machines)
• Flexiblility in the production	Less	More ✓

• Supervision	Difficult	Better supervisioin (Department wise) ✓
• Scope for expansion	Low	High ✓
• Incentive to industrial workers to increase performance	Low	Higher ✓
• Cost of Layout	Expensive	Not so expensive (duplicate of simila machines avoided) ✓
• Flexibility of system	More (✓)	Less
• Any breakdown of equipment disrupt the whole system	Yes	No ✓

Note: All the (✓) ones are advantages The disadvantages are not ticked.

Table 10.10 Comparison between Product Layout and Process Layout

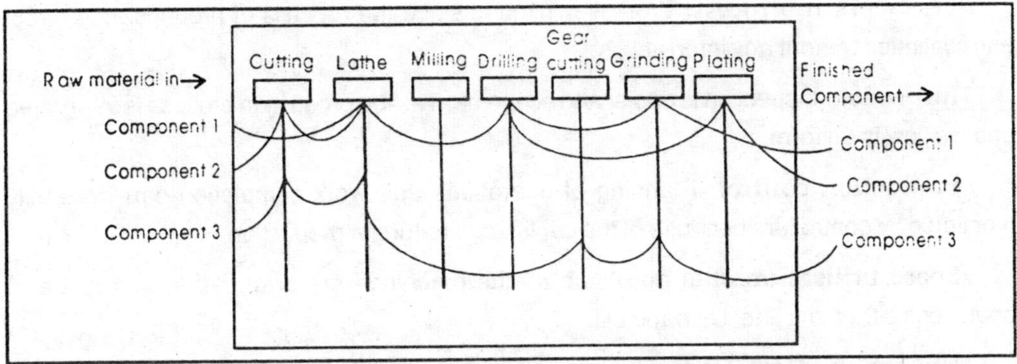

Fig. 10.11 Components Flow in Product Layout

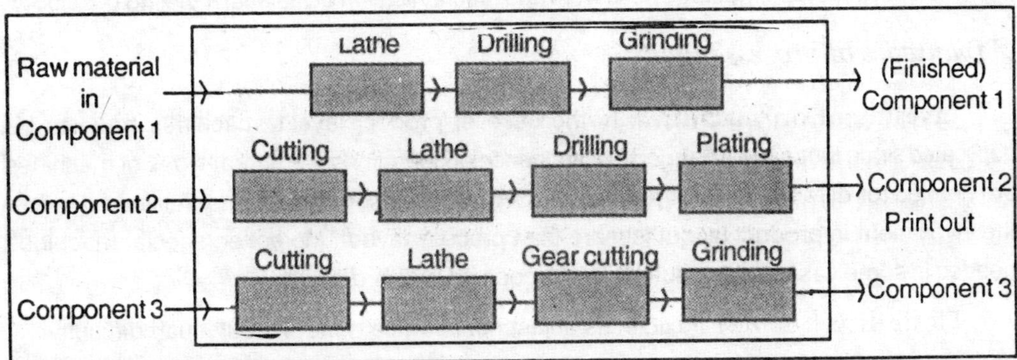

Fig. 10.12 Components Flow in Product Layout

In this case, the machines are arranged serially in a line depending upon the sequence of operations.

Advantages of Product Layout

Smooth flow of Production: It ensures a steady and economical flow of production because by proper arrangement of machines in a sequence, bottle necks are eliminated.

Mechanisation of material handling: As the machines positioned are in a sequence, continuous and quick flow of materials in a line is possible through mechanical devices like conveyors.

Economy in manufacturing item: As the material continuously moves from one end to the other, where the finish product is collected, there is no back tracking. This shortens the manufacturing time since internal transportation time is saved.

Savings in material handling costs: As machines are arranged in sequence of operations, material flows in a line. There is no transportation cost for movement of materials, till the process of manufacturing is completed. There will therefore be savings in material handling costs.

Less work in process: Work is minimum, since the process of production is direct and continues without any interruption.

Inspection: Inspection is easier and economical as the production process is integrated and the flow is uniform.

Production control: Planning of operations and work completion can be easily monitored by controllers because of the continuous nature of production.

Space utilisation: It is maximum as the machines are arranged in sequence of operations either in a line, U shape etc.

Utilisation of available resources: All the resources, such as men, machines and materials can be utilised effectively, since it is continuous production with minimum movement of workers, less material wastage, less work and mechanisation of material handling possibility.

Advantages of process layout

Investment on machines: In the case of product layout, machines have to be duplicated since these are arranged in a sequence of operations and similar types of machines are needed for different lines of production. Sometimes, they may be underutilised. Hence, the investment in product layout is more than process layout. Moreover, special machines needed in some cases for product layout to cope up with production.

Flexibility: It is more flexible, as adjustment can be done without much difficulty.

Supervision: There are separate departments. Hence, supervision becomes easy. Supervisors are more familiar with the types of machines involved, as there are only type of machines of a few types of machines. Here supervisor's salary could be less as there is no neccessity for versatility.

Scope for expansion: it is easier to expand by adding similar type of machines within the department.

Cost of layout: Cost of layout is less since duplication is avoided and space is saved.

No stoppage of work through breakdown: If there is a breakdown, the other machines can take care of the production. This is a major disadvantages for a product layout.

Labour cost: It is not high as every worker is an expert in his line, and during his absence, another worker can take care of his job. Rotation is possible, hence monotony is avoided. Individual incentives work. The other advantages are scope for expansion, maximum utilisation of equipment, better working conditions, higher output rate etc.

10.6.9 Circumstances determining the Product and Process Usage Layouts

Product layouts are preferred where:

- One a few standard products are involved.
- Production is in large quantities.
- Components are such that material handling facilities need to be utilised efficiently (by mechanical means and continuously).
- The same machine is used for less number of products and operations.
- Minimum inspection stages.

Process layouts are preferred where:

- Many types or kinds of products (or special orders) are involved.
- Production is in small quantities.
- Heavy materials or products are used, where material handling facilities cannot be used efficiently.
- A number of products and operations can be used on the same machine.
- The inspection stages are many.

10.6.10 Fixed Position Layout (Static Layout)

In **Fixed position layout** the job is stationary as it is heavy. Men, machines and tools move towards the job. The reason behind this is that as the job is very heavy, it becomes costly and unwise to move the job towards the machine. Fig.4.7 shows an example of fixed position layout.

E.g. Locomotives, Ship building, Satellites, Aircraft, Boilers, Generators etc.

This is also true in the case of site construction, brick kiln, where the materials are moved to the spot. In the case of hospital also, doctors, nurses, medicine (materials) move towards the patient.

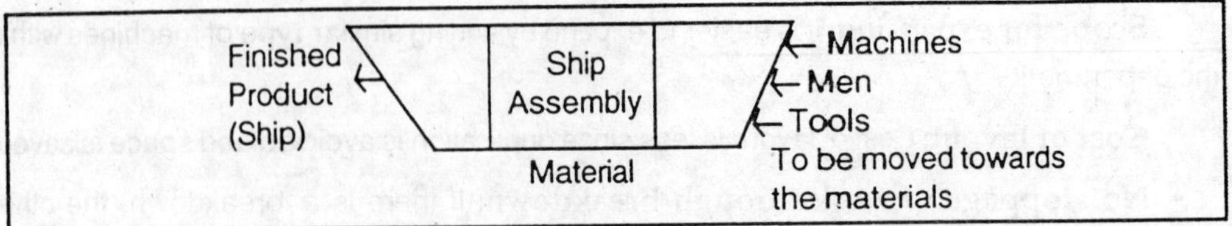

Fig. 10.13 Fixed Position Layout

10.6.11 Advantages and Disadvantages of a Fixed Position Layout

The advantages are:

- Same people and machines can be used on operations producing different products.
- Layout investment is economical.
- Simple portable machines are used to perform the task.
- Workers take pride after the product comes out successfully.
- High cost and difficulty in transporting heavy products are avoided.

The disadvantages are:

- Costly and high precision tooling involved.
- Skilled labour is required as everything depends on accurate tooling, not on the type of machine.

10.6.12 Combined Layout (Hybrid Layout)

Some of the big industries adopted this type of layout, a combination of product and process layouts, with an emphasis on either, to utilise the advantages of both the types of layouts.

It is possibe to combine both types of layouts in an efficient form producing the desired volume of products at the least cost, provided products are similar and not complicated. See the figure 4.8 below:

(i) Machines are arranged in a sequence. Hence the sequence is followed as product layout.

(ii) There are more number of machines at each stage, and they are grouped as mini-departments so that they can take up different components of a similar nature. Process layout principle is followed.

These type of layouts are generally ideal for big engineering industries like BHEL, HMT etc., where type of components, number of components and number of machines are vast. Many of the components can be grouped as they are similar.

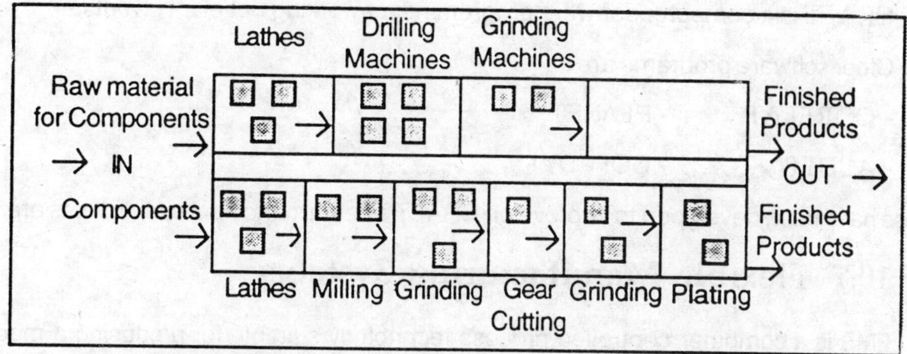

Fig. 10.14 Component Flow in Combined Layout

10.6.13 Group Technology

Similar components varying in diameters, lengths and steps in small dimensions are grouped together to machine them in separate manufacturing cells to save the material movement and time. For example:

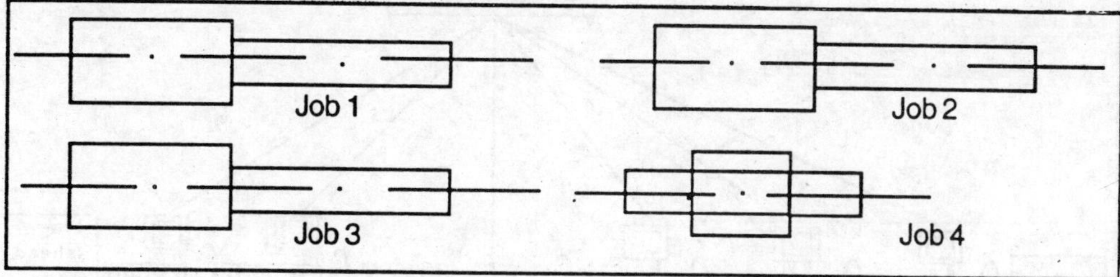

Fig. 10.15 Family of Similar Parts

- It can be used to develop a hybrid between product focused and process focused production systems.
- It enables production of a variety of parts in small batches to achieve economies of line flow production without product standardisation.
- In companies that have a large variety of parts, group technology is helpful in selecting appropriate family of parts that can be processed in the manufacturing cells.

Computer Programs have been developed to help in locating departments in relationship with each other so that the transportation cost is minimised.

- CRAFT (Computerised Relative Allocation of Facility Technique) begins with the expected volume of materials shipment between every pair of departments, the materials handling cost per unit distance, the area needed for each department and an initial layout. CRAFT then iteractively switches pairs of departments as long it can reduce materials handling cost, then prints (**CRAFT** is a computer software programme for working out plant layouts) out a layout showing the recommended location for each department.

- CRAFT is a computer software programme for working out plant layouts.

  Other software programs are :-

  - CORELAP - PLANET

  - ALDEP - COFAD etc.

These have been developed to improve on CRAFT's performance but certain limits are there.

10.7 Flexible Manufacturing Systems

FMS is a computer controlled process technology suitable for producing a moderate variety of products in moderate volumes. FMS consists of a group of production machines known as Flexible Manufacturing cells which are nothing but improved versions of high productive CNC machines. These FMCs are arranged in a sequence, connected by automated materials handling and transferring machines and integrated by a computer system called as FMS (Flexible Manufacturing System). It is a fully computer controlled system.

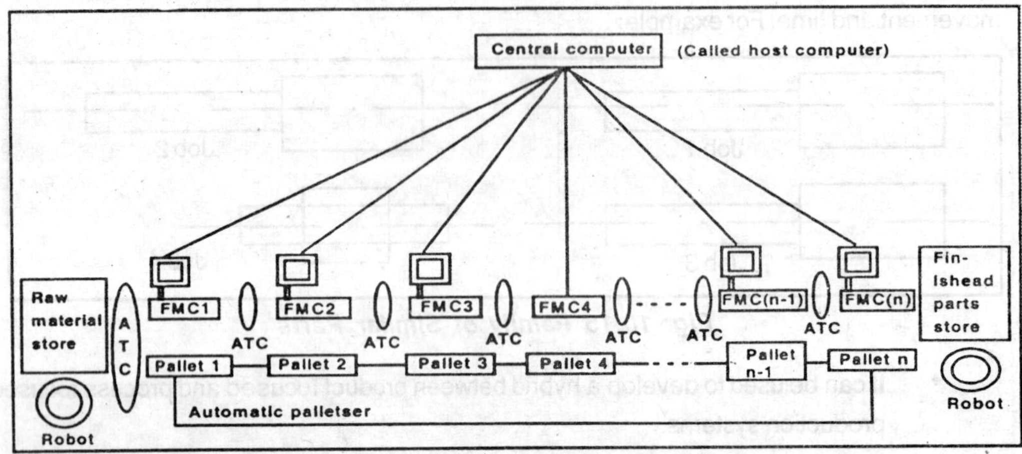

Fig. 10.16 Flexible Manufacturing System.

Robots are provided at both the ends at the start and finish end of FMS. On the Raw materials side, Robot takes the raw material and stacks them in the Raw material stores and also load, the job on pallet. At the finishing end, raw material is converted to the finished components by machining it on various FMCs. Another robot at the finished end moves the finished components from the pallet of the last machine to finished parts store and put them at appropriate places in finished parts store. Work-station machines (FMCs) are automated and programmable.

Each Flexible Machining Cell (FMC) is mounted with automatic tool changers known as ATCs. This will be having a minimum of 100 tools mounted and can perform a number of operations with these tools on each of FMCs. Hundred of tool options are available on each FMC. FMC(n-1) and FMC(n) machines (Last two FMCs) in the line are Flexible manufacturing cells for doing special operations ie., automatic washing and measuring of components.

Automated materials-handling equipment move components to the pallets of appropriate work station, then on to the programmed machines that select, position and actuate the specific tools for each job.

Once the machine has completed one batch of components, the computer signals the next quantity or component and the machine automatically repositions and retools accordingly. In the mean time, the just finished batch is automatically transferred to the next work station in its routing.

FMS has a central computer known as host computer which can coordinate all FMCs properly. The individual computers found on each of the FMCs are responsible for its own individual operations.

- An FMS is generally ideal when:
  - all Products are variations of a stable basic design
  - all products utilise the same family of components
  - the number of components is only moderate (10 to 50)
  - the volume of each component is of medium size (1,000 to 30,000 units annually) but in lot sizes as small as one unit.

Thus FMS technology helps in producing **moderate variety of products in modest volumes** (too quickly and with high quality).

(i) Operating costs can also be reduced by using FMS.

(ii) Lower direct labour costs lead to lower manufacturing costs.

The **disadvantage** in FMS is that it needs very high investments in equipment, planning and control systems, and human resource systems.

FMS has Automated Storage and Retrieval Systems (ASRS) which has three major elements :

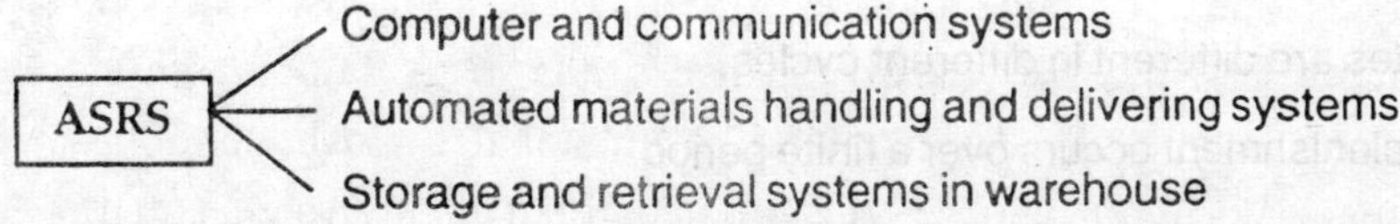

10.8 Quantitative tools in production planning

Three specific tools are discussed below :-

- Economic order quantity approach to Inventory Control.
- Break Even charts
- Learning Curves.

(I) Economic Order Quantity (EOQ)

When the size of an order minimises the total inventory cost, it is known as the '**economic order quantity.**'

Some costs increase as inventory increase and others decrease; there is no ideal order size.

The best lot size will result in adequate inventory to reduce some costs, yet will not be so large that it results in needless expenses for holding inventory. A compromise must be drawn between conflicting costs. EOQ is an important factor in inventory control. It is also known as standard order quantity, economic lot size or economic ordering quantity.

In the order relationship shown in Fig. 17.5, the two costs, ordering costs and carrying costs are taken into consideration.

$$\text{Total inventory cost} = \frac{Q}{2H} + \frac{Da}{Q}S$$

$$\text{Total annual stocking cost} = DaC + \frac{Q}{2H} + \frac{Da}{Q}S$$

Q = Economic order quantity

H = Inventory holding cost

Da = Annual requirement = Yearly usage of items

S = Ordering Cost

C = Purchase cost/unit

EOQ = Economic order quantity = $Q = \sqrt{\dfrac{2DaS}{H}}$

10.9 Situations where EOQ can be Determined Differently

The various situations are:

- When replenishment is instantaneous.
- When rates are different in different cycles.
- When replenishment occurs over a finite period.
- When quantity discounts are allowed.
- When storage is permitted.

The **weaknesses of EOQ formula** are:

- Erratic usages.
- Basic information is faulty.
- Costly calculations involved while working out EOQ.

- No formula is a substitute for commonsense.
- EOQ ordering is based on judgement.

(II) Meaning of Inventory

Inventory is commonly used to indicate materials, raw materials, finished, semi-finished, packing, spares, consumable materials etc. and other stocked in order to meet an expected demand or distribution. though it is termed as an idle resource in the sense, it is not meant for immediate use, but it is absolutely necessary to maintain certain inventories at certain quantities for the smooth functioning of an organisation.

Finished goods inventories - These are called stock in trade, and consists of end products ready for shipment to the customers.

Maintenance, Repair and Operating (MRO) inventories include standard cutting tools, standard tooling elements, raw material for tools, grinding wheels, jigs and test rigs.

Maintenance inventory includes machine tool spares, electrical items such as switches, fuses, lamps, lubricants, spares for transport vehicles, safety equipment such as goggles, gloves etc.

Stationary inventory includes canteen provisions, medical supplies, uniforms, chemicals required for plating and heat treatment baths, gases for welding etc.

Different Types of Inventories

- Inventions are generally categorised into 5 types as shown in figure 10.17(a)

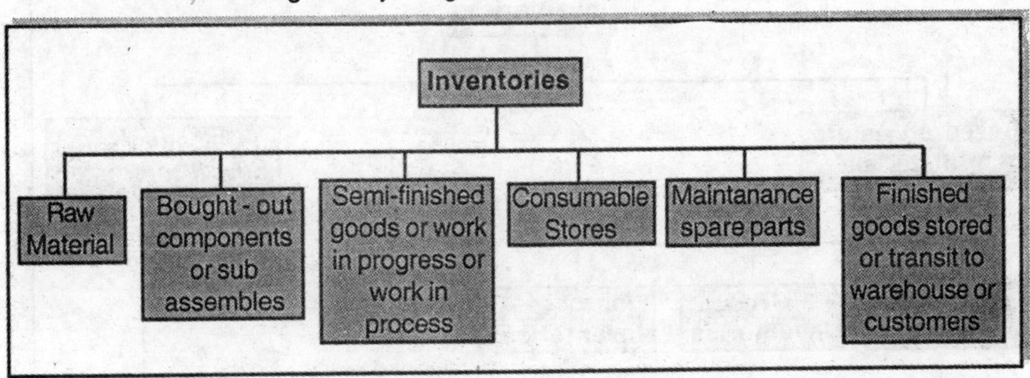

Fig. 10.17 General Classification of Inventory

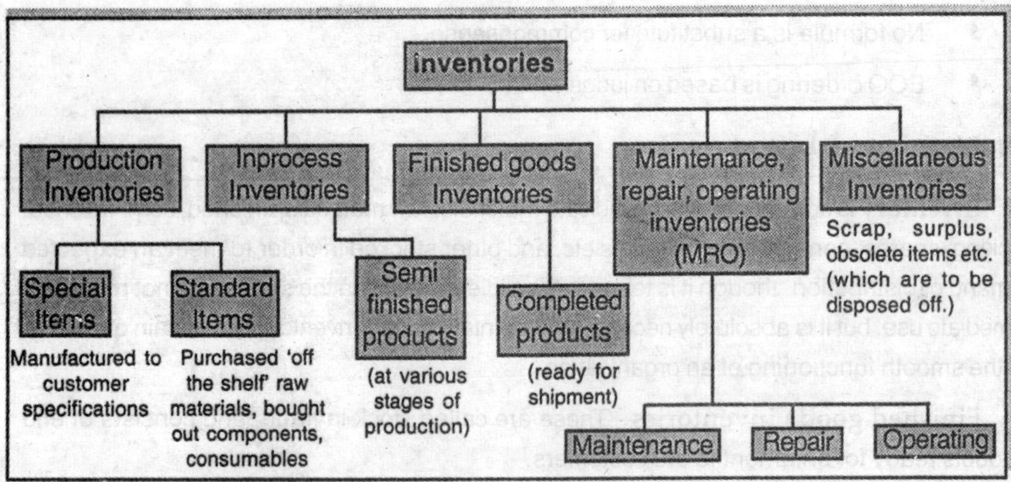

Fig. 10.17 (a) Categories of Inventories

- Other types of Inventories are:

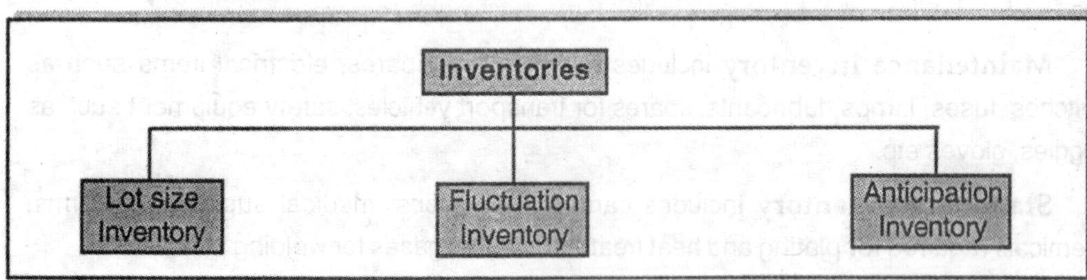

Fig. 10.18 Other Types of Inventories

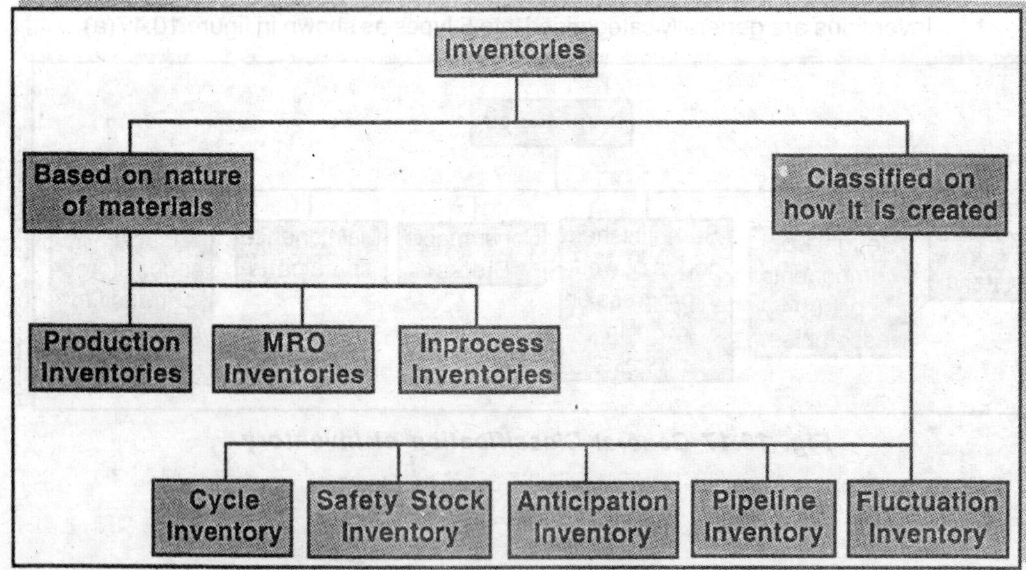

Fig. 10.18 (a) Another Classification of Inventories

- **Cycle Inventory :** is the position of total inventory which varies directly with lot size (i.e., quantity ordered)
- **Safety Stock Inventories :** are held to avoid stock out conditions which causes production stoppages and to protect against uncertainties in demand, lead time, supply and consumption rates
- **Anticipation Inventory :** is materials purchased in bulk quantities in anticipation of price rise and products having seasonal demand produced in quantities more than the demand during off-seasons and held in inventory to meet higher demand rate.
- **Pipeline Inventory :** Inventory moving from point to point in the materials flow system from supplier to a point, from one operation to the next in the plant and from the plant to the warehouse or distribution system to the customer
- **Fluctuation Inventory :** These are held as reserve stock to meet the unexpected fluctuation demand over a period which cannot be predicted accurately

(III) Sensitivity Analysis and Breakeven Charts

Linked with profit planning is the sophisticated concept of 'Sensitivity Analysis' which attempts in graphical form, to indicate how sensitive the profits of any business are likely to be in response to changes in sales volume, prices and costs. Most businesses, however, are more familiar with the well-known **Breakeven chart** which deals with the same basic elements in their simplest forms as shown below :-

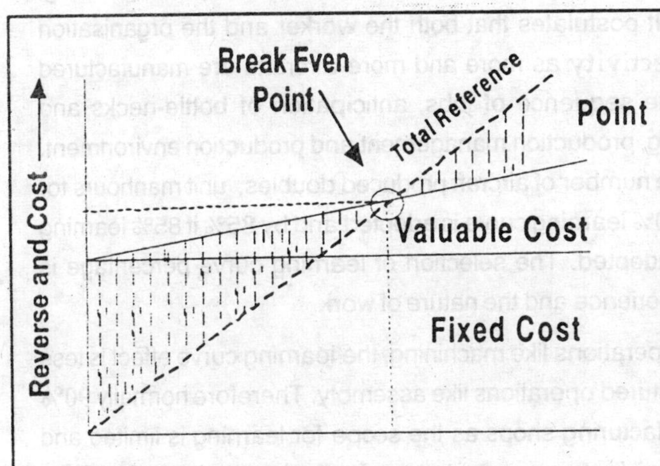

Break Even Point is the level of output (Volume of output) for which total cost (Covering Fixed and Variable Costs Total) equals total revenue.

Fig 10.19 Sales Break-Even chart

Breakeven can be seen as the point at which the total revenue = total costs and beyond which, with more sales (production), a profit can be made.

From this chart, a number of questions can be answered such as :-

- What would happen to profits if total sales were to fall off?
- What would happen to profits if prices were raised, with or without reduction in costs, but less goods could be sold at these higher prices?

The relevance of fixed and variable costs could be appreciated from the **Contribution Theory.** The concept of a product or service covering its own variable costs and making some contribution towards the fixed costs.

There are certain assumptions that have to be made in the use of these charts coupled with a narrow **range** of relevance on either side of the breakeven point. Among these assumptions is the acceptance of a static environment, where a dynamic situation is more likely to be the case in practice. The chart can only be as effective as the extent and accuracy of the data which is built into it. There is an implied assumption that the revenue/cost relationship is linear, which produces its own limitations in applications. Nor can the chart be used beyond the budget period of the firm. Total revenue graph could be curve instead of a straight line. There could be more than one breakeven point given a need for computations at different price levels. However, **Breakeven Charts** have a basic practical value if only as a first approximation, coupled with value judgement and common sense, on the way to more sophisticated analysis.

(IV) Learning Curve

Learning Curve is a technique used in manhour computation and manpower planning, largely in the **Aircraft Industry.** It postulates that both the worker and the organisation improve their **efficiency and effectivity** as more and more aircrafts are manufactured due to better understanding of the sequence of jobs, anticipation of bottle-necks and improvement in manual skills, tooling, production management and production environment. The learning curve states that as the number of aircraft produced doubles, unit manhours for manufacture decrease by 80%, if 80% learning curve is adopted and by 85% if 85% learning curve, which is very common, is adopted. The selection of learning curve percentage is based on a particular Industry's experience and the nature of work.

In standard process - guided operations like machining, the learning curve effect is less compared to relatively more unstructured operations like assembly. Therefore normally 90% **learning curve** is taken for manufacturing shops as the scope for learning is limited and **80% for assembly shops.** for the factory as a whole a **Learning curve of 85%** is assumed.

The underlying mathematics of Learning Curve is explained here :

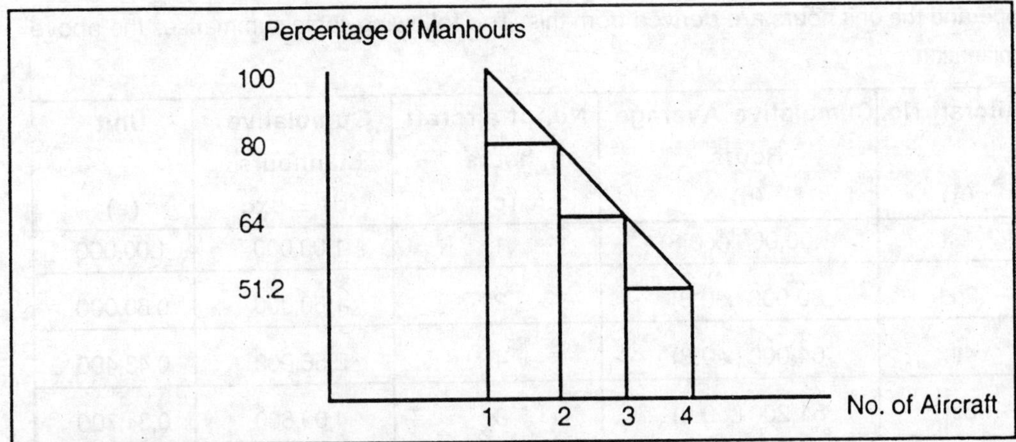

The slope of the line = K.

$$K = \frac{\log \frac{1}{y}}{\log 2}$$

y = The learning curve value as a decimal fraction.

For instance 80% Learning Curve corresponds to 0.8. 1 / y represents the distance analysis between 1st and 2nd aircraft, or 2nd and 4th aircraft or 4th and 8th aircraft etc. 2 represents the ratio of aircraft which is two and is along the x axis.

$$K = \frac{\log \frac{1}{0.8}}{\log 2} = 0.3219$$

$$1 - K = 0.6781$$

The cumulative average manhours of the Xth aircraft =

$$\frac{\text{Manhours of the first aircraft}}{X^{k}}$$

Let the manhours of the first aircraft be 1,00,000

The cumulative average manhours for

$$\text{the } 8^{\text{th}} \text{ aircraft} = \frac{1{,}00{,}000}{8^{0.3219}} = 51{,}200$$

This is the cumulative average approach. The unit learning variant for the Xth aircraft is obtained by multiplying the Xth aircraft manhours above by the factor (1-k).

The unit manhours for the 8th aircraft = 51,200 X (1-K)

= 51,200 X 0.6781

= 34,700.

In case of cumulative average variant the cumulative hours follow the learning curve slope and the unit hours are derived from this. The following table summarises the above explanation.

Aircraft No. (a)	Cumulative Average Hours (b)	No. of aircraft hours (c)	Cumulative Manhours (d) = bxc	Unit (e)
1st	1,00,000 (x 0.8)	1	1,00,000	1,00,000
2nd	80,000 (x 0.8)	2	1,60,000	0,60,000
4th	64,000 (x 0.8)	4	2,56,000	0,43,400
8th	51,200 (x 0.8)	8	4,09,600	0,34,700

Column (b) or column (e) is used for computing the aircraft manhours. The cumulative average learning curve is preferred. The impact of learning curve beyond 100 aircraft is not significant. The possibilities of adopting different percentages of learning curve are shown in the diagram at Fig.

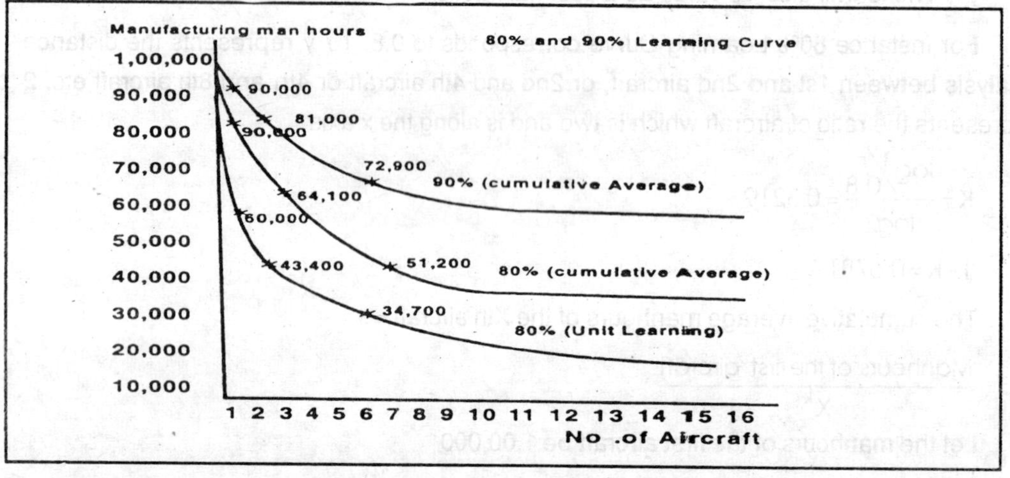

The inferences are :

01. By adopting a steeper learning curve of 80% the requirement of manhours to produce 10 aircraft is 4.76 lakhs (47,654x10) as against 7.05 lakhs (70,469x10) for 90% learning. If the aim is to get more manpower resources with reference to the 1st aircraft manhour, the adoption of a shallow learning curve is advantageous.

02. If the average manhour for the first ten aircraft is fixed and if the objective is to project more resources for building the first aircraft of this batch, it is advantageous to adopt a steeper learning curve. Let the unit average manhour for 10 aircraft be 50,000. At 90% learning curve, the first aircraft requires 50,000 / 0.70469 = 70952 whereas for 80% learning curve the first aircraft will consume 50,000 / 0.47654 = 1,04,922.

Synchronised Manufacturing

Eliyahu Goldraltt, an Israeli developed OPT in 1979, a proprietary capacity - **sensitive scheduling software** for correcting the deficiencies of MRP and MRP II. While implementing that software, he discovered that many of the scheduling problems occurred were the result of not properly recognising the relationships between inventory and capacity. The concepts that he developed came to be known under his software OPT only and explained in his book 'The Goal'. These concepts, are now advocated by many practitioners under the generic name **synchronised manufacturing** and can be used effectively in combination with MRP Software Packages.

☛ 10.10 Flexible Manufacturing System (FMS)

An FMS is a type of flexible automation system which builds on the programmable automation of NC and CNC machines. Materials are automatically handled and loaded and unloaded for machining operations. Programs and tooling set up can be quickly changed and production can be quickly switched on from one job to another with no loss of change over time.

Key Components of an FMS are :-

(I) Several computer controlled machining centres or workstations having CNC machines (Each known as Flexible manufacturing cells - FMCs) and robots for loading and unloading.

(II) Computer controlled transport system (**Automatic Guided Vehicles** called as AGVs) for moving materials and parts from machine to machine and in and out of the system.

(III) Computer controlled robots for loading and unloading stations.

(IV) An **automated storing and retrieval system**.

(V). Each of the CNC machines i.e., FMCs are having **Automated tool changers** - ATCs (about 100 - 120 cutting tools).

(VI) FMS is having a central computer control over realtime routing known as **host computer system** and also provided with an individual computer system for each of the FMCs.

(VII) **Automatic Pallet Changer,** inprocess inspection, parts washing, other CAM technologies. FMS is suitable for intermediate flow strategies with medium level of product varieties and volumes (40 - 2000 units per part). Also an FMS can produce a low variety high volume products in the same way as fixed automation systems.

Advantages	Disadvantages
♦ Improved Capital Utilisation ♦ Lower direct labour cost ♦ Reduced Inventory ♦ Consistent Quality ♦ Improved productivity (Greater output, lesser cost, smaller floor space) ♦ Suitable even for medium level of product varieties and volumes (can be produced even in batches) ♦ Intelligent self correcting systems	♦ High Capital Investment (Initial) ♦ Limited ability to adopt to product changes ♦ Substantial preplanning, tooling and fixture requirements ♦ Standardisation of part designs to reduce number of tools required ♦ Requires long planning and development cycle to instal FMS

☛ 10.11 Factory of the Future (Fully automated factory)

This represents full development of all aspects of computer integrated manufacturing (CIM). All functions of the factory will be computer controlled, integrated and to varying degrees self optimising.

Yamazaki - FMS (in their Machining centres manufacturing plant)

Earlier FMS	Present FMS
♦ 36 Machining Centres	♦ 18 Machining Centres
♦ Employment :- Direct workers 106 Indirect workers 80 Total Manpower: 190	♦ One in toolroom ♦ Four in Loading / Unloading stations (in 2 shifts) ♦ Third shift unmanned: 12
♦ Total time needed for the components of a complete machine - 3 months in Machine shops - 4 weeks in assembly - 1 week for inspection and adjustment Total over 4 months	- Only 4 days in machine shop - 2 weeks in assembly - 1 week inspection Under 4 weeks
♦ Capital costs	♦ Same
♦ Labour costs £ 2,000,000	♦ £ 130,000
♦ Annual profit (on 3 shift operations) £ 800,000	♦ £ 1,900,000

FMS installed by Yamazaki (as per Hartley), a manufacturer of machining centres (themselves FMS components) at its main plant in Oguchi in Japan.

Details	Old Machines	New FMS
• Number of Machining Centres	36	18
• Previous employment (workers)	106 Direct 80 Indirect	Manned by 1 person in Computer room 1 person in Tool room 4 persons at Loading/ Unloading stations
Total	186	6 persons per shift 12 persons on two shifts (Third shift unmanned)
Therefore Comparison is	186	12
• Components for a complete machine to manufacture one machining centre (Time in weeks)	Machine shop 3 months Assembly 4 weeks Inspection and adjustment 1 week Total time Over 4 months (For one machining centre manufacture)	Only 4 days (Average process time of 24 hours) 2 weeks (because work mans are available) 1 week 4 weeks
• Capital costs (See below)*	← Comparable	→
• Labour costs	£ 2000,000	£ 130,000 (Decreased)
• Average Annual profit (3 shift operation)	£ 800,000	£ 1,900,000 (Increased)
• Capital Costs		
Land and building	1.9	1.0
Machinery and equipment	4.0	7.5
Work in process	2.5	0.1
	8.4	8.6

Benefits of FMS : Following are the benefits of FMS :

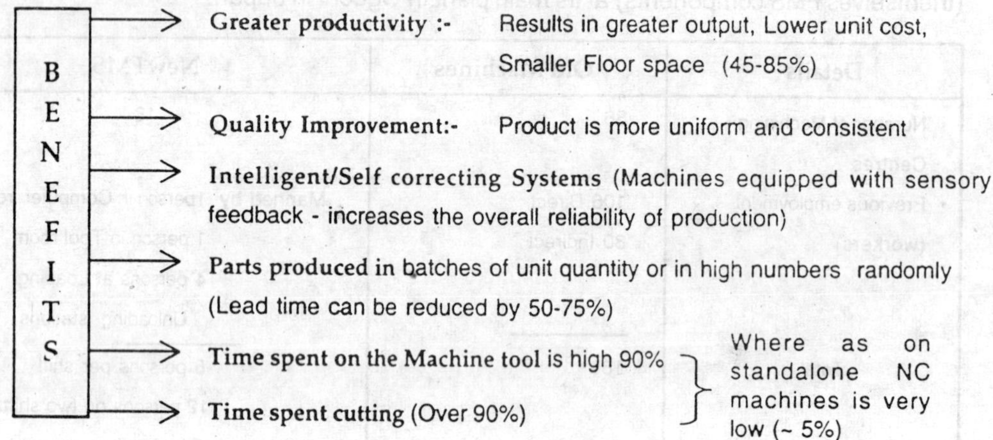

10.12 Production Planning and Control (PPC)

Production planning involves the organisation of an overall manufacturing or service system to product a product (good or service). **Production planning and control** is a management tool employed for the direction of manufacturing operations and their coordination with other activities of the firm.

Production Planning Control (PPC) involves both production planning and control activities. In other words, it involves: the planning of production, a decision about the sequence of operations to achieve what has been planned, the working of a time schedule for starting and finishing production, the issue of necessary orders for commencing operations, follow-up activities to check the progress of operations and to regulate execution to meet the plan requirements (in terms of quantity, quality schedule and the cost of production).

10.12.1 Significance of Production Planning and Control in a Factory

Different authorities have defined production control in different ways. British Standards Institute defines production control as:

"A directive agency which regulates an orderly flow of materials and coordination of the different production operations, following the scientific produce of its principles viz., planning, routing, scheduling, dispatching, and inspecting and taking the objective of producing the right quality, at the right time, and at minimum cost".

Basically, the production control function involves the integration and coordination of operations and activities of different factors of production with a view to optimising efficiency, so that the work may follow on the lines of and according to the standards set by the plans through routing, scheduling, dispatching, and follow-up techniques.

The production planning control (PPC) department in a factory is like a guide to the management. It sees that production is carried out without any hindrance giving due priorities to the right jobs in right quantities, in the right quality, and at the minimum cost. PPC is an important and vital activity of production management, serving not only the management but also the customers who are in need of quality goods.

The management can align the production activities with its sales programme, by keeping the investment in inventories at a minimum. Large-scale economies can thus be achieved and higher profits obtained. For the customers, PPC can help in getting quality goods and services at the right time and at the most economical rate.

10.12.2 Mechanism or Techniques of Production Control Steps In PPC

There are **four techniques on steps** in Production Planning and Control:

- Routing
- Scheduling
- Dispatching
- Follow-up

Fig. 10.20 Techniques of Production Control

10.12.3 Routing

Routing is the determination of path or route on which manufacturing operations will travel, establishing the sequence of operations to be followed in manufacturing a particular item or component. This route path is to be determined in advance.

Routing is defined by Kimball and Kimball as "It is a selection of path or route over which every piece is to travel in being transformed from raw material into finished product".

Bethel, Walter, Smith and Stackman have defined routing as "It determines what work will be done on a product or part, as what, as where and how it will be done?" It forms a pre-activity for most of the scheduling and dispatching functions of the planning department. The activities generally include determining Men, Machines, Materials, volume of production, the type, number and sequence of production operations and the place where production is to be carried out.

"Routing is what, how much, how, where and with which to produce"

10.12.4 Objectives and Benefits of Routing

The objectives of Routing are:

- To decide the most feasible sequence of operations and to ensure that the same are followed.
- To utilise inputs like machines, materials, men etc. in the most economical way.
- To influence the design of the factory layout, building, machines etc.

Benefits of Routing are:

- Efficient use of available resources.
- Reduction in manufacturing costs.
- Improvement in output (both quality and quantity).
- Providing a basis for scheduling and loading.

10.12.5 Steps in Routing

- Analyse the product, its components or parts and determine the processes involved for each of the components to manufacture the same product in a most economical way and to decide what is to be procured to reduce the cost.
- Decide the type of material required, its quality, grade and quantity for the manufacture of individual components. A list of materials with standard of quality, specifications, drawings etc. has to be prepared to enable the routing section to take necessary action to decide on its procurement, after verification.
- Determine the number of manufacturing operations and their sequence as indicated in the route sheet.
- Work out the total process time of each of the operations based on the timings provided by production planning estimation department and work out the type and number of machines necessary to produce the product. This is also called 'Load statement'.
- Decide on the normal scrap allowance, allowance for rejections to be provided during manufacture.
- Design the forms necessary for the production department like Job cards, Inspection cards, Routing sheets, Tools tickets etc.

The person who attends on routing function should be fully aware of all operations, machines, materials, etc. in a plant.

10.12.6 Scheduling

Scheduling involves developing and assigning specific dates for the start and completion of the necessary tasks or operation in a production shop floor. It involves fixing priorities for each job and determining the starting time and finishing time for each operation, the starting dates and finishing dates for each part, subassembly and final assembly.

Scheduling is the next technique of production control after routing. It is the arrangement of different operations involved in manufacturing, to fix priorities (including time, date for commencement and completion of operations). Work scheduling is defined as "the assignment of starting and completion time for the various operations to be performed". "It involves developing and assigning specific dates for the start or completion of the necessary work tasks". Scheduling is performed in two stages.

Objectives of Loading

The objectives are: (i) reduce setup time, (ii) delivery dates fixing, (iii) evenly load the plant and balance workload with available machine and labour capacity, (iv) reduce waiting time for jobs to be loaded on the machines, (v) reduce the idle time of men and machines, (vi) increase the efficiency of utilisation of the plant capacity.

- Loading
- Dispatching

Loading is assigning to a particular work center the task to be performed during some gross scheduling period, say a week. Some desired completion date is usually assigned to each task. The jobs loaded to a work center are considered as a waiting line, or queue, waiting jobs. Even though some of the jobs may not be present physically, loading of work center depends on available capacity in the load report and the expected availability of the material for the job.

Dispatching is explained in the next section.

Activities in scheduling

- Allocation of quantity of each of the components to be produced.
- Indication of the quality required.
- Allocation of time against each operation.

Objectives of scheduling

- To meet the pre-determined demand, make necessary arrangements for the production of goods and services.

- To arrange raw materials, machines, equipments, tools etc. and keeps the inventory of raw materials at the optimum level.
- The production cost should be brought down to the minimum by utilising the production facilities to the fullest extent, so that, the goods and services can be made available as and when they are required. The production facilities are plant, machinery, buildings, men, materials etc.
- To coordinate of the different departments with regard to the production activities, to bring the production cost to the minimum level.
- To arrange for product development and design.
- To arrange the activities of the quality control and inspection department so that the goods may be produced according to the specifications and standards.
- To determine economical batch size and ascertain sequence of operations, so that the setup cost is reduced.
- To arrange for the supply of raw materials and semifinished goods to different machines at a proper time, proper place and in proper quality so that congestion and delays in production may be eliminated.
- To evaluate the route of production, check and inform the management about the production progress from time to time and arrange for proper guidance and control.
- To supply component drawings, process sheets, job cards, routing sheets, tooling (Jigs, Fixtures, Cutting tools etc.). Chasing of jobs from machines, feeding of jobs to every machine without any holdups, arranging inspection, etc. also need to be done.
- To work out a schedule. One should know the date of delivery specified by the customer in the order ie. date of customer's requirement of the product; time required for assembly and sub-assembly, time required for the production of individual components which may be of long and short cycle. Other information required are production capacity of each of the machines, department where it is executed, time required to make or purchase tooling, movement of materials from machine to machine and the time required for the same, time required for inspection, list of priority orders etc. With this information, a detailed schedule can be worked out.

"Routing is the most economic route or path, whereas scheduling acts as a time table; Routing considers 'Where' aspects, scheduling considers 'When' aspects".

10.12.7 Types of Scheduling

Three types of scheduling are:

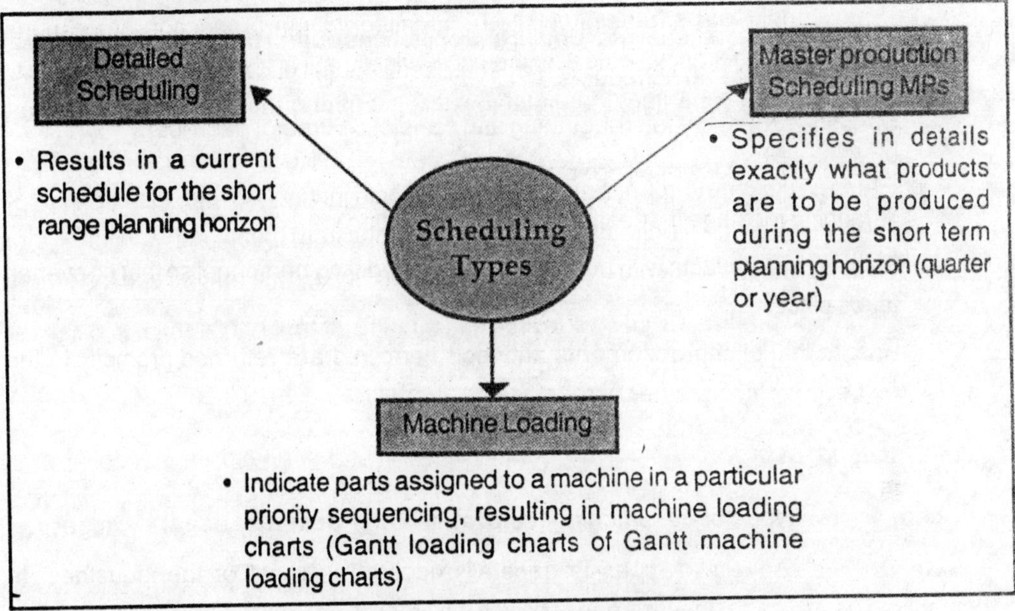

Fig. 10.21 Types of Scheduling

The various types of scheduling are shown in figure 10.21

10.12.8 Dispatching

James B. Dilworth defines **dispatching** as sequencing of the tasks that are waiting to be worked on at a work center and releasing them to be performed at a particular time by a specific machine. It refers to the act of assigning specific tasks to a specific work center, to be performed in a specific sequence.

It is concerned with the issuance of orders, instructions and other communications to the work force, demanding accountability of their performance, exercising leadership and supervision and maintaining supervision and morale of production personnel.

Functions of Dispatching

The various functions of dispatching are:

- Assignment of work to individual machines/work place and men.
- Checking the availability of materials, movement of materials from stores to the machine, providing the tools, jigs, fixtures, dies and gauges for various jobs from the tool stores.
- Giving orders, instructions and production forms to foremen and executives before start of work.

- Obtaining appropriate drawings/specifications, material lists from design office.
- Release of prints of component drawings, part lists, process sheets, job cards, route cards etc. to the shop supervisors.
- Controlling the material movement and operations during processing on the basis of route sheets and schedules.
- Scheduling of every job (beginning and completion time of each job).
- Control of progress of all operations.
- Arranging for stage inspection and final inspection.
- Establishing contacts with both routing and scheduling personnel so that no overlap takes place.
- Ensure that all the documents and tools borrowed are returned promptly to the respective officers, after use.

Types of Dispatching

There are two types of despatching, **centralised and decentralised:**

A mix of the above two types is generally adopted in most of the industries. In decentralised despatching, the foreman receives the orders from central office and it is left to him to determine the sequence within his section. This system is more flexible and avoids red-tapism, delays and the need for elaborate reporting.

10.12.9 Expediting or Follow-up

Expediting or Follow-up activity is meant to examine whether work is going on as per the plan. If variation is found, it is eliminated or adjusted as quickly as possible. A group of people called follow-up men or progress chasers will take up this task.

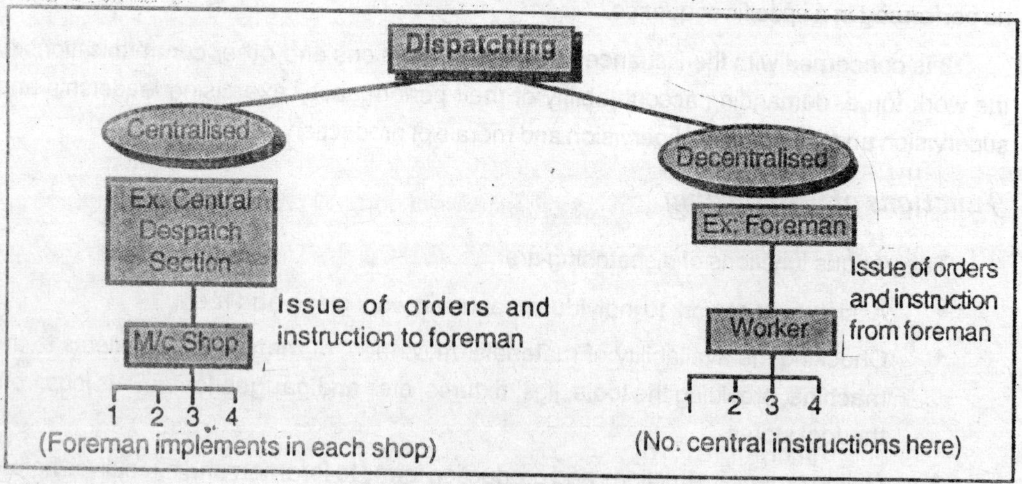

Fig. 10.22 Dispatching

Generally, production progresses as expected. But, sometimes there may be problems due to:

— Non-availability of material or late arrival of materials, tools or men.

— High absenteeism.

— Associated department may not assist due to their own commitments or behind-schedule activities.

— Customers requirements change abruptly.

— 'Acts of God' or strikes which will result in a hold-up of the manufacturing activities (unforeseen circumstances, beyond one's control).

— Errors in drawings.

— Power failures.

— Machine breakdown.

In all these cases, progress chasers will analyse the matter, search for alternate arrangements and reduce the delays or hold-ups.

Current Production Planning and Control Systems

The most widely used ones are :-

- Material requirement planning (MRP or MRP - I)
- Manufacturing Resource Planning (MRP - II)

The other two new methods are :-

- Just in time
- Synchronised manufacturing

☛ 10.13 Material Requirement Planning (MRP -I)

MRP is a technique of working backward from the scheduled quantities and need dates for end items specified in a master production schedule, to determine the requirements for components needed to meet the master production schedule. This technique determines what components are needed, how many are needed and when they are needed, and when they should be ordered, so that they are likely to be available when needed. MRP (Material requirement planning) usually is a computer system, that as the name implies, plans when material (and other components) will be required.

Let us take a simple example to explain this.

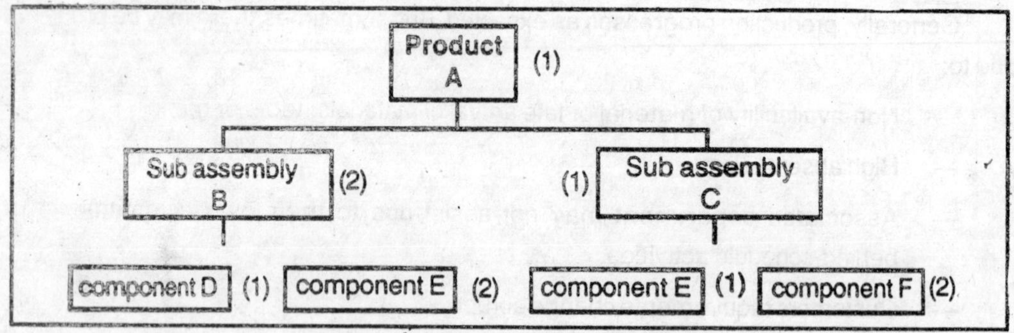

Fig. 10.23 Example of MRP

In the above example, if the product A is to be produced, two sub-assemblies of B one sub-assembly of C are to be assembled.

The requirement of component D will be 1 x 2 x 1 = 2 Nos.

The requirement of component E will be 2 x 2 x 1 = 4 Nos.
(from sub-assembly B)

The requirement of component E will be 1 x 1 x 1 = 1 No.
(from sub-assembly C)

Total requirement of component E will be 5 Nos.

The requirement of component F will be 2 x 1 x 1 = 2 Nos.

This can be represented as under:

Items	Qty.	Component	Qty.
Product A	1	D	2
Subassembly B	2	E	5
Subassembly C	1	F	2

Table 10.24 Requirement of Items

Suppose the sales forecast indicates 100 numbers of product A in the year, then each of the items in the above table have to be multiple by 100, which is to be produced by the firm. Now let us analyse when these items are required.

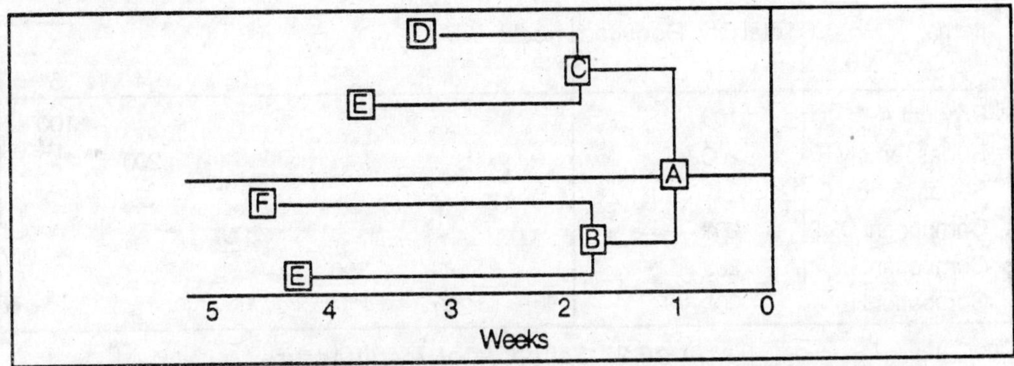

Fig. 10.25 Schedule of Product, Sub-Assembles and Components

0 is the point where the customer needs the product A at his firm.

1 is the point where A should be ready at the manufacturers point and is ready for delivery. The time 0 to 1 is for packing and delivery of the product.

2 is the point where B & C sub-assemblies should be ready for assembling, to get product A.

3 is the point where component D should be ready, since it is a short term production cycle.

4 is the point for component E to be ready.

5 is the point where component F should be ready (Longest production cycle).

Let us also consider stock items already available. If we re-draw the table, it will be as under:

Items	Quality for (100 Production)	Already in stock	Total Quantity required
Product A	100	-	100
Subassembly B	200	-	200
Subassembly C	100	50	50
Component D	200	-	200
Component E	500	200	300
Component F	200	-	200

Table 10.26 Quantity Requirement Considering Stock

Items	Total Qty. Required	weeks					
		0	1	2	3	4	5
Product A	100						100
Subassembly B	200					200	
Subassembly C	50					50	
Component D	200				200		
Component D	300			300			
Component E	200		200				

Table 10.27 Schedule of Manufacture

In the above table, schedule of manufacture is shown. If the product A is required on the fifth week, component F should be ready at the 1st week, component E should be ready at the 2nd week, component D by 3rd week, sub-assemblies B & C should be ready by 4th week and the assembly of B & C takes place by 5th week to get product A. The product A is delivered to the customer in the week.

From the above example, we can understand how complicated the working is what happens if we take big companies where hundreds of products and thousands of components are produced? Is it possible to work like this manually? It needs huge manpower to work on this and finally results in more confusions and mistakes. Hence computerisation is required for MRR In MRR we need quantity for each of the items, list of bought-outs and manufactured items, production cycle of each of the items, number of products required per year, stock position etc. to work out the actual quantities to be manufactured and the commencement of production of each of the items. These can only be done on computers and with software packages.

10.13.1 Bill of Material

Bill of Material shows the list of all the components needed to produce a finished item. Each component which is required in the final product is either purchased on manufactured after the order is received. Many make-or-buy decisions are made at this time. The purchasing department will obtain prices of all the items to be purchased and of all the raw materials for the items to be produced inhouse.

The bill or material example is as under:

Sl. No.	Part Number	Description	Unit of Measure	Source Make/ purchase	Total Qty.
0	10000	Finished Product	1		1000
1	20081	Component A1	1	M	1000
2	30063	Component B2	1	P	1000
3	40181	Component C2	1	M	1000
4	10060	Component C3	1	M	1000
5	21073	Component B3	2	P	1000
6	48070	Component B5	1	M	1000
7	20082	Component B1	1	M	1000
8	30182	Component C1	1	M	1000
9	41816	Component D2	1	M	1000
10	20083	Component C4	1	M	1000
11	33402	Component E2	1	M	1000
12	40116	Component F2	1	M	1000
13	41018	Component C5	1	M	1000
14	50061	Component D3	1	M	1000
15	50110	Component D5	1	M	1000
16	20109	Component E4	1	M	1000
17	18082	Component B6	1	P	1000
18	14583	Component C6	1	M	1000
19	31582	Component F6	1	M	1000
M-Make, P-Purchase					

Table 10.28 Bill of Materials

Manufacturing Resource Planning (MRP - II)

MRP II is a natural outgrowth of MRP I whereas MRP I focuses priorities of materials.

MRP II is a management process for taking the business plan and breaking it down into specific, detailed tasks that people evaluate, agree upon and are held accountable for. It involves all departments like.

- Materials department
- Engineering department (to maintain Bill of Materials)
- Sales/Marketing department (to keep sales plan up to date)
- Purchasing and manufacturing departments (to meet due dates for brought and items

10.14 Just-In-Time

JIT is a method involving very small raw material or in-process inventory quantities, small manufacturing lots and frequent deliveries, such that a small batch of each component or subassembly is produced and delivered 'just in time' to be used in the next production step. It was developed first by the Toyota Motor Company and later adopted by other Japanese companies.

Just-in-Time is a broad philosophy of seeking excellence and eliminating waste in the manufacturing process. It includes:

- People involvement
- Total quality Control
- JIT production

The JIT philosophy of continuous improvement and minimisation of waste considers waste to be any activity that does not add value to the product or serve the customer in some way. One form of waste that is inconspicuous and difficult to combat is the under-utilisation of human talent. JIT seeks to utilise more fully the creative talents of employees, suppliers, sub-contractors and others who may contribute to the company's improvement. **People involvement** includes:

- Team work
- Discipline
- Supplier involvement

Total quality control is the achievement and improvement of quality in a JIT company. It involves every department and every employee in the company. JIT companies consider not only outsiders who buy and use the product as customers but also have the concept that each employee has an immediate customer, who is the next person who uses or further processes the item or information. If each worker sends only good items to his immediate customer, defective products will not be produced.

Total quality control includes:

- The immediate customer
- Quality at the source
- A culture, not a program

JIT Production

The two factors considered under this are:

- Insidious excessive queues (because of lengthy work stoppage at some upstream work center). Items wait in queues for a long time before they are sent further.
- Queues are a waste that JIT fights.

A major objective of JIT is to have items only at the right place at the right time (to purchase and produce items only a short time before they are needed so that work-in-process inventory is kept very low). The goal of JIT production is to make items just before they are needed in order to eliminate the waste associated with queues.

Japan	USA
In Japan, parts coming from other plants are typically delivered one truck load at a time in the JIT system.	In US, with suppliers often thousands of miles away, some adoptations have to be made.
The production line often is fed directly out of the truck that just arrived. This is particularly feasible in Japan, Where manufacturers tend to be located in the Tokyo area.	To make JIT work better, General Motors encouraged suppliers to build parts plants near GM assembly plants.
They have long term relationship with trusted suppliers who are also located in the same area.	To keep assembly plants constantly informed the location of supplied enroute to them., some American tracking firms now carry radios capable of relaying their status to the plant any time via the Geostar satelite.

Questions

Section A:

1. Define production.
2. Give the meaning of production.
3. Explain production function as a system.
4. Discuss the Engineer's role in production activity.
5. Work out sample organisation structure for a single plant of a multiplant company involved in Production, Marketing, Finance, Human Relations, Quality, Designs and R & D with a sketch.
6. How do you compare the working of Japanese companies with US Companies?
7. Explain Synchronised Manufacturing.
8. Explain Flexible Manufacturing System (FMS).
9. Define FMS.
10. What are the key components of an FMS?
11. For what quantities (volume) and batch of production, and product varieties FMS would be ideal?
12. Mention the advantages and disadvantages of FMS.

13. What do you mean be Factory of the future (Fully Automated Factory)?
14. Explain a Fully automated factory.
15. Compare an earlier FMS with the present day FMS. How the present FMS is beneficial?
16. What are the benefits of FMS as compared to conventional or special machines?
17. Compare and contrast how just in time is adopted in US and Japan.
18. What is Plant Location? Define.
19. List five factors affecting the decision of Plant Location.
20. Name the steps in Plant Location.
21. Which are the agglomerating and degglomerating factors for the location of a Plant?
22. Bring out demerits of city site.

Section B:

1. Discuss the factors which should determine the location of a plant.
2. Discuss the steps to be taken in choosing plant location.
3. Explain the relative merits and demerits of urban site to start an industry.

Section C:

1. What are the factors affecting the location of a plant? Discuss.
2. How is a location for plant selected?
3. Discuss the various functions involved in the location of a plant with an emphasis on a sugar plant.
4. What is meant by plant location? Discuss the steps to be taken in choosing a location for the plant.
5. Discuss the various factors which influence the location of a plant.
6. What is plant location? Discuss the factors influencing plant location.
7. You would like to start a software industry. What factors influence your plant location.
8. Discuss the various factors to be considered in the location of a plant, with particular references to a cement plant.
9. Discuss the various factors involved in the location of a plant, with particular references to a cement plant.
10. What factors should be taken into account while selecting a suitable site for a plant?

Add questions on these subjects:

- Plant Location
- Plant Layout
- FMS
- Plant Selection
- Plant Layout software
- Economic order of quantity
- Break even chart
- Learning curves
- Inventory control
- Sensitivity analysis
- MRPI
- MRP II
- Production Planning Control
- JIT

Chapter - 11

11.1 Preview

This Chapter includes :

- *Assuring Product Quality*
  - Some definitions
  - Importance of Better Quality
  - Statistics of Quality
  - Process Control Charts
  - Inspection and Sampling
  - Human aspects of Quality
  - Taguchi Methods
- *Productivity*
  - Productivity defined
  - America's productivity challenge
- *Work Measurement*
  - Introduction
  - Basic Time Study Method
  - Work Sampling
  - Other Methods
- *Maintenance and facilities (plant) Engineering*
  - Scope of Maintenance
  - Types of Maintenance
  - Some Maintenance Management Considerations
  - Other facilities and Plant engineering functions
- *Other manufacturing functions*
  - Human Resources (personal) Management
  - Purchasing and Materials Management

    (Importance of purchasing, the engineer in purchasing, materials management, package engineering)

11.2 Definition of Quality:

(I) **'Quality'** means those features of products which meet customer needs and thereby provide customer satisfaction. Higher quality in this sense usually **'costs more'**.

(II) **'Quality'** means freedom from diffencies - freedom from errors that require doing work again. In this sense the meaning of quality is oriented to costs, and higher quality usually **'costs less'**.

(I) Product features that meet customer needs	**(II) Freedom from deficiencies**
Higher quality enables companies to: * Increase customer satisfaction * Make products saleable * Meet competition * Increase Market Share * Provide sales income * Secure Premium Prices	Higher quality enables companies to: * Reduce error rates * Reduce rework, waste * Reduce field failures, warranty charges * Reduce customer dissatisfaction * Reduce inspection, test * Shorten time to put new products in the market * Increase fields, capacity * Improve delivery performance
Major effect is on sales	Major effect is on costs
Usually, higher Quality costs more	Usually, higher Quality costs less

Fig. 11.1 The Meaning of Quality

This figure helps to explain why some meetings on managing for quality end in confusion.

(III) **Quality - A simple definition is** 'Fitness for use' or **'Conformance to requirements'.**

11.3 Importance of Better Quality

Product quality has eight dimensions. They are:

- Performance
- Feature
- Reliability
- Serviceability
- Durability
- Appearance
- Customer Service
- Safety

The **ten dimensions** of service quality are:

- Reliability
- Responsiveness
- Competence
- Access
- Courtesy
- Communication
- Credibility
- Understanding
- Security
- Tangibles

The role of quality needs no emphasis for a firm because it is the key to success in business addition to price, flexibility and delivery speed to achieve maximum customer satisfaction. Today, "Quality" is the watchword for the survival and growth of any organisation specially in the global business environment. Good quality creation in the product would increase :

- Productivity
- Profits
- Product image
- Brand image
- Company image

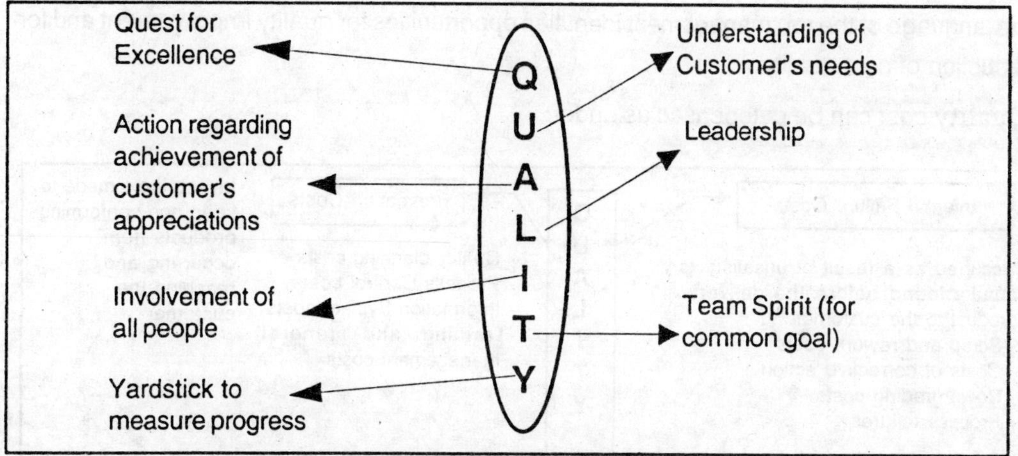

Fig. 11.2 Meaning of Quality

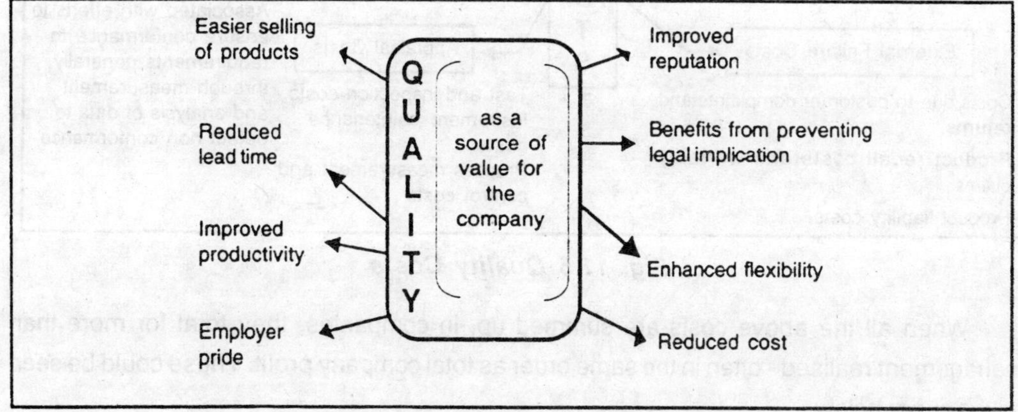

Fig. 11.3 Value of Improvements in Quality

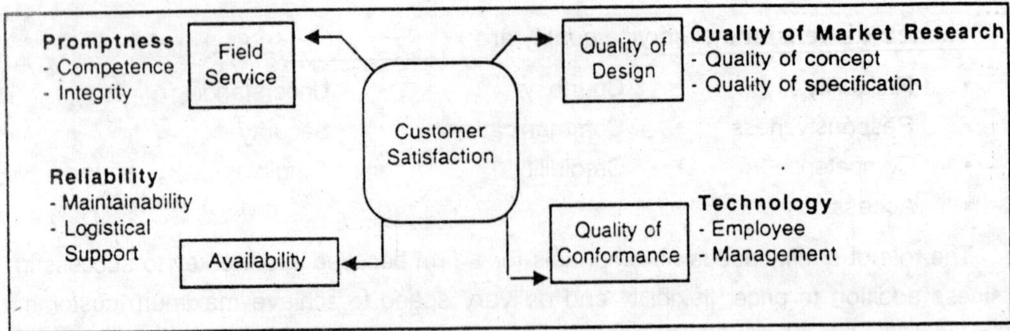

Fig. 11.4 Dimensions of Quality (For Customer Satisfaction)

11.4 Cost of Quality

The 'Costs of Quality' (or the costs of poor quality) were associated with avoiding poor quality or incurred due to poor quality. Quality cost programs translate quality problems into the language of the top management identifies opportunities for quality improvement and for reduction of cost quality.

Quality cost can be categorised as under:

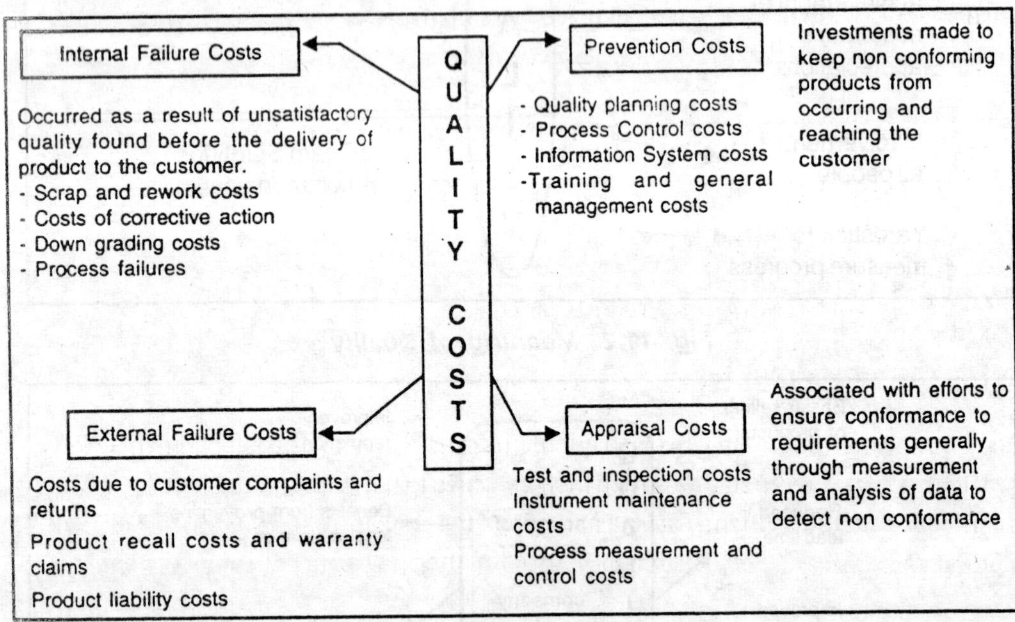

Fig. 11.5 Quality Costs

When all the above costs are summed up, in companies, they total for more than management realised - often in the same order as total company profit. These could be seen on the curve below.

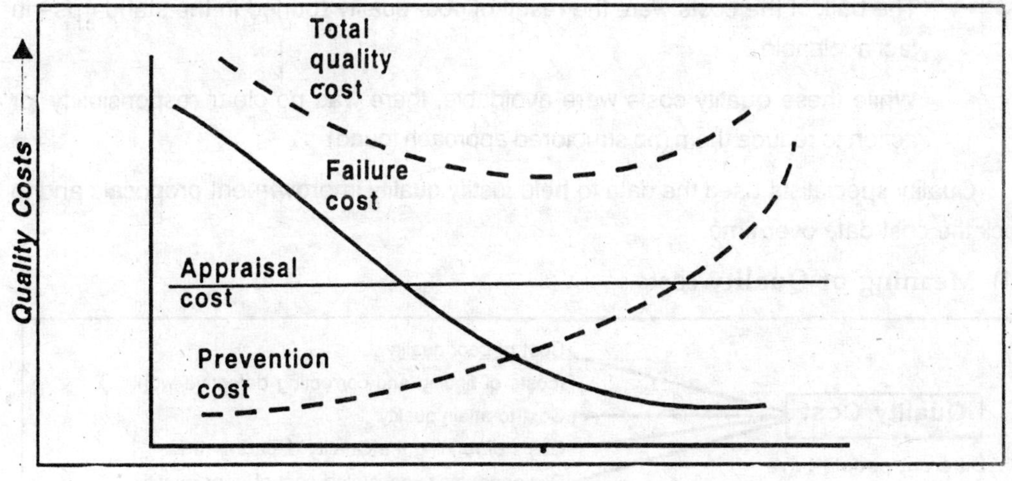

Fig. 11.6 Effect of Quality Conformance on Quality Cost

Prevention Costs are generally found to be a very small percentage of the total. Better prevention of poor quality clearly reduce internal failure costs, as fewer defective items are made. External failure cost also decrease. Appraisal costs are reduced, since top quality production does not require the same intensive level of inspection. The products are made correctly the first time. Figure 11.5 shows the relationship of these components of quality cost with quality level.

Quality cost data can be broken down by product line, process, department, work centre, time or cost category. This categorisation makes data analysis more convenient and useful to the management.

$$\text{Quality cost index} = \frac{\text{Total quality costs}}{\text{Total direct labour costs}}$$

11.5 Quality Costs

(I) During the 1950s, there evolved numerous quality oriented staff departments. The heads of these departments started selling their activities to the company managers. These managers concentrated on money saving and hence the concept of studying quality related costs provided the vocabulary to community between the quality staff departments and the company managers. The results after analysis were:

- The quality related costs were much larger than had shown in the accounting reports. (These were visible and hidden costs)
- The quality costs were not simply the results of factory operations. The support operations were major contributors.

- The bulk of the costs were the result of poor quality (buried in the standards - in fact avoidable).
- While these quality costs were avoidable, there was no clear responsibility for action to reduce them (no structured approach found)

Quality specialists used the data to help justify quality improvement proposals and to track the cost data over time.

(II) Meaning of Quality costs

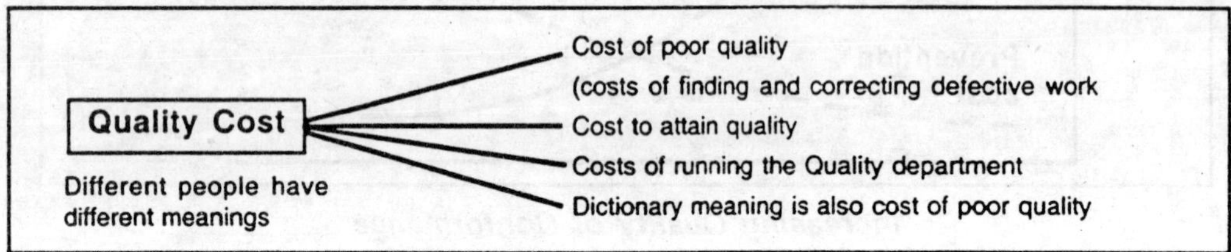

Fig. 11.7 Meaning of Quality Costs

(III) Objectives for tracking and analysing the impact of quality on costs

These are:

- The language of money is essential (Money is the basic language of upper management)
- The meaning of quality costs (See (II) above)
- Quality cost Measurement and publication cost does not solve Quality Problems
- Scope of costs is too limited

(IV) Costs of poor Quality: These are due to :

- Cost of non-conformities
- Cost of inefficient processes
- Cost of lost opportunities for sales revenue

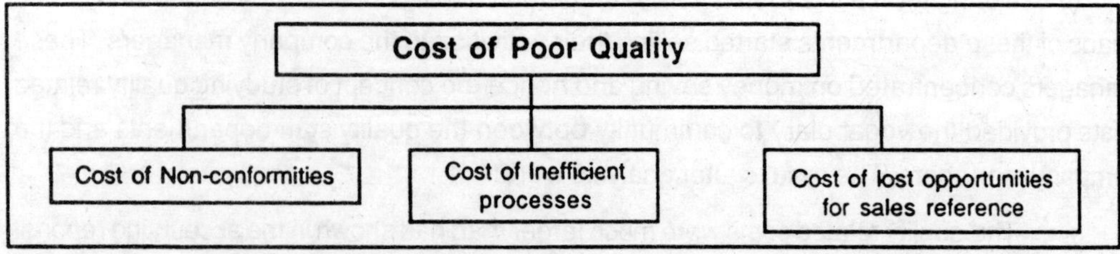

Fig. 11.8 Components of the Cost of Poor Quality

(V) Categories of Quality Costs

Many companies summarise these costs into four categories. Some experts call these as "Cost of Quality"

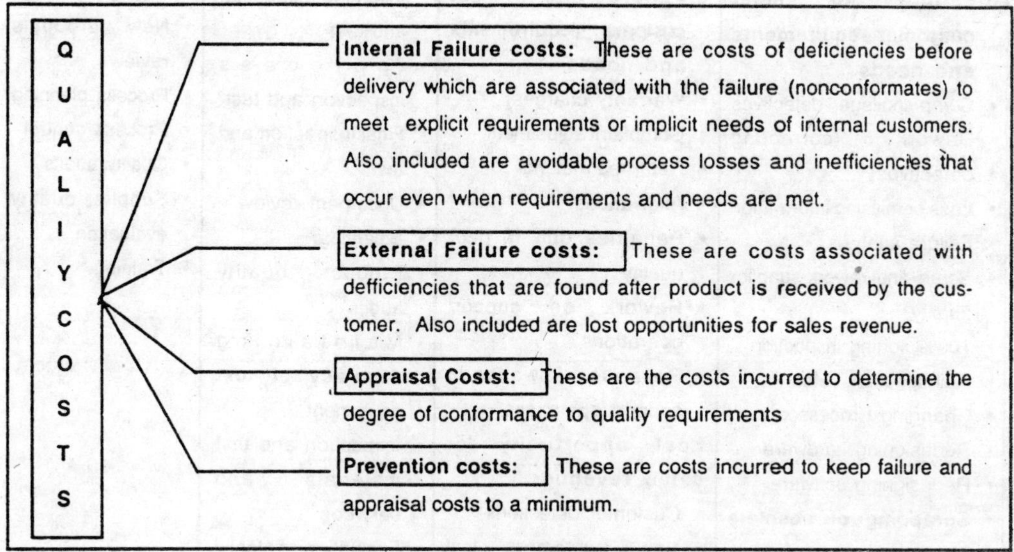

Fig. 11.9 Quality Costs

(VI) Comparison of Various Categories of Quality costs :

Internal Failure Costs	External Failure Costs	Appraisal Costs	Prevention Costs
a) Failure to meet customer requirements and needs • Scrap spoilage, defectives • Rework (correcting defectives) • Loss or missing information • Failure analysis • Scrap and rework-supplier quality • 100% sorting inspection • Reinspection, retest • Changing Processes • Redesigning hardware • Redesigning software • Scrapping of obsolete product • Scrap in support operations • Rework in internal support • operations • Downgrading **b) Cost of Inefficient Processes** Variability of product characteristics Unplanned downtime of equipment Inventory shrinkage Variation of process characteristics from best practice Non-value added activities	**a) Failure to meet customer requirements and needs** • Warranty charges • Complaint adjustment • Returned material • Allowances • Penalties due to poor quality • Rework on support operations • Revenue allowance in support operations **Lost opportunity for sales revenue** • Customer defections • New customers lost because of quality. • New customers lost because of lack of capability to meet customer needs	• Incoming inspection and test • Inprocess inspection and test • Final inspection and test • Document review • Balancing • Product quality audits • Maintaining accuracy of test equipment • Inspection and test materials and services • Evaluation of stocks	• Quality planning • New products review • Process planning • Process control • Quality audits • Supplier quality evaluation • Training

Fig. 11.10 Comparison of Various Quality Costs

Study of Distribution of Quality Costs

The study of the distribution of quality costs over the major categories can be further explored using the model for optimum quality costs.

- **The Failure Costs** : These equal zero when the product is 100% good, and rise to infinity when the product is 100% defective (Note that the vertical scale is cost per good unit of product. At 100% defective, the number of good units is zero and hence the cost per good unit is infinity).
- **The Cost of appraisal plus prevention** : These costs are zero at 100% defective, and rise as perfection is approached.
- **The sum of curves 1 and 2** : The third curve marked as 'Total quality costs' and this represents the total cost of quality per good unit of product.

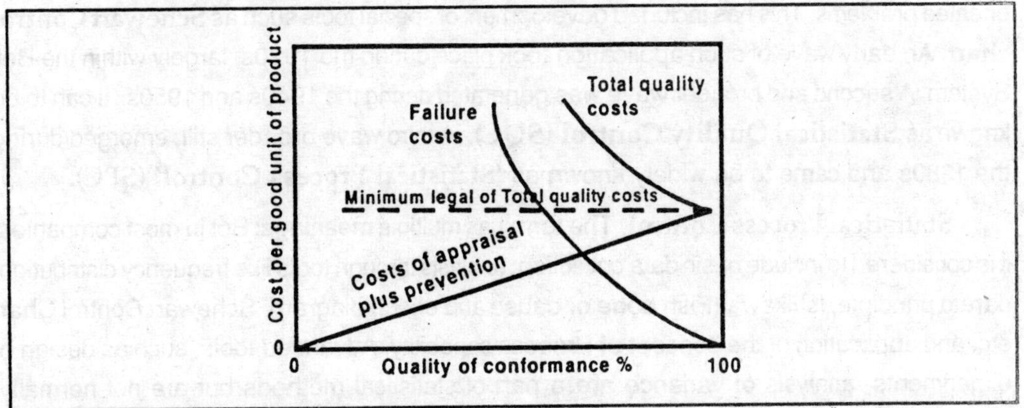

Fig. 11.11 Model for Optimum Quality Cost

11.6 Statistics of Quality

The flow diagram of decisions on conformance and fitness for use is as shown below:

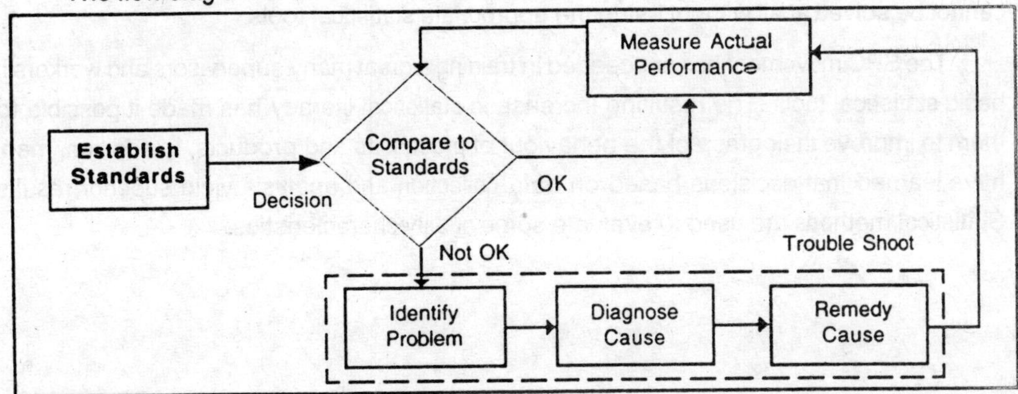

Fig. 11.12 Flow diagram of Decisions on Conformance and Fitness for Use

The feedback loop is short; the feedback often goes directly to the actuator - the energiser for corrective action.

(I) The Role of Statistical Methods

An essential activity within the feedback loop is :

- the collection of data
- analysis of data

This activity falls within the scientific discipline known as **'Statistics'**. The methods and tools are often called **'Statistical Methods'**. These methods have long been used to aid in data collection and analysis in many fields : biology, government, economics, finance, management etc.

During this century, much has happened to apply statistical methodology to quality oriented problems. This has included development of special tools such as **Schewart Control chart.** An early wave of such application took place during the 1920s, largely within the Bell System. A second and broader wave was generated during the 1940s and 1950s. It can to be known as **Statistical Quality Control (SQC).** A third wave broader still, emerged during the 1980s and came to be widely known as **'Statistical Process Control' (SPC).**

Statistical Process Control. The term has multiple meanings; But in most companies, it is considered to include basic data collection; analysis through tools like frequency distribution, pareto principle, Ishikawa (Fish bone or cause and effect) diagram, Schewart Control Chart etc. and application of the concept of Process capability. Advanced tools, such as design of experiments, analysis of variance are a part of statistical methods but are not normally, considered to be a part of SPC.

The statistical methods and tools have contributed in an important way to quality control and also to the other processes of Juran triology - quality improvement and quality planning. For some types of quality problems the statistical tools are more than useful - the problems cannot be solved at all without using the appropriate statistical tools.

The SPC movement has succeeded in training a great many supervisors and workers in basic statistical tools. The resulting increase in statistical literacy has made it possible for them to improve their grasp of the behaviour of processes and products. In addition, many have learned that decisions based on data collection and analysis yield superior results. Statistical methods are used to evaluate some quality characteristics.

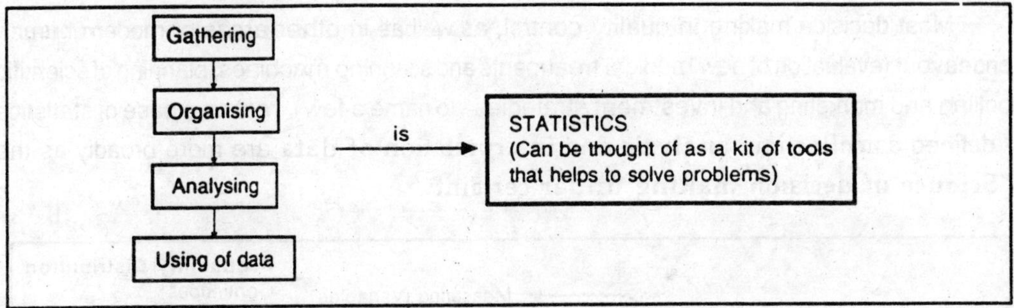

Fig. 11.13 Statistics (as a kit of tools to solve problems)

(II) Control charts

(i) **For variables,** it requires **actual measurements** e.g., length, weight, tensile, strength etc.; go - no go data cannot be used for charts.

(ii) **For attributes,** on the other hand, can be used in situations where we only wish to **count** the number of non confirming items or the number of non conformities in a sample.

Attribute is a quality characteristic which either confirms or does not confirm to specification. It is an 'Accept' or 'Reject' situation. Checking the dimensions of a part by using a go or no go gauge converts a variable into an attribute, whereas **Variable** is a quality characteristic which is checked by measurement. It carries values which continuously vary between the acceptable and non acceptable limits.

Attributes - go, no go information	**Variables** - Measurement information
Defectives - Usually measured in proportion or **percent defective.** This refers to the acceptability of units of product for a wide range of characteristics **(P control chart)**	**Variables** :- Usually measured by the mean and standard deviation. This refers to the distribution of a specific measurable characteristic of the product inspected (X and R charts)
Defects - Usually measured by actual count as a ratio of defects per unit. This refers to the **number of defects found in the units inspected,** and hence can be more than the number of units inspected (Control charts)	

Fig. 11.14 Control Charts

Most decision making in quality control, as well as in other areas of modern human endeavour (evaluation of new medical treatments and scanning machines, planning of scientific polling and marketing and investment strategies - to name a few), rest on a base of statistics - defined as **collection, analysis and interpretation of data** are more broadly as the **"Science of decision making under certainty"**

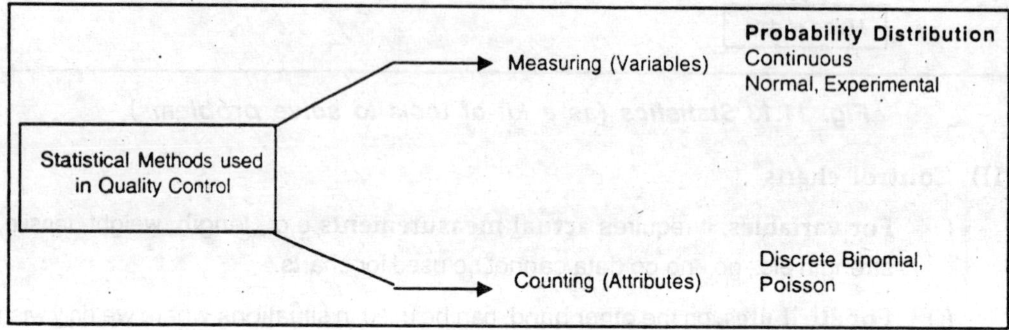

Fig. 11.15 Statistical Methods used in Quality Control

Each probability distribution is designed by a "measure of central tendency" (average) and a measure of dispersion (spread)

11.7 Various Quality Control Techniques

Quality Control is achieved through:

- Inspection
- Statistical Quality Control (SQC)
- Both, Inspection and SQC

Inspection and SQC have already been explained. **Statistical Quality Control** is the application of statistical techniques to accept or reject products already produced, or to control the process and, therefore, product quality, while the part is being made. While the latter is called process control, the former is called **Acceptance Sampling (Product Control).**

11.7.1 Control Chart

Because most manufacturing methods are not perfect, there are variations in the quality of the output. To know the variations and to control the same, control charts are used. **Control charts** are graphs showing the standards, called control limits, for a process, they plot the process measurements obtained from samples over a period of time. Control charts can be used in conjunction with sampling either by variables or attributes.

The essential factors in process control are:

- Standards
- Measurement
- Corrective action

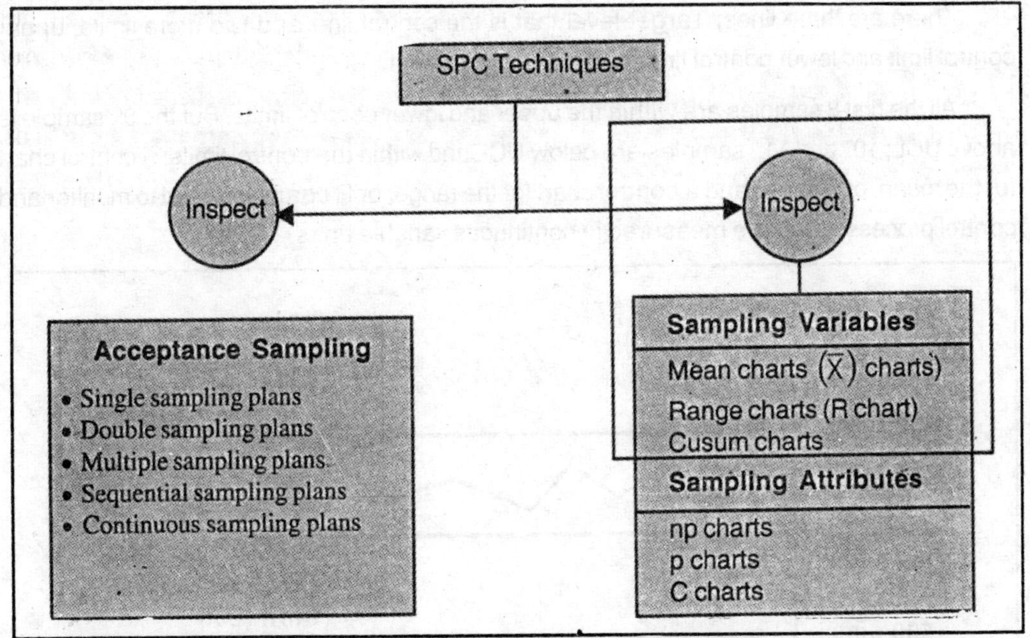

Fig. 11.16 The Different SPC Methods

11.7.2 Samples by Variables

Sampling by variables is done only where measurements can be made, and the reading varies percentage from piece to piece.

Take a few samples at a time from the produced lot. Measure their quality characteristics. Find the mean of the sample. Measure the range of dispersion in the sample. Gather, statistics for the ranges and the means of the various samples taken frequently or at regular intervals of time. These when plotted on a graph paper will show when a particular process needs to be rectified and in what manner.

Let us take an example of filling of coconut oil in bottles in a factory. Suppose 500gms are to be filled in an automatic filling machine, the readings are different for each fillings, even if you set the machine exactly for 500 gms. The readings may be 490, 500, 500, 510, 505 gms, if you take 5 samples and examine their measurements. In one case the customer is going to loose, in two cases the customer neither gains nor loose, in other two cases the customer is benefited. In all cases, the company should ensure that their customers should not loose any quantity of oil, to keep up to it's reputation. Hence the setting may be kept at 505 gms or more to start with, so that even in the case of lower reading, it should not fall below 500 gms. Instead, if the machine is set at say 520 gms, the customer is benefited always and the company loses in every filling. Hence the optimum should be worked out by using a formula. Examine a graph, below:

There are three lines; Target level that is the central line and two more limits, upper control limit and lower control limit and lower control limit.

All the first 8 samples are within the upper and lower control limits. But the 9th sample is above UCL; 10th and 11th samples are below UCL and within the control limits. A control chart for the mean, or $\overline{X}$ chart and a control chart for the range, or R chart, are used to monitor and control processes that are measured in continuous variable units.

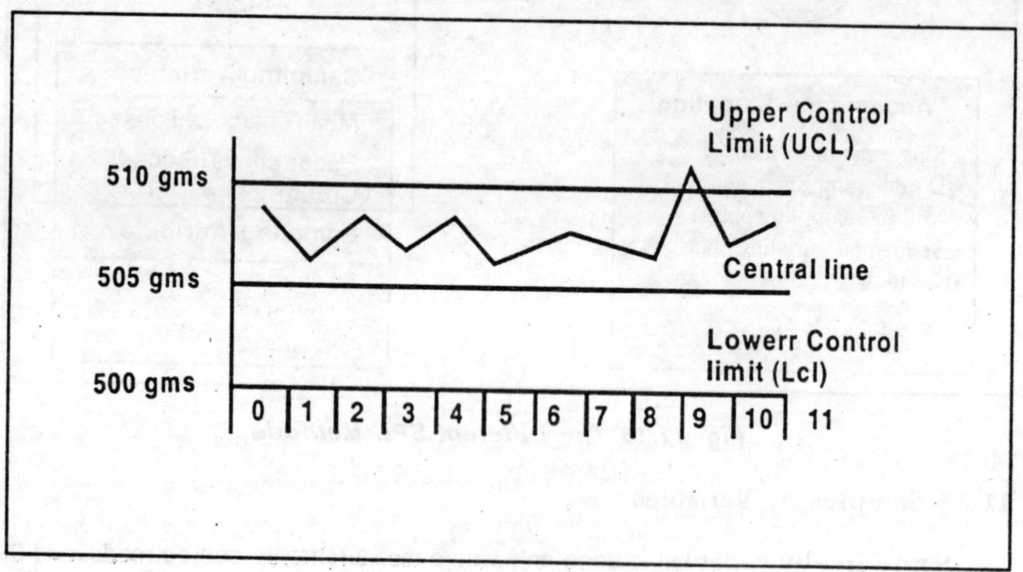

Fig. 11.17 Readings Plotted

11.7.3 $\overline{X}$ Chart

$\overline{X}$ **chart** checks whether a process is under statistical control and has been properly centered. In the example of coconut oil, 505 gms may be the correct central limit, instead of keeping the machine setting at 500 gms or 520 gms. A process under statistical control will conform to normal frequency distribution (the variations in the parameter values are due to random causes and not assignable causes). In the same example, sample numbers 1 to 8 and 10 to 11 are within the control limits, variations in the process measurements are assumed to be the result of 'chance causes,' small random variations naturally inherent in the process, when it is working correctly. However, sample No.9 goes above the UCL. Such an event would cause alarm to the production personnel, who would conclude that the automatic filling process was probably 'out of control,' not working as it should. A similar thing might also happen if the $\overline{X}$ values (average of sample readings) fell below the LCL. An out of control signal in this case also would cause the production/ quality control personnel to begin looking for an 'assignable cause' of the variation and to correct it. Of course, a type I error could have occurred and the process could be working properly.

11.7.4 Example of an $\overline{X}$ Chart

Take 5 samples of 10 readings each, on a lathe which produces a cylindrical part. The readings are: (in mms.)

Sample No.	1	2	3	4	5
Readings ($\overline{X}$)	5.75	5.60	5.712	5.81	5.66
	5.83	5.80	5.48	5.80	5.80
	5.80	5.81	5.86	5.79	5.74
	5.62	5.65	5.64	5.69	5.69
	5.68	5.73	5.73	5.82	5.81
	5.72	5.84	5.81	5.63	5.52
	5.71	5.76	5.66	5.47	5.51
	5.99	5.80	5.71	5.60	5.71
	5.81	5.79	5.81	5.71	5.75
	5.80	5.68	5.82	5.85	5.84
Total of 10 readings	57.71	57.46	57.23	57.17	57.03
$\overline{X}$ (Total % 10)	5.77	5.75	5.72	5.72	5.70

($\overline{X}$ Average of X in each sample)

Note $\overline{X} = \dfrac{\Sigma X}{10}$ (Total) and rounded off to the nearest 2nd decimal

$\overline{X}$ = 5.77+5.75+5.72+5.70+5.72 = 28.66%5 $\quad \overline{\overline{X}} = \dfrac{\Sigma X}{5}$

= 5.73 mms

Note $\overline{X}$ = Total of $\overline{X}$ divided by number of samples

11.7.5 Range Chart (R chart)

R is the range (Minimum to Maximum Value difference in each sample)

Sample No.	1	2	3	4	5
Min. Value	5.62.	5.60	5.48	5.47	5.51
Max. Value	5.99	5.84	5.86	5.85	5.84
Difference (R)	0.37	0.24	0.38	0.38	0.33

$$\overline{R} = \frac{0.37 + 0.24 + 0.38 + 0.38 + 0.33}{5} = \frac{1.70}{5} = 0.34\text{mms}$$

To calculate UCL and LCL in the case of $\overline{X}$ chart

The former used is :

$$\sigma\overline{X} = \sqrt{\frac{\Sigma(\overline{X} - \overline{\overline{X}})^2}{K}}$$ Where K is the number of samples

Sample No.	$\overline{X}$	$\overline{\overline{X}}$	$(\overline{X} - \overline{\overline{X}})$	$(\overline{X} - \overline{\overline{X}})^2$
1	5.77	5.73	0.04	0.0016
2	5.75	5.73	0.02	0.0004
3	5.72	5.73	-0.01	0.0001
4	5.72	5.73	-0.01	0.0001
5	5.70	5.73	-0.03	0.0009
		Total		0.0031

$$\sigma\overline{X} = \sqrt{\frac{0.0031}{5}} = \sqrt{0.0006} = 0.0246\text{mm}$$

$3\sigma\overline{X} = 3 \times 0.0246 = 0.738$

The Upper control limit (UCL) is

$\overline{\overline{X}} + 3\sigma\overline{X} = 5.73 + 0.738 = 6.468\text{mm}$

The Lower control limit (LCL) is

$\overline{\overline{X}} - 3\sigma\overline{X} = 5.73 + 0.738 = 4.992\text{mm}$

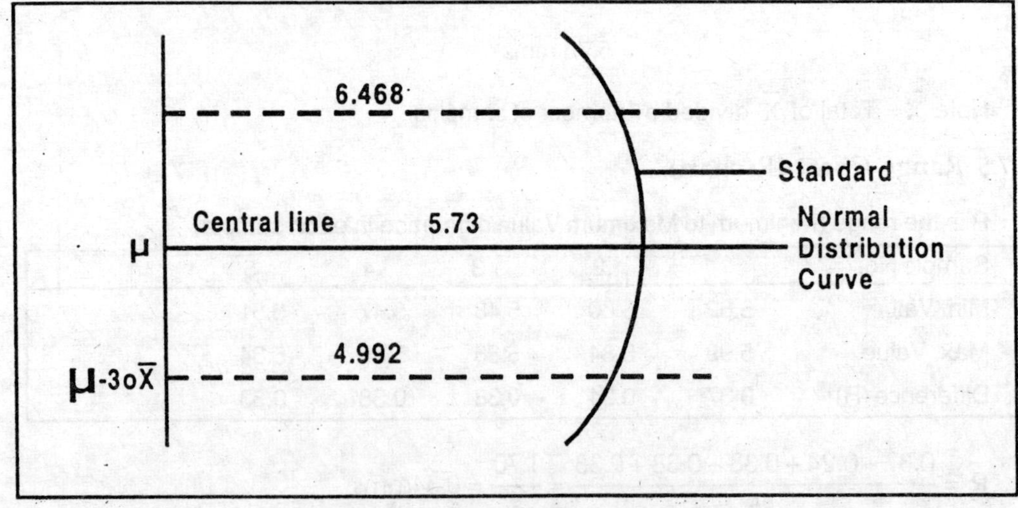

Fig. 11.18 Readings Plotted

Settings for 2 σ for Precaution

Two more lines above and below m can be added i.e., $\bar{\bar{X}} + 2\sigma\bar{X}$ and $2\sigma\bar{X}$ respectively as an early warning signal to the operator so that he can adjust the process when the parameter values exceed these limits. Inspection is only concerned with UCL and LCL and it will ask the operator to reset the machine if the sample average readings go beyond the control limits.

11.7.6 Example of a R Chart

In the $\bar{X}$ Chart, we were keeping a control on the central tendency. The standard deviations as well as the range will give an indication of the dispersion R and $\bar{R}$ values i.e., Range and average value of ranges respectively have already been worked out for the above example.

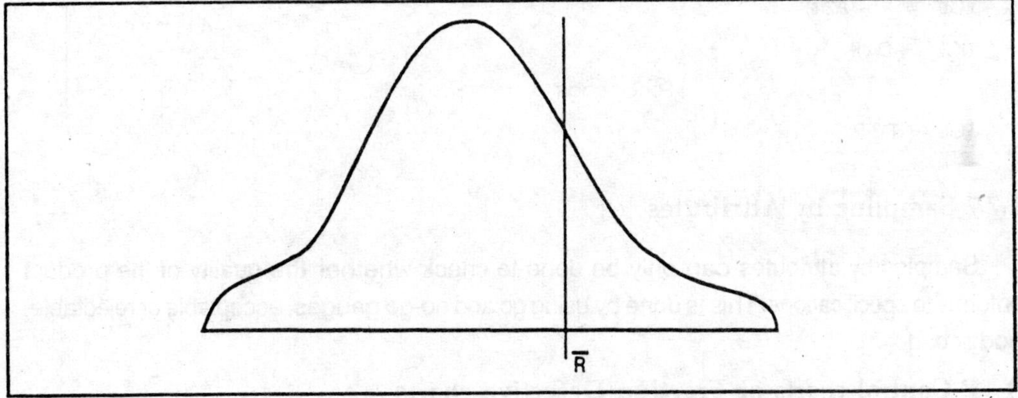

Fig. 11.19 Frequency Distribution of Range

Sample No.	R	$\bar{R}$	$(R - \bar{R})$	$(R - \bar{R})^2$
1	0.37	0.34	0.03	0.0009
2	0.24	0.34	-0.10	0.0100
3	0.38	0.34	0.04	0.0016
4	0.38	0.34	0.04	0.0016
5	0.33	0.34	-0.01	0.0001
		Total		0.0142

$$\text{Average value of Ranges} = \frac{\Sigma(R - \bar{R})^2}{K} = \frac{0.0142}{5} = 0.0028$$

$$\sigma R = \sqrt{\frac{\varepsilon(R - \bar{R})^2}{K}} = \sqrt{0.0028} = 0.0529 \text{ [K = number of samples = 5]}$$

$UCL = 0.34 + 3\sigma R \quad = 0.34 + 3 \times 0.0529$

$= 0.34 + 0.1587 \quad =0.4987$

$LCL = 0.34 - 3\sigma R \quad = 0.34 - 0.1587 = 0.1813$

Calculation of UCL and LCL by using the direct method.

Instead of using the formula as above, the UCL and LCL can be calculated in a simpler way using ready made table of co-efficients, where A2, D3 and D4 are constants from the table (Table values not shown here).

$UCL = \bar{\bar{X}} + A2R$

} For $\bar{X}$ chart

$LCL = \bar{\bar{X}} - A2R$

$UCL = D4\bar{R}$

} ForR chart

$LCL = D3\bar{R}$

11.7.7 Sampling by Attributes

Samples by attributes can only be done to check whether the quality of the product conforms to specifications. This is done by using go and no-go gauges, acceptable or rejectable, good or bad.

(I) P Control charts or Fraction Defective charts

These charts are used to control the quality of the components which are inspected by "attributes." They check if the fluctuations in product quality are due to chance causes or assignable causes. An example of a control chart is given below.

	Sample size (n)	Defective Parts	% Defective (P)
Day 1	100	8	8%
2	100	10	10%
3	100	9	9%
4	100	12	12%
5	100	6	6%
6	100	9	9%
7	100	11	11%
8	100	13	13%
9	100	12	12%
10	100	10	10%
Total	1000	100	

Total defectives are 100 for 1000 components

$$\bar{P}\text{ (Average defective)} = \frac{100}{1000} \times 100 = 10.00$$

A Chart is drawn with 10.00 as the center line allowing for variations down to (lowest value) and up to (highest value)

$$3sp = \sqrt{\frac{P(100-P)}{n}} = \sqrt{\frac{10.00(100-10)}{100}} = \frac{10\times 90}{100} = 3$$

SP = Standard deviation

Upper control limit (UCL) = $\bar{P}$ + 3Sp = 10+3 = 13

Lower control limit (LCL) = $\bar{P}$ - 3Sp = 10 - 3 = 7

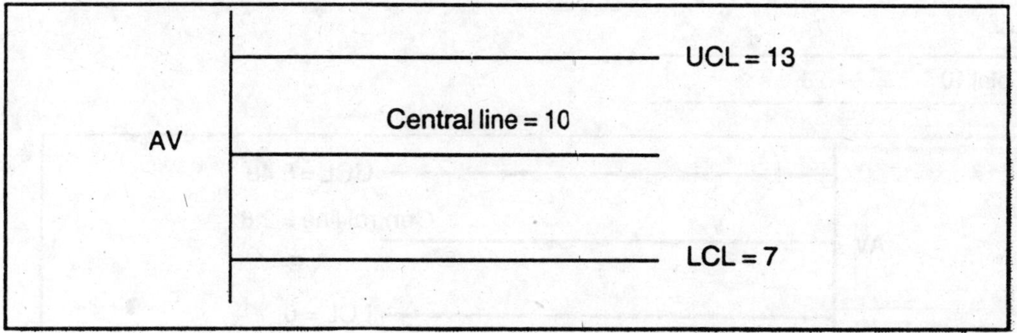

Fig. 11.20 P Chart UCL for LCL for the Example

(II) Control Chart (Number of defectives Chart)

In the case of certain products, such as castings, defects per unit is an important indication of quality. This is also applicable in the case of attributes, where measurements are not done. A sample of 10 castings or forgings are taken from a lot and inspected, and the defects found in each casting or forging are calculated.

Casting No.	No of Defects in each
88	2
167	4
173	1
210	0
310	4
322	5
401	3
406	1
452	1
464	7
Total 10	28

Average defects $\bar{C} = \frac{28}{10} = 2.8$

The distribution follows Poission distribution and the standard deviation is

$SC = \sqrt{C}$

$UCL = \bar{C} + 3SC = 2.8 + 3\sqrt{2.8} = 8.48$

$LCL = \bar{C} - 3SC = 2.8 - 3\sqrt{2.8} = -2.88$

(Negative value is taken as Zero)

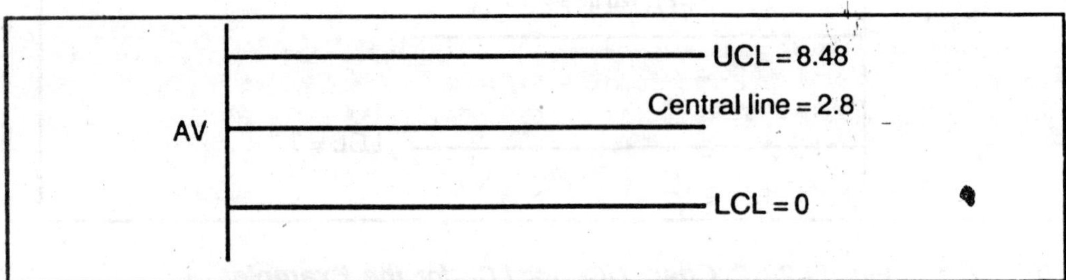

Fig. 11.21 Chart UCL & LCL for the Example

11.7.8 Sampling Plan Classification

Sampling Plan may be classified as:

- **Sampling by attributes or variables**
- **Lot by lot sampling or continuous sampling**

11.7.9 Acceptance Sampling

Acceptance sampling is based on the premise that a sample represents the whole lot from which the former is drawn.

This sampling by attributes is carried out by extracting a random sample from some larger lot of materials to determine whether to accept or reject the entire lot or whether to subject it to 100% inspection and separate the good from the bad. This process may be used in:

- Receiving • Process • Final Inspection

But, it is generally adopted for receiving (Purchased raw materials).

A rejected lot is returned to the supplier or charged for 100% screening of rejected lots, after which only the defective items are returned for a refund. A high rate of rejection is generally expensive to the supplier, even if he is able to find another source.

The sampling is done in several ways:

- **Single Sampling Plan**
- **Double Sampling Plan**
- **Multiple Sampling Plan**

11.7.10 Single Sampling Plan

This plan is for a single sample, specified for two numbers n and c where n is the sample size, c is the acceptance number i.e., maximum number of defects that may be found in the sample if the lot is to be accepted. If more than c defective items are found in the sample, the entire lot will be rejected or fully screened.

Dodge and romig in 1944, adopted a standard sampling plan table, wherein one of the following options would be selected, depending on the confidence level of the vendor in the process.

- Tightened Inspection
- Normal Inspection
- Reduced Inspection

11.7.11 Difference between Inspection and Statistical Quality Control (SQC)

Inspection is done after all the components are produced and hence, there are no chances of preventing or correcting the defects during the production process stage. It is very time-consuming and in some cases, it is highly impracticable to inspect all pieces. There is no feedback system as in SQC and there is also no corrective action procedure.

SQC is meant for detecting and correcting faults in the production process. It aims at prevention of defects at the very source. It relies on an effective feedback system. It is a corrective action procedure (Preven the issue of wrong tool and to have a setup approval procedure prior to starting continuous production and keeping of simple check during production). It alerts the operator against poor performance prior to his commenting the work in an effective prevention oriented atmosphere. It arrests the incidence of defects in the job on hand and helps to plan the prevention of similar defects in future. It is a plant-wide activity. It is self-controlled, control of quality by the operator and a system where control is delegated down to the worker's level where the action takes place. Standards, measurements and corrective actions can be applied. It keeps the process running adequately so that defects are seldom produced. For destructive tests, SQC is ideal since it is a localised activity.

The **disadvantages of SQC** are:

Sampling errors may lead to erroneous conclusion about the process.

Type I and type II errors (Producers risk and Consumers risk) are not as accurate as 100% inspection.

Human Aspects of quality

Lester Thurow in 1992 in his book 'Head to Head' has mentioned that the skills of the work force are going to be the key competitive weapon in the twenty first century.

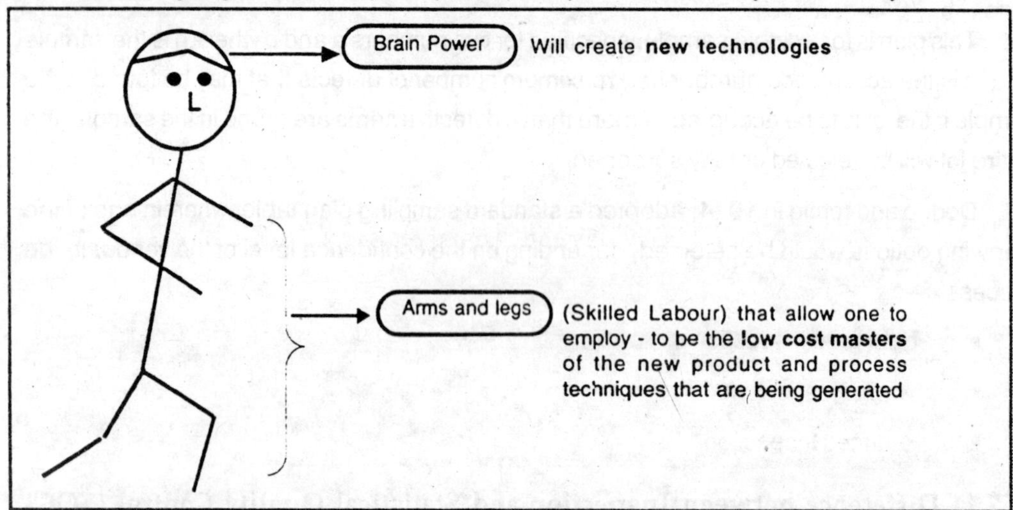

Fig. 11.22 Key Competitive Weapon is - Skills of the Work Force

Those organisations that get the highest performance from employees who can work together effectively with the technology of their systems are projected to be the **long term maximisers**.

Every good company would be working to make itself a high performing organisation. The list of characteristics below might explain why successful implementation does not always occur. High performance organisations require :

- Paradigm shifts
- New Culture
- Long term vision
- Relinquishing management control

- Investment in training
- Careful selection of employees
- Effective communication

Competitive advantages are never easy to get and are sometimes hard to keep. The advantage of a high performing workforce is difficult to build but capable of sustaining a long term advantage.

Human resources can be the most effective sustainable competitive advantage

High quality and reliability levels needed in modern products has reduced the emphasis on sampling inspection, with its notion that a stated fraction detective is somehow 'good enough'. Today's emphasis is on designing and manufacturing quality into a product instead of sorting out defectives after they are created.

Steps

- Designs need to be reviewed first
- An item can only be assembled the right way.
- production and tooling is capable of the precision required
- operators have the training to know what tolerance must be held and why?

Production workers are the final determinants of quality. Their willing and informed involvement in the quality effort is essential. One effort to achieving this is through the institution of **quality circles.**

11.8 Quality Circles :-

Quality circle is a philosophy of workers direct involvement in solving problems that affect their work, their work output and their workplace.

This was first started in Japan, other countries immediately followed the suite.

11.8.1 Formation and Working of Quality Circle in an Engineering industry

Quality Circle is a collective effort where 3 to 15 volunteers from various disciplines form a group and meet regularly, weekly or bi-weekly for about one or two hours. They identify and analyse work-related problems and search for solutions and the ways of implementing the same. In fact, it was quality circles which gave birth to TQM. QC is not involved only with product quality. It aims at individual and group development. QC, though appears to be simple, requires a massive effort on the part of the management to effect successful implementation.

The structure which supports QC is:

- Steering Committee
- Facilitators
- Circle leaders
- Circle members

The Steering committee consists of top management officials who provide overall guidance, suggest problems for the circles to take up, receive recommendations and follow up through facilitators for implementation.

Each Facilitator looks after a number of circles and is responsible for providing training to the circle leaders as well as circle members. He is the man who has to provide information to the circle leaders and circle members, arrange meetings, communicate all decisions taken in the circle to the steering committee and receives instructions from the top. Hence he should be well connected with other mangers in the organisation and receive support from the top.

The circle leader is generally a supervisor from the area where the circle is formed. He imparts training to the circle members in problem identification and solution methods. He interacts with the top through the facilitator.

Circle members are members selected from the concerned area like a senior worker, a production planning man, a designer, an inspector etc. These members are deeply involved in the problems and try to arrive at solutions with the assistance of the circle leader. Based on preliminary findings, the group focuses on a problem and works out a solution and a strategy to implement it. Finally, the decision is sent to the steering committee through facilitator for acceptance. The circle is kept informed on its progress. If the decision is not acceptable, reason for rejection is given to the circle. Through QC, the circle members gain sufficient experience in communication with colleagues, working together in harmony and sharing their findings with other circles. In India, many Public sector undertakings like BHEL, HMT etc. and also many private sector companies have formed QCs to solve most of their problems.

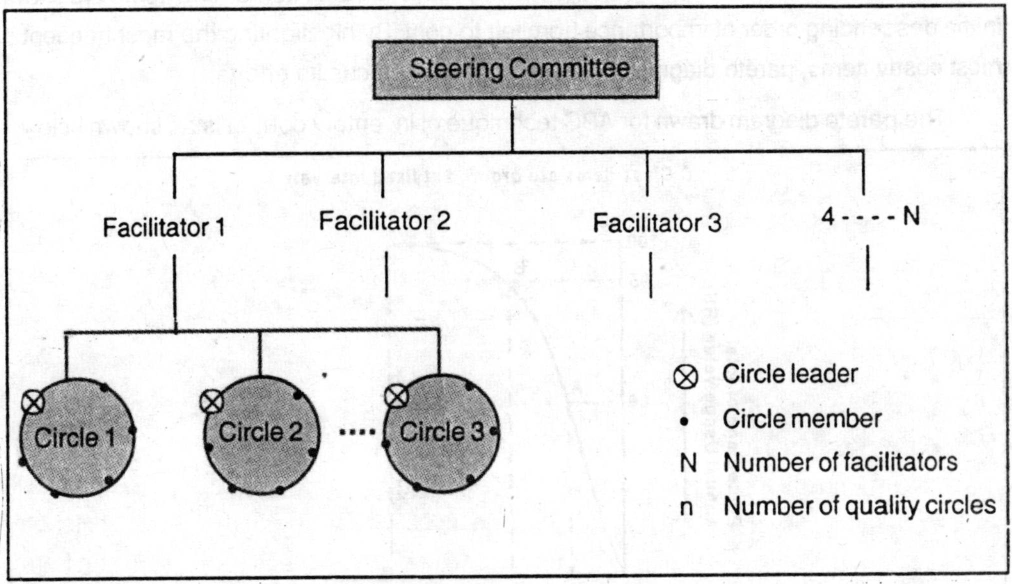

Fig.11.23 Team in QC

11.8.2 Benefits of QC

Quality Circle is a small group of employees who meet frequently to resolve company problems, QCs were initially developed in Japan as employee participation programs to identify the variations in quality and management programs to eliminate sources of those variations.

QC has many benefits, like

- Constructive use of workers, intimate familiarity with their own work problems.
- Providing opportunities to finding solutions to problems.
- Personal and professional growth of circle members.
- Team building
- Compel the organisation to have more and more workers participation programmes.

These quality circles are taught some basic methods of statistics and problem solving, and then proceed to identify problems within their work area, develop alternatives, and formally propose a solution to management.

One example of techniques a quality circle might be taught is **Pareto analysis,** named after an Italian **economist.**

Pareto Analysis / Pareto Diagrams / Pareto Charts. It is a technique based on the pareto principle of "the vital few and trivial many". The pareto principle is also called 80-20 rule i.e., approximately 20% of a group of items, people, inventory, causes and the like accounts for 80% of the work, effort, problems and the like. A **pareto diagram** is a bar chart that illustrates the frequency of recurrence or the cost of a set of items. The items are shown in the descending order of importance from left to right. By highlighting the most frequent or most costly items, pareto diagrams can help a team to focus its efforts.

The pareto diagram drawn for ABC technique of inventory control is as shown below.

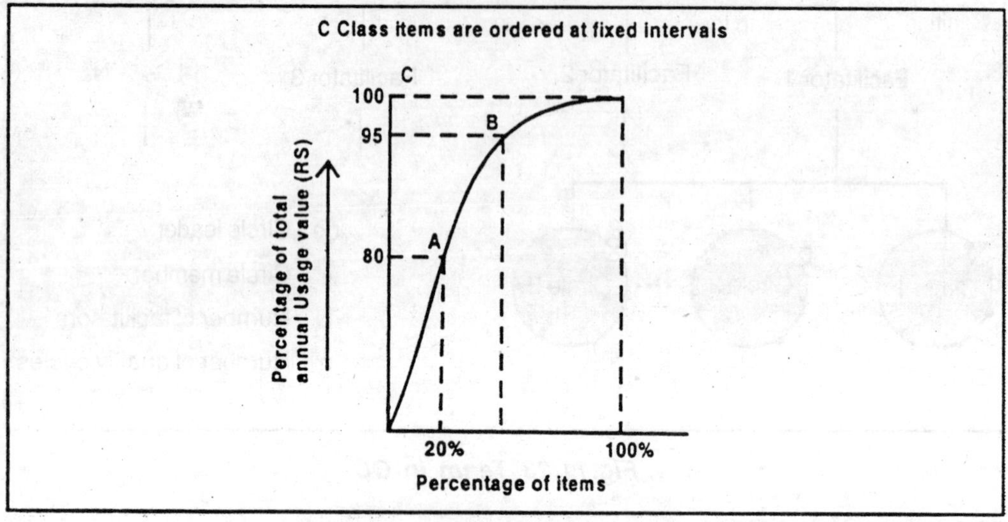

Fig. 11.24 Pareto's Principle

Elephant-Sized and Bite-Sized Projects

Some projects are very **big 'elephant sized'**. They cover so broad an area of activity that they must be subdivided into **multiple 'bite sized' projects.** In such cases, one project team can be assigned to **'cut up the elephant'.** Other teams are then assigned to tackle the resulting **bite sized projects.** This approach shortens the time to complete the project, since the teams work concurrently. Alternatively, if a single team works out everything, they take several years. Frustration sets in, team membership changes due to attrition, the project drags and morale declines.

A most useful tool for cutting up the elephant is the **pareto analysis.** This pareto principle states that in any population that contributes to a common effect, a relative few of the contributors - the vital few - account for the bulk of the effect. **The principle applies widely in human affairs.**

- Relatively small percentage of the individuals write most of the books.
- Commit most of the crimes.
- Own most of the wealth etc.

Nowadays engineers feel **quality engineering** a satisfying career field, involving as it does making products higher in quality and is more competitive in both national and international markets. Quality engineers establish criteria for inspection and process control charts and lead the investigation of the cause of failure and the search for solutions.

Suppliers of materials and parts are partners in the quality control efforts. They are chosen and retained more on the basis of demonstrated product quality rather than on insignificant differences in their last bid price, since savings in quality costs such as acceptance inspection, scrap and rework and unproved customer satisfaction covers more than the small differences talked out. **"Quality doesn't cost - it pays"**.

Taguchi Methods

A Japanese engineer **Dr. Genichi Taguchi** proposed the use of **statistically planned experiments** for **parameter designs. Experimental design** or **design of experiments** is one of the most powerful techniques for improving quality and increasing productivity. Through experiments, changes are intentionally introduced into the process or system in order to observe their effects on the performance characteristic or reference of the system or process. Any experiment that has the flexibility to make desired changes in the input variables of a process to observe the output response is known as **experimental design.**

The primary goals of a designed experiment are to :

- determine the variables and their magnitude that influence the response
- determine the levels for these variables
- determine how to manipulate these variables to control the response

As per Taguchi, it is not sufficient to :

- control processes
- inspect output
- identify and remove defects
- rely on customer feed back

To improve quality, one must look upstream at the design stage since that is the place where quality design begins. His strong belief in the design of quality and cannot be inspected later. To obtain better design, is experimentation on variables that contribute to a product's performance. This has brought Design of Experiments (DOE) into wider use by quality experts, designers and other members of design build teams. Taguchi believes in robust design.

Taguchi's statistical approach to quality control is based in three concepts :

- **Quality robustness** (All processes, procedures and products should be designed for quality robust)

- **Taguchi loss function** (This indicates the relationship of production effort and quality)
- **Target specification** (The target of production should always be the quality standard, not some lower or upper level of allowable variation)

Quality Loss Function is a simple quadratic formula

$L = D^2C$ where

L = Loss in rupees

D = Deviation from the target quality standard value

C = Cost of deviation

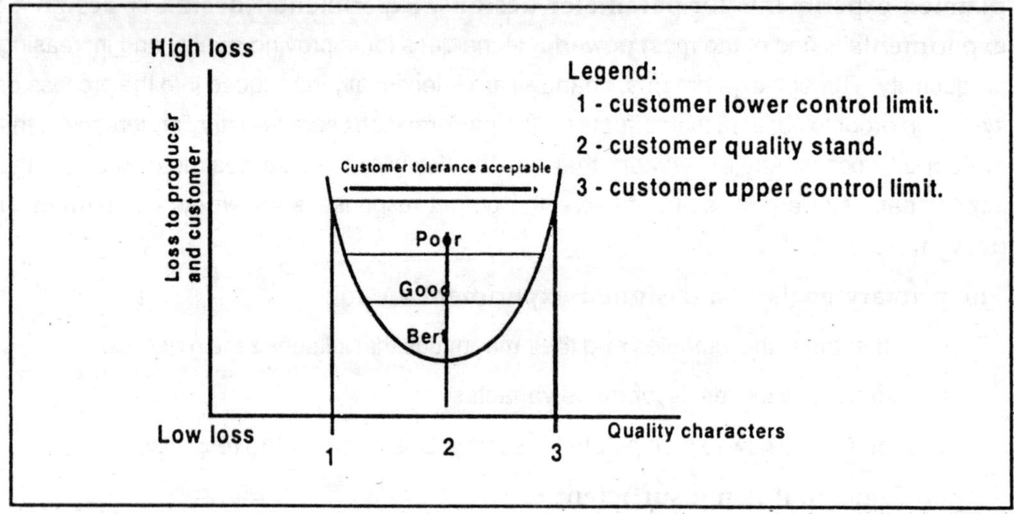

Fig. 11.25 Taguchi Loss Factor

Taguchi explains the need for a continuous quality improvement program to reduce the variations of product performance characteristics of their target values. The more the product deviates from the quality standard, the more likely it will breakdown and cost the user customer (downtime costs) and the producer warranty or guarantee costs.

Taguchi's methods include :

Extensive experimentation in which product and process parameters are varied in a statistical matrix of tests; Results are then evaluated using ANOVA (**Analysis Or Variance**) methods to identify the values that lead to least variation.

His methods were employed extensively in various US industries starting from automobile industry in 1982.

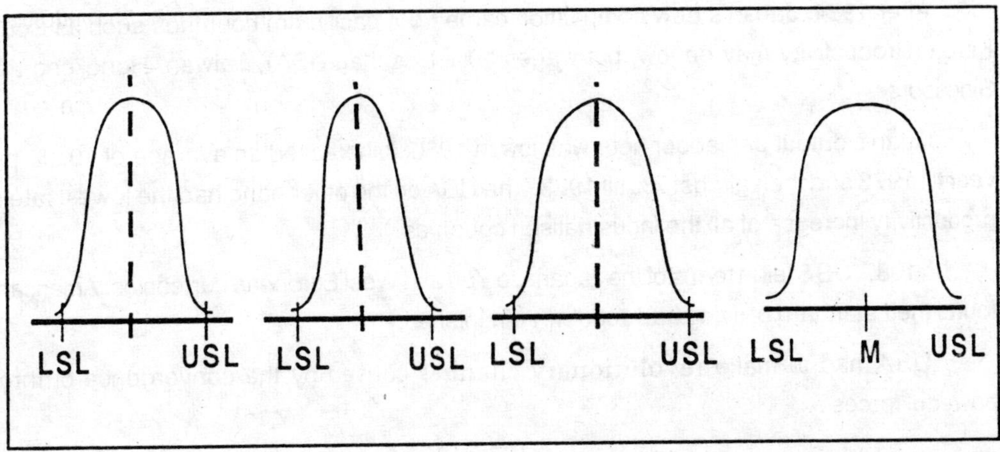

Fig. 11.26 Various Distributions of a Quality Characteristics in Terms of the Upper and Lower Specification Limits (Midpoint m)

Definition of Productivity

The term 'Productivity' describes how well a production manager achieves productive use of the resources of his firm. It is an index or measure of the effective use of resources. It is usually expressed as a ratio of output to input.

$$\text{Productivity} = \frac{\text{Output}}{\text{Input}}$$ The outputs are goods and services

Whereas the inputs are resources such as materials, labour, energy, and other resources to produce the outputs.

$$\text{Total Productivity Measure} = \frac{\text{Output or services (Goods produced)}}{\text{All inputs used to produce them}}$$

11.9 America's Productivity Challenge

- Around 1970, USA was the industrial giant of the world
- Labour costs per unit of production in 1970

	1970	1980	1984
-Japan labour costs	50% of USA	60% of USA	Wages increased in Japan
-Output per hour (Productivity) of Japan	44% of USA	84% of USA	Productivity increased in Japan
-Western' European economies (except UK) Labour cost		Between USA and Japan	

After 1984, Japan's new competition came from pacific rim countries such as South Korea (Productivity may be low, but wages 10% less than USA), Taiwan, Hongkong and Singapore.

Japan's output per labour hour was low in 1960; It increased an average of 10.5% per year till 1973 and then almost 7% till 1983. The USA on the other hand had the lowest rate of productivity increase of all the industrialised countries.

In 1987, US $ fell in terms of the Japanese Yen and West European currencies. Americans found their standard of living had suddenly diminished.

USA had to make **revolutionary changes** caused by the convergence of three powerful forces :-

- All over the world, **the rapid spread of manufacturing capabilities** created intense competition.
- The emergence of **advanced manufacturing technologies** is dramatically changing both the products and processes of modern manufacturing.
- **Growing evidence of :-**

  Changes in traditional management, labour practices, organisational structures, decision making criteria are needed to (i) improve the effectiveness of manufacturing operations (ii) provision of new sources of competitiveness and (iii) introduction of new strategic opportunities.

Hence the greatest challenge for USA in the last decade of the 20th century is to recognise the above mentioned forces and to take corrective action.

Average Annual percentage in Manufacturing output per hour as per US Bureau of Labour Statistics 1985 is as under :-

Country	1960-1973	1973-1983
Canada	4.7	1.8
France	6.5	4.6
W Germany	5.7	3.7
Japan	10.5	6.8
UK	4.3	2.4
USA	3.4	1.8

☛ 11.10 Work Measurement

11.10.1 Work Study

Industry use new work methods and techniques to produce goods of required quality at reasonable costs. This will involve techniques like work simplification, job design, value analysis etc. All these are called together as **methods engineering, industrial engineering, work design, work study** etc.

Early researchers in the field of management were concerned with motion study. Frederick W. Taylor, Frank B. Gilbreth and Lillian M. Gilbreth were some of the pioneers in the field of work study. Dr. Taylor's conclusion was "The greatest production results when each worker is given a definite task to be performed in a definite time in a definite manner". This is the foundation on which modern work study stands, today. Work study is constituted of Method Study and Work Measurement.

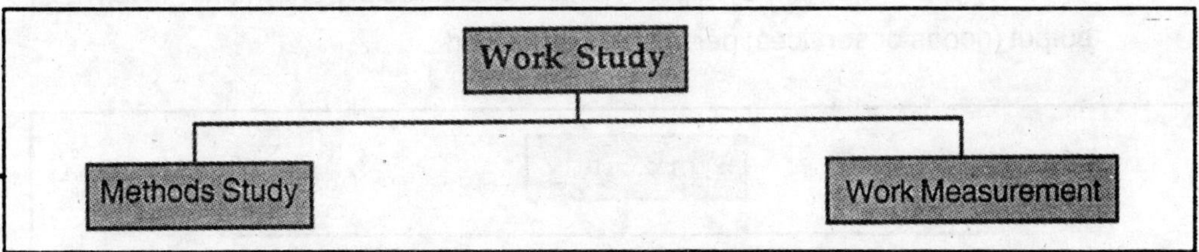

Fig. 11.27 Work Study Constituents

Russel M. Currie defines **work study** as "The systematic, objective and critical examination of all the factors governing the operation efficiency of any specific activity in order to effect improvement."

11.10.2 Need for Work Study

Work study is needed under the following circumstances:

(i) Process time consuming and delays found in work performance

(ii) High rate of rejection

(iii) Low efficiency in production

(iv) Incentives and bonus schemes are to be introduced

(v) The unwanted working habits of the untrained workers

(vi) Layout problems

11.10.3 Techniques of Work Study

The techniques of work study are:

(a) **Methods study or method analysis or operational analysis or work simplification** (the technique of improving the method of performing a job or task)

(b) **Work Measurement** [the technique used to measure the work content of a job in terms of standard time units (seconds, minutes or hours) and thereby establish the standard output of a worker while performing a job]

Scope of work study

Work study is a discipline of management tool is concerned with:

- Better ways of performing tasks/job
- Exercising control over the output by setting standards of performance in terms of output (goods or services) per want of time period

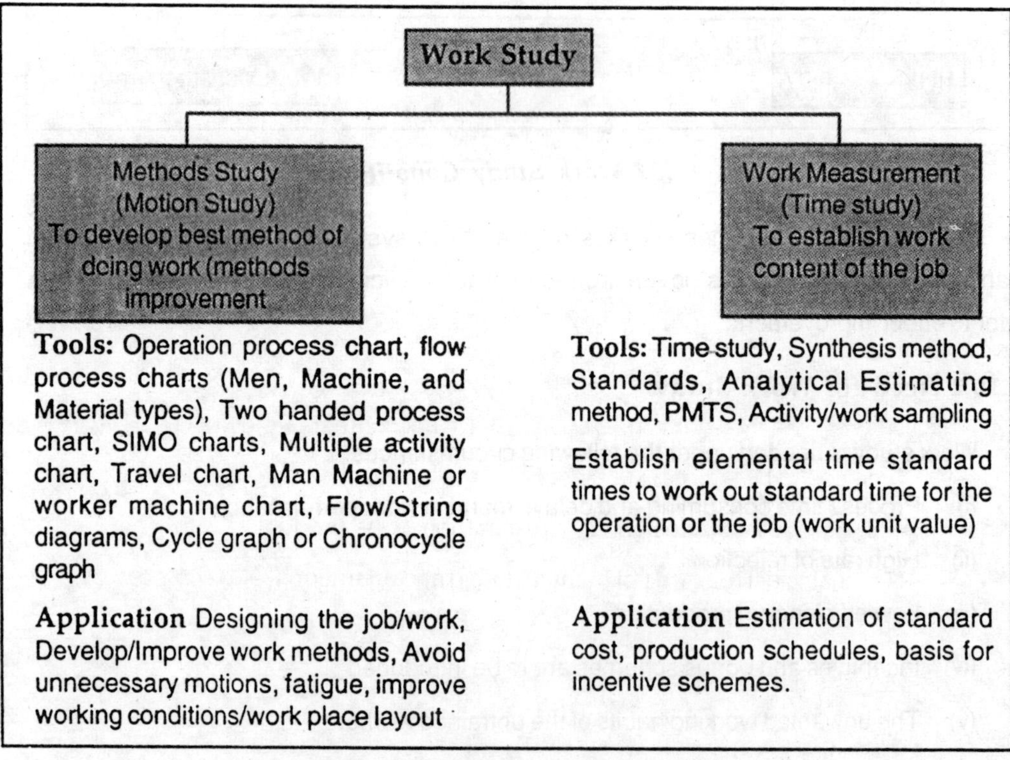

Fig. 11.28 Scope of work study

11.10.4 Methods Study

Methods study is the systematic recording and critical examination of existing and proposed ways of doing work in order to develop easier and more effective methods which will also reduce costs.

Method study involves:

• Making an efficient shop layout, • Planning the proper movement of workers in the shop reduce fatigue, • Devising efficient flow and handling of materials, • Methods improvement and better working conditions, • Motion study.

The modern concept of method study is a development of Gilbreth's technique of motion study.

Methods Analysis: Methods analysis is also known as method study is a scientific technique of observing, recording and critically examining the present method of performing a task or job or operation with the object of improving the present method and developing a new and less costly method. This is also known as methods improvement/work improvement involving the study of:

• Work processes, • Working conditions, • Equipments and tools used to carry out the job.

11.10.5 Work Measurement

Work measurement is the application of scientific techniques to establish the time required for a qualified worker to carry out a specified job at a defined level of performance. It is also known as time study. Method or work design is a pre-requisite for effective work measurement.

Work measurement attempts to measure:

- Unavoidable minimum time for the basic work content of the job.
- Time added by factors, such as:
  - Defects in the design and specification of the product.
  - Inefficient methods of manufacturing and operations.
  - Ineffective time within the control of management and workers.

And suggests measures to minimize this time.

11.10.6 Techniques of Work Measurement

Work measurement consists of five techniques.

(a) Time study (with the help of a stop watch)

(b) Analytical estimating (with Standard data)

(c) Work sampling or Activity sampling or Ratio delay method

(d) Synthesis method

(e) Predetermined Motion Time System (PMTS)

The standard timings are worked out based on any one of the three methods.

Steps in Work Measurement:

(a) Break the job into elements.

(b) Record the observed time by time study, synthesis or analytical estimation.

(c) Establish elemental time values by making observed time into normal time for each element with a rating factor.

(d) Assess allowances (personal allowance 5%, workshop allowance 5%, fatigue 5% approximate). These % varies from firm to firm (type of jobs involved).

(e) Add contingency allowance if any to arrive at the standard time to do the job.

11.10.7 Time Study

Time Study is the art of observing and recording the time required to perform an element of an operation; the operation may be manual, mental or machining operation. Manual time is for the handling of tool, job, machines and material; mental time is for thinking and machining time is the time taken by the machines to process the work pieces.

Procedures for conducting the Time Study

The procedure for conducting the time study with a stop watch are:

- Analyse the work, split the job into operations; operations into elements.
- Standardise the method of doing the work.
- Decide the speeds, feeds, depth of cuts, number of cuts etc.
- Select an average worker.
- Instruct the operator not to perform any unwanted operations and advise him to work in a normal way.
- See that all the jobs, tooling etc. are kept at convenient places before starting, so that the operator can reach these without fatigue.
- There should be no disturbances for the operator. Don't start the time study in the beginning of the shift.
- Take the studies using a stop watch atleast for a minimum of 8 pieces; record

timings for each of the elements. Eliminate the timings of 4 pieces (2 high and 2 low figures). Then take the average for each element from the remaining 4 readings.

- Add all the timings of different elements to arrive at the total.
- Rate the operator for his speed and dexterity and multiply with the total timings.
- Make allowances for personal, workshop delays, and fatigue (10-20%)

11.10.8 Standard Data

For calculating the standard time of each of the operations, the following data is used:

(a) Rationalised elemental time standards fixed by an inter-factory committee of industrial engineers.

(b) In-house time studies of elemental timings.

(c) Experience of other comparable industries.

(d) Data supplied by ILO, Geneva or REFA standards, France.

(e) Special studies carried out by committees.

Such time standards are used to synthesis the standard time for various manufacturing operations.

Synthesis is a technique of work measurement for building up the time required to do a job a defined level of performance by synthesising or totalling elemental time values obtained from previous time studies or other jobs containing similar job elements or from standard data or synthetic data or built up time standard.

Application is to estimate standard time for new jobs; to estimate production time for determining the prices of products to be sold; used as a basis for designing incentive schemes.

Analytical engineering is a technique of work measurement to determine the time values for jobs having long and nonrepetitive operations. The time values are determined by using synthetic data or on the basis of the past experience of the work study engineer, when no synthetic or standard data is available.

11.10.9 Estimation of the Standard Time from the Standard Data

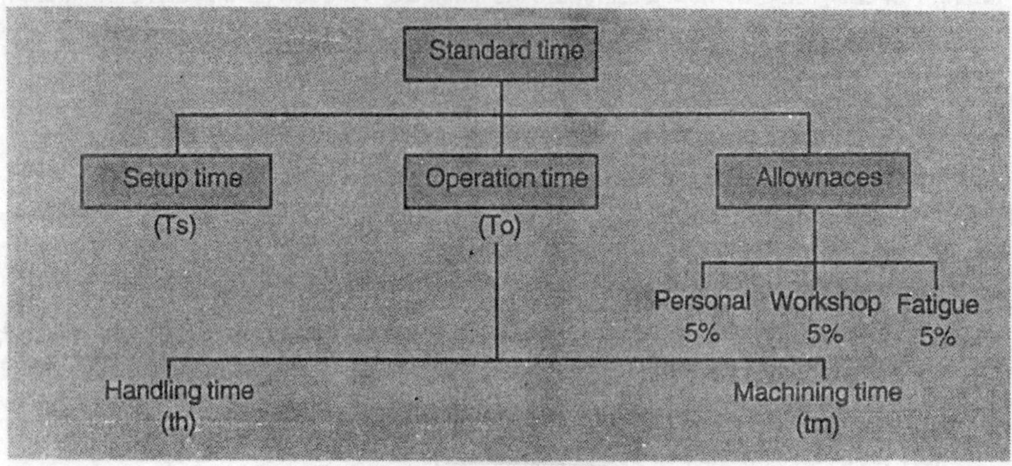

Fig. 11.29 Standard Time

Note:

(i) Ts is always for a batch; To is always per piece.

(ii) To = th + tm

(iii) Standard time = $\left(T_o + \frac{T_s}{\text{Batch}}\right)$ + Allowances (as % of T_o or T_s)

The procedure for estimating the standard time is:

- Study the drawing and the operations from the operation process sheets.
- Split the operations into elements.
- Indicate the standard timings for each of the elements from pre-established time standards.
- Add all the timing separately for both th (handling time) and for tm (machining time).
- Set-up time Ts is calculated separately by adding the timings for each of the elements (needed for the batch), taken from pre-established time standards. This has to be divided by the bath quantity to set-up time per piece.
- Add allowances for both To and Ts (approximately 15% generally)

11.10.10 Work Sampling

Work sampling, also known as **activity sampling**, is a simple method of establishing standard time either for a part of an operation or an operation as a whole by conducting a sampling study during which time it is noted whether the manufacturing activity is in progress or not. It can be carried out by rate fixers with little training and costs much less. It however, has its limitations.

11.10.11 A work sampling was conducted on a machine as under

(i) Period of study 100 hours.

(ii) Number of observations made 3000 (Total)

(iii) No activity was noticed during 500 observations (worker was idle)

(iv) Manual to machine elements of time ratio is 2:1

(v) Rating factor (estimated) as 1.20

(vi) Personal allowance and fatigue assumed 10%

(vii) 10,000 components produced during the study period.

With the above data, standard timings can be calculated as under:

$$\text{Proportion of working time} = \frac{3000-500}{3000} \times 100 = 84\% \text{ (app)}$$

$$\text{Time to make one article} = \frac{100 \times 0.84 \times 60}{10000} = 0.50 \text{ min}$$

$$\text{Manual time} = 0.50 \times \frac{2}{3} = 0.33$$

$$\text{Machine time} = 0.50 \times \frac{1}{3} = 0.17$$

$$\text{Basic time} = 0.33 \times 1.20 + 0.17 = 0.57$$

$$\text{Standard time} = 0.57 \times 1.10 = 0.63 \text{ minutes}$$

11.11 Maintenance and Facilities Engineering

Definition of Plant Maintenance

Maintenance is defined as "that function of production management concerned with the day-to-day problem of keeping the physical plant in good operating condition.

Maintenance management is concerned with the direction and organisation of resources in order to control the availability and performance of the industrial plants to some specified level.

Plant maintenance is concerned with actions taken by the plant user to maintain an existing system and facilities or to restore it to an operating condition.

11.11.1 Scope of Maintenance

The maintenance department performs two distinct functions primary and secondary.

Primary Functions

- These are with respect to maintenance of assets like plant and machinery. (Electro plants include mechanical installations like air conditioning plant, electro-planting plant, boiler etc. Machinery covers all types of machine tools, coil winding machine, textile machinery etc. depending on the type of the equipment installed).
- Maintenance of existing plant, buildings and ground areas (Shop buildings like Machine shop, Assembly shop, Tool Room, etc., Auxiliary buildings like Stores, Canteen, Office buildings, Township, Residential quarters, Amenity buildings like Hospitals, Schools etc., Built-up area and open area).
- Maintenance of equipment like material handling equipments, factory equipments, heat treatment equipments, inspection equipments, electrical equipments etc.
- Maintenance of services both internal and external (Internal services are like power wiring for the machines, lighting for buildings, compressed air for operating portable tools, steamlines for heating, plating baths and air conditioning for metrology room; external services like electric cables, roads, drains, streetlighting etc., which are outdoors).
- Maintenance of mobile assets (material handling equipments like mobile cranes, fork lifts, pallet tracks, jeeps, lorries and buses).

Secondary Functions

- Plant Protection (including fire fighting)
- Waste disposal
- Pollution and noise reduction.
- Sanitorial service
- Storekeeping, accounting etc.

11.11.2 Categories and Types of Maintenance

The **three categories** of maintenance are:

- **Breakdown Maintenance** (Corrective Maintenance)
- **Preventive Maintenance** (PM)
- **Predictive Maintenance**

11.11.3 Breakdown Maintenance or Corrective Maintenance

Break down maintenance allows a machine or any other facility to run without much routine attention, till it actually breaks down and then it is put back into commission. It leads to disruption of productive plans. Repairing the machine after it breaks down is called Breakdown maintenance.

11.11.4 Preventive Maintenance

Preventive maintenance is repairing of the machine at planned intervals so that sudden breakdowns could be prevented and costly down time avoided. This work is done at a time when the shop can spare the machine for repairs, generally during off-shift hours, Sundays, and holidays. This is only a part of a good maintenance program. It also consists of routine actions taken in a planned manner to prevent breakdowns and to ensure operational accuracy to the extent possible, economically and practically. Lubrication and Inspection are the two constituents of PM. Lubrication ensures long life and the safe working of the equipment without mishaps. Inspection tries to detect faults in an equipment and facility so that repairs and replacements may be undertaken before the faults lead to a break down.

11.11.5 Predictive Maintenance

Also known as **'Condition Monitoring,' predictive maintenance** is a form of preventive maintenance. By tracing the performance of the machine over its operating life, deterioration that can occur at various intervals of time is predicted. Early symptoms of failure are identified and proper maintenance measures developed.

11.11.6 Control of maintenance Function

Since maintenance involves cost, sometimes high cost, there is a need for control. This is done through:

- A maintenance official holding high responsibility authorises the work, by preparing a maintenance schedule indicating the timing of maintenance, number of staff, place of maintenance etc.
- Maintenance budgets are prepared to control the actual costs in comparison with the planned costs.
- Equipment records, history files of machines and equipment records, are maintained. This information is helpful to know the earlier problems and parts used to plan for future work/repairs.
- Management needs certain vital information to control the cost of maintenance is provided.

11.11.7 Maintenance Policies

A company may consider several options and trade off as maintenance policies. Some of them are:

- Centralised vs. Decentralised maintenance.

- Use of contract vs. In-house maintenance.
- The number of standby machines held.
- Repair vs. Replacement of defective equipments.
- Individuals vs. Group replacement when large number of similar items are employed in operation.
- The amount of maintenance capacity that should be kept ready.
- Extent to which the preventive maintenance and remedial maintenance to be used.

The maintenance function may be thought of as a sub-system under a total production system. The maintenance sub-system runs parallel with the product manufacturing system. The maintenance works must be scheduled, inventories of spare parts maintained, prescribed quality standards fulfilled, and labour standards and wage payment systems established.

If a component within a system fails, the entire system will collapse. Similarly, if maintenance fails to achieve its objective, production is bound to lag behind its target in terms of quality, quantity and cost of production. Hence, the various maintenance policies have to be thoroughly examined and correct maintenance policies are to be strictly adhered.

A well conceived maintenance programme should contain the following features:

- Proper identification of all items to be covered in the programme.
- Records to be covered in full, volume of work, cost etc.
- Scheduled inspection (with standing orders on specific assignments) followed by check lists.
- An inspection frequency schedule (may be six hours to even yearly once).
- Well-qualified inspectors (capable of making repairs also as soon as trouble is noticed).
- Use of budgets meant for repairs of major requirement.
- Administrative procedures involved.

11.11.8 Plant Maintenance

Every manufacturing organisation needs maintenance because, machines break down, parts wearout and building's deteriorate over a period of time. All segments of a factory, buildings, machinery, equipments, tools, cranes, jigs and fixtures, heat treatment plants, generating equipment, civil engineering equipment, medical equipment, wash rooms, etc. all whatever found in the plant need attention. It has two functions:

Primary Function	Secondary Function
• Maintenance of existing plant/ equipment, existing plant buildings and ground • Equipment inspection and lubrication • Utilities generation and distributing • Alterations to existing equipments and buildings • New installations of equipments and buildings	• Store keeping (stock of spare parts keeping) • Plant protection • Fire protection • Waste disposal • Salvage • Insurance administration (for theft, fire, pilferage etc.) • Sanitorial services • Property accounting • Pollution and noise control • Any other service delegated towards maintenance by the plant management

11.12 Purchasing

Definition of Purchasing

Purchasing is a window to the outside world. Purchasing is to produce the materials, supplies, tools, equipment etc. The objectives of the purchase department is to follow the 5 R's of purchasing i.e. to buy the right material in right quantity from the right source at the right time and at the right price.

11.12.1 Objectives of Purchasing

The major objectives of purchasing are:

- Procurement of required quality and quantity of materials at the most economical price.
- Procurement of materials which suits the product best.
- Purchasing the materials well in advance to meet the needs of the production department, to save production losses from lack of materials.
- Buying an optimum quantity, which is neither too much nor too less, affecting capital or holding up the regular supply for production respectively.

- Improvement of the product with reference to quality and distribution by means of selection of adequate material.
- Maintaining supply continuously to ensure production schedule at minimum of investment.
- To keep the top management aware of costs involved in the company's procurements and any market changes that would affect the company's profits or growth potential.
- To avoid duplication of materials, leading to wastage of materials and equipment.
- Company's competitive position in the market, is maintained by maintaining company's quality standards in accordance with demands of the customers.
- To develop fullest cooperation, coordination and maintenance of internal relationship with departrnents in the company.
- To maintain effective communication linkage between the company and its suppliers or potential suppliers.
- To initiate, if necessary, and cooperate in cost reduction programs, value analysis, make or busy studies, market analysis, and long range planning. Purchasing should keep abreast with the trends and projections in prices and the availability of the inputs that a company must have.

11.12.2 Importance of Purchasing

The distribution of costs in large manufacturing firms are shown in Fig. 19.1 below:

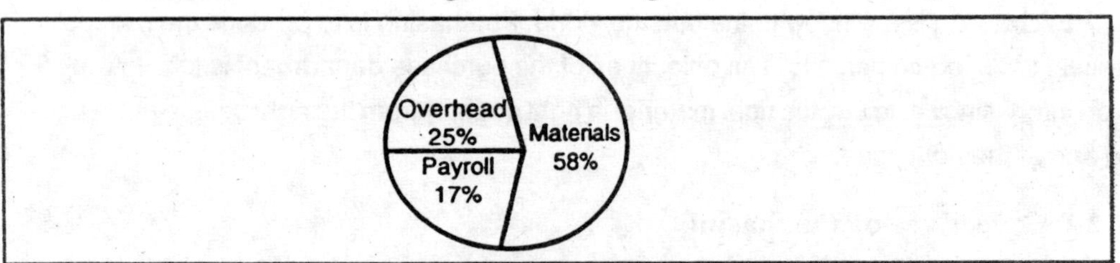

Fig. 11.30 Distribution of Costs

(**Source:** Production and operations management - James B.Dilworth, Mc.Graw Hill publication co., p. 221)

(i) The purchasing department spends most of the money in procurement of materials, which account for more than 50% of the company's expenditures. The purchasing department is usually placed high in a company's organisation so that it has direct communication with top management.

(ii) It is also important that right type of materials are to be purchased in right quantities at the right time. Otherwise, production will be hampered.

(iii) The manufacturer spends a lot of money on purchases and even if there is one percent savings, it is equivalent to 10% increase in the turnover. Hence, efficient buying is resorted to.

(iv) Many of the components if produced in-house will cost much more than buying from outside. Hence buying is preferred.

(v) For any big project, buying becomes a vital activity.

(vi) Many a times purchasing contributes to import substitution and saving of foreign exchange.

(vii) The purchasing function has become so active, that it has to be treated many a times, as an exclusively separate function. In some organisations, there is a chief commercial manager, who looks after purchasing and reports to the Vice President or President of the firm.

(viii) Material cost increases, shortages, high competition, growing international markets etc. have resulted in proper planning and procurement of materials for survival of the organisation.

11.13 Materials Management

11.13.1 Definition of Materials Management

Materials are any commodities used directly or indirectly in producing a product or service such as raw materials, component parts, assemblies and supplies. Management of materials in most organisations is crucial to their success because the cost of purchasing, storing, moving and shipping materials account for over half of the products cost.

11.13.2 Importance of Materials Management

Goods that enter the product directly consists of:

- Raw Materials (such as agriculture products or natural gas normally enter the production process with little or no alteration)
- Manufactured Materials (all type of raw materials that are subjected to some amount of processing before entering the manufacturing process). Eg.: Copper formed into wire.
- Component Parts (Switches, motors) can be installed directly into products with little or no additional changes.

11.13.3 Functions of Materials Management

The functions of Materials Management are:

(i) Materials planning and programming, (ii) Raw material purchase, (iii) Receiving, store keeping, and warehousing, (iv) Issuing of material, (v) Inventory control, (vi) Value engineering and value analysis, (vii) Transportation of materials, (viii) Materials handling, (ix) Vendor development, (x) Vendor rating, (xi) Disposal of scrap and surpluses

11.13.4 Objectives of Materials Management

The main objectives of Materials Management are:

(i) Maintaining the flow of production, (ii) Contribution towards higher productivity, (iii) Reduction in inventory cost, (iv) Elimination of extra materials (through product design), (v) Increasing the profit margin of the organisation, (vi) Contribution towards competitiveness, (vii) Buying the best item at the lowest cost

Questions

1. Define Quality.
2. Give the Meaning of Quality.
3. What is the importance of better Quality?
4. Give the value of improvements in Quality.
5. Explain the dimensions of Product Quality.
6. Define Quality cost. Bring out the different categorisation of Quality costs.
7. Which are the ten dimensions of Service Quality?
8. Explain the terms :- Appraisal costs, Prevention costs, Failure costs.
9. Explain the effect of Quality conformance on Quality cost.
10. What do you mean by Quality cost index?
11. What do you mean by costs of poor Quality? Why it happens?
12. Work out a comparison of various categories of Quality costs.
13. What are the components of the costs of poor Quality?
14. Explain a model for Optimum Quality Cost.
15. Write down a flow diagram of decisions on conformance and fitness for use.
16. What is the role of Statistical methods?
17. Explain the terms Statistical Quality Control (SQC) and Statistical Process Control (SPC).
18. What is Statistics?
19. What are control charts? Name the different types of control charts. Explain them briefly.
20. Define Attributes and Variables.
21. Define Inspection.
22. State the meaning of Quality Circle.
23. What are the benefits of Quality Circle?
24. What is X Chart? Explain.

25. What is R Chart? Explain.
26. What is P Chart? Explain.
27. What is C Chart? Explain.
28. Explain Sampling by Variables.
29. Explain Sampling by Attributes.
30. What is SQC? How is it different from Inspection? Discuss.
31. Explain the various Quality Control techniques.
32. Explain Material Requirement Planning. (MRP I)
33. Explain Manufacturing Resource Planning (MRP II)
34. Define Purchasing.
35. What are the objectives of Purchasing?
36. Explain the importance of Purchasing.
37. Explain Pareto analysis.
38. What is materials management? Explain the functions of management.
39. Explain the objectives of Materials Management. What is the importance of materials management?
40. What is Work Study? What is the need for Work Study?
41. Explain the techniques of Work Study.
42. Define Work Measurement. Explain the techniques of Work Measurement.
43. Explain the basic steps in time study procedure.
44. What are the steps to be followed sequentially for Work Measurement?
45. Outline the procedure of time study.
46. How time studies are useful?
47. What is Standard data?
48. How do you estimate the standard time from the standard data?
49. What is Work Sampling? How do you work out the standard time for Work Sampling?
50. What do you mean by allowances?
51. Name the different allowances considered in standard time.
52. Give the meaning of time study, work study, work measurement.
53. Define Maintenance.
54. Define Maintenance management.
55. Define Plant Maintenance.
56. Define Maintainability, Reliability, Availability.
57. Discuss the scope of maintenance.
58. What are categories and types of Maintenance? Explain each one of them.
59. Explain Maintenance policies.
60. Describe the control of Maintenance Function.
61. Explain Taguchi's statistical approach to Quality Control.
62. Define Productivity.
63. Explain America's productivity challenge.
64. Explain the human aspects of quality.

Chapter - 12

12.1 Preview

This chapter covers the following Topics :

- *Marketing and the engineer.*
  - Transaction based relationships
  - More sustained relationships
  - Highly committed relationships
- *Engineers involvement in marketing industrial products*
- *After sales service*
- *Engineers in service organisations*
  - Importance of service industries
  - Comparison with manufacturing
  - Technical employment in the service sector
- *Some specific service industry applications*
  - Public works
  - College teaching and research
  - Biomedical engineering and health services

12.2 Marketing

Marketing embraces selling and covers the full gamut of:

- Analysis
- Promotion
- Coordination

This involves studying the environment, assessing the outlook, analysing actual and potential markets, finding out what goods and services customers want, where they want them, how best to advise them and what is available, weighing up the strength of competition, anticipating changes in demand, and other policy considerations.

Marketing function focuses on selling and/or promoting the goods and services of the organisation. It is responsible for assessing customer needs and wants and discovering or developing demand for the organisations goods or services and also maintain a responsive working relationship with customers and potential customers.

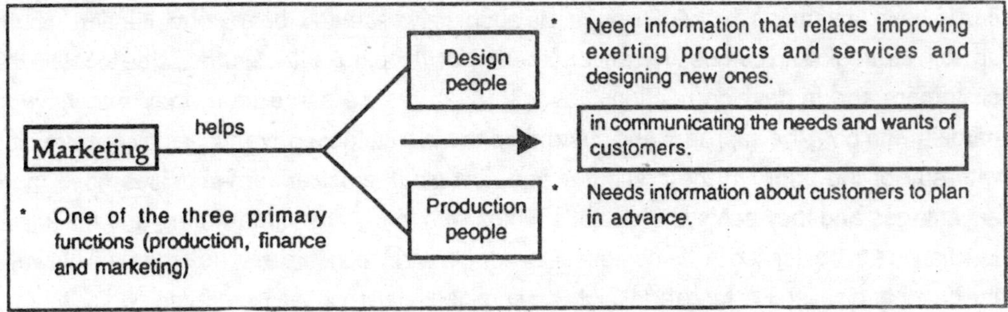

Fig 12.1 Purpose of Marketing Function

12.3 Relationships

I) Transaction based relationships

Market related tasks prior to sale such as:

- Identifying the customers needs
- Studying the customers needs
- Opportunity to submit an offer to the potential customer
- Closing a deal etc. are very common in transaction oriented types of firms. In the recent days, we find customer relationship management, supply chain management have become prominent to establish continuous relationship with good suppliers and customers. Old customers are to be retained at any cost and new customers are to be attracted.

II) More sustained relationships

If the contact between the parties to a transaction is more sustained and good report is built up, over days, months and years, the tasks of marketing may be more encompassing including the customer.

- to inform the status of the order
- shipment delays, shipment position
- determining the disposition of damaged or below standard deliveries
- determining the user requirements and his satisfaction etc.
- to understand customers delight

III) Highly committed relationships

After developing the relationships with the customers, the firm is more committed in transfer of standard goods and services. After the electronic commerce and Internet developed, the customers need not have the same firm for supply. They can go globally and select any firm to have advantage for them. Hence it is absolutely essential for any supplier firm to build up both strategic and competitive advantages by developing suitable strategies to retain the customers and to develop relationships with them. At the same time, they may have to bargain with both the suppliers and customers to have suitable advantages by not straining with any of the firms. In the computer age, **Internet worked enterprises** have more advantages and they can sustain relationships with many firms. Marketing and marketing function are to be defined in the context of the length of relationship and environment between the buyer and seller. For long term, highly committed relationships, marketing people have to work hard and of many faceted.

12.4 Engineering involvement in Marketing Industrial Products

The Industrial products can be divided into eight :

(I) Installations	(V) Component parts
(II) Accessories	(VI) Fabricated items
(III) Raw Materials	(VII) Maintainence, Repair and Operating (MRO) Items
(IV) Process materials	(VIII) Services

The product or service produced determines the complexity of the marketing function. The characteristics of the items are :

(I) **House hold items** - Mass produced at lowest costs; uniform or near uniform requirements; purchase of small quantity.

(II) **Industrial purpose items** - Unique, manufactured in special purpose machines or with special tools; Bought to be resold (repair parts sold by wholesalers)

(III) **More complex products** - Like sheet metal components used in cabinets rivets used for fastening metal pieces; Items orders on large quantities by customers

☛ 12.5 The engineers role is different while marketing industrial products

Types of Product	Description	Engineers role
(1) **Installations** (eg. In particular buildings, airports, sanitation stations, turn key allignments for new factories, oil refinery, etc)	These are special, large in size; custom built; process is interactive leading to changes, often subject to a bidding process; Hence competitive quality. Service and price are the criteria.	Selling; performance of design service.Estimatation of cost construction supervision, Delivery to be met. Price to be competitive specially in construction bid.
(II) **Accessories** (may include standard office machinery, copiers, desks, other furniture, automobile fork lifts, std machine tools, electrical items etc.	Not all the accessories used by all short lived capital goods; lesser durability; Faster depreciable items.	Design engineers design based on requirements of customers
(III) **Raw materials** (Ore, tobacco, tea leaves, coffee seeds)	Extracted; Agricultural enterprises	Quality to be assessed
Process materials (Basic manufactured goods like metal bars or rods made as screws, drawn as wires etc.	Goods that change form during production	Buyers engineers develop suitable specifications
Component parts (Generally sold by distributors, agents and by sales force)	Catalog items; Do not loose identity in production	Buyers engineers develop suitable specifications
(IV) **M R O items** (cotton waste, coolant, lubricants, fuels, air filters, spark plugs, office stationery etc).	Consumed in process of production, use	Repair parts and methods specified by supply firms engineering involvement.
(V) **Fabricated items**	Custom built	Engineers sell and perform
(VI) **Services** (Market offerings)	By only incidental use of product	Buyers engineers develop specifications. Seller bids on manufacture

Fig 12.2 Engineer's Role

12.6 The level of service varies on the type of clients :

(I) For less sophisticated clients or clients, with little investment, the level of service will be more fundamental like :

- Periodic inspection, servicing, calibration and maintenance. The more fundamental the service, the larger the investment in field service.

(II) For a support activity required at the centralised location includes :

- Analysis of reported failures to determine the rate of production of spares, to note weakness that may require redesign of the system or some portion, to note and trace retrofit etc.

(III) For large systems, continuing support may include :

- The provision of maintenance beyond the capability of that possible on site e.g. maintenance of ocean going vessels, rebuild of airliners etc.

12.7 Importance of Service Industries

The service sector in US has the following statistics to show that it is important:

Employment :	*	70% of the total employed (2/3rd of GNP).
1970-86 :	*	US employment increased 37% overall employment (From 81.7 mln to 111.6mln)
	*	In manufacturing, employment actually decreased by 2 % (From 19.4 mln to 19 mln)
	*	Agricultural employment decreased over 7% (From 3.5 mln to 3 mln)
	-	Increase in service producing industry employment of 58% (From 47.1 mln to 74.4 mln)
	-	Whole sale and retail trade increase - 15.7% (15mln to 23.6 mln)
	-	(Eating and Drinking places) - 128% (2.6 mln to 5.9 mln)
	-	Health services increase - 115% (3.1 mln to 6.6 mln)
	-	Business services increase - 185% (Building services, personnel supply computer and data processing etc.)
	-	Legal services increase 3 times to 0.7 mln
	-	Government federal up only 6% (2.7 mln to 3 mln)
		Local Government up 41% (9.8 mln to 13.8 mln)

12.8 Manufacturing Vs. Servicing

Service producing industries has a wide variety and it is difficult to identify common characteristics with manufacturing. There are only a few common.

Details	Manufacturing	Servicing
(1) Intangibility	Tangible goods produced	Most of them are more intangible (health care, hair dressing, travel service, legal advice, marriage consultancy)
(II) Performance in real time often in the presence of customer	No	Yes
(III) Inventoried	Yes	Not (Hence performed on a schedule that fits the needs of a customer. A challenge in staffing)
(IV) Most professionalor - consulting services	-	Customised, personalised, labour intensive
(V) Airlines transportation telephone or electrical services	-	Standardised, capital intensive
(VI) Front office customed approach to the needs and interests of the client	Mass production philosophy	To be carried out efficiently and accurately
Back room - the clerical functions carried out		
(VII) Customer contact	Little	Extensive
(VIII) Capital/Labour intensive	Capital intensive	Labour intensive
(IX) Lead time	Long	Short
(X) Determination of Quality	Product quality easily determined	Service quality determined with difficiency
(XI) Investments in assets	High	Low

Fig 12.3 Manufacturing VS Servicing

12.9 Some specific service industry

Computer Applications

In this super highway information age, Information are stored and manipulated at super fast speed in nano seconds. or even faster than that further very large scale integrated (VLSI) circuits have made possible computers of increased capability at low cost which have made our lives easier. Now a days all industries are using computers of which can have connections with internet and world wide web for access to quick information. From 1st generation computers to 4th generation computers, (ie from 1960 to 2005), computers have come down in size, miniaturised to a great extent, Semi conductors technology have changed to transistors and to Integrated circuits, now to VLSI. The capabilities of computers have increased with greater band width and speed of access at decreased cost, size and power requirements. Small computers now a days smaller than Lap top computers like personal digital assistant, pocket calculators etc. have come with the same capabilities of other bigger computers. For rural side, computers are being developed in India by Intel known as **'community computers'**. The computers price is also coming down. PCs are now sold at Rs 10,000 in India, with more or less good features. Further down in prices also may be possible

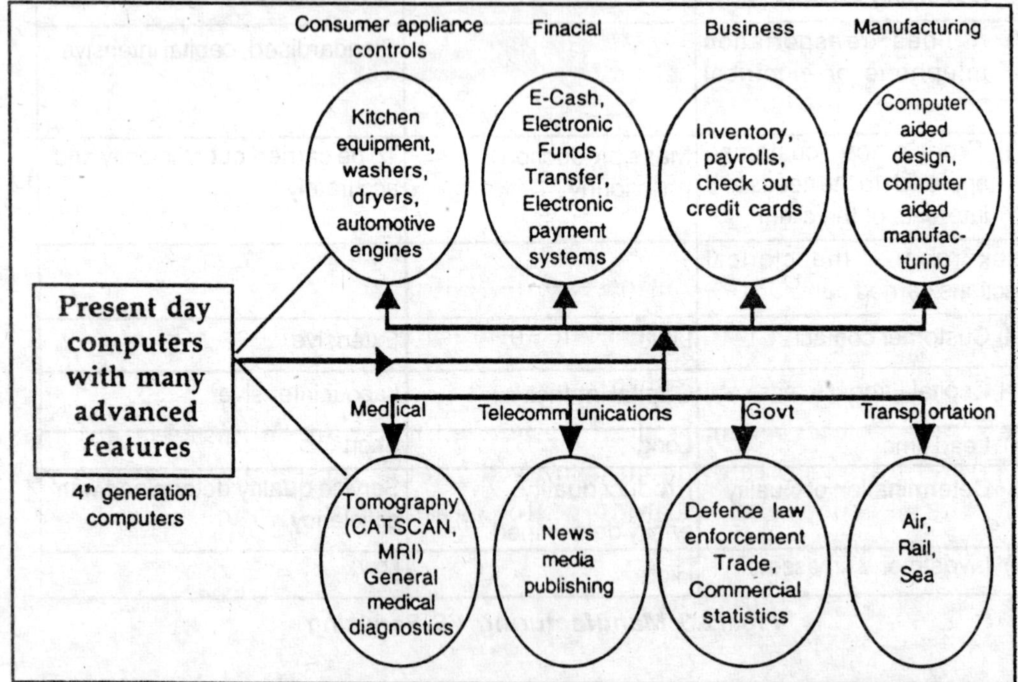

Fig 12.4 Impact of Computer Technology on Service Producing Industry

i) **Public works :-** Engineers who are mostly civil, head these and take up many responsibilities needed by the public. Here the various services are to be provided by them for infrastructure development and for other social works.

ii) **College teaching and research work**

iii) **Biomedical Engineering**

iv) **Health Services**

These are the areas where engineers are needed and lots of responsibilities they have to shoulder.

(I) After sales service

- Engineers are also involved with client related tasks after the sales transaction, (after delivery and payment is completed). For example :

♦ Installation	♦ Training	♦ Supply of spares and supplies
♦ Warranty	♦ Provisioning	♦ Documentation
♦ Field service	♦ Providing repair facilities	♦ Retrofit, rebuild, overhaul

- Industrial and military purchases are very expensive; May involve several millions of rupees per unit, Hence commitment to a long service life is needed to justify the expenditure. Units can be discarded when they malfunction ; may need repairs to be done by suppliers engineers. The buyers may have sufficient expertise to repair still the suppliers could help at times when needed. Split in the responsibility for maintenance is likely between buying and selling organisations.
- Sellers firms typically form departments for servicing the continuing needs of their clients. Field service personnel are responsible for:
  - travelling to their clients site where equipment is located.
  - making on-site repairs etc.

eg :- Telephone repair personnel, office PC service technicians, electric department servicing, water department servicing tasks involved may be : Installation, reconfiguring the customers equipment by updating or addition, repair and servicing, some cases customer, demonstration and training.

- Suppliers can improve their relationships with customers by improving the level of service offered to them. This can involve :-
  - providing more reliable delivery
  - fast just-in-time delivery
  - setting up computerised reorder systems
  - offering fast, accurate quotes,

- reducing defect levels

In so doing, the customer gains by :

- Lower inventory costs
- Smoother production runs
- Lower waranty costs

By creating systems that link the customers to the supplier, for example through :

- reorder systems
- Just-in-time delivery

Switching costs may be built making it more expensive to change supplier

- ♦ **Risk reduction**

This may involve free demonstrations, the offer of products for trial at zero or low cost to the customer, product and delivery guarantees, preventive maintenance contracts, swift complaint handling and pro-active follow ups. These activities are designed by engineers to provide customers with reassurance.

- ♦ **Suppliers also can give following supports to the customers.**

(I) Technical Support

This may be in the form of :

- R & D cooperation
- before sales and after-sales service
- providing training to the customers staff

The supplier is thus enhancing the customer's know how and productivity.

(II) Expertise

This may be :

- offer of design and engineering consultancies
- dual selling where the customer's sales force is supplemented by the supplier

The customer benefits through acquiring extra skills at low cost.

(III) Resource support

Suppliers can support the resource base of customers by :

- extending credit facilities
- giving low interest loans

- agreeing to cooperative promotion
- accepting reciprocal buying practices (Where the supplier agrees to buy goods from the customer)

♦ A major task of marketing management is to manage supplier to customer relationships. Buyers and increasingly treating trusted suppliers as strategic partners, and devoting dedicated sales teams to key accounts. By helping customers by the provision of free or low cost services, suppliers can buy goodwill, and foster close relationships with them.

Questions

1) Define Marketing.
2) What does the Marketing function focuses ?
3) Explain the purpose of marketing function.
4) Explain the involvement of engineering in marketing industrial products.
5) The product or service produced determines the complexity of the marketing function. Explain the characteristics of the products with examples.
6) Explain the role of engineers in the activities of after sales service.
7) How do suppliers improve their relationships with customers by improving the level of service. ?
8) How does the level of service varies on the type of clients?
9) Explain the importance of service industries.
10) Differentiate manufacturing Vs servicing.
11) Explain on your own, some of the specific service industries.

Chapter - 13

Project Planning and Acquisition

13.1 Preview

This chapter deals with the following topics:

- *Characteristics of a project*
- *The project proposal process*
  - Proposal effort
  - Proposal preparation
  - Proposal contents.
- *Project planning tools*
  - Statement of work
  - Mile stone schedule
  - Work breakdown structure
  - Gantt (Bar charts)
  - Network scheduling system
  - PERT treatment of uncertainty
- *Other project Network Models.*
  - Precedence Diagram Method (PDM)
  - GERT (Graphical Evaluation and Review Technique)
  - PERT / LOB (Line of Balance)
  - Resource allocation
- *Types of contracts*
  - Fixed price contracts
  - Cost type contracts

13.2 Project Definition

A **Project** is an organised endeavour to accomplish a specified non-routine or low volume task. Although projects are not repetitive, they take significant amount of time to complete and are large-scale or complex enough to be recognised and managed as separate undertakings.

A **project** is a collection of inter-related activities leading to the achievement of a desired set of objectives. This chapter is concerned with engineering projects. Examples are:-

- Construction projects : Dams; highways ; oil pipe lines
- R & D projects : Super conductivity ; Solar energy
- Chemical and Pharmaceutical projects : Fertiliser, Antibiotics
- Consumer items : Metal boxes, Household plastics
- Manufacturing projects : Machine tools, transformers and switch gear

Program : A group of related **Projects.**

Project Management is the planning, organising, monitoring and controlling of the tasks and resources to accomplish a defined objective usually with constraints on time and cost.

13.3 Characteristics of a project

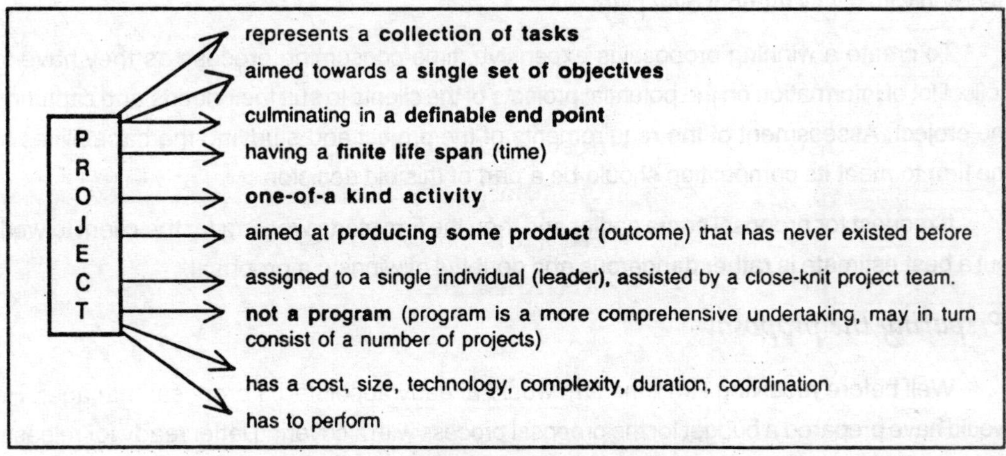

Fig. 13.1 Project Characteristics

The **characteristics of a project** are shown above.

13.4 Project proposal process

Every project should indicate:

- Detailed description of what is to be accomplished
- A proposal or estimate of the time (Duration and schedule)
- Cost required

Preproposal effort

Efficient organizations work on this well before RFP (Request for proposal) is received from a potential customers from whom they have already collected the information.

Request for proposal (RFP) is a document defining what the organisation promises to do regarding the project for its client and how much it will cost? The organisation identifies new business opportunities or types of activity where attractive projects are likely to be funded. Following details will be explored at the same time.

- Estimating the resources.
- Capability needed to meet expected future needs of potential customers.
- Present resources of the customers. Comparison with the expected resources
- Development of the needed technical skills.
- Identify or to help them acquire needed sources.

The efficient organisations have a group of people exclusively to work for the customer needs well in advance of their coming with RFP so that the firm will work out a preliminary bid decision with a well thought over plan.

To create a winning proposal is expensive, time consuming process as they have to collect lot of information on the potential projects of the clients to suit their needs and capturing the project. Assessment of the requirements of the project and studying the capabilities of the firm to meet its competition should be a part of this bid decision.

If request for proposal come earlier and then the firm starts working for the client to work out a best estimate is rather dangerous and doubtful of winning a proposal.

Preparing the proposal

Well before receiving RFP, the firm would already appointed a proposal manager. He would have prepared a budget for the proposal process with a covering letter ready for release. All the functional managers would have been appraised on this issue. When RFP is received, it will be quickly examined with the concerned without any surprises and tentative decision to prepare a bid is reconfirmed.

RFP generally includes:-

- A covering letter
- Statement of the work (to be performed)
- Time schedule
- Specification of the length and content (as required by client)
- Standard clauses (Boiler plate is the name given) for quotation format with all legal terms and arbitration, penalty clauses etc.

A **'kick off meeting'** after a good preparation of the proposal team launches the proposal process.

All projects in general have certain common features and pose similar problems. The driving parameters of the project are **three**:

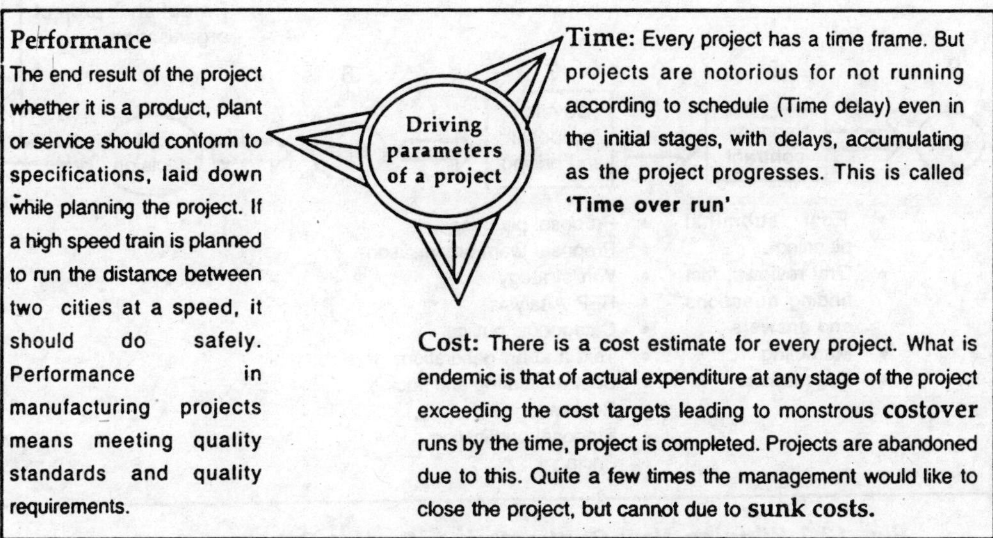

Fig. 13.2 Driving Parameters of a Project

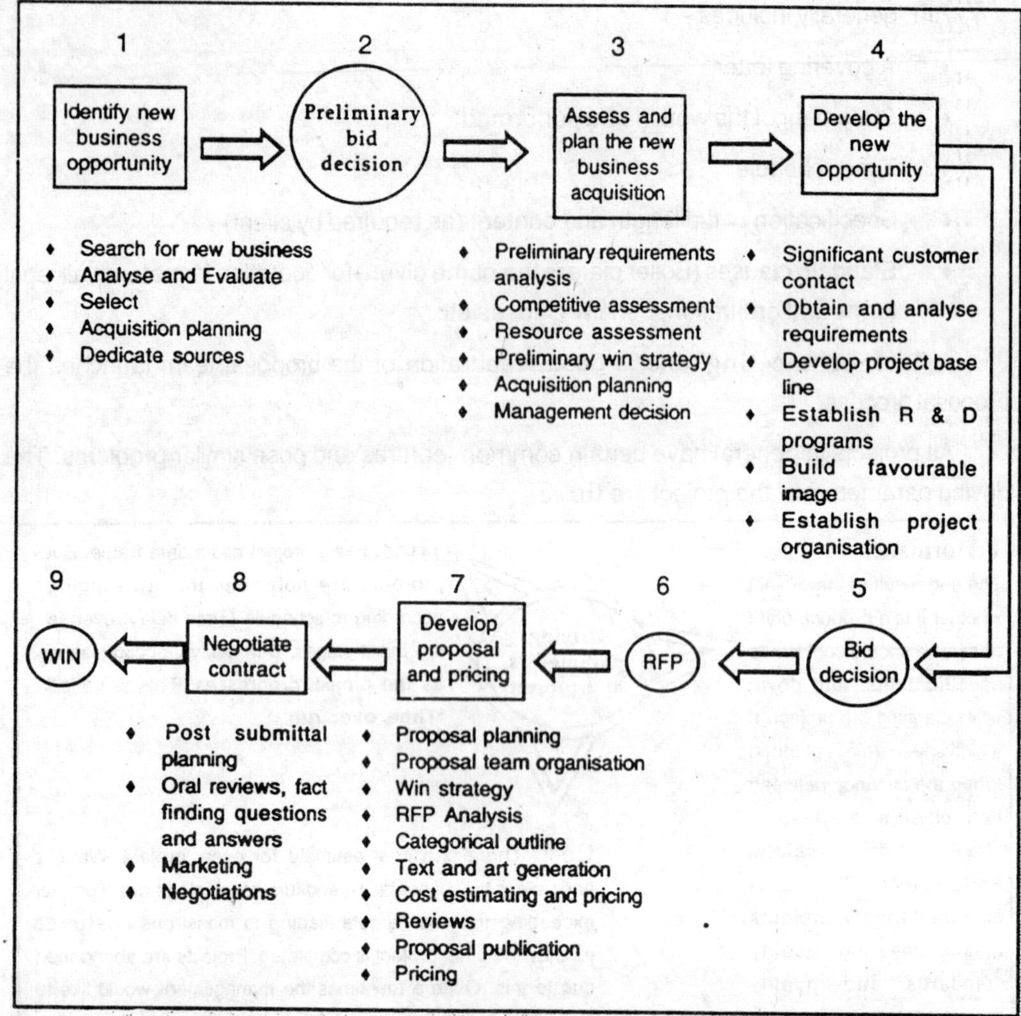

Fig. 13.3 Winning New Contracts in a Project Oriented Business (Steps 1 to 8)

Project personnel are highly qualified, experienced and trained people to enable them to work out proposals fast on their own. However, they interact with the concerned, prepare drafts quickly overnight and will be ready for discussions in the morning. They may use word processing, desktop publication using laser printers. (Reviews and revisions are carried out rapidly)

13.5 Proposal contents

For the project envisaged, RFP will specify separate management, technical and cost proposals involving:

Management proposal	Technical proposal	Cost proposal
• About the company its organisation, its experience, Its management methods and control systems, describes the personnel proposed to lead the project.	• The design concept proposed to meet the clients needs, with special emphasis on the approach planned to resource the most difficult technical challenges posed by the project.	• A detailed price breakdown. • Aspects of inflation • Contingencies • Contract change procedures.

Typical organisation chart for a major proposal

A **proposal package** has been worked out by the proposal manager and his peers review the same (Company senior management also reviews), revised, printed and delivered to the customer.

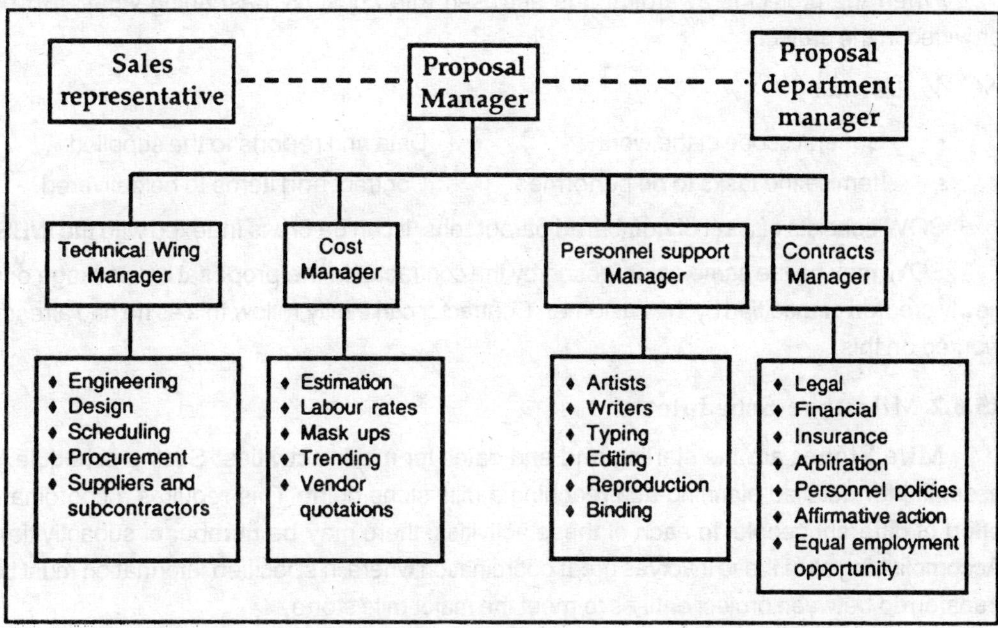

Fig. 13.4 Typical Organisation Chart for a Major Proposal

13.6 Project planning Tools

Project planning includes all activities that result in a course of action for a project. Planning begins with setting well defined objectives (such as implementing a new Management Information system), decision making regarding resources to be committed, completion times, priorities of activities etc. Areas of responsibility must be identified and assigned time and resource requirements to perform the work activities must be forecasted and budgeted. Planning also involves establishing project boundaries and identifying controllable and uncontrollable variable that must be managed. Also, the performance criteria should be stated related to the project objectives and in measures of time, cost and quality characteristics.

Planning Tools

These are many and include:

- Statement of work (SOW)
- Milestone Schedule
- Work Breakdown Structure (WBS)
- Gantt (bar) charts
- Network Scheduling Systems (PERT or CPM)
- Resource allocation methods.

13.6.1 Statement of work

When the project is awarded, it is enclosed with an SOW describing what is to be provided in the project.

SOW Details

- General scope of the work
- Itemise the tasks to be performed
- Data and reports to the supplied
- Contract end items to be delivered.

SOW consists of a set of numbered paragraphs. It can be cross indexed with the WBS.

SOW may be the same as proposed by the contractor in the proposal bid package or a newly created or modified by the customer. Contractor can easily follow this as he had already worked on this.

13.6.2 Milestone Schedule

Mile Stones are the starting and end dates for major activities. Such a schedule is essential for detailed planning and reaching a mile stone point. This requires a coordinate effort of different people. In each of these activities, there may be number of subactivities. Accomplishing all of these involves great coordination where in specified information must be transferred between project entities to meet the major mile stone.

Milestone	2004												2005											
	1	2	3	4	5	6	7	8	9	10	11	12	1	2	3	4	5	6	7	8	9	10	11	12
Activity 1			▲																					
Activity 2							▲																	
Activity 3												▲												
Activity 4																			▲					
Activity 5																					▲			
Activity 6																							▲	

Fig. 13.5 A Typical Milestone Schedule

13.6.3 Work Breakdown Structure

This planning technique, as the name suggests, enables the organisation to break the project into manageable and recognizable elements. The work breakdown structure has the format of a hierarchical tree with the following nomenclature for each successive level from the top.

1 st - level - work block

2nd - level - work block elements

3rd - level - work packages

4th - level - work sub-package

A large project could have 20 work blocks, 100 work block elements, 500 work packages and 2000 work sub-packages. For each work package/sub-package, a statement of work (SOW) is written identifying the agency, work centre, working group, officer accountable, resources, budget allocations, time schedules and performance targets. There are two types of WBS - One is product - oriented and the other is function-oriented. The product oriented WBS is somewhat akin to product explosion and is shown in Fig 3.6 for a missile project. The second type of WBS is function-oriented and is shown in fig 3.7 for an aircraft project.

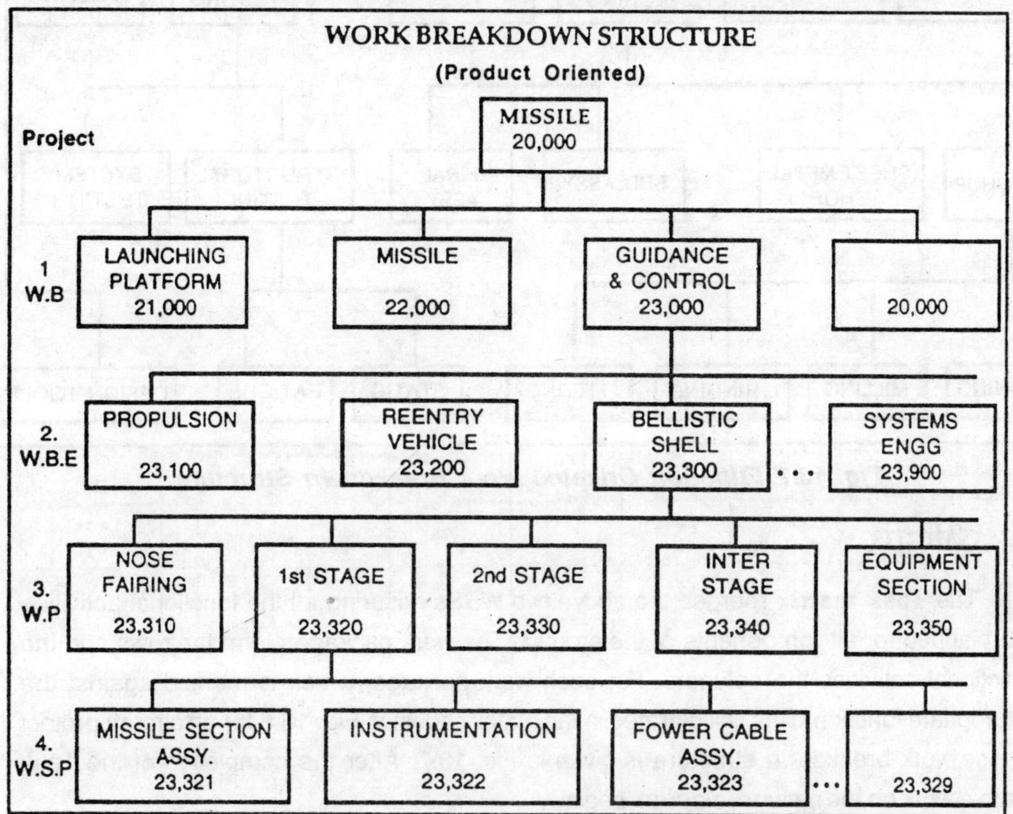

Fig. 13.6 Work Breakdown Structure (WBS)

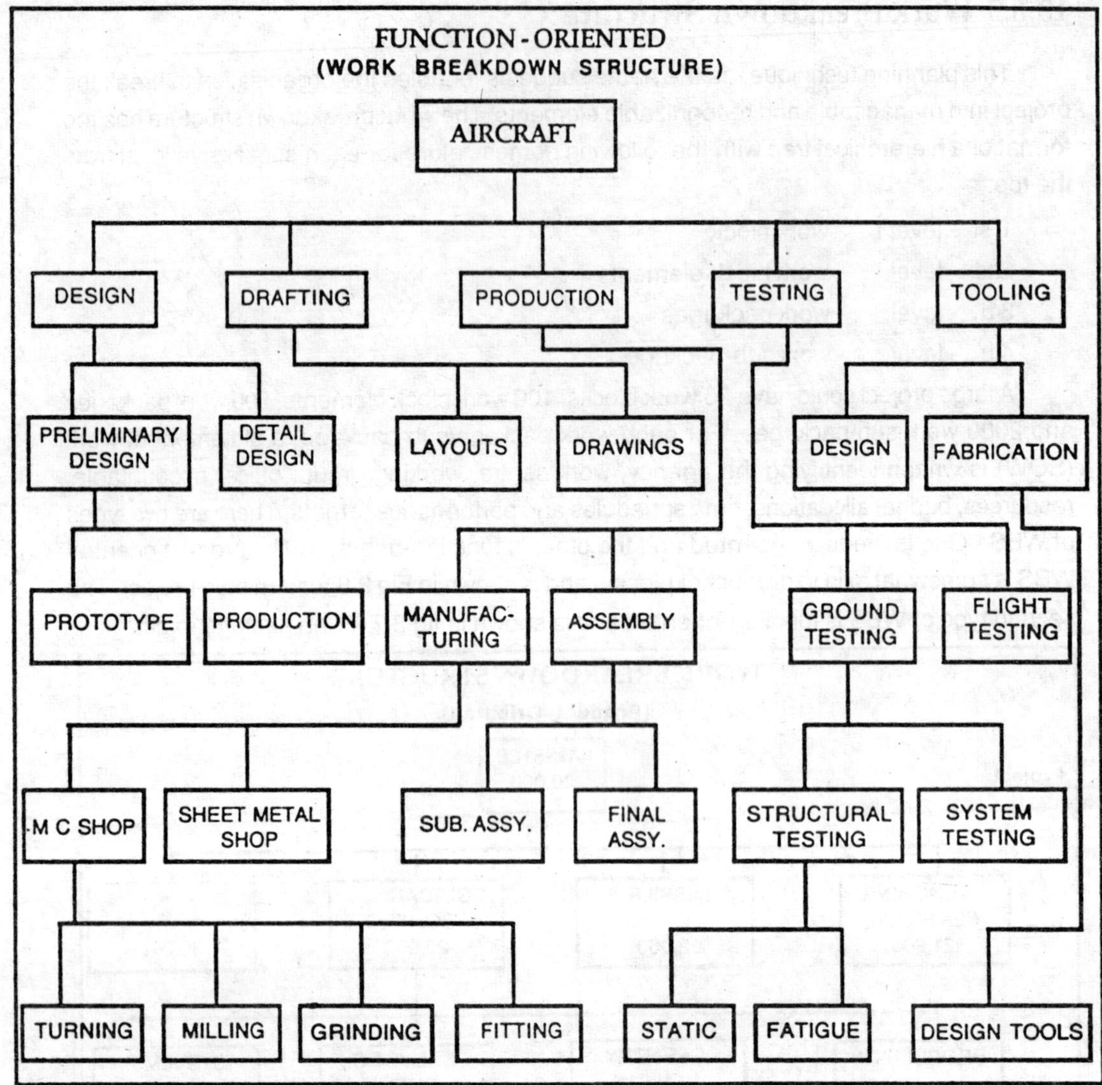

Fig. 13.7 Function Oriented Work Breakdown Structure

Task Matrix

The **Task matrix** merges the above two WBSs ensuring all the functional activities are planned for all components of the product. The work packages form the rows and the functional activities the columns. For each work package, a tick is marked against the appropriate function. This is illustrated in the matrix shown in Fig. 13.8 for an aircraft project whose work breakdown structure is given in Fig. 13.7. After the completion of the Task Matrix, work on the network diagram begins.

TASK MATRIX

TASKS	DESIGN DEPT			DRAFTING		MANUFACTTURING	
	GROUP 1	GROUP 2	GROUP 3	LAYOUT	DETAILING	FABRICATION	ASSEMBLY
FRONT FUS-BULK HEADS	X	–	–	X	X	X	X
FRONT FUS-LONGCRONS SKINS	X	–	–	X	X	X	X
CENTRE FUS-BULK HEADS	X	–	–	X	X	SUB CONTRACT	
Centre Fus-LONGCRONS & SKINS	X	–	–	X	X	X	X
Rear Fus-BULK HEADS	–	X	–	X	X	X	X
Rear Fus-LONGCRONS & SKINS	–	X	–	X	X	X	X
WIND-SPARS	–	X	–	X	–	– OUTSIDE PURCHASE	X
WING RIBS & SKINS	–	X	–	X	–	– OUTSIDE PURCHASE	X
SYSTEM-MECHANICAL	–	–	X	X	–	– OUT SIDE PURCHASE	–
SYSTEM-AVIONICS	–	–	X	OUTSIDE PURCHASE	–	–	–

Fig. 13.8 Task Matrix

13.6.4 Scheduling Chart (Gantt Chart or Horizontal Bar Chart)

The chart is the most frequently used tool to manage small projects. The chart indicates-*what must be done and when it must be done.* As the project progresses, the chart is updated to indicate the amount of accomplishment towards the plan. In this way, the project managers can compare actual project work accomplishment with planned project progress. This chart time phases activities. Every activity should have a start date and a finish date. Fig 13.9 shows a typical Gantt chart to Horizontal bar chart for a building construction project.

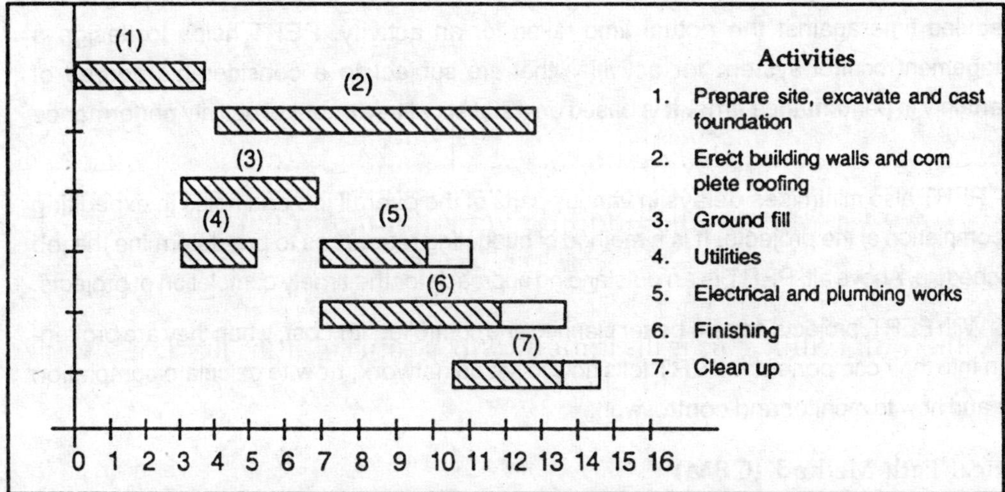

Fig. 13.9 Gantt Chart for Construction of a House

Source: (Seetharam L. Narasimhan, et. al., Production planning and inventory control,) P.H.I, p.586

The chart is prepared in advance of the project to plan and schedule the activities of the project. After the bar chart is initially prepared, managers can be assured that, all the activities of the project are planned for, the order in which the activities must be performed is taken into account, the time estimates for completing each activity are included and finally the overall estimated time for completing the project is developed. The horizontal bar chart becomes the overall plan for the project.

As the project progresses and the activities are completed, actual progress is recorded by shading in the horizontal bars.

These charts are easy to understand and to modify. They are of low cost. The drawback is that, these charts do not adequately indicate the degree of inter-relationships among the project's activities.

13.6.5 Programme Evaluation and Review Technique (PERT) and Critical Path Method (CPM)

PERT is the name given to a networking approach to planning, monitoring, controlling and evaluation of complex projects. It consists of a network diagram which is a two-dimensional schematic of the relationships between tasks in a project. PERT is used for non-repetitive projects that have been done before and will not be done again in precisely the same manner. The technique has been used for projects such as developing missiles, nuclear powered submarines and for the programme that landed the first man on the moon. It is a planning tool which enables the project manager to estimate the time required to complete a proposed project. It also provides a time schedule for various project activities and for checking of the scheduled time against the actual time taken for an activity. PERT helps to design a management control system for activities that are subject to a considerable degree of uncertainty in performance time. It is based on a statistical treatment of activity performance time.

PERT also minimises delays in various parts of the overall job and helps in expediting the completion of the projects. It is a method of budgeting resources to pre-determine the job on schedule. Above all, PERT is an outstanding approach for the timely completion of projects.

With PERT, projects can be better planned and controlled for cost, when they are broken-down into their components. PERT tells how to set up network, how to calculate completion time and how to monitor and control work.

Critical Path Method (CPM)

CPM refers to a quantitative technique which, when applied to network planning, is helpful in calculating the minimum time and the sequence of tasks needed to complete a project. This technique is mostly used for construction projects such as bridges, building, dams and canals, where engineers and contractors try to complete the job at the earliest to avoid rising costs. In CPM technique, the precedence, the relationships between activities and their mutual dependence are suggested, leading to the final objective of reducing the cost and completion time of the project.

The **network techniques** are famous in project management literature but not so widely used in real life project situations. Networks are overkill for small projects; large projects do not establish the required data and organisational discipline to exploit the full potential of this technique. But even those, who do not intend to use a network for project monitoring will do well tő try this out as an one-time exercise because of the following benefits:

1. A network is a great planning tool as it forces the project team to make an exhaustive list of all activities. The WBS and Task Matrix techniques are aids to ensure that no element or activity is missed out.
2. The logical sequence of all the activities have to be visualized - what activities precede or succeed what, what can be done concurrently and what sequentially etc. After this the network is drawn.
3. Thirdly rough estimate of the duration of each activity is made in order to complete the network.
4. Once the network is completed, the critical activities can be identified and the project duration established.

The **critical Path Method** was developed in 1957 in the USA by Morgan Walker of the Engineering Services Division of DU Pont and James Kelly of Remington Rand: It is reported that this technique was successfully used to compress the time taken to repair and overhaul chemical plant machinery. CPM finds application in carrying out repetitive jobs like those in the maintenance department, eg. the overhaul of diesel generators. The activity time is estimated based on experience. This model is said to be **deterministic**.

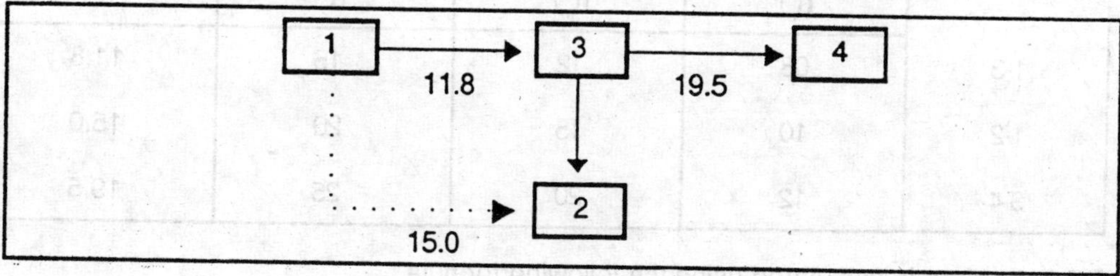

Fig. 13.10 An example of CPM

1, 2, 3 & 4 are called events, which are points in time signifying the start and finish of an activity or group of activities. They do not consume resources like time or money.

1 - Begin breakfast / Begin reading newspaper

2 - Finish reading newspaper

3 - Finish breakfast / start for factory

4 - Reach factory

1-3 is an activity, viz breakfasting

3-4 is another activity viz driving to factory

1-2 is yet another activity viz reading newspaper.

There are four events and three activities.

1-3 and 3-4 are sequential activities; 1-3 and 1-2 are parallel activities.

There are two constraints for starting activity 3-4 - Finish breakfast and Finish reading newspaper.

The first constraint is obvious; the second constraint is shown by creating a dummy activity (shown in dotted lines) with zero time duration. The direction of the arrow indicates the consumption of a resource be it time, money or manpower. Mostly it is time.

Let it be assumed that due to changes in the breakfast menu, the news content and the traffic conditions, exact duration of the three activities cannot be given. In this situation statistical methods are applied to arrive at the expected time durations. For each activity optimistic, pessimistic and most likely durations are assessed based on the knowledge of similar activities.

The three time estimates, it is assumed, conform to **Beta distribution**. It is further assumed that t_o and t_p occur equally and the probability of occurance of t_m is four times that of t_p or t_o. An example

Activity	Optimistic time (t_o)	Most likely time (t_m)	Pessimistic time (t_p)	Expected time (t_e)
1-3	08	12	15	11.8
1-2	10	15	20	15.0
3-4	12	20	25	19.5

Realistic time is calculated using the following formula.

$$t_e = \frac{t_o + 4t_m + t_p}{6}$$

for 1-3 activity,

$$t_e = \frac{8 + 4 \times 12 + 15}{6} = 11.8$$

Standard deviation (s) calculation

$$\sigma = \frac{tp - to}{6}$$

for 1 - 3 activity

$$\sigma_{1-3} = \frac{15 - 8}{6} = 1.17$$

for 1 - 2 activity

$$\sigma_{1-2} = \frac{20 - 10}{6} = 1.7$$

for 3 - 4 activity

$$\sigma_{3-4} = \frac{25 - 12}{6} = 2.17$$

Standard deviation s_r of the total project duration. Therefore becomes the root mean square of the standard deviations of activities lying along the critical path is 1 - 2, 2 – 3, 3 – 4

$$\sigma r = \sqrt{\sigma_1^2 + \sigma_2^2 + \sigma_3^2}$$

$$= \sqrt{\sigma_{1-2}^2 + \sigma_{3-4}^2} = \sqrt{(1.7)^2 + (2.17)^2} \sim 2.79$$

Critical Path

The time required to reach the factory is 15 + 19.5 = 34.5 minutes.

1 - 2 - 3 - 4 is the critical path, as this represents the earliest completion of the project which is to reach the workspot from the house. If the breakfast duration increases to 17 minutes, then the earliest project time is 17 + 19.5 = 36.5 and 1-3-4 becomes the critical path. Under normal circumstances, there is a slack of 3.2 minutes available for activity 1-3, in other words, a more leisurely breakfast can be had without affecting the project time of 34.5 minutes.

CPM Network

Consider the CPM network at Fig.13.11 The following terms will be defined with respect to this network.

An Activity, which is bound by two events, is an element of project work; in networks even waiting time is considered an activity. eg. waiting for government sanction.

The start event is at the tail of the arrow and hence called the **tail event**. The **Earliest start time (EST)** is the earliest possible time at which an activity can start. The finish event is at the head of the arrow and hence called the **head event**. The **earliest finish time** (EFT) is obtained by adding the activity time to the earliest start time. All earliest times are calculated during what is known as the **forward pass**. By convention the first event starts at zero time. Later any specific date can be assigned to this event. The events are numbered in increasing order. The earliest finish time of the last event gives the **project duration.** Unless a scheduled time t_s is given, the latest finish time (LFT) and earliest finish time (EFT) of the last event are the same. If the EFT is less than the T_s, there is a slack or float; in case EFT exceeds the scheduled time, **network must be crashed** to **reduce the project duration** either **by inputting extra resources** or **reallocating the available resources.** The latest finish times are calculated by making a **backward pass.** The activity time is subtracted from for LFT to get the LST starting from the last event and ending at the first event.

Purpose of CPM

1. To ensure logical discipline in planning, scheduling and controlling project.
2. To encourage more long range and detailed planning of projects.
3. To provide management with periodic reports as the project progresses.
4. To identify the most critical element of the plan.

Procedure for drawing up a CPM Network

The general procedure has two major activities, namely

(a) Structure Analysis
- (i) Draw up lists of **activities**
- (ii) Draft of structure / **network**
- (iii) Numbering of **events.**

The ***critical path method (CPM)*** *and* ***program evaluation and review technique (PERT)*** are network techniques for analysing a system in term of activities and events that must be completed in a specified sequence in order to achieve a goal. Some activities can be done concurrently where as others have precedence requirements.

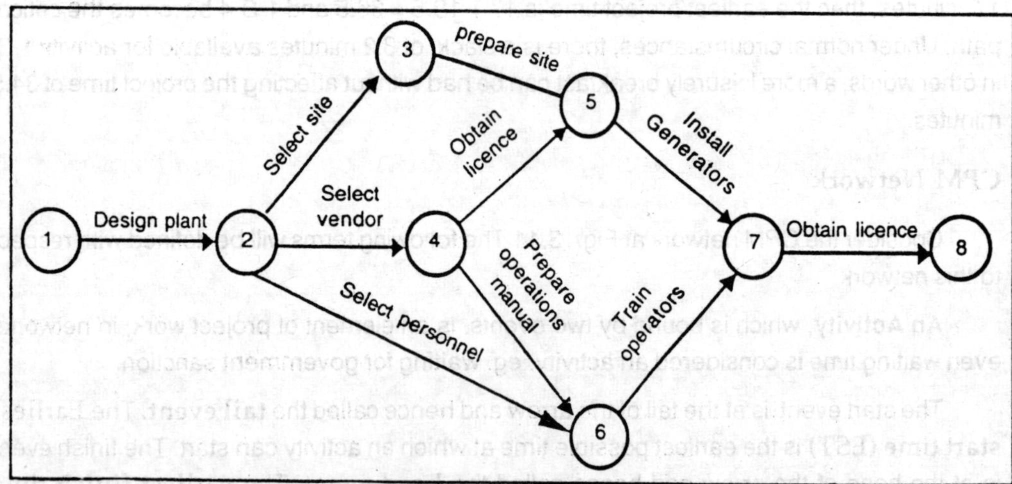

Fig. 13.11 Network diagram for Power Plant Construction.
(Source: Joseph G. Monks. Operations Management. 3rd Edn., Mc Graw Hill International Edition. p.553)

Commonly Used Network Symbols

Symbol	Meaning
——→	Activity
- - - →	Dummy Activity
○	Event
(1) —A→ (2) —B→ (3)	Activity A must be completed before activity B can begin.
(1) —A→ (3), (2) —B→ (3), (3) —C→ (4)	Activities A and B can occur concurrently, but both must be completed before activity C can begin.
(1) —A→ (3), (2) —B→ (3), (3) —C→ (4), (3) —D→ (5)	Activities A and B must be completed before activities C and D can begin, but C can begin independently of D and vice versa.
(1) —A→ (3) —D→ (5), (2) —B→ (4) —E→ (6), (4) - - C - → (3)	Activities A and B can occur concurrently, but both must be completed before activity D can begin Activity E can occur only after activity B is completed. Activity C (dotted line with arrow head) is a dummy activity which shows a precedence relationship but has a zero time duration.

Fig. 13.12 Some of the Commonly Used Network Symbols

There are two types of resources analysis.

Time limited analysis suggests ways and means of rescheduling activities within floats available in order to smoothen the peak demands on the resources. In this analysis, the project time is sacrosanct; and in order to meet the schedules, the required resources are provided.

Resources limited analysis is similar to the above analysis except that there is a ceiling on the resource availability and stretch of project duration to the extent unavoidable is accepted.

CPM and PERT

The terminologies relating to the two techniques are correlated below.

PERT	CPM
Network	Arrow Diagram
Event	Node
Activity	Job
Scheduled Time	Duration
Slack	Float

Critical path Analysis: In recent years a great deal has been heard about **'critical path analysis' (C.P.A)**, which is simply a systematic way of programming economically in sequence. Known also as **'network analysis'** and **'programme evaluation and review technique'** (P.E.R.T), and other names emphasizing slight differences in practice, its aim is to ensure the shortest possible time between inception and completion, to keep delay and cost to an absolute minimum. Thus a diagrammatic network of 'events' is drawn up in logical order, with a time-scale for each part, the total time being determined by the shortest way home, through taking the critical path.

C.P.A is basically an operational research technique, and in line with that it is essential to construct a progressive model of the real system. In this case it takes the form of an arrow diagram such as that shown below. The example given is a simple one, but in practice, particularly with regard to construction projects, the network can be highly complicated, the critical path threading its way through a veritable maze of high ways and by-ways to achieve a minimum sequence of significant events. It will be seen that each event is given a progressive reference number in a circle, called a 'node', and that between adjacent events, conveniently placed in a square, there is a figure indicating estimated duration, usually expressed as so many units of working days. A refinement includes minimum and maximum times of expected duration.

The critical path in the example given is the horizontal line extending right across the centre of Fig 13.13.

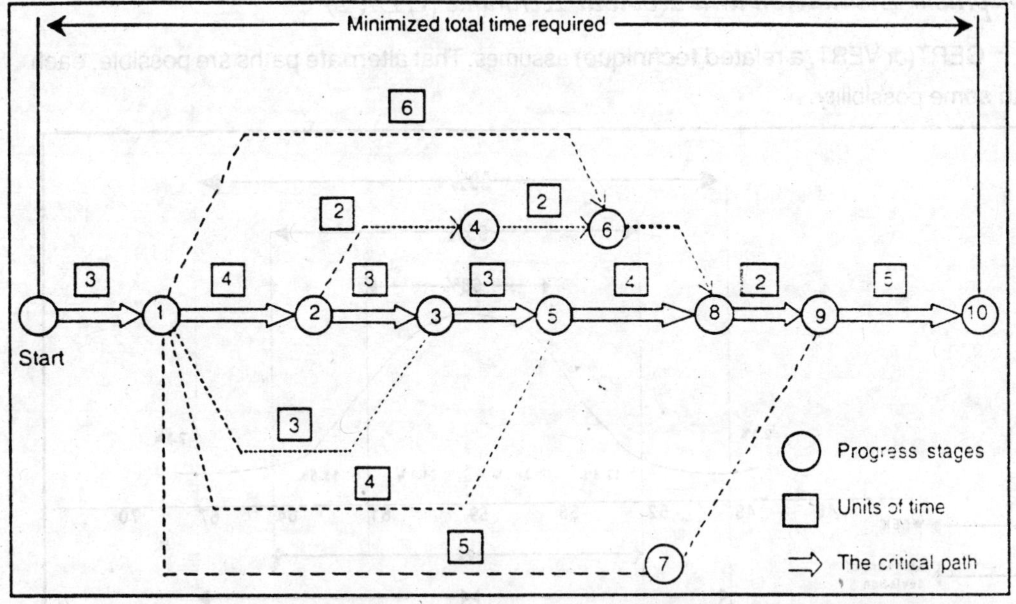

Fig. 13.13 Critical Path Analysis

This shows that stage (1) takes three units of time to complete from the start of the programme; at this point certain side sequences are set in motion to slot into and help complete stages (3), (5), (8), and (9) along the critical path. By the time stage (8) is reached, for example, side programmes (4) and (6) have been finished, there by enabling stage (8) to be completed. By stage (10) the programme as a whole has been finally achieved in the least possible total time.

13.7 Other project network models

A few variations and extensions of PERT and CPM have been developed to provide additional capability. They are as under:-

Precedence diagramming method: (PDM)

PERT and CPM assume that the next activity can begin, with certainty only after the preceding activities have completed. There are many times when greater flexibility is needed eg., After concrete is laid on the floor, it has to be cured for about 10 days atleast before we start building on it. In CPM, we add another activity called cure concrete with a time duration but no cost. In PDM, the two can be connected with a 'Finish to start' (PS) delay constraint of 10 days. It can be even "start to start" (SS) or 'finish to finish' (FF) constraints.

Graphical Evaluation and Review Technique (GERT)

GERT(or VERT, a related technique) assumes. That alternate paths are possible, each with some possibility.

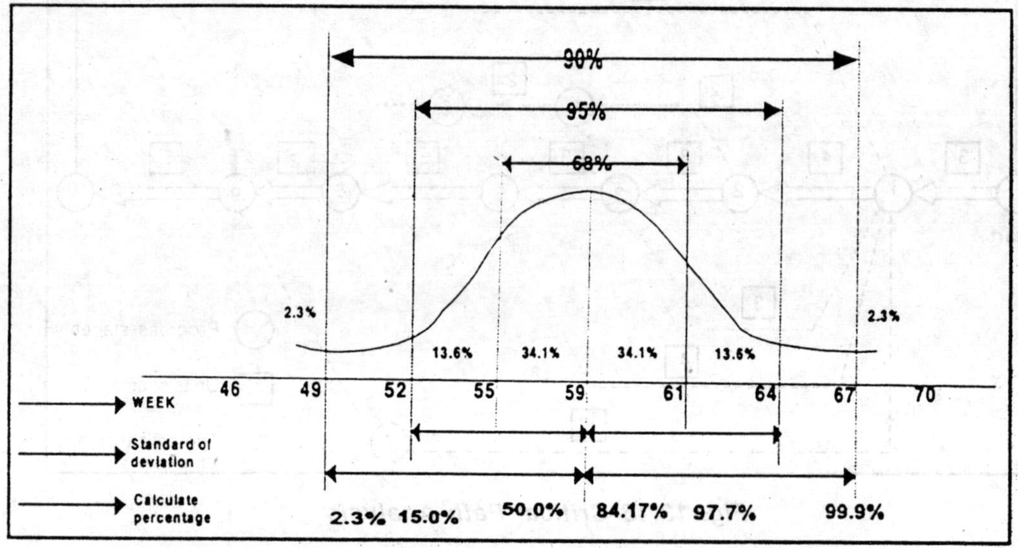

Fig. 13.14 Normal possibility Distribution of Project Critical Path

Time durations for complex project, using GERT can be estimated by running them many times in **Montecarlo Simulations.**

PERT / LOB

PERT and CPM are designed projects (unique) with one of a kind activities. If series of identical items are to be produced, each following the same network logic, PERT is combined with Line of Balance (LOB) methodology developed for production planning.

13.8 Contracts

Contracts can be classified on the basis of contract costs borne:

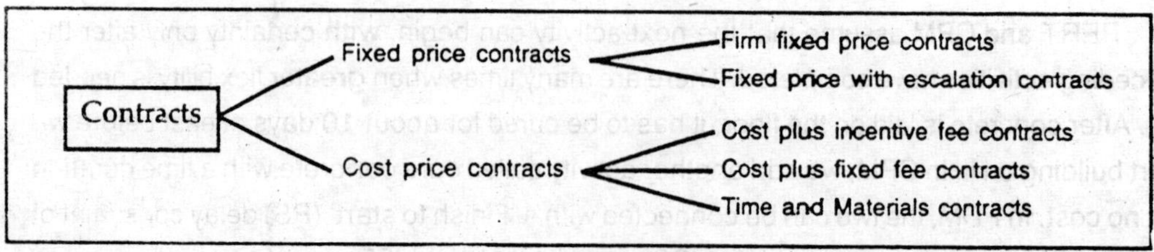

Fig. 13.15 Contracts

A. Fixed Price Contracts:

(i) **Firm fixed price contract** Here the contractor has to provide an agreed product and for service for a **specified price**. He has the maximum motivation to eliminate waste as he realises the total profit / loss.

(ii) **Fixed price with escalation contracts:-** These are firm fixed price except that the contractor's price can be adjusted to incorporate any increases in specified labour and material rates.

B. Cost Type Contracts are of three types:

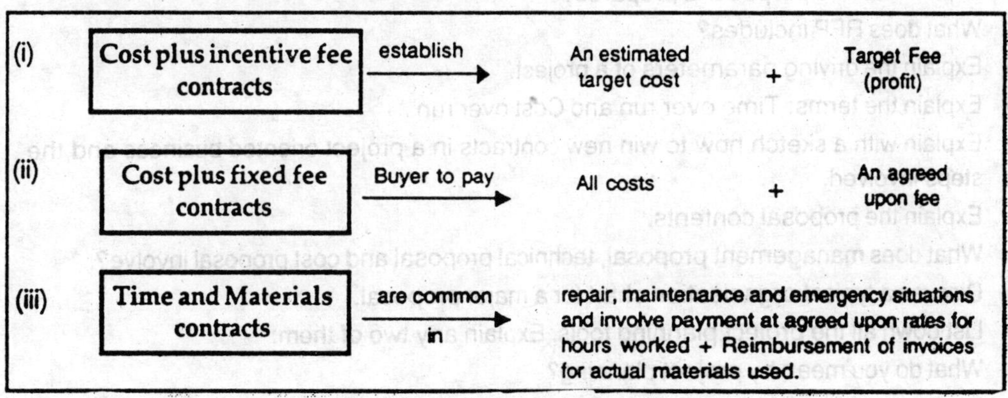

Fig. 13.16 Cost Type Contracts

Example for (i)

Target cost (estimated cost ------- \$ 100 ml^{n}

Target fee 8% \$ 8 ml^{n}

Customer / contractor sharing ratio 70:30

(with a variation of $\pm$ 20% of target)

The contractor will get either \$ 2 ml^{n} min

or \$ 14 ml^{n} max

If \$ 80 ml^{n} plus 30% of 20 %

(i.e \$ 6ml^{n}) saving

Total \$ 14 ml^{n}

If \$ 150 ml^{n}

contractor would only have to share 30%

of 20 \$ ml^{n} overrun = \$6ml^{n}

Target fee received = \$2ml^{n}

Example for (ii)

In this case, the contractor would receive fee rate agreed as 8% in 8 ml^{n} fee regardless of cost over runs.

Example for (iii)

The only motivation for efficiency is the hope of future work . The advantage is its speed and economy for small jobs not worth detailed estimating.

Questions

1) Define project.
2) Define program.
3) Define project management.
4) Explain the characteristics of a project.
5) Explain the project proposal process.
6) Define 'Request for proposal' in a project.
7) Explain the preproposal effort.
8) Explain how the proposal is prepared?
9) What does RFP includes?
10) Explain the driving parameters of a project.
11) Explain the terms: Time over run and Cost over run.
12) Explain with a sketch how to win new contracts in a project oriented business and the steps involved.
13) Explain the proposal contents.
14) What does management proposal, technical proposal and cost proposal involve?
15) Discuss a typical organisation chart for a major proposal.
16) List down all the project planning tools. Explain any two of them.
17) What do you mean by project planning?
18) Explain statement of work.
19) Explain Milestone schedule with a sketch.
20) Discuss work Breakdown structure with sketches.
21) What do you mean by Task Matrix? Explain with a sketch.
22) Explain Gantt chart with a sketch
23) Explain programme evaluation and review technique (PERT) and Critical Path Method (CPM).
24) Discuss network techniques.
25) Explain PERT taking an example.
26) Discuss in the terms:- optimistic time, most likely time, pessimistic time, expected time and establish a relationship between them.
27) What do you mean by standard deviation and standard deviations of a activities lying along the critical path?
28) Write down commonly used network symbols.
29) What is the purpose of CPM? Give an example of a network diagram.
30) Distinguish PERT and CPM.
31) Explain Critical Path Analysis with an example.
32) Explain some of the other network models like PDM, GERT.
33) Explain PERT / LOB.
34) Discuss the meaning of contracts and various types of contracts.
35) Explain: Fixed price contracts and Cost type contracts.

Chapter - 14

Project Organisation, Leadership and Control

14.1 Preview

This Chapter deals with the following topics :

- *Project Organisation*
  - The project - driven organisation
  - Elements of the project - driven organisation
  - Projected versus functional organisation conducting projects within the functional organisations
- *The Projectised Organisation*
  - Comparing the functional organisation with the projectised organisation
- *Matrix Management*
- *Organisation structure and project success*
  - Characteristics of effective project managers
  - Various skills
- *Developing project management skills*
- *The managers charter*
- *Motivating project performance*
  - Team building
- *Managing conflict*
  - Sources of conflict
  - Methods of conflict management
- *Keys to project success*
- *Customer (client) communications*
- *Early learning path*
- *Controlling cost and schedule*
  - Project control systems
  - Reducing project duration
  - Crashing the project
  - Earned value system

14.1 Project Organisation

Kerzner classifies organisation broadly into two groups:

- The project driven organisation
- Traditional organisation (non-project-driven)

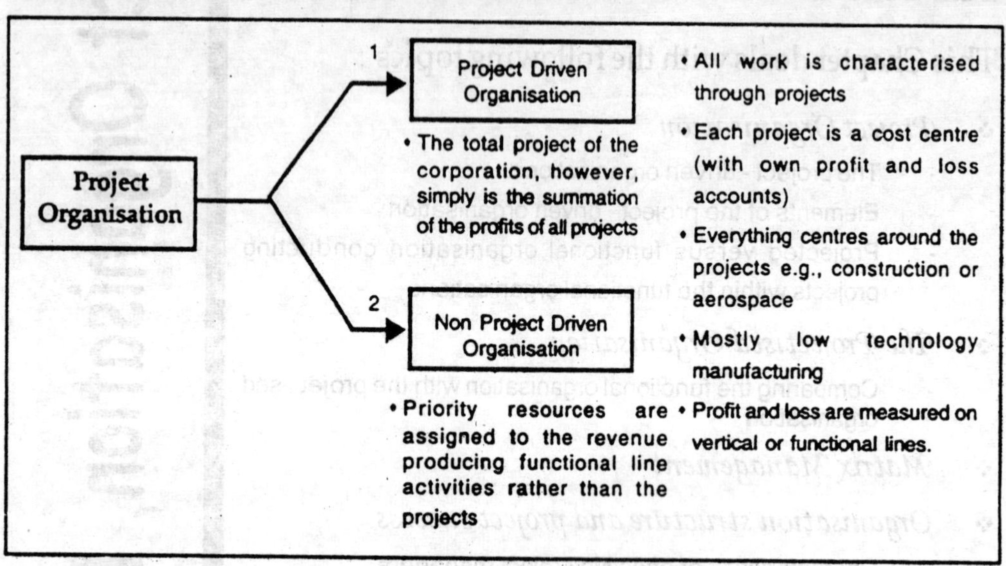

Fig. 14.1 Project Organisation

4.3 Project Driven Organisation

This needs four different categories/types of elements. Project organisations are characterised by the number of the categories coming under the direct control of the individual project manager :-

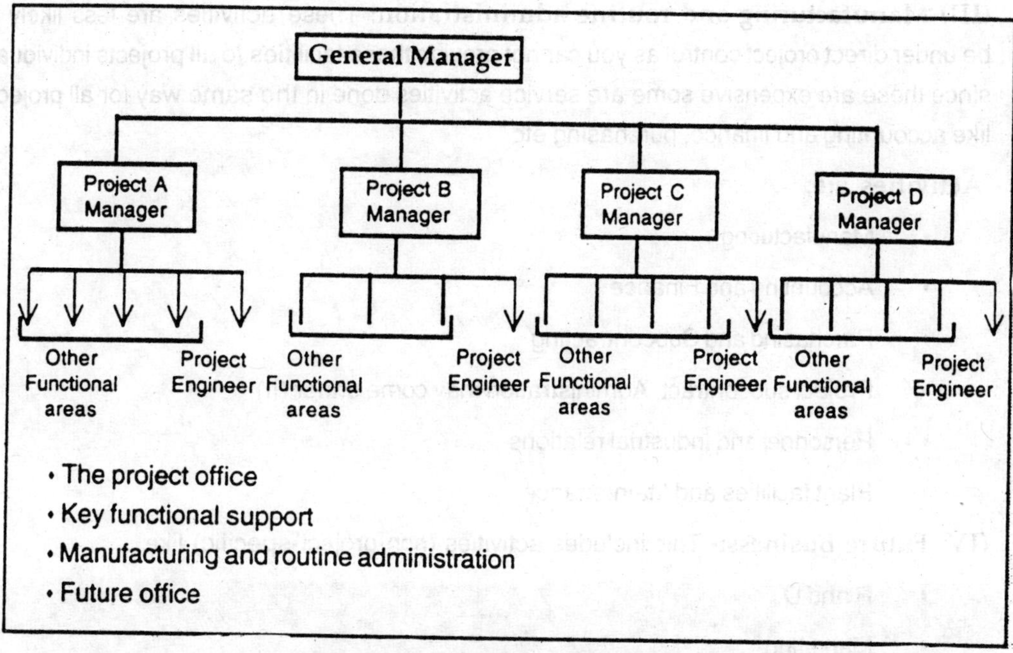

Fig. 14.2 Project Organisation

(I) The Project office:- In every project, the project manager has to take the overall responsibility. In a small project, the project office will be completely looked after by the project manager. In large projects, he takes the assistance of a project engineer responsible for the technical integrity of the project and the cost and schedule of engineering activities. There will be a project administrator who is responsible for:

* Project planning and control systems
* Documentation

Other functions include: Design review, configuration/change control.

(II) Key functional support: Project success depends on support received from certain key functional areas which is tailored to the specific needs of the projects. These are:-

- Systems analysis, systems engineering and systems integration
- Product design and analysis.
- Quality assurance and reliability
- Production planning
- Product installation and testing
- Training, logistics planning and field support

(III) Manufacturing and routine administration: These activities are less likely to be under direct project control as you cannot provide these facilities to all projects individuals since these are expensive some are service activities done in the same way for all projects like accounting and finance, purchasing etc.

Activities are:

- Manufacturing
- Accounting and Finance
- Purchasing and Subcontracting
- Project subcontract, Administration may come under (II)
- Personnel and Industrial relations
- Plant facilities and Maintenance

(IV) Future Business:- This includes activities (non-project-specific) like

- R and D
- Marketing

The above are not part of specific projects but necessary for the continuation of the project-driven organisation

Projectised versus Functional organisation

Working of projects within the functional organisation

The following organisation depicts a typical functional organisation If a project connected with many of the functions are to be conducted in this functional organisation, a project manager or coordinator or expeditor is to be recruited or selected from the same organisation who has some experience of these functions to coordinate the various activities of working on the project. This person may be directly attached to the chief of the organisation like General manager or at different places as shown below with osterik mark (*) He may be a staff to the GM over all the functions involved or may be the supervisor of the function most heavily involved in the project or a key subordinate of that supervisor.

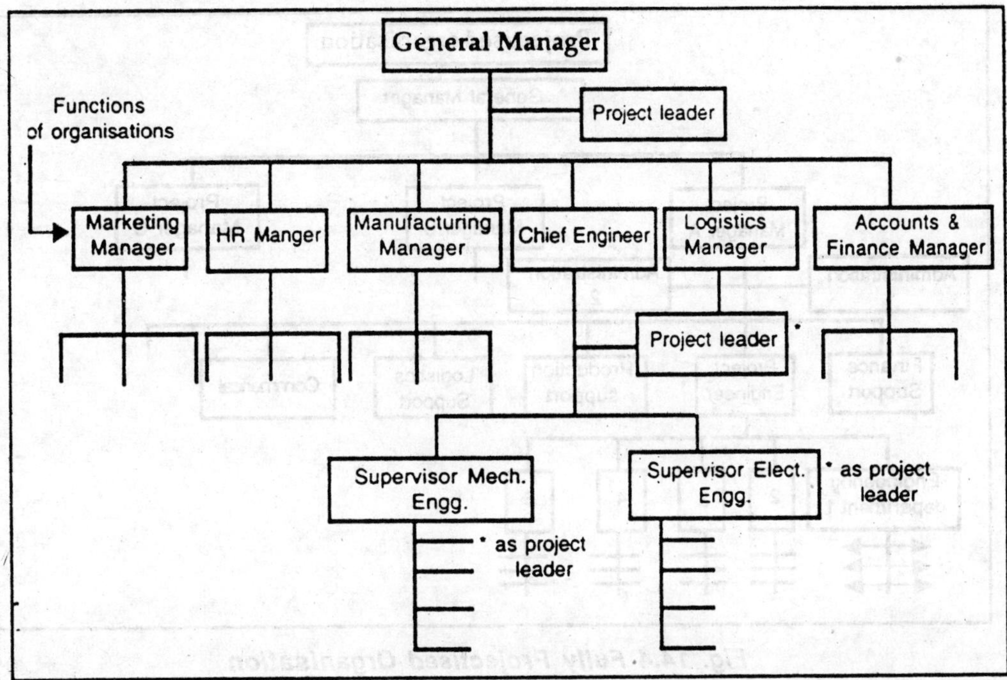

Fig. 14.3 Typical Functional Organisation from which a Project Manager can Work and Lead the Team

The designated project leader usually has no line authority over the bulk of project personnel-only over the immediate project office. In case the project is establishing a new product in the organisation proves successful, the project leader 's designation is changed later on and he will become the chief of manufacturing of that product.

14.4 Projectised Organisation

In this type of organisation, the project or program manager is in direct control of all the activities to be done on this project. This is ideal for projects of large size, long duration projects, complex, involving a number of different organisations requiring advancing the state of technology. In the case of projectised organisation, though this solves some problems in the short run, it is expensive, waste resources and as projects phases out, difficulties arise in balancing work loads and reallocating personnel who in such circumstances develop a feeling of insecurity.

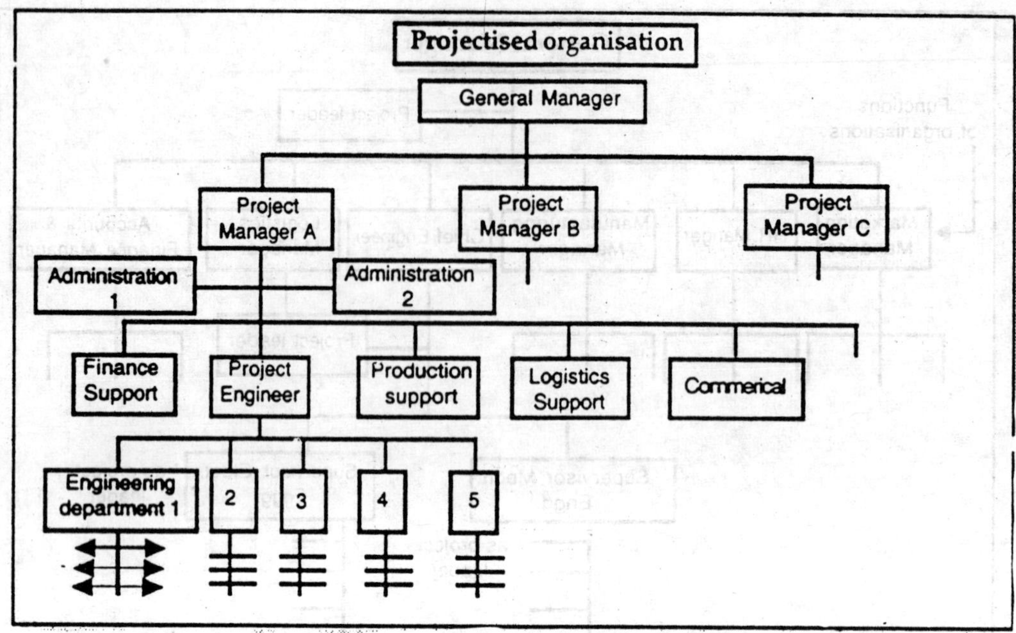

Fig. 14.4 Fully Projectised Organisation

Advantages and Disadvantages of Functional and Projected Organisation

The advantages and disadvantages of both the types of organisations are as shown below :-

Functional organisation	Projected organisation
• Efficient use of Technical personnel of different functions • Career continuity and growth of technical personnel • Good technology transfer between projects • Good stability, security and morale	• Problems solved in the short run • Good project schedule and cost control • Single point for customer contact • Rapid reaction time possible • Simpler project communication • Training ground for general management
• Weak customer interface • Weak project authority • Horizontal communication poor • Slower work flow • Technology rather than program oriented	• Expensive • As projects phase out, balancing of work loads is difficult. • Water resources • Reallocating personnel use in such circumstances develop a feeling of insecurity • Uncertain technical direction • Inefficient use of specialists • Insecurity regarding future job assignments • Poor cross feed of technical information

Fig. 14.5 Advantages and Disadvantages of Functional organisation and Projected organisation.

14-5 Matrix Management (Relationship of programma management to Functional Management)

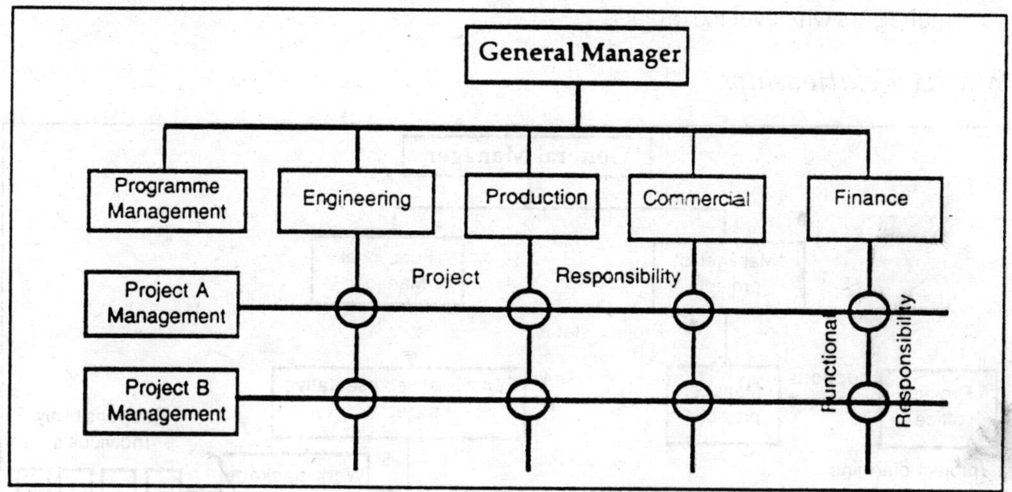

Fig. 14.6 Matrix Organisation

(II) The functional manager, has primary responsibility for :

- Assignment of functional specialists
- Distribution of key specialists among the several projected non-project assignments competing for them.
- Also responsible for assuring the quality of work done on projects or elsewhere in that speciality
- For selecting, evaluating and rewarding work done in that speciality.

The specialists, on the other hand benefit from :

- Communication with peers
- Having a congenial 'technical home' to return after completion of the project

The Functional specialists (assigned temporarily to the projectised organisation) develop :

- An understanding of other functions that enhances their personal growth in the organisation.
- Contacts outside their narrow function that persist for some time.

Application of Matrix organisation

- **Shifting matrix organisation** is common in aerospace industry. Personnel are shifted between projects depending on the work load and project cycle. Project team is disbanded at the end of the project.

In fixed matrix organisation, the project manager is responsible for a successive series of projects, and functional personnel are always assigned to the same project managers whatever the project.

Matrix Relationships

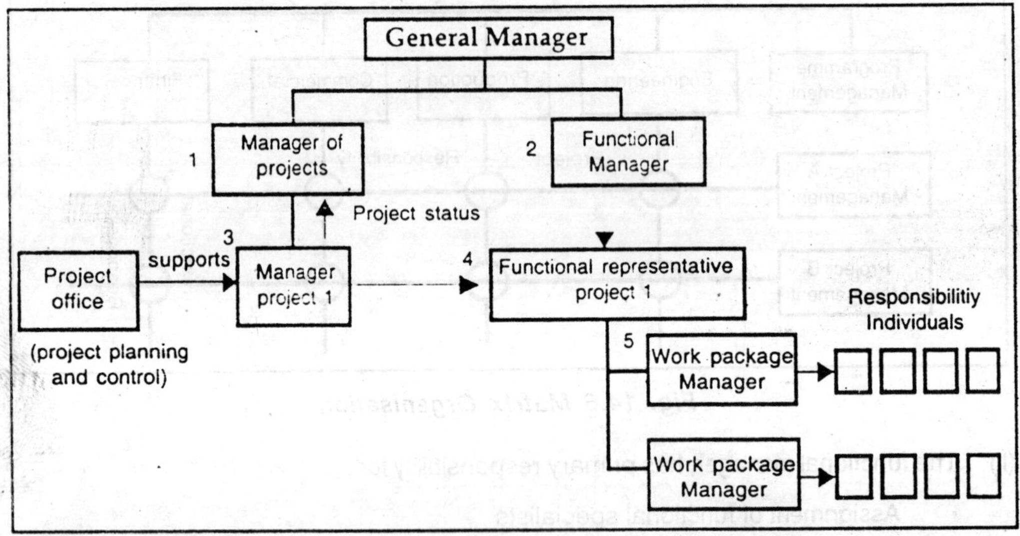

Fig. 14.7 Matrix Relationships (Responsibilities of different individuals are shown separately in a table below)

Organisation of the project Management

The organisation of the project management department itself is shown in figure 14.8 below. This follows the conventional line and staff organisation

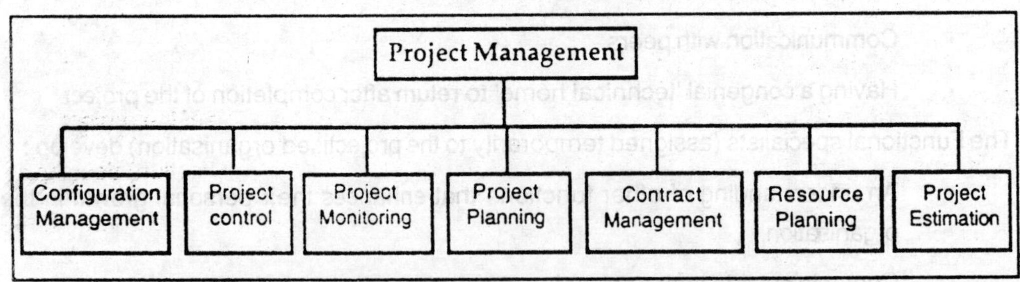

Fig. 14.8 Project Management

Matrix Management

It is a **composite organisation structure** that combines many of the advantages of both functional and projectised management. In this system, the person assigned responsibility for a specific functional speciality on a specific project is accountable in two dimensions, reporting to both functional and project managers. Reporting to two bosses relationship defies the **'unit of command'management principle as per Henri fayol,** and, indeed, most early management scholars. It is very real source of conflict unless the nature of these two reporting relationships is clearly understood.

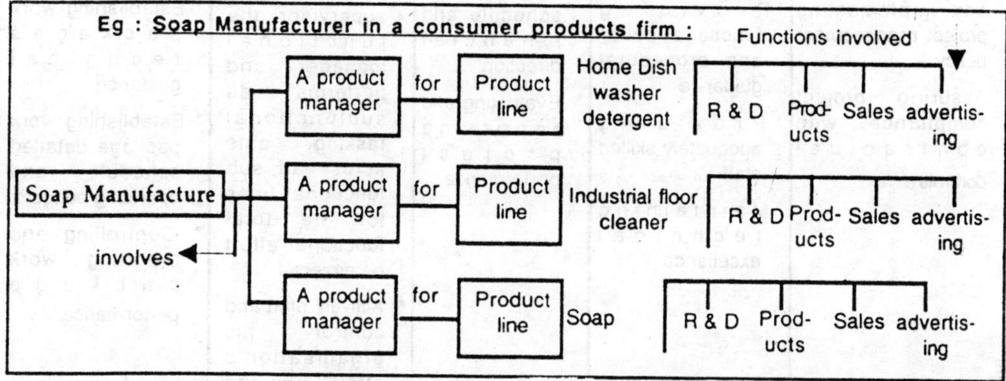

A Simplified Matrix Organisation Showing one of the Several Projects with one Functional Manager

This example explains the nature of the relationships and benefits of the matrix organisation

(1) The horizontal relationships are pertaining to the project manager who has control over the three key factors in projects control

- **Projects tasks and performance** (what has to be done?)
- **Projects schedule** (when it must be done?)
- Projects **budget** (how much in the way of resources will be allocated ?)

The project manager is the central local point for:-

- Customer contact
- Decisions on project changes
- Project communication

1. Manager of projects	2. Functional Manager	3. Manager project 1	4. Functional Representative Project 1	5. Work package managers
• Directing and evaluating Project manager activity • Planning, proposing and implementing project management policy • Assuring project compliance with contractual commitments	• Accomplishing work package tasks on schedule and within budget • Providing functional policy and procedural guidance • Providing adequately skilled staff • Maintaining technical excellence	• Developing and maintaining project plans. • Giving project schedule and financial direction • Evaluating and reporting project performance	• Focal point of all activation on project 1 • Alter ego of his supervisor, the functional manager and performs all subfunctional tasking, cuts across all sub functional lines for the total functional effort on project 1 • Actively plan and control his organisation's effort on the project	• Develop and maintaining work package plans for accomplishment • Establishing work packages technical guidance. • Establishing work package detailed schedule and operating budgets. • Controlling and reporting work package performance.

Fig. 14.5 Responsibilities of Individuals in the Matrix Organisation

☛ 14.7 Organisation Structure and Project Success:-

Larson and Gobeli describes five project Management structures:-

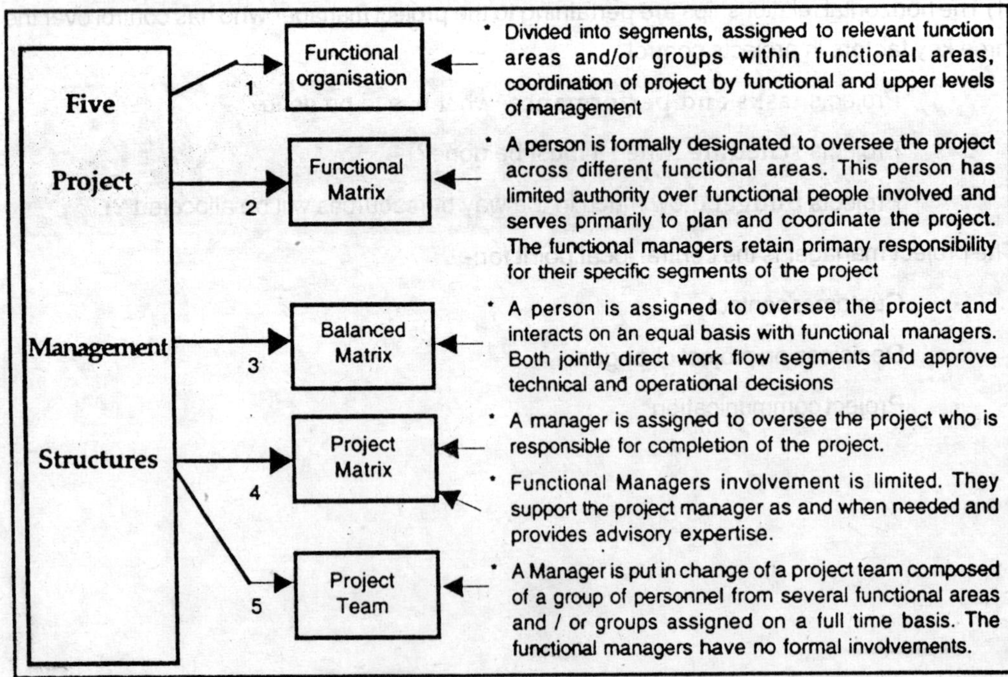

Fig. 14.10 Five Project Management Structures

Analysis of Larson and Gobeli of the above project Management structures

(With reference to : a) Meeting schedule b) Controlling cost c) Technical performance and d) Overall performance.

1 Functional Matrix .... More successful than Functional Organisation

2 Functional Organisation

3 Balanced Matrix
4. Projected Matrix
5. Project team

} .... Better than 1&2 in all a), b), c), d) aspects.

- Project matrix 4 was considered best in b) controlling cost
- Project matrix 4 and project team 5 were best in meeting shcedule a)

Characteristics of effective and efficient Project Managers:-

The project managers have

- Leader ship qualities
- To work hard
- To show enthusiasm,
- High degree of dedication to work.

The project managers should have tremendous responsibility for the success of the project and hence they should be from senior positions. They should work closely work with functional managers with whom they should negotiate. They need a blend of **skills** such as **technical, administrative, interpersonal** to provide effective leadership.

SKILLS		
TECHNICAL	ADMINISTRATIVE	INTERPERSONAL
• Certain key technologies are important for project success • Project manager should understand the importance of using such key technologies for quality work. • Project manager should also deal with unfamiliar technologies by quickly grasping the implication if any involved in it for implementation.	• Project managers must be experienced in planning, organising, staffing, and control techniques as they apply to projects. • They should understand the project planning techniques, such as work break down structure, network systems and others, design control methods such as design review, and configuration / change control and project cost control methods	• Expect in fully projectised organisations, project managers depend heavily on the work of others not within their control. • The ability to inspire, cajole, negotiate and persuade others • Project managers need a good understanding of conflict resolution methods.

Fig. 14.11 Skills

14.8 Developing Project Management Skills

In big projects where managers put both their efforts while working in some speciality of engineering or business, learned project planning and control applying their speciality in a project environment. They were assigned responsibility for a major project only after they work in a series of projects and functional assignments of increasing responsibility.

Engineers are assigned to small projects with little or no preparation. Many short courses are also available offered by consultants, professional societies and at universities. Many books are available for study on the subject of project management. Nothing would substitute, the experience really gets while working. Several publications of the Project Management Institute of engineering management divisions of the major engineering societies and of the American Society for engineering management also help in acquiring project management skills.

The Project Manager's activities

The importance for a project manager is:

- His charter or **scope of authority**
- His **responsibilities and authority** are to be defined in writing in advance to clarify the interfaces between the project manager, functional managers and others.
- To reduce the potential for conflict and confusion.

Areas of a project manager to be covered

- **Project** priority specification relative to other activities.
- **Designation** as the primary contact with the customer.
- **Authority**: To define the work to be performed by supporting departments in terms of cost, schedule and performance; to constitute and chair the make or buy and source selection board.
- **Control, over the, project budget,** with signature authority on all work authorisations.
- **Responsibility for:** Configuration and change control and for approving changes, to schedule and hold design reviews, determine the agenda and representation, and establish responsibility for follow-up action, for regular reporting to general management of project status and identification of any factors inhibiting project success.
- **Participation** in the merit review process for all personnel on loan to the project.

Some of the project managers would have been granted all the authorities suggested above; But authority relationships with functional managers and among projects should be clarified.

Team Building

It is one of the prime responsibilities of the project or program manager

It involves a whole spectrum of management skills required to:

- Identify
- Commit
- Integrate

Various task groups from traditional functional organisations into a single program management system, known for centuries.

It is a complex work and requires more specialised management skills.

When a team is newly formed it lacks clarity, about purposes, responsibilities, expectations and communication, commitment and team spirit. Hence following suggestions have been made by Thamhain to prevent the above and to eliminate the potential to such problems for developing.

- Project importance to the organisation, its principal goals and objectives are to be clear to everyone who is involved in the project
- Defining of project leadership positions, staffing at the beginning of team formation stage. The capabilities, interests and commitments to the project should be assured before any of the lead personnel are signed up. One-on-one interviews are recommended where in the scope, project requirements and the management philosophy, organisational structure, rewards can be explained.
- Members of the newly formed team are to be closely to facilitate communications and development of a team spirit. Locating all in one area is ideal. Regularly scheduled meetings are recommended after the formation of new project team and necessary specially when team members are geographically separated and do not meet on day-to-day basis.
- All project assignments to be negotiated individually with each prospective team number to know clearly on the specific task, the outcome, timing, responsibilities, reporting relation, potential rewards and the importance of the project to the organisation.
- The basic team structure together with the operating concepts during the project formation stage has to be defined by the management.
- The project manager should involve most of the key personnel in the project definition

and requirement analysis; conduct team building sessions throughout the project life cycle. Intense effort is needed during the team formation stage.

- Project leaders should try to determine lack of team member commitment early in the life of the project; eliminate negative news. If non cooperative team member is found, the leader should examine ways to bring him to line or consider replacement.
- Senior management is to provide the proper environment for the project to function effectively.
- Project managers to understand the various barriers to team development. They have to build a work environment conducive to the team's motivational needs by watching barriers such as:

- disinterested team members	- role conflict and power struggle
- uninvolved management	- incompetent project leadership
- unclear goals and priorities	- lack of project charter
- funding uncertainty	- insufficient planning and project definition
- poor communication	- excessive conflict (personal conflict)

- Project leaders should watch for changes in performance on an ongoing basis. Performance problems are to be dealt quickly by the team taking the help of organisational development specialists if any.

14.9 Managing conflict

Conflicts cannot be escaped. They are natural and found everwhere in any organisation like in relationship. These are due to:

- Pettiness
- Lack of understanding (person or group)
- Intolerance
- Stems from honest disagreement on priorities
- Use of scarce resources

Seven Potential conflict sources as per Thamhain

These are conflicts over:-

- Schedules
- Project priorities (including conflict over the sequencing of activities and / tasks to be undertaken)
- Workforce resources (obtaining the desired quality and quantity of personnel from

other functional and staff support areas)

- Technical opinions and performance trade-offs
- Administrative procedures (how project managed definition, the project manager's reporting relationships, responsibilities and authority)
- Personality
- Cost and funds allocated to functional support groups.

The relative importance of these seven conflict sources varies over the **Project life cycle'**

(i) According to Thamhain, the largest concern at first phase of project life cycle project formation is with administrative procedures (establishing the relative authorities of project and functional managers). As per posner from research a decade later, that this source has diminished as project management organisations have been institutionalised.

(ii) As the project progresses into the next two phases of project life cycle. the overall level of conflict increases

- staffing concerns - first

- Then with priorities,schedules, costs and the technical issues.

(iii) Toward the end of the project, the overall level of conflict is reduced. Most likely forms of conflict relate to schedule slippages that delay project completion and project costs.

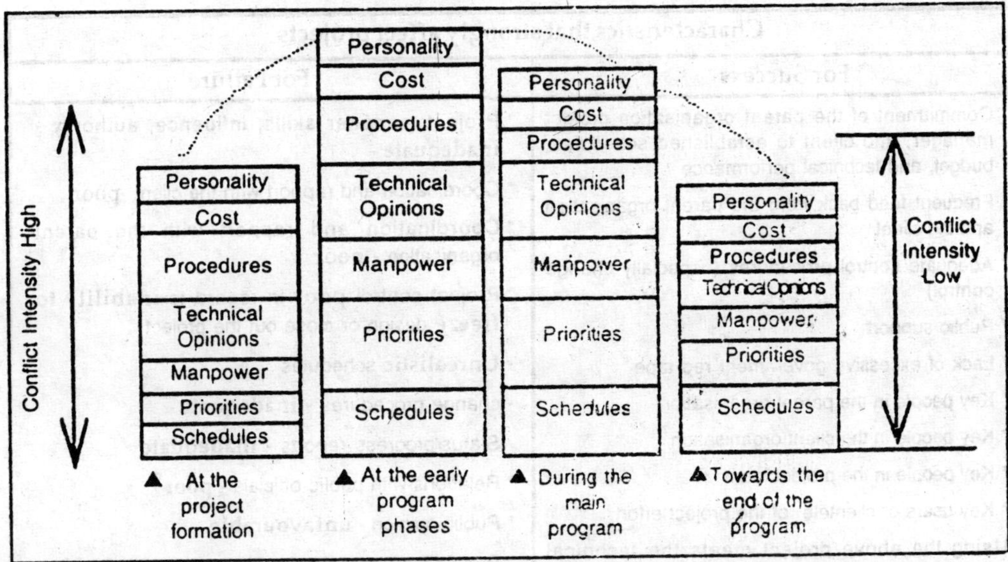

Fig. 14.9 Conflict Sources over the Project Cycle

Methods of conflict Management

Blake and Mouton identified five methods for dealing with conflict:-

(i) **Withdrawal or Retreat**	- from actual or potential conflict
(ii) **Forcing one's view point**	- at the potential expense of the other party
(iii) **Smoothing or Emphasising**	- the points of agreement or deemphasising areas of conflict
(iv) **Compromising or Negotiating**	- in which each party must give up something but each walks away partly satisfied.
(v) **Confronting or Problem solving**	- in which the parties focus on the issues, consider alternatives, and look for the best overall solution.

Fig. 14.10 Five Methods of Dealing with Conflict

Thamhain and wilemon examined the above 5 methods and their views are:-

Most favoured:- Confrontation (problem solving) i.e. (v) followed by compromising and smoothing (iv) and (iii)

Next to best choice is Forcing ... (II) ; Last is withdrawal (I)

Note:- In the reverse order, it, is preferred:

Characteristics that strongly affect projects	
For Success	**For Failure**
• Commitment of the parent organisation project manager, and client to established schedules, budget, and technical performance • Frequent feed back from the parent organisation and the client • Adequate control procedures (especially change control) • Public support • Lack of excessive government red tape • Key people in the parent organisation • Key people in the client organisation • Key people in the project team • Key users or clientele of the project effort Using the above project meets the technical performance specifications, mission to be performed, high level of satisfaction concerning the project outcome.	• Project manager skills, influence, authority - **inadequate** • Coordination and rapport with the client -**poor** • Coordination and rapport with the parent organisation - **poor** • Project control **poor** in regard to **inability to freeze** design or close out the project - **Unrealistic** schedules - change procedures - **inadequate** - Status/progress reports - **inadequate** • Relations with public officials - **poor** • Public opinion - **unfavourable** • Project team participation and team spirit - **lacking** • Project of different type or **more complex** than handled previously • Projects initially **underfunded**

Katz and Allen says that project performance reaches its highest level " when organisational influence is centred in the project manager and influence over technical details of the work is centred in the functional manager"

14.10 Early learning path

In any development process, the key management task is strategic creation of early **learning path.** During the phases of engineering design process at the beginning of chapter 11, emphasising the need to reduce uncertainty in the early phases of the process, so that the later, more expensive phases are attempted only when early as much early uncertainty as possible has been eliminated. The project activities has been scheduled to gain maximum learning in the early period when cumulative project expenditure is still low.

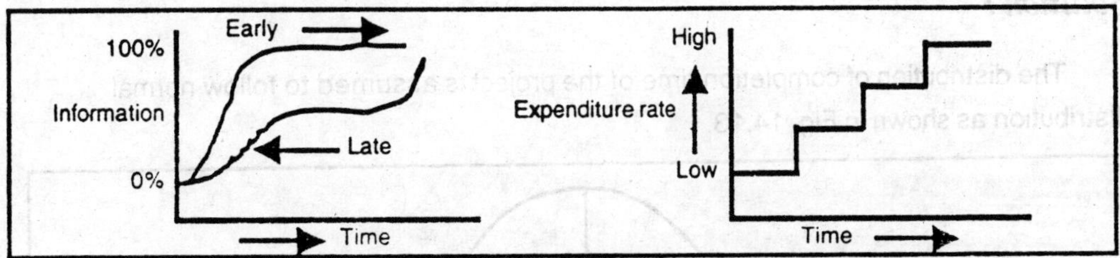

Fig. 14.11 a) Learning Path b) Expenditure rate vs time.

14.11 Controlling cost and schedule

Essential management function of control was discussed long back . It has been simply defined as "compelling events to conform to plans". The first step in control was to establish standards. This was done in planning process. The other essential project planning methods was also explained like work breakdown structure, G'antt (bar) chats and network scheduling systems such as PERT.

Determining Probability of Meeting Scheduled Date in PERT Analysis

Cumulative expected time of an event T_E represents a 50-50 chance. If a scheduled date T_S is given for an event and if it indicates a value higher than T_E value, then the probability of completing the event by the scheduled date is greater than 50%. It T_E is lower than T_E then, the probability of completing the event by the scheduled date is less than 50%

Determination of the probability of meeting the scheduled date can be, best illustrated with the help of an example given below:

Fig. 14.12 represents the critical path in a PERT network.

(1) —— t_e = 5 days, $\sigma_1 = 5$ ——▶ (3) —— t_e = 7 days, $\sigma_2 = 1.4$ ——▶ (6) —— t_e = 9 days, $\sigma_3 = 3$ ——▶ (9) —— t_e = 4 days, $S_4 = 2$ ——▶ (14)

Fig. 14.12 Activities along critical path with expected times and standard deviations.

The cumulative expected time T_E of event 14 is say 25 days.

(*a*) Determine the probability of completing the project in 28 days and 21 days.

(*b*) What is the expected time of completion which assures the management a 95% confidence level of completing the project ?

Solution :

The distribution of completion time of the project is assumed to follow normal distribution as shown in Fig. 14.13.

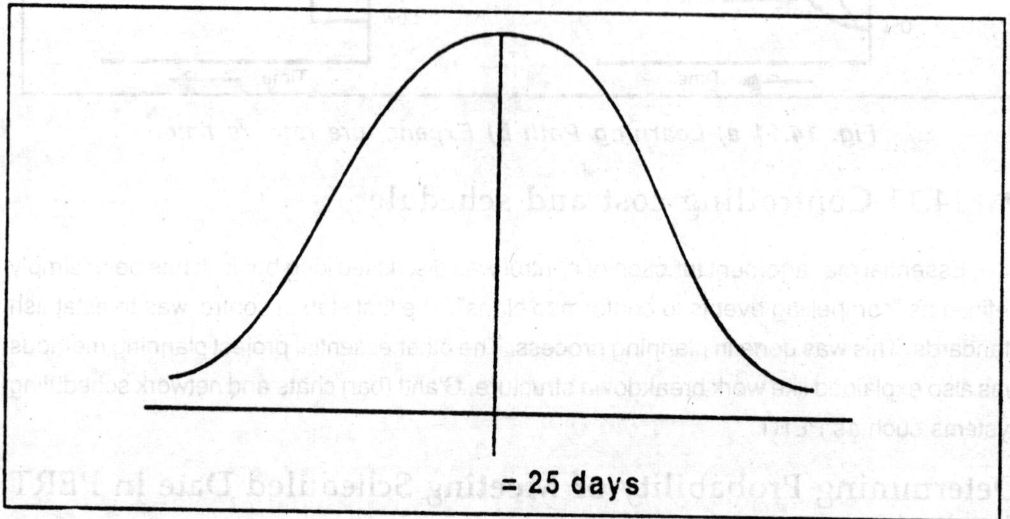

Fig. 14.13 Distribution of completion time of the projects

Standard deviation for the end event (event number 14) is

$$\sigma_{TE} = \sqrt{\sigma_1^2 + \sigma_2^2 + \sigma_3^2 + \sigma_4^2}$$

$$= \sqrt{1 + 1.96 + 9 + 4}$$

$$= \sqrt{15.96}$$

To determine the probability of completing the project by 28 days : Since this completion period of 28 days is more than the expected completion time of 25 days, the probability is greater than 0.5. But the question is by how much. To find this, the number of standard deviations (Z) has to be calculated as :

$$Z_1 = \frac{T_S - T_E}{\sigma_{TE}} = \frac{28-25}{4} = 0.75 \text{ standarddeviatior}$$

Where T_S = Scheduled time;

T_E = Cumulative expected time and

σ_{TE} = Event standard deviation.

Fig. 14.14. shows the area under the normal distribution curve which corresponds to 0.75. This can be ascertained from the table of values under a normal curve (Appendix A) that the area corresponding to 0.75σ is 0.27337. The probability of completing the project by 28 weeks is 0.5 + 0.27337, *i.e.*, 0.77337 or a probability of 77 %

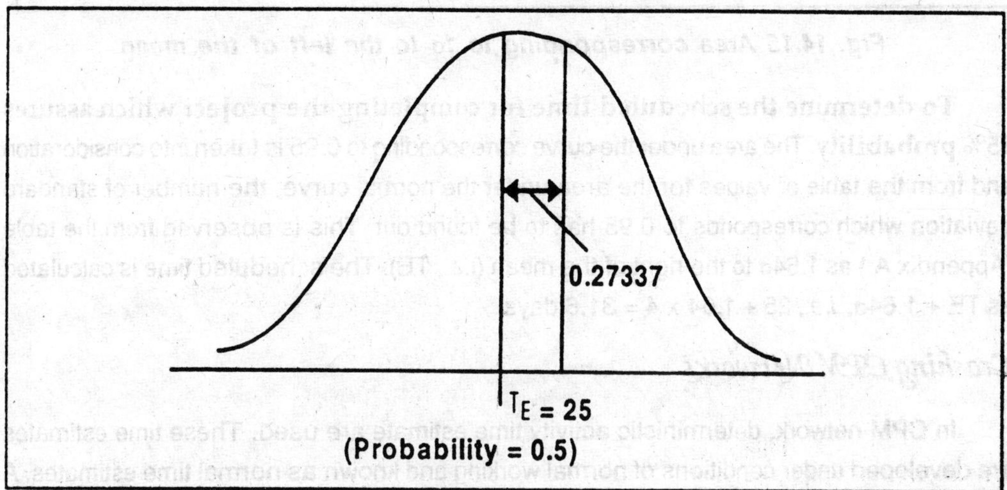

Fig. 14.14 Area corresponding to 0.75σ to the right of the mean

In a similar manner, the probability of completing the project by 21 days is determined as below :

The number of standard deviation $Z_2 = \frac{T_S - T_E}{\sigma_{TE}}$

$$= \frac{21-25}{4} = \frac{-4}{4} = -1\sigma$$

From the table of values of area under normal curve (Appendix A), it is found that 1σ corresponds to an area of 0.34134 (Refer Fig. 14.15)

The probability of completion of the project in 21 days is found by subtracting the area under the curve corresponding to 1σ *i.e.,* 0.34 from 0.5 which is equal to 0.16. This means The probability of completing the project in 21 days is 16%.

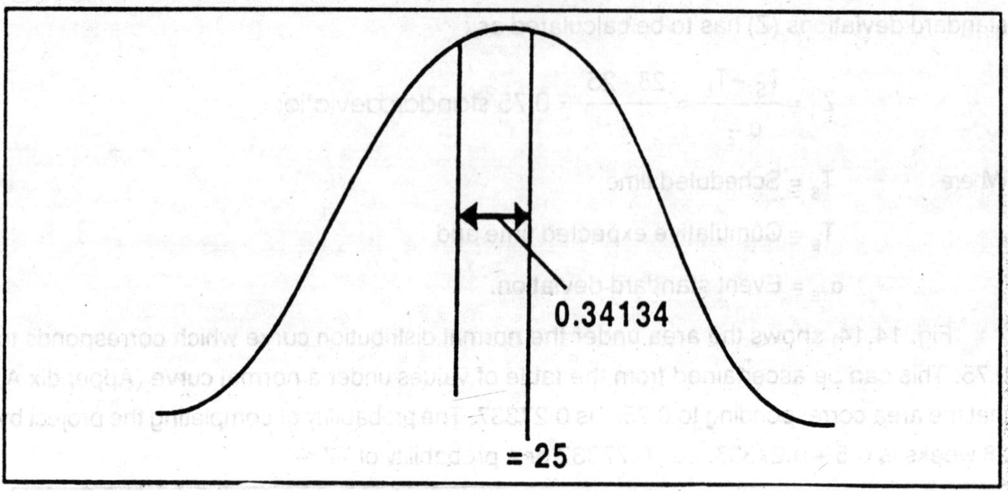

Fig. 14.15 Area corresponding to 1σ to the left of the mean

To determine the scheduled time for completing the project which assures 95% probability. The area under the curve corresponding to 0.95 is taken into consideration and from the table of values for the area under the normal curve, the number of standard deviation which corresponds to 0.95 has to be found out. This is observed from the table (Appendix A) as 1.64σ to the right of the mean (i.e., TE). The scheduled time is calculated as TE + 1.64σ, *i.e.,* 25 + 1.64 x 4 = 31.6 days.

Crashing CPM Networks

In CPM network, deterministic activity time estimate are used. These time estimates are developed under conditions of normal working and known as normal time estimates. A normal time estimate does not take into consideration overtime working or use of abnormal resources for completion of an activity. The project duration time in CPM networks is determined based on normal time estimates for various activities in the network. Hence, this project duration time is known as *normal time* to complete the project. However, if the project manager desires to reduce the total duration of the project to be below the normal duration, it is necessary to analyse the critical path for a possible reduction of the original time estimates for some of the activities on the critical path. This reduce time estimates is called "crash time estimate". The project manager has same options such as hiring additional workers and machines or increasing control with supervision on critical activities to reduce their completion time.

In these instances, the goal is identify the time versus cost trade-offs and to evaluate alternative plans for minimising the sum of the indirect and direct project costs.

The cost of resources required to complete an activity in the normal time is known as '*normal cost*' and the cost of completing an activity in less than normal time by crashing or reducing the duration by using more resources is known as '*crash cost*'. The crash cost is bound to be higher than the normal cost.

To compress the normal project duration to the desired duration time, we have to concentrate on the crashing of activities lying on the critical path. As we crash the activities on the critical path, we must ensure that no other path on network becomes critical. If in the processing of crashing the activities, some other path becomes critical then the activities on that path must be considered for crashing.

Steps in Network Crashing

Step No.1 : Determine the time-cost ratio for each activity in the network. This ratio represents the increase in cost for a unit decrease in time.

$$\text{Time - cost ratio} = \frac{\text{Increase in cost}}{\text{Decrease in time}}$$

$$= \frac{\text{Crash cost} - \text{Normal cost}}{\text{Normal time} - \text{Crash time}}$$

Step No.2 : Identify the activities on the critical path and select that activity on the critical path which has the smallest time-cost ratio and crash that activity to the extent possible.

Step No.3 : Observe whether there is any change in the critical path *i.e.,* any other path becomes critical. If so, calculate the time-cost ratio for the activities in the new critical path.

Step No.4 : Repeat step no.2 and 3, till the activities are crashed to reduce the project duration to the desired time period.

Earned value system

While planning a project, activities are scheduled against time. In budgeting the project, a cost for each activity is estimated.

i) Budgeted cost of work scheduled (BCWS) is represented as a cumulative cost versus time.

ii) As the project progresses, labour, material and other costs are carefully recorded. The actual cost of work performed (ACWP) cannot be compared effectively with the work scheduled to be accomplished by the same data, as some tasks will be lagging (behind schedule) and some ahead of schedule (beyond schedule)

iii) What is needed is the budgeted cost of work performed (BCWP) ?

iv) This earned value system works as under:-

When a task or (separable part of a task) has been completed, the project is considered have "earned the value" (BCWP) originally estimated (budgeted) for the task or segment, it then becomes possible to compare the budgeted (estimated) and the actual costs of work performed to date to determine the **cost of variance** known as (CV) (CV = BCWP - ACWP)

(v) One can compare the value BCWP of work actually completed (performed) at some point in time with the value of BCWS of work scheduled for completion by that time. to obtain the **scheduled variance (SV)** (SV = BCWP - BCWS)

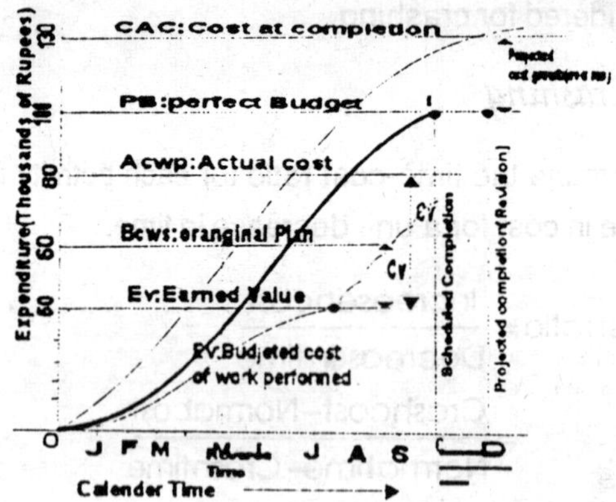

Fig. 14.16 Illustration of earned value system

Questions

1. Define project organisation.
2. Explain project Driven organisation with a sketch.
3. Differentiate projectised is organisation with Functional organisation.
4. What is a projectised organisation ? Explain a projectised organisation with a sketch.
5. Explain Matrix management ? Give an example.
6. Discuss Application of Matrix organisation.
7. Explain Matrix relationships in an organisation with a sketch.
8. How do you organise the project management department ?
9. Show a matrix organisation showing one of the several projects with one functional manager.
10. Explain the responsibility of individuals in the matrix organisation.

11. Explain the five project management structures and the analysis made from this.
12. Explain the characteristics of effective and efficient project managers and the skills involved.
13. How do you develop project management skills ?
14. Explain the project managers activities in developing project management skills. What are the areas of a project manager to be covered and team building activities involved ?
15. How do you manage the conflicts in the project organisation ? Explain the reasons for conflict, potential conflict sources over the project cycle and the Methods of dealing with conflict.
16. Explain Methods of conflict management.
17. Discuss the characteristics that strongly affect projects for success and failure.
18. Discuss on the early learning path and earned value system while planning a project.
19. How do you a crash a network ; What are the steps involved ?
20. Discuss on determining probability of meeting scheduled dates in PERT Analysis.

References

1. Forecasting and Management of Technology by ALAN-L. PORTER; A. THOMAS ROPER, and THOMAS W. MASON; FREDERICK A. ROSSINI; JERRY BANKS; BRADLEY J. WIEDERHOLT; Johnwiley & Sons, INC Publication

2. Managing Engineering and Technology (An introduction to Management for Engineers) Prentice Hall, Englewood cliffs, New Jersey by Daniel L. Babcock.

3. Management of Technology (The key to competitiveness and wealth creation); Jarlk M. Khalil, Mc Graw Hill Publication

4. Management by William F: Coventry (Revised by John L. Barker) Rupa & co, Calcutta

5. Total Quality Management, Himalaya Publishing House (by K. Sridhara Bhat) 2002

6. Human Resource Management by Dr P. Subba Rao, 2004, Himalaya Publishing House.

7. Management Information Systems by CSV Murthy, Himalaya Publishing House.

8. Business Ethics Revised Edition 2005 by CSV Murthy, Himalaya Publishing House.

Index

- D -

- E -

- F -

- G -

- H -

- I -

- J -

- K -

- L -

- M -

- N -

- O -

- P -

- Q -

- R -

- S -

- T -

- V -

- W -